In the Shadow of Hitler

the MODERN SOUTH

series editors
Glenn Feldman & Kari Frederickson

In the Shadow of Hitler

Alabama's Jews, the Second World War, and the Holocaust

Dan J. Puckett

THE UNIVERSITY OF ALABAMA PRESS
Tuscaloosa

The University of Alabama Press
Tuscaloosa, Alabama 35487-0380
uapress.ua.edu

Hardcover edition published 2014.
Paperback edition published 2016.
eBook edition published 2014.

Typeface: Caslon

Manufactured in the United States of America
Cover image: Religious service held at Temple Beth-Or, Montgomery, Alabama; courtesy of the Jacob Rader Marcus Center of the American Jewish Archives, Cincinnati, Ohio, americanjewisharchives.org
Cover design: Kate E. K. Barber

∞
The paper on which this book is printed meets the minimum requirements of American National Standard for Information Science–Permanence of Paper for Printed Library Materials, ANSI Z39.48-1984.

Paperback ISBN: 978-0-8173-5868-6

A previous edition of this book has been catalogued
by the Library of Congress as follows:
Library of Congress Cataloging-in-Publication Data
Puckett, Dan J.
In the shadow of Hitler : Alabama's Jews, the Second World War, and the holocaust / Dan J. Puckett.
pages cm.—(The modern South)
Includes bibliographical references and index.
ISBN 978-0-8173-1328-9 (trade cloth : alk. paper)—ISBN 978-0-8173-8107-3 (ebook)
1. Jews—Alabama—History—20th century. 2. World War, 1939–1945—Jews—Alabama. 3. World War, 1939–1945—Refugees—Alabama. 4. Alabama—Ethnic relations. 5. Holocaust, Jewish (1939–1945) I. Title.
F335.J5.P83 2013
305.892'40761—dc23
2013016593

for Mae—

Contents

Acknowledgments ix

Abbreviations xiii

Introduction 1

1. Alabama's Jews and Nazism, 1933–38 19
2. The Refugee Crisis, 1938–41 40
3. Zionism in Alabama, 1933–45 74
4. The Alabama Press, Nazi Antisemitism, and the Holocaust 105
5. The War 131
6. Antisemitism and Racism during the War 185
7. Postwar Alabama 206

Postscript 225

Notes 235

Bibliography 293

Index 313

Illustrations to follow page 166

Acknowledgments

This book on Alabama's Jews and the Holocaust grew from my earlier research on the subject. I had originally planned to write a book that described how Nazism, war, and the Holocaust affected African Americans' demands for civil rights, which at the time was my primary focus. I also planned to include a small section devoted to the Jewish community. I began working on the Jewish reaction first, which I had relegated to roughly two chapters, largely to get them out of the way. In the course of further research and writing, it became clear that a separate study of Alabama's Jews was required. The University of Alabama Press, which had agreed to publish my original study, encouraged this decision, and editor Dan Waterman has been both supportive and patient as I steadily worked on the book. As this project progressed, southern Jewish history, not African American history, became my overriding interest. The result is a book significantly different from what I had originally imagined.

This book would not have been possible without the assistance, both great and small, of a number of individuals. First, special thanks should go to four individuals who have shaped my professional career. As an undergraduate at the University of West Alabama, I was fortunate to have Joe B. Wilkins, Fred Sakon, and the late David W. Bowen as professors. The three were as different as could be, but their obvious love of history and their support and encouragement of a clueless undergraduate student inspired me to follow them into the historical profession. My graduate advisor at Mississippi State University, Johnpeter H. Grill, taught me how to be a historian. I am grateful for the lessons I learned in his seminars and in the many hours sitting in his office. I'm especially grateful for his encouragement as my research floundered. In many ways, this book is a product of their faith in me. Thank you all!

Two individuals deserve special mention in connection with this book: Sol Kimerling and Mark Bauman. I met Sol Kimerling years ago at a panel discussion at the Birmingham Civil Rights Institute where he was speaking about Birmingham's Jews and the civil rights movement. As one who grew up Southern Baptist, I knew little about Alabama's Jewish community. Sol was the perfect tutor. He served as a sounding board, patiently reading and responding to what I wrote. He introduced me to many people in the Jewish community, which eventually diverted my research into areas I had not expected. I will never forget the kindness and generosity of Sol and his late wife, Rita. They truly made me feel welcome, and it is something that I will always treasure. Mark Bauman is perhaps the most relentless editor I have ever encountered. I became acquainted with Mark in 2006 when he contacted me about publishing some of my work in *Southern Jewish History*, a journal he edits. I was, of course, familiar with Mark's work, but had never met him. Over the years I have had the opportunity to work with Mark, at times a victim of his merciless red pen. His critiques, often many, have made me a better historian. When Dan Waterman of the University of Alabama Press asked my opinion as to who should review the manuscript, I did not hesitate to recommend Mark (and his red pen). His comments, suggestions, and advice made this a much better book. Thank you, Mark.

There are many people who have generously contributed their time and energy to reading portions of the manuscript. I am in their debt for their insight and advice: Jim Arlandson, Jennifer Brooks, David Isaacs, Tom Kolasa, Sara Kosiba, the late Wayland Marler, Jeffery Marlett, Scott Merriman, Stuart Rockoff, Jennifer Treviño, and Phyllis Weinstein. Much of the credit for chapter 4 belongs to Claire Rosenson. A large part of that chapter appeared in *Holocaust and Genocide Studies* 25 (Fall 2011), of which Claire is an editor, and I appreciate Oxford University Press for granting permission to reprint part of it. A special thanks goes to Jack Salzman who read the entire manuscript and who generously offered his sage advice. He and his wife, Cecily, welcomed me to New York and entertained me while I was there. Jack and Cecily, thank you for your hospitality (and the sushi)!

While Alabama is often lacking in resources and services when compared to other states, such is not the case when it comes to the quality of our professional archivists and librarians. Indeed, this study could not have been completed without their invaluable assistance. One of the most enjoyable places in which to work is the Birmingham Public Library Department of Archives and Manuscripts. Director Jim Baggett, Don Veasey, and the staff have made researching in Birmingham a real pleasure. The staff at the Alabama Department of Archives and History, particularly the former director Ed Bridges, director Steve Murray, Norwood Kerr, the late Rickie Brunner, and Patricia Wilson, to name but a few, should be commended not only for their willingness to assist everyone who walks into the reading room, but also for their professionalism while doing so. Ed Bridges should also be commended for his commitment to Alabama and Alabama history. Under his leadership, the state archives has become one of the finest research centers in the United States. My time at the Hoole Special Collections at the University of Alabama was made easier by its excellent staff, particularly Holli Connell, who went above and beyond the call of duty in assisting a wayward researcher. Thanks also to Marty Olliff at the Wiregrass Archives, Scotty Kirkland at the University of South Alabama Archives, Anne Coleman at the University of Alabama in Huntsville Archives, and Susan Thomas at Springhill Avenue Temple Archives. My friends at Troy University's Rosa Parks Library, director Kent Snowden, Alyssa Martin, and Debbie West, also deserve special thanks. They never complained about some of the more difficult requests I made of them. They never once let me down.

My research visits to New York were made easier thanks to the people at the Center for Jewish History. While everyone who works at the center deserves recognition, a special thanks goes to Fruma Mohrer and Gunnar M. Berg at the YIVO Institute for Jewish Research and Rivka Schiller at the American Jewish Historical Society. Thanks also to Shelley Helfand and the staff at the JDC offices in New York City and Kevin Cawley at the University of Notre Dame Archives. In Cincinnati, Dr. Gary Zola and his excellent staff at the Jacob Rader Marcus Center at the American Jewish Archives, Kevin Proffitt, Dana Herman, Nathan Tallman, and Elisa Ho, were a joy to work with.

There are many others who have contributed to this project and deserve recognition: Emily Allen, Hanna Berger, John Boncek, the late Morris Capouya, Raymond Cohen, the late Leo Drum, Mickey Feldman, Susan Finkelstein, Phyllis Feibelman, Gina Friday, Stephen Grafman, Anne Goldsmith Hanaw, the late Eugene Heilpern, Max Herzl, Eric Goldstein, the Jewish Federation of Central Alabama, Sam Kayser, Milton Klein, Adalien Feidelson Kahn, Denise Lewis, Kathleen Lowe, Joseph Miller, Ann Mollengarden, Mary Ann Neeley, Norman Niren, Arthur Prince, Jerry Rosenberg, Bert Rosenbush, Rosalyn Siegal, Henry Stern, Temple Beth-Or, Rita Whitlock, Itamar Yakir, and the late Sidney Ziff. Ralph and Francis Capuoya always made me feel welcome, and I sincerely appreciate their advice and the additional leads in the Montgomery Jewish community.

It has been a pleasure to work with the University of Alabama Press on this book. Thanks go to Dan Waterman for his encouragement to pursue this project, and the entire editorial staff, especially Jon Berry and Dawn Hall for their careful reading of the manuscript.

A special thanks to Troy University, which has generously funded my work. Faculty development grants and the financial support from the College of Arts and Sciences and the History Department has allowed me to undertake the research necessary to complete the book. Without the unwavering support and the encouragement of my associate dean, Fred Beatty, and my department chair, Annette Allen, this project would not have been possible.

Most importantly, I would like to thank my family who have been so supportive, not just of this project but also of everything that I have undertaken. My parents, Charles and Barbara Puckett, and my sister, Kimi Knisley, have provided unconditional love and encouragement, which I can never repay. To my wife, Heather, I would like to express my gratitude and love. To my beautiful daughter, Mae, who numerous times interrupted me so she could sit in my lap and practice her letters on my keyboard: thank you. It is my hope that when she reads this in the coming years, she will know just how much I love her and how much that time with her meant to me. To her I dedicate this book.

Abbreviations

ACJ	American Council for Judaism
ADAH	Alabama Department of Archives and History
ADL	Anti-Defamation League
AFL	American Federation of Labor
AJA	American Jewish Archives
AJC	American Jewish Committee
AJHS	American Jewish Historical Society Archives
AP	Associated Press
BHEC	Birmingham Holocaust Education Center
BPL	Birmingham Public Library Archives
BWR	Bureau of War Records
CCAR	Central Conference of American Rabbis
CIO	Congress of Industrial Organizations
CZO	Central Zionist Archives
DP	Displaced Persons
FBI	Federal Bureau of Investigation
FEPC	Fair Employment Practices Committee
FSA	Federal Security Administration
GJCA	German-Jewish Children's Aid
HSC	Hoole Special Collections, University of Alabama
IRO	Industrial Removal Office
ILD	International Labor Defense
JDC	Joint Distribution Committee
JFM	Jewish Federation of Montgomery Papers
JWB	Jewish Welfare Board
MMA	Mobile Municipal Archives
NCC	National Coordinating Committee for Aid to Refugees Coming from Germany
NCCJ	National Conference of Christians and Jews
NCCS	National Catholic Community Service

NCDPP	National Committee for the Defense of Political Prisoners
NCJW	National Council of Jewish Women
NJWB-AN	National Jewish Welfare Board—Army-Navy Division
NJWB-BWR	National Jewish Welfare Board—Bureau of War Records
NRS	National Refugee Service
NYA	National Youth Administration
NYPL	New York Public Library Archives and Manuscripts
ODK	Omicron Delta Kappa
ORT	Organization for Rehabilitation and Training
PCA	Production Code Administration
SCHW	Southern Conference for Human Welfare
TBO	Temple Beth-Or Archives
TCI	Tennessee Coal and Iron Company
UCLA	University of California at Los Angeles Special Collections
UJA	United Jewish Appeal
UJF	United Jewish Fund Minutes
UNC	University of North Carolina at Chapel Hill
UNCF	United Negro College Fund
UNDA	University of Notre Dame Archives
UP	United Press International
UPA	United Palestine Appeal
USA	University of South Alabama Archives
USNA	United Service for New Americans
USO	United Service Organization
WPA	Works Progress Administration
WRB	War Refugee Board
WRS	War Research Service
YIVO	Institute for Jewish Research
YMCA	Young Men's Christian Association
YMHA	Young Men's Hebrew Association
YWCA	Young Women's Christian Association
YWHA	Young Women's Hebrew Association
ZBT	Zeta Beta Tau
ZOA	Zionist Organization of America

In the Shadow of Hitler

Introduction

In 1982 the Orthodox congregation Ahavas Chesed in Mobile reconsecrated a Torah scroll from the Altneuschule in Prague, Czechoslovakia, that the Nazis had seized in the midst of the Holocaust. The Nazis, over the course of their occupation of Czechoslovakia, confiscated 1,564 Torah scrolls from Jewish communities throughout Bohemia and Moravia, among numerous other Judaic ceremonial objects, cataloged them, and planned to exhibit them after the war in a museum to the extinct Jewish race. Ahavas Chesed acquired the scroll from the Czech Memorial Scrolls Trust to honor the members of those communities who had perished in the camps, and "in order to remind us all that we are the lucky (the living) ones, that ours is the 'awesome obligation' and wondrous privilege to live as Jews—for the sake of the Six Million, and for our own."[1]

> We have a Holocaust Scroll in order to remind us: of each Jewish individual, in the Six Million, whose life was ended solely because he was a Jew; of the failure of education, law, and science; of the near-complete failure of Christianity in Nazi Europe; of where anti-Semitism can sometimes lead. We must be reminded, by this scroll, to be prodded to speak up against injustice done to any group; to remember that civilized nations cannot always be counted on to do what is right; to do more to aid Jews anywhere than American Jews did in the Hitler years for European Jewry; to recall how final restraints on human behavior were, and can be, abolished—but also how, despite the cruelty and indifference of most other people, compassion can be shown and assistance rendered if a person truly wills it. We need a Holocaust Scroll to recall Jewish heroism in fighting back in living human beings. We need this scroll to remember.[2]

The impact of the Holocaust went far beyond the Orthodox community. Adolf Hitler's persecution of European Jewry and the subsequent Final Solution profoundly affected Jews everywhere, including the German Reform Jews in the United States who emphasized adaptation and acculturation to Christian-dominated American culture. This study examines the response of Alabama's Jews to Nazism and the effect that war and the mass murder of approximately six million European Jews had on them and the Jewish communities throughout the state.

In many ways, the response of Alabama's Jews to Hitler and Nazism mirrored the experience of Jews elsewhere in the United States. They recognized the dangers that Nazism posed for Germany's Jews and loudly protested the Nazis' increasing antisemitic persecutions throughout the 1930s. They organized themselves locally and at the state level to support persecuted European Jews and became politically and socially active in advocating for their relief and rescue. Indeed, Alabama's Jews were not silent. A number of them assumed leadership roles at both the regional and national levels, and local groups coordinated their actions and campaigns with national organizations. Yet their raised voices—part of a cacophony of voices nationwide, both Jewish and Christian—were not heeded by those in a position to assist the persecuted Jews of Europe, ultimately resulting in the death of hundreds of thousands more Jews in the Holocaust. Moreover, like other Jews nationally, Alabama's Jews refused to criticize President Franklin D. Roosevelt and his administration for inaction in regard to saving European Jewry.

Alabama's Jews also vigorously supported the American war effort, although most of their attention naturally focused on the war against Nazi Germany. This is not surprising given their concern for German Jewry and their attention on the antisemitic Nazi regime. Even journalists and editors of the Alabama press, based on newspaper accounts during the war years, focused much more on the European theater of war than on the Pacific. As a result, Alabamians, whether Jewish or non-Jewish, were well informed of European events, including the Nazi persecution of the Jews. While the press in Alabama placed greater emphasis on Europe than on the Pacific, it also covered the events of the Holocaust extensively and generally supported local Jewish efforts to aid persecuted Jews in Europe, showing greater sympathy for European Jewry than has been generally perceived in the national press.

Jews supported the war both as members of the armed forces and on the home front. They served in the military in numbers proportional to their population, including in the infantry and other hazardous fields that regularly placed them in harm's way, contradicting a common antisemitic stereotype of Jewish servicemen. Many of those Jews who served believed the war against Nazi Germany had greater and deeper meaning for Jews than for non-Jews. The many Jewish communities around the state also played a significant role in maintaining the morale of soldiers stationed at nearby military bases through their cooperation with the Jewish Welfare Board (JWB), a Jewish agency and component of the United Service Organization (USO). Such wartime experiences unified, and in some ways even transformed, numerous Jewish communities in the state. Because many of the military installations used during the war were situated in rural or semirural areas, the Jewish communities closest to those installations—whether in the South, Midwest, or the West—were small in size. In order to support the goals of the USO adequately, or in some cases at the barest minimum, the JWB had to rely on virtually every member of the local Jewish community. Again, this was consistent among Jewish communities throughout the United States. While it is doubtful that Alabama's Jewish communities participated in such USO-JWB efforts to a greater degree than other Jewish communities nationally, no previous study has examined the interworkings of community support in depth.

In Alabama, as in America generally, deep rifts had formed between the established Central European Jews and the newer Jewish immigrants from Eastern Europe who clung tightly to their Jewish heritage and identity. Because of the Nazi persecution of European Jewry, Alabama's Jews began to coalesce, to put aside their not-insignificant differences and work together in response to the events that began in 1933, most of which were driven by Nazi aggression, brutality, and racial intolerance. Indeed, the persecutions of the 1930s and the war in the 1940s forced these disparate communities together to aid European Jewry, in the process mitigating some of the mutual distrust and suspicion. Significant and divisive issues remained, such as cultural and religious clashes over Zionism, but the crisis the antisemitic persecutions caused and the war forced Alabama's Jews to work together more closely and with greater purpose than they had ever done before. By 1948, with the horrors of the Holocaust fully exposed, Alabama's Jews moved to accept a Jewish state in Palestine. In fact, support for the state of Israel by individuals, community organizations, and congregations of all traditions is the most obvious way that Nazism affected Jews in Alabama. For example, in the Reform temples, often the center of non- or anti-Zionist activity in the 1930s and early 1940s, one can find numerous programs devoted to Israel or perhaps even an Israeli flag, something inconceivable prior to the rise of Hitler. An examination of the Jewish communities in Alabama today reveals that although certain divisions still exist, the cultural rift that was a chasm in the years prior to 1933 has all but closed. The cooperation to aid and then save European Jewry, the returning veterans from the war, the murder of six million European Jews, and the establishment of the state of Israel built the foundation for closer cultural and religious cooperation in the decades that followed.

Southern Jews before 1933

Before the arrival of the Eastern European immigrants in the late nineteenth and early twentieth centuries, the majority of Jews in America came from the German states, essentially from what became Germany in 1871. Jews from Prussian Poland, Russian Poland, Lithuania, England, and other nations also came in lesser numbers before the large influx from Eastern Europe after 1881. Both Ashkenazim from Central Europe and Sephardim from Spain and Portugal arrived in the southern colonies in the mid-eighteenth century. Only a century later, most Sephardim had all but lost their identity through assimilation and intermarriage, and German Jews began arriving in greater numbers. By 1880 Germans comprised the vast majority of the Jewish community in the United States, which numbered around 250,000, a great many of whom lived in the South.[3] These German Jews of the mid-nineteenth century established the Reform temples that dominated much of southern Judaism by the 1890s. As these German Jews embraced southern culture and accepted southern mores, subsequent generations maintained their Jewish identity, an identity, as Stephen Whitfield notes, that was deeply braided with southern and American roots.[4] The new wave of Eastern European Jewish immigrants who arrived after 1881 preferred to remain in the northern industrial cities—a majority in New York City—which not only had greater opportunity for the newly arrived but also a significant Jewish population with its cultural familiarity. Those who did move south established small congregations, but only a few joined with the previously established Reform congregations. During the 1920s, immigration was restricted and the Eastern European Jews who had migrated south, and especially their children, moved further along the road into the middle class toward Americanization.[5] By the mid-1930s, the population of Jews in the American South totaled approximately 214,000, a far cry from the approximately two million who lived in New York City.[6]

Jews had arrived in Alabama as early as 1785, although they settled in greater numbers by the 1830s. By 1844 German Jews in Mobile established the state's first Jewish congregation, and one of the first in the South after Charleston, New Orleans, Richmond, and Savannah. The experiences of Jews in Alabama, and of those in the South generally, have received comparatively little attention next to the Jewish experience in New York, where Jewish immigration from Eastern Europe transformed Jewish culture in the

United States and helped transform American culture itself.[7] But this attention to the New York experience, which many Americans have assumed is *the* Jewish experience, has overshadowed the achievements and experiences of Jews living elsewhere, including those in the South. In one of the first attempts to examine the southern Jewish experience, Eli Evans writes that southern Jews, in stark contrast to those in the vibrant, colorful Jewish culture in New York, have been characterized as "the provincials, the Jews of the periphery, not destined to triumph but just to survive." Evans's part-memoir, part-historical examination of southern Jewry argues that southern Jews, overlooked by popular culture and literature, nonetheless thrived in their southern surroundings and became an integral, "blood-and-bones" part of the South.[8] Within the past quarter century, more historians have examined southern Jewry and built upon the work Evans, Leonard Dinnerstein, and Harry Golden began. Many have concluded, as Evans did, that the South affected Jews, often profoundly. As Melvin Urofsky notes in the preface to *Turn to the South: Essays on Southern Jewry*, "the Southern-Jewish experience differed both qualitatively and quantitatively from that of Northern Jewry. Far fewer Jews, both in absolute numbers and as a percentage of the total population, settled in the South, and this fact significantly affected their self-perceptions, as well as the way others saw them."[9]

Such conclusions, however, are not universally accepted. Mark K. Bauman, in a purposefully "provocative essay," challenged those assertions and argued that the influence of the South on Jews was only marginal. Where southern Jews had been "most influenced, the causal factors were ecological and were not unique to the South." Despite the regional differences that Bauman acknowledges existed, and despite the fact that southern Jews identified themselves as southerners, Bauman argues that these differences and this identification overshadow "the substantial amount of continuity and similarities between Jewish experiences in similar local environments." Only by comparing Jews in southern communities to similar communities outside of the region—not to the Jewish experience in New York City—can one recognize that patterns in mobility, occupation, institutional development, and cultural values crossed regional boundaries.[10]

Bauman's argument, however, has been vigorously challenged by scholars of the southern Jewish experience who argue that "to dismiss the impact of region on Jewish identity is to underestimate the power of place." Marcie Cohen Ferris and Mark I. Greenberg, in *Jewish Roots in Southern Soil: A New History*, have argued that Jews in the South have been, and continue to be, shaped by the region's history and culture, creating a distinctive southern Jewish identity. Because of the omnipresence of southern Protestantism, to identify as Jew meant that "you had to *want* to be Jewish." Even today, they conclude, "being a Jewish southerner still requires a level of commitment and a consciousness of identity that sets this region apart from others."[11] More recently, Eric L. Goldstein has argued that both sides of the debate have become too monolithic, too concerned about whether a "distinctive" southern Jewish experience exists. Recognizing that a southern regional identity does exist, Goldstein suggests weaving "both distinctive regional patterns and ties to the larger, national scene into a complex and coherent history" that demonstrates southern distinction and an interregional, even national continuity.[12]

While this study does not propose to explicitly address southern Jewish distinctiveness, the subject is, perhaps, unavoidable. Alabama's Jewish history during the 1930s and 1940s fits into many of the national patterns that Bauman explicates, and Alabama's Jews were intricately involved with national organizations and international events. As individuals increasingly joined and even led regional and national Jewish organizations, and local and state groups coordinated their actions nationally to influence political events both in the United States and abroad, Alabama's Jews were clearly cosmopolitan, not provincial.

This does not mean that the South as a region has had no impact on Jews living there. Regional "distinctiveness," for lack of a better term, can most clearly be illustrated in the issue of race. Obviously, racism, discrimination, and racial violence were not unique to the American South—northern cities, for instance, had black ghettoes and experienced numerous race riots—but southern Jews, especially those in Deep South states such as Alabama, had to live within the confines of Jim Crow, a social construct of tradition, custom, and law that was unique in American society, something Goldstein has argued that allowed southern Jews to retain "important elements of distinctiveness."[13] As southern Jews adapted to their surroundings, often blending their Jewish culture with southern culture, this acculturation meant accepting, or at least abiding by, the Jim Crow system. That their whiteness corresponded with that of the southern Anglo-Saxon allowed southern Jews to enjoy the benefits that white supremacy provided, albeit with some limitations. Historian Leonard Rogoff has argued that "for southerners the Jew's racial identity was not fixed and, consequently, neither was their social place. Racial thinking confused biology, religion, and culture, and prejudice in practice reflected the incoherence of the underlying ideology." Rogoff may well be correct in claiming that race did affect how southerners viewed Jews, that "their racial difference was still assumed," and Gentiles' references to a Jewish "race" lends a certain credence to Rogoff's argument. But the very incoherence of southern racial ideology meant that Jews in Alabama and in the South by the 1930s considered themselves and were considered by the Gentile population as being part of the white community.[14] As an observer from the American Jewish Committee noted at the time, southern Jews "are, in fact, inclined to emphasize and perhaps exaggerate this identification precisely because they are aware of being Jews in a Christian world."[15]

White southerners focused their attention on the "Negro problem" rather than on the racial status of Jews. African Americans, not Jews, provided the target for southern Gentiles' prejudice. As members of white society, Alabama's Jews adopted the same or similar attitudes on race as white Gentiles, although scholars have suggested that southern Jews were perhaps more liberal than other southern whites, but less liberal than northern Jews.[16] Yet most liberal southerners generally refrained from publicly opposing segregation. Thus southern Jews supported, tacitly accepted, or quietly "bent" the boundaries of Jim Crow racism.[17] This examination of distinctiveness is, by necessity, only a brief summary of a nuanced and often controversial issue. The South, and the southern Jewish experience, was not homogenous, and life in small-town Mississippi or Alabama differed considerably from experiences in environs such as Atlanta, Memphis, or New Orleans.

With Hitler's rise and the expansion of antisemitic statutes and persecution, Nazi Germany joined with the American South in producing the most distinctive and rigid racial-caste systems in the Western world.[18] Both systems relied upon the idea of racial supremacy, whether white Anglo-Saxon supremacy or Aryan supremacy, and used legal and extralegal means to enforce segregation and discriminate against those considered inferior. The similarities of these two racial systems were so profound that pioneering scholars in this area have argued that there existed "a natural racial connection" between the American South and Nazi Germany that neither white southerners nor Nazi leaders fully recognized.[19] Nazi propaganda never took advantage of this, and white southerners, as well, failed to make any connection, instead condemning Nazi racial ideas largely on the basis of the Nazis' brutality and aggression. African Americans, however, clearly recognized the similarities between Nazi racism and Jim Crow, pointing this out as early as 1932. So deeply were white southerners wed to white supremacy and segregation that they failed, or in some cases refused, to see the similarities between the two systems of racial thought.

Such cognitive dissonance extended to Jews as well. Like the southern white Gentile majority, Alabama's Jews also failed to recognize the similarities between the persecution of Jews in Germany prior to the war and the situation of African Americans in the Jim Crow South. The irony of this failure was rich. Jews should have recognized it, due to their history of diaspora and persecution. Theoretically, they should have been the ones to point out the gross injustices inherent in Jim Crow segregation. It should not be surprising, however, that Jews did not publicly make the connection, since the Scottsboro trials that began in 1931 had inflamed racial and antisemitic passions in the state, making dissent or criticism of southern social customs dangerous, but they apparently did not make the connection privately either. Jews living outside of the South certainly did, but most southern Jews did not. Alabama's Jews spoke out loudly and forcefully against the antisemitic discrimination of Jews in Germany, but not against similar injustices perpetrated against blacks in the American South. Could they not see the similarities, or did they choose not to see? Were they fearful of Gentile reaction if they spoke out, as some scholars would claim of the succeeding generation during the civil rights movement?[20] Or perhaps acculturation into such a racial-caste society led them to assimilate the racial ideas of the white majority and mute criticism of the racial status quo. A non-southern Jewish observer suggested shortly after the war ended that southern Jews frequently suffered "inner conflict" over the treatment of African Americans in the South. Because of "their experience of oppression and their religious ethics, [they] should be concerned about the Negro's welfare, [but] they also feel that they are not in a position to take any action."[21] While the answers are not entirely clear as to why southern Jews failed to make the connection between the treatment of Jews in Germany and blacks in the American South, one thing is certain: had Jews in Alabama linked Jim Crow with Hitler, as had African Americans, their call for aid for European Jews would have fallen on deaf, even hostile, ears. This differed significantly from the northern Jewish experience and provides a vivid regional distinction in regard to race that cannot be found elsewhere.[22]

While scholars continue to debate whether a distinctive southern Jewish identity exists, no such disagreement exists over whether Jews differed from non-Jewish southerners. W. J. Cash, who in 1941 authored *The Mind of the South*, a penetrating analysis of southern culture, characterized the Jew as "everywhere the eternal alien; and in the South, where any difference had always stood out with great vividness, he was especially so."[23] More recently, historian David Goldfield has argued that southern Jews could not "overcome fully the distinctions between themselves and white Gentiles . . . the South has always been ambivalent about Jews, sometimes embracing those in their midst but railing against 'foreign' or Yankee Hebrews; at once exuding an almost embarrassing philosemitism while at the same time propagating the crudest stereotypes of Jews."[24] Precisely because of this perceived difference, southern Jews—perhaps more so Reform German Jews than Eastern European Jews—largely sought to be indistinctive in society, keeping opinions about social or political matters to themselves.[25] This attitude prompted Harry Golden, who rarely kept his opinions to himself, to comment, "The Jews of the Southern communities live in deadly fear of a disturber. . . . The studied attempt to avoid all debate, except on purely Jewish matters, has been in force so long that it would be hard to find six Jews below the Mason–Dixon Line who hold sufficiently strong convictions to be accused of anything."[26]

Although many Jews openly embraced southern culture and values, and had acculturated to a greater degree than Cash gave them credit for, they still fitted imperfectly into a biracial and culturally homogenous southern society that both revered and rejected them. Their inescapable "otherness" created a fine, if sometimes illusory, distinction between the Jewish minority and the white Gentile majority—far less severe than that between whites and African Americans—that certainly limited Jews' social opportunities but rarely affected the economic or civic possibilities of the most acculturated southern Jews. For the less-acculturated Eastern European Jews, antisemitic prejudice and social discrimination was much more pronounced. Indeed, no other place better illustrated the paradoxical nature of Jews in adaptation and interaction with non-Jews than the American South.

The antisemitism that most commonly placed social limitations and even social isolation on Jews in Alabama and the South was complex: part religious, part xenophobic, and it included the "conspiratorial International Jew—'half banker and half Bolshevik'—theme" so prevalent in antisemitic literature.[27] Much of this can be blamed on ignorance, too, as many southerners who subscribed to such antisemitic stereotypes had never met a Jew. Moreover, southern Protestant pastors and laymen, paradoxically, characterized Jews as "Christ-killers," while at the same time the Protestant fundamentalist culture in the South influenced whites to see Jews as people of the Bible. None of this was uniquely Protestant, fundamentalist, or even southern.[28] In fact, Americans since the nineteenth century have had difficulty differentiating between the nameless and faceless stereotypical Jews popularized in antisemitic literature—those whom historian Jonathan Sarna calls the "mythical Jew"—and Jews who lived and worked among, and perhaps even alongside, local non-Jews—the "Jew next door." As Sarna argues, "Mythical Jews could, depending on the circumstances, personify either evil or virtue. Real Jews fell somewhere in between. Mythical Jews were uniformly alike. Real Jews displayed individuality, much as all people do."[29] Indeed, white southerners generally directed their antisemitic venom at "outsiders" such as the stereotypical Jewish Communist, labor radical, or lawyer, as in the case of the notorious Scottsboro defense—a Yankee rabble-rouser who would agitate and disrupt the status quo—but not necessarily at southern Jews, who had adapted to southern culture and its prevailing ideology of white supremacy.[30]

In many ways, the German people initially approached Jews in a similar fashion. Rita Steinhardt Botwinick argues that Germans separated Jews into two categories: "First, there were their Jewish neighbors, the ones they knew in flesh and blood. They were viewed as ordinary people, no better or worse than most Germans. And then there were the other ones, the despicable ones. They lived somewhere else, in some vague sphere beyond their horizon."[31] Despite the similarity in how Americans and Germans categorized Jews as either "mythical" or "next door," or in the resultant antisemitism, the treatment of Jews in the United States could hardly be considered similar to the treatment of Jews in Nazi Germany.

The Milieu—Alabama

Throughout the nineteenth and into the twentieth centuries, Jews thrived in Alabama, with communities in Birmingham, Montgomery, Mobile, Dothan, Tuscaloosa, Selma, Gadsden, Sheffield, and small towns throughout the state. In the 1930s, Alabama's Jewish population hovered around 12,000, or less than 1 percent of the state's total population.[32] Nevertheless, Jews played a more prominent role in their communities than the numbers suggest. While discrimination limited Jews' social opportunities, they nonetheless became an integral part of their community's economic and civic leadership, holding not only prominent positions in civic organizations such as the Community Chest, the Kiwanis, and the Rotary Club, but also serving in such elected positions as mayor, sheriff, school board member, and councilman, in many cases for multiple terms.

Alabama's Jews, like Jews throughout the South, had to deal with the conservative social values southern Protestants who controlled the social climate espoused, and Alabama's Jews often faced a dilemma when confronted with a choice between their own values and those of the southern Protestant majority. For example, under the auspices of the Birmingham Sunday School Council, the city's public school system gave academic credit to students for Sunday School work, going as far as to take a religious census of all the students in the public schools. Although such academic credit was offered to Jewish students for attending temple/synagogue, the council did not always recognize their attendance, leading to frustration for a number of Jewish parents. The goal of the council, in fact, was to create "weekday schools of religion" and "the spread of the Christian religion" within the public schools and communities of Birmingham.[33]

Groups such as the Ku Klux Klan more aggressively expressed conservative and reactionary values, and during the 1920s the Klan exerted a major influence throughout the state. Often these extremist groups threatened minorities with retribution unless they conformed to their views. Most moderate or liberal Gentiles condemned such groups' excesses but not necessarily the views and ideals to which they adhered. Some Jews, such as respected attorney Irving M. Engel, fled Birmingham and the South because the city had "accepted complete domination by the Klan." Only a few Jews practiced law in the city "because Klan-influenced judges often ruled against Jewish attorneys." Like Engel, Isadore Shapiro also left Birmingham because he claimed that he "could not get favorable judgements in Jefferson County." Yet Engel, a member of the Reform Temple Emanu-El, admitted that he had not "suffered any inconvenience or harassment at the hands of the Klan," and Klan leadership urged him to reconsider leaving the city because he "was not the kind of Jew they were after."[34] Indeed, most prominent and acculturated Jews in Birmingham, as was the case in Mobile and Montgomery, escaped such harassment and often belonged to the same civic organizations as did Klan leaders. A number of Jews in small towns in Alabama also avoided Klan discrimination. Elmo Ellis, who grew up in the mining town of West Blocton, recalled that "the Klan was anti-Semitic and anti-black, but it always accepted the Jews who lived in that particular community, because they were considered different," fitting Sarna's description of "Jews next door." Ellis had been "taught not to be personally afraid of them; that they would pose no threat to our family. But, at the same time, I disliked . . . what they stood for and my family did also."[35]

The Klan's favorite targets included Catholics, blacks, and immigrants, and such vigilante groups often sought out radicals or those whom they perceived to be a threat to the status quo. The Eastern European Jews who had begun to immigrate to Alabama in the last decades of the nineteenth century more commonly bore the brunt of antisemitic hostility rather than the older, more established and respected Reform Jews, such as Engel. As Glenn Feldman notes in his study of Alabama's Klan, some Birmingham business leaders claimed that "'Russian Jews of the low intelligence type' comprised the leadership cadre for Alabama's black communists," a group that most certainly challenged the status quo.[36] The Klan's dominance throughout the state in the 1920s produced tremendous "emotional distress and psychological anxieties" for Jews, particularly those from Eastern Europe. In his history of Birmingham's Jews, Mark Elovitz argues that "there seems to be precious little, documented or anecdotal, to indicate that there were any noteworthy, negative, discomfort-producing incidents in which Jews were prominently harassed, picketed, boycotted or otherwise inconvenienced in a physical sense by the Klan and its activities in Birmingham."[37] While Elovitz seems to minimize the effect of the Klan to "emotional distress and psychological anxieties," these are conditions that should not be dismissed easily. Moreover, the threat the Klan posed was ubiquitous, even for acculturated Reform Jews. In 1933, for example, Montgomery's mayor threatened a Klan-led boycott of Jewish businesses to silence an outspoken Reform rabbi who condemned racial injustice.[38] Klan dominance in Alabama clearly produced an atmosphere unattractive and oppressive to those not part of the religious and ethnic majority.

Southern Jews, of course, had the benefit of not being the primary target of southern white prejudice, a position decidedly reserved for blacks. Some creative Jewish merchants even profited by marketing their wares to such hate groups. One popular Jewish merchant in Birmingham sold pistols and the occasional sheet to Klansmen who frequented his shop.[39] Another, Robert Kaplan, a Jewish merchant in Columbiana, a small town thirty miles south of Birmingham, brazenly tried to enter a Klan meeting at the Shelby County courthouse to announce that he was "overloaded on sheets." Although Kaplan was not allowed into the meeting, a friend made the announcement for him and, according to his nephew, Norman Niren, "the next day was the best day he ever had . . . he sold out every damn sheet he had."[40]

The more pervasive antisemitic policies and practices that excluded Jews from prestigious social clubs led to the establishment of parallel Jewish social associations, such as the Standard Club in Montgomery and the Hillcrest Club in Birmingham. These organizations, instead of providing a social haven for all Jews, illustrated the stark cultural, religious, and class division within the Jewish community that existed between the acculturated and prominent German Jews, whose families had settled in Alabama throughout the nineteenth century, and the more recently arrived, less acculturated, and less prominent Eastern European Jews and the Sephardim from the Isle of Rhodes and the Levant. For example, the Standard Club in Montgomery had been founded by members of the Reform Temple Beth-Or, who themselves could not join the elite Montgomery Country Club. Yet the members of the Standard Club refused to allow the Sephardim to join because of their poor financial resources and lack of social standing. Such snobbishness on the part of the Reform Jews—Beth-Or Rabbi Eugene Blachschleger admitted as much—led many members of the Orthodox Agudath Israel to refuse to accept membership to the Standard Club because its exclusionary policies "reflected the Reform community's desire to mirror the traditions of gentile society."[41] Cultural and religious divisions existed within Birmingham's Jewish community, too. Barred from joining Gentile clubs such as the Birmingham Country Club, Reform Jews of Emanu-El founded their own, the Hillcrest Club, while Eastern European Jews, largely excluded from the Hillcrest Club as well, followed suit by forming the Fairmont Club. In Mobile, members of the Orthodox Ahavas Chesed built the Progressive Club in 1930 for athletics, meetings, and banquets, an unusual undertaking for an Orthodox congregation. It was to be open to all of Mobile's Jews, and funds were solicited from the entire community, but the Reform Jews contributed little to its construction and used it infrequently due to the cultural differences between the two subcommunities. Conversely, members of the Reform congregation Sha'arai Shomayim across town had their own social clubs, including an exclusive Mardi Gras Society, created because of the exclusionary policies of Mobile's non-Jewish Mardi Gras societies.

In many ways, the divisions among Birmingham's 5,300 Jews, the largest and most active Jewish community in the state, reflected the division among the German Reform Jews and Eastern European Jews in other Alabama cities and, in fact, throughout the United States. The relatively young city of Birmingham, founded in 1871, had three synagogues: the Reform Temple Emanu-El, founded by German Jews in 1882; K'nesseth Israel, the Orthodox congregation Eastern European immigrants organized in 1889; and Temple Beth-El, a congregation established in 1907 by rapidly acculturating members of K'nesseth Israel. Although Temple Beth-El initially practiced Orthodoxy, it moved toward Conservatism in the early part of the twentieth century but formally identified with the Conservative movement only in 1944. By the 1930s, Birmingham's Reform Jews were the most prominent and wealthiest by far, and the city's Gentiles recognized Temple Emanu-El's Rabbi Morris Newfield as the spokesman of the city's Jewish community. Newfield's leadership and influence in the community mirrored that of other Reform rabbis who ministered in the South and nation. Eli Evans has characterized a number of southern Reform rabbis, including Newfield and Montgomery's Blachschleger, as men with "powerful personalities, many of them the first rabbis in the South who spoke English without an accent. Deep-voiced, dramatic men, they deeply impressed the fundamentalist community with their appearance and bearing. To rock-ribbed Baptists they seemed the very embodiment of the prophets themselves. Every sermon was a soaring, learned, carefully honed presentation of the roots of Christian thought in Jewish law, and the little country churches showered them with adulation as bearers of the 'word' from the chosen people."[42] Despite the embellishment frequently endowed on these men, they nonetheless served a crucial role in how Jews and the Jewish communities related to non-Jews, acting as ethnic brokers or "ambassadors to the Gentiles" in order to build cultural bridges within their specific community.[43] Birmingham's Newfield, who served Emanu-El from 1895 until his death in 1940, did this to great effect by emphasizing two commonalities that Jews and Christians shared—the Bible and American citizenship.[44]

Further reinforcing Emanu-El's prominence among non-Jews, numerous members of the congregation achieved both citywide and statewide success and recognition. In the late nineteenth century, businessman and educator Samuel Ullman presided over the Birmingham Board of Education. In the late 1920s, attorney Leo Oberdorfer became president of the Birmingham Bar Association and, in 1933 and 1934, presided over the Alabama Bar Association. Milton Fies, the vice president of operations for DeBardeleben Coal, served as president of the Birmingham Chamber of Commerce, and investment banker Mervyn H. Sterne led numerous civic organizations as well as the Birmingham Community Chest. Sterne's father had fought for the Confederacy, giving him a richer southern pedigree than many southern Gentiles.[45]

The Eastern European Jews of Beth-El and K'nesseth Israel, on the other hand, could not claim the same prominence in civic affairs, although they comprised the largest and arguably the most vibrant element of the city's Jewish community. Economic and social disparity had existed between the city's German Jews and Eastern European Jews since the latter's influx in the late nineteenth and early twentieth centuries, a disparity one Beth-El member described as being "like two different worlds." Sidney Ziff, a Beth-El member during the 1930s and 1940s, remembered that "during World War II, a lot of our members made money, and because they had money, they felt it was better if they elevated themselves and went down the street [to Emanu-El]. But down the street, all they said was 'we don't need you down here, either.'"[46] This social and cultural division lingered until after World War II, with the return of World War II veterans and the intermarriage of the succeeding generations. Some of Emanu-El's members, however, were of Eastern European origin, including Rabbi Newfield, who emigrated from Hungary in the late nineteenth century and married Samuel Ullman's daughter. Many Eastern European Jews "went down the street" and joined Emanu-El, although some joined the Reform congregation but also maintained their membership at Beth-El. Successful merchant and philanthropist Louis Pizitz joined Emanu-El later in his life "as a token member," while Beth-El remained his primary synagogue. His son, Isadore Pizitz, however, moved his membership fully to Emanu-El.[47] Such actions were not uncommon for successful merchants who wanted to broaden their appeal to potential customers.

Only the large cities of Birmingham, Montgomery, and Mobile had a significant population of Eastern European Jews, but cultural disparity and division also existed in smaller communities that had fewer Jews. Other cities and towns throughout the state had small numbers of Eastern European Jews who, more often than not, attended the local Reform temple, as no Orthodox synagogue existed outside of those three cities. Even when no local house of worship existed, most tried to observe their religious practices. Yet differences remained. Lee Shai Weissbach, in his study of small-town Jewish life, notes, "the lack of harmony between Reform and Orthodox congregations . . . in many small communities reflected a more general cultural subdivision. The friction that kept Reformers and traditionalists from uniting, even when doing so might have made practical sense, was based as much on cultural differences between German and East Europeans as it was on strictly religious considerations."[48] With the rise of Adolf Hitler and the Nazis in the 1930s, and the outbreak of World War II and the revelations of the Final Solution in the 1940s, events transpired that began to transform the cultural disparity and division of Jews throughout Alabama.

Upon Hitler's rise to power in 1933 and the subsequent antisemitic persecutions in Germany, Jews and Jewish organizations throughout Alabama immediately began organizing protests against Nazi Germany whose protestors included politicians at the local, state, and national levels as well as numerous Christian and civic groups. Chapter 1 examines how Alabama's Jews responded to the Nazi persecution of the Jews, working together and either creating or expanding existing organizations to address the humanitarian crisis unfolding in Germany, from Hitler's assumption of power to *Kristallnacht* in November 1938. German Jews and Eastern European Jews (and the Sephardim in Montgomery) participated in these efforts, often using the community Jewish federation as the vehicle for such cooperation. By working together to aid European Jewry, the various communities within the state began the process of dissipating the cultural and social divide that had existed since the Eastern European Jews' arrival in the late nineteenth century.

As a result of the increasing Nazi terror in the 1930s, many Jews fled, or attempted to flee, Germany and Austria. Chapter 2 looks at how Alabama's Jewish communities organized themselves and worked with national refugee organizations to resettle Jews who had fled from Nazi persecution. Many Jewish refugees had been brought into the United States and into Alabama by family members who served as sponsors, but by 1938 Jewish communities and organizations in the state began to participate in resettling refugees, working with national organizations such as the National Coordinating Committee (NCC) and National Refugee Service (NRS). The resettlement of refugees in Alabama by local Jewish communities and the NRS, and the problems associated with this resettlement, mirrored the situation in communities throughout the United States. Small towns, especially those that had a tiny Jewish population, faced the same problems, problems that were not isolated to small-town Alabama, or even the South: few employment opportunities for refugees and a distinct lack of Jewish culture and life. Despite the many problems, the cooperation to assist refugees further brought the disparate Jewish subcommunities together, although many areas of disagreement remained.

The most vehement disagreement between Eastern European and German Jews centered on Zionism. Chapter 3 explores the conflict over the creation of a Jewish state in Palestine. Eastern European Jews, as well as the Sephardim, had long supported the Zionist ideal of a Jewish state and comprised the bulk of Zionists in Alabama. The movement grew substantially after the Nazis assumed power and increased their persecution of the Jews in Germany. Because of their desire to acculturate into American society, German Reform Jews rejected the idea of a Jewish political state and feared that support for it would raise questions about their loyalty to the United States. When Great Britain threatened to restrict Jewish immigration to Palestine in 1938, the state's Jews came together to lobby their representatives and even collaborated with national Zionist organizations to ensure Palestine remained open as a refuge for persecuted European Jews, although they differed significantly over whether a Jewish state should be established. By 1942 Birmingham and Mobile's Reform congregations had hired Zionist rabbis who increased support for Zionism within the Reform community. The question of whether Palestine should serve as a haven for the oppressed or a Jewish state began to change with the revelations of the mass killings as more Reform Jews began to believe that a Jewish state was necessary. Surprisingly, given Alabama's history and reputation for racial discrimination and oppression, the state stood at the forefront of all American states in proclaiming its support for the creation of a Jewish state in Palestine. Politicians, of whom so many had been complicit, or at least silent, in the implementation and continuation of Jim Crow, lobbied—in some cases loudly—for assistance for oppressed and persecuted Jews abroad. Only with the creation of the state of Israel in 1948 did the majority of Reform Jews accept the Jewish state; a number of them, however, remained firmly anti-Zionist.

Chapter 4 examines the Alabama press and how it covered major events taking place in Germany from the rise of Adolf Hitler and the Nazis in 1933 through the Nuremberg Trials in 1946. Journalists in the state provided extensive coverage, and editors opined frequently on the persecution of the Jews in Europe. As a result, Alabamians were fully aware of Hitler's discriminatory policies, the antisemitic pogroms that targeted German Jews throughout the 1930s, and the mass murder of the Final Solution. Yet like the national press, Alabama's white-run, Gentile-owned press failed in the end to explain the events as a singularly Jewish tragedy. The state's African American press, on the other hand, used the news of the mass killings of the Jews to warn their readers against the danger of racial superiority—a primary concern for blacks living in the Jim Crow South.

World War II had a profound impact on the state of Alabama and on its Jewish citizens. Chapter 5 looks at the war's impact on both Jewish communities and individual Jews who served in the armed forces. The war clearly gave many of Alabama's Jewish servicemen a deeper and more meaningful purpose, especially those who witnessed the results of Nazi atrocities firsthand, that affected not only their outlook toward Judaism but also their participation in Jewish life in the postwar years. On the home front, Jewish communities throughout the state, especially the small communities near rapidly expanding military installations, worked with the JWB and became vital components in building the morale of the Jewish servicemen stationed in Alabama by taking part in USO programs and, in some cases, operating entire USO facilities. The JWB-USO events not only united the Jewish communities that participated, but also strengthened communal ties between Jews and non-Jews whose participation in these events was necessary for success. While the community efforts to aid the troops were not directly related to Hitler's persecution of the Jews, these episodes provide related experiences tying prewar attitudes and actions together with postwar events.

Chapter 6 deals with the antisemitism and racism that increased throughout the state, and indeed the nation, during the war. African American agitation for more opportunities in national defense industries and greater civil rights further fueled racial reactionaries' fears of miscegenation and suspicion of liberal Jews, perceptions that began with Scottsboro in 1931 and only increased after the United States entered the war. Although the South arguably experienced less antisemitism during the period than other parts of the country, Jews in Alabama still faced numerous instances of bigotry and antisemitism—in one case a subversive Catholic priest who denied that the Holocaust took place—and had to navigate the increasingly tense racial atmosphere black demands for equality and white reaction caused. Much like the Jewish efforts to aid Jewish soldiers stationed in Alabama, the examination of antisemitism during the war years only touches on the impact of Hitler and Nazism, but it nevertheless carries through with the expansion of antisemitism during the 1930s, to which Hitler and Nazism substantially contributed, and provides essential context for Jewish actions and reactions in regard to antisemitic and racial turmoil during the 1940s.

In the aftermath of World War II, Alabama's Jews had to grapple with the realization of the death of millions of European Jews, how to care for the survivors of Hitler's Final Solution, and the still-raging conflict over Zionism. Chapter 7 examines how Alabama dealt with the fallout of war's end. Like the years preceding the war, Alabama's Jews assumed responsibility for the resettlement of Displaced Persons (DPs) who had been liberated from Nazi camps, and these newcomers often presented challenges unique to their experiences. The returning veterans of World War II also offered an infusion of new leadership in the Jewish community, influencing the direction of Jewish affairs for more than a generation. These veterans, often second- or third-generation immigrants, contributed significantly to the healing of the cultural breach that had existed within the Jewish community since the late nineteenth century. At the same time, the establishment of the state of Israel in 1948 all but settled the contentious issue of Zionism, if only as a fait accompli. Even by the early 1950s, Nazism, war, and the Holocaust had transformed Alabama's Jews profoundly.

Today, both Israel and the Holocaust have become integral to Jews and to Jewish memory and have assumed a central place within American Jewish communities. Like many other states throughout the nation, Alabama has an active Holocaust Commission that sponsors educational programs for the larger community and for schools at the elementary, secondary, and postsecondary levels, including lectures by both scholars and survivors. In addition to the numerous Yom HaShoah observations at many of the state's synagogues, the state of Alabama also sponsors a Yom HaShoah commemoration at the state capitol in Montgomery that includes participation by the active and vibrant survivor community as well as numerous politicians, including the governor. How the Holocaust has been remembered and memorialized, not only by Alabama's Jews but also by the state's non-Jewish population in the decades following the war's end, will be discussed in a brief postscript.

1
Alabama's Jews and Nazism, 1933–38

The confluence of two events, the Scottsboro case in 1931 and the rise to power of Adolf Hitler in Germany in 1933, produced antisemitic reactions and fears as strong and vibrant as had existed under the Klan in the 1920s. For Alabama's Central European and Eastern European Jews, these two events clearly increased the awareness of their vulnerability to antisemitic violence. Where the former only raised the threat of violence against Jews, the latter vividly illustrated it. As antisemitism in the United States steadily increased during the 1930s, Leon Schwarz, the president of the Reform Sha'arai Shomayim congregation in Mobile, observed, "the Anti-Semitic situation, wherever it exists in America at this time, may be accounted for as the 'backwash' from Germany and other unhappy countries in Europe."[1] Indeed, the Nazi pogroms against the Jews in the 1930s, and later the exposed atrocities during the war, demonstrated the dire threat that Nazism posed to all Jews. As a result, Jews in Alabama worked together for the relief and rescue of persecuted German Jews, as did Jews throughout the United States. Yet these coordinated efforts on behalf of Jews in Germany helped to bridge the divide between Alabama's Eastern European and Central European Jews and brought together the disparate Jewish communities in the state.

Scottsboro

The arrest of nine African Americans, collectively known as the Scottsboro Boys, for the rape of two white women in March 1931, began a decades-long legal odyssey that linked Jews, Communists, and African Americans together to challenge Alabama's white-dominated judicial system. For white Alabamians, it confirmed the perception of northern Jews as agitators and radicals due to the participation of defense lawyer Samuel Leibowitz and Joseph Brodsky, the lead counsel for the Communist-sponsored International Labor Defense (ILD). As journalist Joseph Lelyveld observed, "White Alabama didn't see a Democrat and a Communist. It didn't see two lawyers. It saw two New York Jews."[2] This perception promulgated harsh antisemitic rhetoric throughout the state. For example, an editorial in the *Andalusia Star* questioned Leibowitz's patriotism and asked, "we would like to know what a man with Samuel's last name would be expected to know about American ideals and traditions—we feel sure that he knows a lot about 'the bolshevism of Moscow.'"[3] Prosecutors at the Haywood Patterson trial, one of the nine defendants, also used this perception to great effect when Wade Wright, the Morgan County solicitor, urged the jury to "show them that Alabama justice cannot be bought and sold with Jew money from New York."[4] The jury quickly found Haywood Patterson guilty of rape and sentenced him to death, despite the lack of credibility of the defendants' "victims."[5] As Oscar Adams, the editor of the African American *Birmingham Reporter*, wryly observed, "it seems it would take a whole heap of 'Jew Money' to overbid this sacred personal thing of violation . . . to buy 'Alabama Justice.'"[6]

Wright's inflammatory speech had no effect on the jury—indeed, the verdict was a forgone conclusion—but it certainly had an impact on how white Alabamians perceived Jews. Many people in Decatur, the site of Patterson's trial, and those in the surrounding Morgan County, voiced their preference for Judge Lynch to "settle this damn Scottsboro case once and for all." The targets of these threats included Leibowitz and the ILD lawyers, whom whites regarded as trying to obstruct justice and, more ominously, to overturn the racial status quo. As one Decatur citizen warned, "if them lawyers, especially that Jew lawyer, Leibowitz, comes here, it will be a one way trip."[7] Numerous others expressed contempt for "those damn Jew Bastards who are defending the 'Niggers,'" and suggested that Decatur "ought to [lynch] the Jews to teach them a lesson."[8] Robert Burns Eleazer, who attended the Patterson trial for the Commission on Interracial Cooperation, noted that "even though Southern Jews had 'more freedom and suffer less prejudice than in the north' . . . the shylock image was never far beneath the surface. The chant of 'Jew money' at Decatur had 'damaged the standing of southern Jews' even more than the fulminations of the Ku Klux Klan during the 1920's." Charles Feidelson, the Jewish editorial writer for the *Birmingham Age-Herald*, also noted that those in Decatur "took for granted that a Jew was a Communist or at least in secret sympathy with the reds." Because of this, Feidelson said, "Jews in Alabama leaned over backwards to show they were not sympathetic with the ILD."[9]

Alabama's Jews did not support the Scottsboro Boys' defense or demand changes to the state's inherently discriminatory and racist judicial system, but the antisemitism Scottsboro sparked understandably alarmed Alabama's Jews and made them more self-conscious of their Jewishness, as Feidelson testified. Although this antisemitic vitriol targeted "outsiders" and radicals—northern Jews—many critics often failed to distinguish between northern and southern Jews in editorials, speeches, or private conversations, much to the consternation of Jews throughout the state. Despite such antisemitism emanating publicly from the press and politicians, and even more intense rhetoric being uttered privately, Scottsboro did not unleash a wave of antisemitic violence or increase antisemitic discrimination in the state to any perceptible degree. Of course, the same could not be said about the persecution of African Americans.

Although the Klan's power had waned by the time of the Scottsboro trials, the memory of Klan violence had not. In his study of the Ku Klux Klan in Alabama, Glenn Feldman notes that "at the end of the 1920s, Alabama had only about 5,500 Klan members left. Though the numbers of active, dues-paying, uniform-wearing Klansmen probably fell during the 1930s, Alabama kept a climate favorable to Ku Kluxism. Ku Kluxism and a basic propensity for vigilantism were part of Alabama's social fabric."[10] Such a propensity for vigilante violence showed itself clearly with the desire by white citizens in Decatur and Morgan County to have the Scottsboro Boys and their lawyers lynched. Although such vigilante violence never came to fruition in and around Decatur at the time, it clearly manifested itself elsewhere in the state.[11]

In June 1933, with Alabama still inflamed by the ongoing Scottsboro trials, the arrest of three African American men for the murder of a white woman in Tuscaloosa led to tragedy. ILD lawyers attempted to intervene in the case, but Judge Henry B. Foster barred them from court and they had to sneak out of town "in disguise, under the reluctant protection of the national guard" after rumors that Communist Jews had taken a hand in the case. The three African American defendants had no such protection as Tuscaloosa deputies turned them over to a lynch mob who succeeded in murdering two of the three defendants. Weeks later, another mob lynched an invalid, middle-aged African American man for the rape of a mentally deficient white woman.[12] Whites in Alabama quickly blamed the ILD for causing the violence. J. Gilbert Balfour, the editor of the Black Belt *Marion Times-Standard*, declared that while "there can be no defense for mob rule," the ILD's attempts "to block the course of justice" probably incited the lynch mob that was "impatient with slow justice and outside interference." Because of this provocation, "Alabama need not apologize for this incident" caused by "those Kike lawyers, who are excellent examples of the scum of humanity." The *Birmingham Messenger* also argued that "the Negroes of the South have the ILD to thank for the anarchic behavior of the mob that perpetrated the terrible crime against civilization and law and order." Had the ILD not interfered in Alabama justice, the *Messenger* declared, the three Negroes "would be safe in the Tuscaloosa jail . . . [and] they would have received in due course a full, fair and just trial."[13] Even the liberal University of Alabama professor Clarence Cason blamed the lynchings on "the resentment directly created by the three Communist lawyers who deliberately irritated a disturbed situation by their offensive presence."[14]

The blame the press and Tuscaloosa officials placed on the involvement of the ILD lawyers conveniently ignores the fact that "a mob of several hundred" unsuccessfully attempted to lynch the suspects on the evening of June 21, just five days after the arrest of the first suspect. A few days later, a grand jury, at Judge Foster's urging, indicted three white men for "unlawful assembly and attempt to commit a felony" for their participation in the foiled lynch mob. The ILD did not become involved in the case until July 18, almost one month later. In the days just prior to the lynching, the tension in Tuscaloosa had become palpable. The reactionary *Tuscaloosa News* encouraged outrage toward the "outsiders" in the ILD, although no ILD lawyers remained in the city or involved in the case. Local Jews, who worried that such sentiment against the Jews in the ILD would reflect badly on them, had the *News* publish a letter sent from William P. Bloom to Rabbi Stephen Wise in New York that requested he use his influence so "that no representatives of the International Labor Defense be allowed to come to Tuscaloosa when the case comes up for trial again. . . . We wish to use every possible means to the end that this harmonious contact (between the Jews and Gentiles in Tuscaloosa) shall not be disrupted by outsiders coming in to spread hatred and malice among the classes."[15] John R. Steelman, a professor of sociology at Alabama College in Montevallo, investigated the Tuscaloosa murders for the Southern Commission on the Study of Lynching. He determined that "the lynchings were generally satisfactory to Tuscaloosa's white people," and the "outsiders" of the ILD made "a convenient scapegoat" for the racial violence that occurred.[16] Nevertheless, ILD involvement further reinforced the prevalent notion of Jewish radicalism. Despite the hysteria that surrounded the Tuscaloosa lynchings—Clarence Cason observed that the atmosphere in Tuscaloosa presented "an impression of horror"—the tension produced by the Scottsboro trials overshadowed all else and extended throughout the state.[17]

In Montgomery, Rabbi Benjamin Goldstein of the Reform Temple Beth-Or believed racism lay at the heart of the Scottsboro case and publicly supported the defendants. His outspoken and brash action alarmed members of his congregation who feared his perceived radicalism would reflect badly on members of Beth-Or. When Goldstein had been hired, the temple's search committee warned him "to leave the Negro question alone," a warning he clearly ignored.[18] Because of his public support for the Scottsboro Boys—he was the only white minister to visit them at Kilby Prison, he participated in an interracial Scottsboro Aid rally at a black church in Birmingham, and he openly proclaimed their innocence to his congregation—and his support of the black Tallapoosa Sharecropper's Union, Beth-Or's board of trustees forced Goldstein from his pulpit in April 1933, even though some members privately agreed with his views. Just prior to the Birmingham rally, the board had urged him "to desist from going to Birmingham under all circumstances" and to cease speaking out on behalf of the Scottsboro Nine.[19] Even after his appearance in Birmingham, a few Beth-Or members still supported him. The teachers of Kahl Montgomery's Religious School petitioned the board of trustees to retain the beleaguered rabbi and characterized criticism of Goldstein as "unfair" and "unmerited." They endorsed him as "a leader . . . who stands for the ideal of universal justice, one of the essentials of religion, and wish to commend him for his sincere and courageous attitude in upholding this ideal."[20] Goldstein's outspokenness about Scottsboro, however, created an "open threat to the welfare of the congregation," which William Gunter, the mayor of Montgomery, confirmed when he accused him "of being a southern agent for the ILD." Gunter also warned Beth-Or members of a Klan-led boycott of all Jewish businesses in Montgomery if Goldstein continued his support for the Scottsboro Boys.[21] To fend off charges of radicalism due to Goldstein's activities, the trustees of Beth-Or issued a press release condemning outside agitation and affirming their wholehearted support for segregation. Others, such as former trustee Leo Straussburger, stressed that Goldstein did not represent the "better element of Montgomery's Jews," while businessman Charles Moritz admitted, "he doesn't fit in our Southern civilization."[22]

Goldstein clearly did not fit in with southern society. He had come to Montgomery in 1928, a graduate of Rabbi Stephen Wise's Jewish Institute of Religion in New York. His liberal beliefs and attitude frequently clashed with southern convention, as did his uncompromising personality with the quiet and reserved Montgomery Jewish community, leading to lower attendance at his synagogue. When asked if he resented that he did not have a large congregation, Goldstein replied that "he'd just as soon talk to empty benches than empty heads."[23] He had been a member of a Marxist study group in Montgomery that included Beatrice and Louis Kaufman, members of his Beth-Or congregation, and Olive Stone, a professor of sociology at nearby Huntingdon College. In his study of Alabama Communists, historian Robin D. G. Kelley described the study group as "teachers, social workers, and wives of upper-middle-class Jews interested in world peace and domestic social reforms." Although Goldstein and the other members of the group had not joined the Communist Party, they "provided crucial financial and moral support for Communist activities in Birmingham, Montgomery, and the cotton belt," a situation that, had it been publicly known, could have had even more dire consequences.[24]

This tension-filled atmosphere the Scottsboro trials produced prompted Birmingham's Rabbi Morris Newfield to remain silent about Scottsboro and abandon his friend Goldstein to quell any further antisemitic outbursts and protect his own congregation. Newfield, however, had spearheaded numerous campaigns for greater social justice in his forty-five years as rabbi of Birmingham's Temple Emanu-El and had played a major role in combating the insidious influence of the Klan in the 1920s. Newfield biographer Mark Cowett calls the rabbi's record "mixed" when it came to championing civil rights. While the evidence points to Newfield "bowing to well-placed political pressure" not to support the Scottsboro Boys, Cowett points out that "he supported black rights not when it was convenient for him to do so as a white man, but when it did not conflict with what he perceived his role as leader of Birmingham Jews to necessitate."[25]

Like Goldstein, Joseph Gelders, too, did not fit in with southern society. Gelders, a southern Jew and member of Newfield's congregation at Temple Emanu-El in Birmingham, had taught physics for six years at the University of Alabama before moving to New York to assume a leadership role in the Communist-oriented National Committee for the Defense of Political Prisoners (NCDPP). In September 1936, not long after Gelders's return to Birmingham to direct the local NCDPP, four men kidnapped and viciously flogged him, injuring him severely.[26] Gelders's flogging reinforced the perceived Bolshevik-Jewish connection. Alabama's press vigorously denounced the beating but, as with the Scottsboro case, cared more about the bad publicity it generated for the state than about seeking justice. Indeed, as "a mountain of evidence" showed that Tennessee Coal and Iron Company (TCI) detectives had assaulted Gelders, and Birmingham business and political leaders colluded to suppress the investigation, Grover Hall of the *Montgomery Advertiser*, who had won a Pulitzer Prize for his crusade against the Klan in 1928, remained silent, and the *Birmingham News* and *Birmingham Age-Herald* "defended the steel giant from complicity and reminded readers that TCI had recently pumped $31 million into the Birmingham district."[27] Two grand juries, moreover, refused to indict the assailants after George Lewis Bailes, the Jefferson County solicitor and a former Klansman, called Gelders "a Jew, a Communist, and a supporter of the Scottsboro Boys." Bailes's description of Gelders as an agitator ended any attempt to prosecute the assailants, and the Birmingham press "quietly endorsed" the decision.[28] While the assailants flogged Gelders for his agitation rather than because of his Jewishness, the publicity surrounding the case, and certainly Bailes's reference to Scottsboro, linked the two.

Alabamian William Bradford Huie also explored the idea of northern Jews as radicals in his 1942 autobiographical novel *Mud on the Stars* when his alter ego in the novel explained that "the first people who sat in my apartment and told me they were communists were New York Jews. So I concluded that all American communists were New York Jews—a false and hardly original conclusion which many Southerners share to this day."[29] He described the interaction between southern and northern Jewish students after the latter's influx to the University of Alabama in Tuscaloosa in the late 1920s and 1930s, due to antisemitic quotas at eastern universities. The University of Alabama, out of all southern universities, proved to be "an especially welcoming admissions haven" for northern Jewish students.[30] These northern Jews faced hostility and resentment from southern students, and "no group hated the 'kikes' as fiercely as the Southern Jews." Prior to the arrival of northern Jews at the university, Huie wrote, "the members of the two old Jewish fraternities had been accepted everywhere. Sons of the established Jewish families in Birmingham and Montgomery and Mobile, these boys were more Southern than Jewish. They had the manners of high-born Southerners. They had never heard the term 'kike' applied to them, and except for their own religious and racial clannishness they could have forgotten they were Jews. But they couldn't forget now."[31]

Of the 4,700 students enrolled in the University of Alabama in 1935, 375 were Jewish. When Elizabeth Eldridge of Alpha Epsilon Phi sorority visited the Tuscaloosa campus in 1935, she reported that "the Jewish student body is a conglomerate one. . . . Alabama raises no barriers and has no restrictions. It is known as a campus with little Jewish prejudice. Accordingly, it attracts many Jewish students from New York who cannot get into schools elsewhere and are 'undesirable.'"[32] Her observation of the campus as having little prejudice, however, was not entirely accurate. Greek letter societies often imitated Gentile social clubs in excluding Jews from membership, although some Sephardim and German Jews had been accepted in select fraternities. In 1898, Zeta Beta Tau (ZBT) became the first recognized Jewish fraternity, and by 1916, ZBT had established a chapter at the University of Alabama. Because ZBT recruited from the older, more established German families, Eastern European Jews formed their own fraternities. While the small number of southern Jews on southern campuses "experienced insignificant prejudice," the influx of northern Jews in the mid-1930s aroused resentment between the southern Gentile and southern Jewish populations.[33]

Huie's experience with Jews at the University of Alabama is similar to that of Arthur Prince of Mobile who enrolled at Alabama in 1942. Prince, who attended the Orthodox Ahavas Chesed synagogue, joined the Kappa Nu fraternity, comprised almost exclusively of southern Orthodox and Sephardic Jews. Of northern Jews who attended Alabama, Prince recalled, "we didn't really hate them, but we didn't want them in our fraternity, either . . . we segregated ourselves pretty much because of our backgrounds. . . . And we probably did the same number on them that the German Jews did on the Eastern Europeans, but not to that extent." Like much of Jewish society at the time, Jewish fraternities remained largely separated by ethnicity. While the Orthodox members of the fraternity accepted Sephardim, they derogatorily referred to them as "Scallaboochers." "We accepted them completely," Prince said, "but we still made fun of them."[34]

Initial Reactions to Nazism

At the same time that the Scottsboro trials increased antisemitic tensions in the state, the Nazi persecution of the Jews in Germany directed the attention of Alabama's Jews toward Europe. Indeed, the first antisemitic persecutions in Germany in March 1933 motivated Alabama's Jews to action. Because their civic and economic connections extended throughout the state, Alabama's Jews secured the support of local, state, and national leaders who frequently spoke out in support of Jewish causes. Alabama governor Benjamin M. Miller, for example, sent a letter to the American National Conference against Racial Persecution in Germany proclaiming that "in this day of enlightenment, no race of people should be persecuted, nor their liberties destroyed. The Jewish people have done much, and are doing so much, for civilization, that other races should seek to prevent their ill treatment." He was not alone. The Mobile City Commission, lobbied by the city's Jews, passed a unanimous resolution expressing "regret for examples of racial and religious intolerance in Germany." City commissioner R. V. Taylor told the commission that "how a Christian nation can have antagonism for the Jew is unthinkable to me." Taylor, along with fellow commissioner Leon Schwarz, president of the Reform Sha'arai Shomayim congregation and a former mayor of Mobile, offered the resolution that stated that the commission, "with goodwill for the German people," condemned the "intolerant abuses [that] have been practiced by reason of racial or religious intolerance," and trusted "that steps will be speedily taken by competent authorities which will ensure adequate protection for the lives and property of all the citizens of Germany irrespective of creed or religious origin."[35] Both of Mobile's Jewish congregations, the Reform Sha'arai Shomayim and the Orthodox Ahavas Chesed, contributed to the relief effort, joining together through Mobile's Federation of Jewish Charities to form the Mobile Joint Distribution Committee (JDC) to raise money to "relieve distress" among the persecuted German Jews and "to protect the good name of the Jew."[36] The committee raised over $1,000 by September 1933. In addition, Mobile's Beth Zur Lodge of B'nai B'rith petitioned President Roosevelt to use his influence to stop the violence in Germany. The petition garnered a thousand signatures, including "all Protestant and Catholic clergymen, city and county officials, judges, and others in prominence" throughout Mobile.[37]

The Jewish Federation of Montgomery responded in similar fashion. From its inception in 1930, the federation had sent aid and relief to Jews in Europe and Palestine, although some of its members questioned the propriety of disbursing funds to areas outside of Montgomery.[38] Federation leaders, however, argued that they distributed funds according to need, that Europe and Palestine represented the greatest need, and "that Jews and their welfare were the business of Jews regardless of national boundaries." As such, relief to Jews in Europe and Palestine became an "integral [part] of the Federation."[39] The Montgomery Ministerial Association also responded in sympathy by declaring their "concern and anxiety" over the recent persecutions and demanded Germany "take all necessary steps to see that full amends, as far as possible, be made to all Jewish residents, who may have suffered maltreatment of any kind."[40] In late 1933, Ernest Mayer, the president of Temple Beth-Or, described the Jews in Germany as "being robbed of their possessions, deprived of all means of making a livelihood and subjected to the most brutal and inhuman treatment imaginable." He urged Beth-Or congregants that "we must come to their rescue, we must not, we dare not, fail them."[41]

In Birmingham, Morris Newfield, rabbi of Temple Emanu-El and president of the Central Conference of American Rabbis (CCAR) in 1931, prepared a statement for the Central Conference that deplored the "ill-treatment" of the Jews, "despite the fact that they have been so loyally identified with the fortunes and hopes and destiny of Germany." Newfield later commented that he did not believe "that the published accounts of various atrocities and slaughter of Jewish people should be accepted as having actually happened," but felt confident that they originated "on the basis of a large number of individual persecutions that have been perpetrated by fanatic and youthful members of the Nazi storm troops." He did believe, however, that the Nazis used "economic and social pressure" on the Jews in order "to eliminate as far as possible the human rights of economic and social equality of the Jewish people in Germany."[42]

Over the following months of 1933, Newfield continued to condemn the persecution of the German Jews from his pulpit. In a sermon on "Hitler and the German Jew Situation," the rabbi suggested that the Nazis sought to "annihilate the Jews economically and culturally" in order to distract the German people from other problems in Germany. In an address to the joint meeting of the Methodist Laymen's Club and the Catholic Club, Newfield called Hitlerism a movement "not alone against the Jews," but a threat to "Catholic Centrists as well as to all forms of liberalism." "Unless there is a change in Germany," he continued, "it is doomed. It will drop to a third or fourth class nation. Hitlerism came 200 years too late. Public opinion all over the world will not allow it to spread."[43]

In June 1933, at the CCAR convention in Milwaukee, the Committee on Social Justice dealt with "the social and racial injustice" of Scottsboro and the "threat to world peace" Hitler posed. The conflict between Rabbi Goldstein of Beth-Or in Montgomery and his congregation over the rabbi's outspokenness in his support of the Scottsboro Boys prompted the committee's condemnation of the "inability of the Negro to secure economic or social justice" in the South. Concerning Hitlerism, Newfield, the Central Conference's president, criticized "a lack of unity of American Jewry in meeting the problems created by Hitler's anti-Semitic activities."[44] Where Newfield worked to aid the victims of Nazi persecution, he said little in regard to Scottsboro.

With the first wave of antisemitic persecutions in Germany in early 1933, Jewish communities throughout the state began organizing themselves to aid their persecuted co-religionists in Germany, rallying their own community and eliciting the support of the local Gentile population. In doing so, Alabama's Jewish communities acted similarly to Jewish communities throughout the United States who raised money through local Jewish organizations for Jews suffering under the heel of Nazism, and who contributed significantly to the American Jewish Joint Distribution Committee, which operated the vital relief programs abroad as well as enabled persecuted Jews to escape Germany through emigration. Alabama's Jews also spoke frequently among themselves and to civic groups at large about the threat of Nazism and antisemitism. They sponsored public lectures on the growing international crises and lobbied state and local governments, as well as their representatives in Congress, to take action against Nazi Germany.

Birmingham

The effort Alabama's Jews expended to assist European Jews persecuted by Nazism also helped to alleviate tensions between Central and Eastern European Jews as the entire Jewish community united in a common cause. Such was the case in Birmingham as the breach between the city's Jews narrowed. In his history of the city's Jews, Mark Elovitz argues that the changing relationship was marked by "accommodation, [a] blurring of disparities and a growing, though perhaps unconscious, expression of a willingness among the 4,500 Jews of Birmingham to coexist and even draw together for their mutual well-being."[45] The closing of America's shores to new immigrants and the gradual acculturation of the Eastern Europeans, coupled with their economic gains and entrance into the middle class in the 1920s, as Elovitz notes, accounts for the change, although this cooperation did not fully bridge the social divide between the two subcommunities. The critical turning point for Birmingham's Jews, however, occurred when both subcommunities consciously and deliberately worked together, primarily in the interest of aiding and later rescuing European Jews who suffered at the hands of the Nazis. Although the two subcommunities did not see eye to eye on many things, such as religious rituals and practices or the creation of a Jewish state in Palestine, Nazi Germany provided a common and tangible threat that drove community cooperation. As this cooperation increased, the divide that existed between the two subcommunities gradually dissipated.

A Federation of Jewish Charities, begun in Birmingham in 1924, aided local Jewish families in need. Emanu-El's Rabbi Newfield served as the president of the organization, although its main function, the dispersal of funds for relief of local families or transients, centered on the Young Men's Hebrew Association (YMHA) and relied heavily upon the services of Beth-El's Benjamin Roth, the head of the YMHA, and his wife, Dora Roth.[46] Ostensibly, the federation should have provided common ground for intra-Jewish cooperation, but meaningful interaction failed to occur. The Depression forced the unwieldy and disorganized Federation of Jewish Charities to create the United Jewish Fund in 1936, the primary organization that both Central and Eastern European Jews used to aid the persecuted European Jews and to contribute to the overall well-being of their own community. The fund served as the vehicle for this intracommunity cooperation even as it also maintained services to local and national charities. With the fund serving as the heart of Birmingham's Jewish charity and relief activities, the Federation of Jewish Charities continued to exist only as a beneficiary of the fund and quickly became irrelevant to any relief efforts.[47] The reorganization of the fund, moreover, mirrored similar actions other American Jewish communities took to better address the economic pressures of the Depression and the growing need to aid European Jewry. For example, the Memphis, Tennessee, Jewish community established a Jewish Welfare Fund in 1935, while the Atlanta Federation of Jewish Charities reorganized in 1936 in order to meet the expanding needs of the international and local communities.[48]

Birmingham's United Jewish Fund had been in the planning stages since shortly after Hitler assumed power in Germany in 1933, as representatives from various local groups and charities conscientiously worked to alleviate any conflict or jealousy that might arise from the allocation of funds. Once established, the fund supported numerous and varied Jewish charities—sixty-five different agencies in 1936 and 1937—and became the main vehicle for Birmingham's Jews to aid the persecuted Jews abroad through its contributions to the JDC, the United Jewish Appeal, the National Labor Committee for Palestine, Hadassah and Junior Hadassah, and yeshivot in Europe and Palestine. In addition to raising money for Jewish relief organizations, Birmingham's Jews, through the United Jewish Fund, sponsored and conducted seminars and lectures on Judaism and the European situation with B'nai B'rith and the YMHA, drafted petitions, and cultivated political connections on the state and national levels in a largely futile attempt to alter the course of events in Germany. They also sponsored ecumenical gatherings designed to promote interfaith goodwill in the city.[49] Moreover, the fund financially sponsored refugees and found jobs for them in the Birmingham area. With the strong support of the rabbis of the three congregations as well as their most prominent congregants, the organization united the Jewish community in a way that it had not been united before by appealing to its generosity and willingness to aid Jews in distress.[50]

Because of the prominence of Emanu-El's members in Birmingham's economy and civic society, the Gentile community considered Rabbi Newfield the spokesman for the city's Jews, despite the fact that the Eastern European Jews, who belonged to the less prosperous Temple Beth-El and K'nesseth Israel, outnumbered the Reform Jews and played the most active roles in supporting and perpetuating Jewish life and culture in the city as well as serving as the driving force behind many of the relief efforts. Although Newfield believed that "the United Jewish Fund was the spokesman for the Jewish people" of Birmingham, the ecumenical nature of the Reform tradition and the acculturation of Reform Jews caused non-Jews, including those in the press, to look to Newfield and Emanu-El for the Jewish perspective.

Rarely did they consider that other rabbis and congregations might have different views. Although the press reported the activities of the Jewish community, such as events at the YMHA, it rarely commented editorially, covered in-depth, or granted any great importance to the activities at K'nesseth Israel and Beth-El unless Newfield or Emanu-El also participated.

Montgomery

The phenomenon of the rabbi as an ethnic broker or "ambassador" to the Gentiles could also be seen in Montgomery, where the city's non-Jews viewed the Reform Jews at Temple Beth-Or, and their rabbi, Eugene Blachschleger, as representative of all Jews in Montgomery. After the controversial tenure of Rabbi Benjamin Goldstein, and his forced resignation in April 1933, Temple Beth-Or's trustees quickly appointed Blachschleger, who worked diligently to repair the relationship between the city's Jews and a suspicious Gentile public. His success was such that later congregants referred to him as "an ambassador of goodwill between the Jews and Christians." His interfaith cooperation led to his election to the Montgomery Ministerial Association, a first for a Montgomery rabbi.[51] Conversely, non-Jews gave little consideration to the wide divergence of Judaic culture and practices in the city, as Montgomery was also home to Orthodox Eastern European Jews and a significant Sephardic community, the largest in the South outside of Atlanta. Montgomery's approximately 3,000 Jews had formed three congregations. The oldest and largest was the Reform Temple Beth-Or. Originally Orthodox when it formed as Kahl Montgomery in 1852, by 1873 the congregation had embraced the Reform ritual. In 1902, Eastern European Jews, who began arriving in Montgomery in the late nineteenth century, formed the much smaller Congregation Agudath Israel. By 1906 a new influx of Sephardim from Rhodes arrived, led by Ralph Cohen. In 1912 they founded Congregation Etz Ahayem.[52]

As was common throughout the South, the long-established Reform Jews remained the most prominent in the city's Jewish community organizations and in the eyes of Montgomery's Gentiles. Its members headed nearly every civic organization in Montgomery and served in leadership roles for organizations ranging from the Rotary, the Kiwanis, to the Huntingdon College Board of Trustees. Jews had been a part of Montgomery's civic and economic fabric since the city had been founded. Abraham Mordecai, a veteran of the Revolutionary War and the first white settler in Montgomery County, established a lone trading post in 1785 that preceded Montgomery's founding. As the city grew in the mid-nineteenth century, due to its prime location on the Alabama River, Jews became intertwined in the city's economic success. With the arrival of Henry Lehman from Bavaria in 1844, followed shortly after by his brothers Emanuel and Mayer, the Lehmans parlayed their success as small shopkeepers into a wildly successful cotton brokerage firm. After the Civil War, Lehman Brothers expanded their interests into finance, closed their Montgomery offices, and moved their operation to New York. Other German Jews found success in Montgomery as well. Jacob Kohn and the Weil brothers, Josiah, Heinrich, and Jacob, also arrived in Montgomery from Germany in the 1840s and became successful merchants. Jews also thrived politically as Mordecai Moses became the first Democratic mayor of Montgomery after Reconstruction, winning the mayoral election in 1875.

The newly arrived Eastern European Jews and the Sephardic immigrants from Rhodes and the Levant did not have the same desire to assimilate into American culture as did their co-religionists from the Reform Beth-Or. Like other Eastern European Jews who immigrated to the United States, the Jews of Agudath Israel held tightly to their Orthodox practices and culture. Similarly, the Sephardim in Montgomery remained committed to their heritage, conducting their services in Ladino, a mixture of Spanish and Hebrew. While initially they did not attain the level of success established German families enjoyed, both Sephardim and Eastern European Jews found economic security as grocers and merchants.[53] Mary Stanton argues in her study of Montgomery's Jewish community that the relationship between the various subcommunities proved to be so amicable in some regards that the idea "Montgomery is different" resonated among Montgomery's Jews.[54] Such amity, however, could be scarcely found prior to World War II, as intractable cultural differences remained until well after the end of the war that resulted in a rigid social division between the subcommunities. For instance, a Reform leader of the National Council of Jewish Women became "indignant" when members of Agudath Israel's Sisterhood "thought that an invitation to join the Council Chapter 'means they can mix with us socially.'"[55] Rabbi Elchonon Oberstein, whose father had immigrated to the United States from Poland in 1924, grew up in an Orthodox household in Montgomery where they "were never unobservant or assimilated." As an Orthodox Jew, Oberstein recalled, "don't assume we were really friends with [the Reform Jews of Beth-Or]—they were much richer and 'higher class'—but we tried to build bridges."[56] Such bridges, however, rarely extended to the Sephardic community. Rabbi Samuel S. Lerer of Agudath Israel admitted in 1945 that "his congregants avoid association with the Sephardic Jews," whose "misconduct" some Jews blamed for the increase in antisemitism. According to Montgomery's leading Reform Jews, "these Sephardim . . . are not held in good repute by the majority of the Jews in Montgomery," as they operated as "bootleggers" during Prohibition and "at the present time, they operate . . . liquor stores and engage in other business enterprises allegedly without much regard for ethical considerations."[57] Such criticism of the Sephardim, however, reflected the insecurities of Reform Jews who had established themselves within Montgomery's economic and civic leadership, a position of which those at Beth-Or were proud and consciously strove to maintain. Beth-Or members took care to assimilate into the larger Christian-dominated culture in Montgomery, and intermarriage with non-Jews occurred frequently among the Reform community. Such intermarriage was virtually unheard of among the Orthodox and Sephardic communities. Beth-Or member Leo Drum observed that a "wide gulf [existed] between the Reform Judaism at Temple Beth-Or and Etz Ahayem and Agudath Israel" that only narrowed toward the end of the twentieth century as more members of Agudath Israel and Etz Ahayem also became members of Beth-Or. Another member of Beth-Or averred that "they worshiped at [Agudath Israel and Etz Ahayem] and they came to the Temple to become Americans, or become Americanized."[58]

Like Birmingham, cooperation among Montgomery's subcommunities existed within the local Jewish community organization, the Jewish Federation of Montgomery, which originated around 1930. The majority of the work by the federation, however, took place at Temple Beth-Or, but federation board members actively worked to include Agudath Israel and Etz Ahayem members by scheduling meetings at both of the synagogues "in the hopes that this would bring to the attention of the members of these congregations that they were a part of the Montgomery Jewish Community and that the responsibility of the Federation rested just as much upon them" as it did upon members of Beth-Or.[59] The federation served as the vehicle through which Montgomery's Jews collected and distributed funds to aid Jewish "educational, philanthropic, and charitable organizations," and it incorporated the city's earlier benevolent organizations, the United Hebrew Charities and the Hebrew Ladies Benevolent Society.[60] While the federation existed to aid Jews locally, federation president Walter Lobman observed that few Jews in Montgomery required such aid, a somewhat surprising admission given the economic devastation of the Depression. Despite the financial hardships the federation and the synagogues experienced—like other institutions across the nation—they continued to assist transients, but apparently few Jewish individuals or families in Montgomery required such help. Historian Mark Bauman argues that southern Jews, who generally lacked a working class, did not suffer the severe economic dislocations that Jews in northern industrial cities experienced during the Depression. This phenomenon, however, was not limited to the South. The Jewish community in Indianapolis, Indiana, for instance, fared better during the 1930s because Jews, like those in Montgomery, were "conspicuously absent" in the heavy industries the Depression most affected. Without the need for such local aid, the majority of the funds the Montgomery federation distributed went "for the relief of our suffering brethren in Germany," as well as to yeshivot in Eastern Europe and Palestine.[61] Throughout the 1930s, the federation increased the funds distributed for those suffering overseas and for the aid to refugees from Nazi terror. The federation worked with the American Jewish JDC, the National Coordinating Committee for Aid to Refugees Coming from Germany, and its successor, the National Refugee Service, to sponsor Jewish refugees who had arrived in the United States.

Mobile

Similar intracommunity cooperation occurred in Mobile, coordinated by the Mobile Federation of Jewish Charities, formed by the consolidation of Jewish charities in 1914. The federation served as clearinghouse for other Jewish charities, with the Ladies Hebrew Benevolent Association, the United Hebrew Charities, the Orthodox Federation of Jewish Charities, and the Philanthropic Committee of the Council for Jewish Women undertaking the majority of welfare work in Mobile.[62] Home to Alabama's oldest Jewish community, Mobile had two congregations that served the city's approximately 1,000 Jews. The Reform congregation Sha'arai Shomayim had been organized in 1844. One of the oldest Jewish congregations in the South, only the congregations in Charleston, Savannah, Richmond, and New Orleans antedated it. The Orthodox congregation Ahavas Chesed, organized in 1894 by primarily Russian and Polish immigrants, remained small and had no consistent rabbinical leadership.[63] Like many Orthodox congregations in the South, Ahavas Chesed had difficulty attracting and keeping a rabbi because of poor pay and location. While the Orthodox community had little in the way of wealth or status, the members did comprise the most vibrant element of Jewish culture in Mobile, as their congregation had "most of the young people and large families" in the city's Jewish population, in contrast to Sha'arai Shomayim, which had "few children."[64]

Mobile's Jews enjoyed extremely cordial relations with the city's Gentile majority, with Gentiles often contributing to Jewish fund-raising drives. Members of Sha'arai Shomayim had even been invited to join the Mobile

Country Club. Yet not everyone accepted this premise. Merchant Arthur Eppstein thought Mobile's Reform Jews "guilty of snobbishness" and questioned "the belief of Jews in Mobile that they are well integrated." According to Eppstein, Gentiles had extended membership to the Mobile Country Club to Reform members "only because their money was needed."[65] The city's Jewish community, however, mirrored Montgomery and Birmingham in that it remained divided by religious and cultural differences. Jake Linnick, the president of the Jewish Progressive Club, observed that the "gap between the Orthodox and Reformed groups is greater than between the Jews and Gentiles." Much of the long-standing divide between the two groups came down to differences in wealth, status, and acculturation, and the Orthodox group not surprisingly viewed the Reform congregation as "snobbish." Linnick also suggested that "the schism" persisted because "the Orthodox group [will] go ahead and do things whereas the Reform groups sit back."[66] The desire to aid persecuted European Jews brought the two groups together in a common endeavor, at least temporarily.

The Reform congregation in Mobile remained active and mobilized to aid persecuted Jews in Germany largely due to the efforts of Leon Schwarz. Schwarz, who cultivated and maintained long-standing friendships in Alabama politics, took the lead in the Jewish community to raise funds to aid Jews in Germany and to curry political support for Jewish relief. He had served as Mobile's sheriff and mayor and remained one of the city's foremost civic leaders. When the Nazis began persecuting German Jews in March 1933, Schwarz, the president of Sha'arai Shomayim, invited Sam J. Ripps, the president of Ahavas Chesed, to form the Mobile JDC. The group included Sha'arai Shomayim's Rabbi Alfred G. Moses, James G. Adler, Aaron Lowenstein, Herbert C. Brown, Leo M. Brown, and Sol Kahn. The Mobile JDC raised $1,295 from the Mobile Jewish community its first year and distributed the funds to national Jewish aid societies, including the American Jewish JDC, the American Jewish Committee, the American Jewish Congress, the Hebrew Immigrant Aid Society, and B'nai B'rith. The amount the Mobile JDC raised exceeded the amount that the Federation of Jewish Charities annually provided to local charities.[67] Unlike the federation, the Mobile JDC provided common ground for the Jewish leaders of each subcommunity to work closely together to aid persecuted Jews abroad.

Rabbi Alfred Geiger Moses had fulfilled the position of "ambassador to the Gentiles" in Mobile since his installation as Sha'arai Shomayim's rabbi 1901, but throughout his rabbinic tenure he suffered from acute mental illness and dementia, which ultimately led to his resignation and replacement by Rabbi Sidney Berkowitz in 1940.[68] In the rabbi's stead, Schwarz and other lay members such as Ben May took the lead in regard to community relations. Schwarz had established friendships and political contacts throughout the state that allowed him to lobby governors, senators, and representatives directly, such as when he lobbied Alabama senator Hugo L. Black in early 1934 to support the resolution of Maryland senator Millard Tydings requesting that President Roosevelt communicate to Nazi Germany "an unequivocal statement of the profound feelings of surprise and pain experienced by the American people" caused by the persecution of the Jews in Germany.[69] These connections, as well as Schwarz's and May's sterling reputation with Mobile's Gentiles, meant that Mobile Jewry would not want when it came to solicit community support for Jewish endeavors.

Schwarz had served in the Spanish-American War in 1898 and in World War I. He played a leading role in Alabama's American Legion and had even been at the founding meeting of the legion in Paris in 1919. His honorable service and his advocacy for the legion further strengthened his friendships with Alabama politicians such as governors William Woodward Brandon, David Bibb Graves, and Frank Dixon, veterans all. Schwarz had even roomed with Brandon when they attended the University of Alabama Law School in the early 1890s. In 1936, when the CCAR endorsed a resolution supporting the "exemption of Jews from military service in accordance with the highest interpretation of Judaism," the *New York Times* published the headline: "War Exemption for All Jews Urged." Schwarz quickly objected, citing "a feeling of deep personal resentment, and one of dismay for the welfare of Jewish people" in the United States. Schwarz considered the resolution a profound insult to himself and to all American Jews, and he cynically responded that the CCAR should adopt another resolution that "should endorse the political and governmental stand of one Adolf Hitler of Germany, for he asserts that the Jew is never a real citizen, or national, of a country—but merely one who lives in or on a country." Mobile's Government Street Temple had a roll of honor naming those in the congregation who served in World War I. It stated clearly that "Judaism commands that its adherents shall love and serve the State to which they belong with devotion, promote its national interests with all their hearts and might, and willingly sacrifice property and life for its honor, welfare and liberty." This not only mirrored the tenets of Reform Judaism, but it also embodied Schwarz's idea of civic and moral virtue and was, for him, "in accordance with the highest interpretation of Judaism."[70]

The federation, the two congregations, and other Jewish organizations frequently brought speakers to Mobile to highlight and discuss the plight of Jews in Germany. One such speaker told the Mobile audience that the "atrocities [were] not only of a physical nature, but of spiritual, mental and emotional natures" as well. The crimes perpetrated against the Jews constituted a "war against civilization, which Germany has begun and which, unless we beware, they will finish."[71] Moreover, to ensure that their own members fully understood the danger that Nazism posed to Jews, both B'nai B'rith and Sha'arai Shomayim made available to the community copies of *Mein Kampf*.[72] Such programs to spotlight the ongoing tragedy in Germany, and active support of these endeavors by the Mobile press, helped the Mobile JDC to raise funds for their ongoing Jewish relief efforts. Yet even as they criticized and condemned the treatment of Jews by the Nazi regime, Mobile's Jews remained wary of efforts that might cause further harm to those for whom they worked most diligently. B'nai B'rith warned Jews not to use "anti-Hitler" stamps—stamps promoting the boycott of Nazi products—for their correspondence as their use might cause "considerable harm" to their already suffering brethren in Germany.[73]

Kristallnacht

Even as Alabama's Jewish community labored to aid their persecuted brethren in Europe, Nazi-sponsored violence spiraled out of control. The assassination of German diplomat Ernst vom Rath in Paris by Herschel Grynszpan, a disaffected German-born, Polish Jew, on November 7, 1938, unleashed a wave of murderous violence directed at Jews in Germany. After vom Rath finally died from his wounds on November 9, Hitler approved the pogrom that became known as *Kristallnacht*, the Night of Broken Glass. *Kristallnacht* raged over two days, and the Nazi-directed violence destroyed over 7,500 Jewish shops and businesses and all but one of the 275 synagogues in Germany. Mobs murdered one hundred Jews and injured countless more. The Gestapo and the SD, the security force of the SS, also arrested 30,000 Jews and sent them to concentration camps throughout the country. Despite Joseph Goebbels's characterization of the event as "an impulsive reaction by an enraged nation," other nations condemned Germany for its barbarity. President Roosevelt, outraged over the violence, recalled the American ambassador from Berlin in protest but took no further action against the Nazi state.[74]

Kristallnacht galvanized Alabama's Jews to a greater extent than at any time since the Nazis assumed power. Unlike the state press's reaction, no one in the Jewish community mistook the murderous violence as anything but a concerted, state-sanctioned effort to grind the Jews under the Nazi heel and either drive them from Germany or eliminate them altogether. It was, they recognized, open season on Jews. Such recognition profoundly affected not only their understanding of the enormous threat Jews in Europe faced but also their own sense of well-being and security. Ida Newman Fisher, a member of K'nesseth Israel in Birmingham, recalled that her Gentile neighbors did not understand why the "Hitler oppression" had distressed the Jewish population so profoundly. It infuriated her when they said, "this doesn't affect you, you're not that kind of Jew." Yet Fisher maintained that "I'm a Jew just like all the other Jews. They could turn against me just like against my people. . . . Why do you think I'm any different, because I speak without an accent?"[75] Fisher's response to her Gentile neighbors reveals the divide between Jews and Gentiles regarding how each perceived the Nazi threat. But as Rabbi Alex Klein of K'nesseth Israel noted, after *Kristallnacht* attitudes toward Germany's persecution of the Jews began to change among Jews and Gentiles. Many national magazines had altered their attitude toward "the Jewish question," recognizing the real danger Nazism posed, and Klein believed "that the recent persecutions in Germany are largely responsible for this."[76]

The violence of *Kristallnacht* also produced numerous protests and reactions from Gentiles. Birmingham mayor Jimmie Jones and Alabama governor Bibb Graves sent telegrams to President Roosevelt condemning the attack upon the Jews in Germany. As will be discussed in chapter 3, it challenged Baptists such as L. L. Gwaltney to reexamine long-held beliefs, and the state newspapers vigorously condemned the attacks. In Mobile, the Lamar Y. McLeod Post of the American Legion and the Mobile County Federation of Women's Clubs condemned the Nazis, who governed "by brute force and terrorize[d] helpless minorities." Leon Schwarz played a large role in organizing the Mobile protests.[77] Mobile's clergy, moreover, participated in a day of prayer for the Jews suffering in Germany. Rabbi Moses led a "quiet demonstration of sympathy" for an overflowing crowd at the Government Street Temple. Catholic bishop T. J. Toolen of the Mobile Diocese commented that "Hitler has proved himself insane. He is unjust, inhuman and a barbarian. . . . How can the Jewish people in Germany be blamed for the act of one lone boy, carried away by the injustices to his race? Yes, it is an act of cruelty and insanity on Hitler's part. No American could think otherwise." Presbyterian minister John Alexander stated the "Christian conscience must unite in opposing such inhuman brutality." Hoyt Horace Harwell of West End Baptist Church told his congregants that the Nazis "simply have to take it out on the Jews because of the inferior feeling they have in comparison to the members of this noble race in their midst. Out of it all will grow some good."[78] Other religious organizations followed suit. The Alabama Baptist State Convention met in Gadsden only a few days after *Kristallnacht*, and

Alfred J. Dickinson, pastor of First Baptist Church of Mobile, addressed the convention and lamented the treatment of the Jews in Europe. In his sermon, "A Militant Christianity and a Terrorized World," Dickinson condemned Nazi antisemitism but also warned his audience against prejudice in Baptist denominational life. The Alabama Baptist Convention subsequently passed a resolution protesting the "injustices" against the Jews.[79]

After *Kristallnacht*, Alabama's Jews clearly recognized the murderous intent of Nazi antisemitism. They placed greater emphasis on rescuing the Jews remaining in Germany—after the *Anschluss* in March 1938 and the Munich Conference in September 1938, an emphasis on Jews in Austria and Czechoslovakia as well—a task made infinitely more difficult by the outbreak of a general European war in September 1939. Individuals, congregations, and Jewish organizations worked incessantly, lobbying for increased immigration into the United States, sponsoring refugees who had managed to flee Europe, and working to open Palestine as a possible refuge for European Jews. As the United States entered the war in December 1941, Jews responded, as did most Americans, with patriotic fervor and concern for family and friends in the service. Unlike other Americans, many Jews had relatives trapped in Nazi-occupied Europe, and they watched helplessly as the horrific revelations of the Nazi mass killings became public in November 1942. The Final Solution only confirmed the lethal threat of Nazism to Jews everywhere, and it transformed a majority of the Reform Jews, who had viewed Palestine as a logical place of refuge for European Jews fleeing persecution, from being opponents of a separate Jewish state to a grudging acceptance of Zionism.

2
The Refugee Crisis, 1938–41

As the Nazis enforced increasingly restrictive antisemitic measures such as economic boycotts, professional and social segregation, and the legal removal of their civil rights and citizenship, German Jews were systematically isolated and marginalized. By 1938 the Nazis' efforts to expunge the Jews from German life, as well as from the recently annexed Austria, took the form of forced emigration. The Nazis, however, placed enormous obstacles in the way of emigration by confiscating Jewish property, imposing a steep emigration tax, and limiting the amount of money that Jews could transfer from German banks.

Few nations opened their doors to the impoverished Jewish refugees. The two nations best suited to aid the Jews, the United States and Great Britain, both maintained strict limitations on immigration. In the United States, the public outcry against a wave of refugees and entrenched antisemitic sentiment in the federal government resulted in thousands of Jews being denied entrance into the country during the 1930s. The US State Department imposed antisemitic-driven, bureaucratic hurdles—what historian David Wyman has called "paper walls"—that prevented Jewish refugees from entering the United States in greater numbers.[1] Approximately ninety thousand Jewish refugees entered the United States between 1933 and 1939, a far smaller number than the immigration quotas from Nazi-dominated lands allowed. Those Jews generally came to New York, often with only the clothes on their backs. The rapid influx of Jewish refugees to New York created tremendous financial and social strains on the New York Jewish community. Many Jewish leaders worried that overcrowding "was creating another Jewish ghetto," prompting intensive efforts to resettle refugees throughout the country.[2] Great Britain, like the United States, also erected barriers to fleeing European Jews. Britain had issued the Balfour Declaration in 1917 that promised the creation of a homeland for the Jews in Palestine. Despite this pledge and the desperate plight of the Jews in Europe, Britain ignored the cries for aid from Jewish and humanitarian groups and refused to open Palestine as a haven for the Jews. Indeed, the Nazi policy of forced emigration of Jews failed because of the restrictive and often antisemitic immigration policies of these nations.

Because of the dire threat to Jews driven under the Nazi heel, made more explicit after *Kristallnacht*, Alabama's Jews, like Jews throughout the United States, clearly recognized a responsibility to aid and support Jews worldwide. They organized at both the local and state level to work for the rescue of those still trapped in Nazi-dominated Europe. These efforts included lobbying for relaxed immigration policies and opening Palestine as a refuge for persecuted European Jews as well as sponsoring refugees who wanted to flee or who had already fled Germany, Austria, and Czechoslovakia. Although these lobbying efforts had little effect on the immigration and refugee policies of either the United States or Great Britain, the sponsorship of refugees by Alabama's Jews had a profound effect on both the individual refugees and Alabama's Jewish community at large.

Non-Jewish Attitudes toward Jewish Refugees

Public opinion in Alabama, as well as throughout the United States, generally sympathized with the Jews attempting to flee Nazi persecution, but this did not translate into demands to provide refuge for them in the United States. As early as 1934, editors at the *Birmingham Age-Herald* called for "sympathy and understanding" from the US government to fill its immigration quota from Germany, although its motive "is not on behalf of Jews merely but of all Germans who are under the Nazi heel." At no time did the editors of the *Age-Herald*, or anybody else, advocate exceeding existing quotas. Later that same year, the *Age-Herald* suggested Palestine as the solution to the great "burden" that German refugees placed on the nations of the world, a common refrain when discussing the plight of Jewish refugees.[3] Even after the intense violence of *Kristallnacht* in 1938, there is little evidence to suggest that Alabamians made any extraordinary effort to aid suffering Jews above advocating filling existing immigration quotas, a position consistent with national opinion. In the immediate aftermath of *Kristallnacht*, a poll by the National Opinion Research Center in Chicago revealed that 94 percent of Americans "disapproved of Nazi treatment of Jews," but 72 percent of those polled opposed "admitting a large number of German Jews into the United States."[4] The *Birmingham News* spoke for many non-Jews concerning the refugee crisis when it reasoned that in the midst of the lingering Depression, no country could be "expected to increase immigration beyond present legal limits," and that "there should be ample latitude within existing immigration quotas to take care of most, if not all, of the refugees." Yet the *News'* sister paper, the *Age-Herald*, noted the problems associated with increased immigration and still argued that "the overshadowing fact still stands out that there is really no reason great enough to justify a failure to help these pitiful women, children and men." It asked, "why could not those nations of the earth which deserve to be called humane work out a system of special quotas for receiving these people. . . . Sure it would be hard. Sure it would call for sacrifice. But whose earth is this anyway? Does it not belong to all God's children or only to certain fortunate ones?"[5] Such questions proved to be only rhetorical as the *Age-Herald* failed to follow up on that line of inquiry. Little more was said in the press about increased quotas. In the months following *Kristallnacht*, attention on immigration peaked. By 1940, few in the press or public addressed the issue. Instead, the drive to open British Palestine for Jewish refugees gained momentum.

Uncertainty and Jewish stereotypes frequently characterized the discussion in the public and the press over the issues of refugees and immigration. In late 1938, David Akins from Jasper expressed his disgust with Nazi brutality but argued that Jewish immigration to the United States would cause problems because "the Jews are not as a race accustomed to living in the lower brackets of society. And a great influx of them to this country would be bound to cause an anti-Jewish feeling in time to come, and we do not want that to take place here." He offered no solution to the problem of persecuted Jews and took a position similar to many of those in the press: "someone no doubt in the near future will advance a workable plan for caring for these unfortunate Jews, but what untold suffering must take place before it can be put into effect!" "I think any old place," he surmised, "will be better than those European countries where they now live."[6] Akins's reference to Jews as a race, not as an ethnicity or religion, reflected a common perception that was readily apparent in the comments and correspondence of non-Jews during the period.

An intriguing solution to the refugee problem came from J. B. Lockhart of Talladega who suggested that the six hundred thousand persecuted German Jews settle in Alabama. Lockhart pointed to the abundance of uncultivated land in Alabama—he estimated twenty-five million acres—which "would allow each persecuted Jew 40 acres of land" and believed that should all six hundred thousand Jews resettle in the state, Alabama "would take on the greatest boom in its history." This suggestion, he wrote, "should be considered by those . . . who are selfish enough to be willing to see a race of people persecuted and abused because we are not willing to share our abundant resources with them."[7] The *Birmingham News* had previously discounted such possible settlement plans when it argued that "the Jew of today is not well adapted socially and by nature to pioneering colonial enterprises. . . . As a race, the European Jew is ambitious and eager to acquire educational and cultural advantages for himself and family." Because of the Jew's nature, the *News* called any plan to settle Jews in frontier areas ill-advised because the colony would, "in all probability, disintegrate and the colonists would drift back to more civilized areas."[8] The National Refugee Service (NRS) in New York came to the same conclusion after it had previously considered settling refugees in rural areas and on farms, even instructing selected refugees in agriculture at the National Farm School in Pennsylvania. Rabbi Joseph Krauskopf had founded the National Farm School in Doylestown, Pennsylvania, in 1896 so its graduates would "act as leaders of Jewish colonies now in existence or hereafter to be planted. In this way, perhaps, the pressure in the large cities within a few trades may be relieved, and instead of slaving in the sweat shops, the sons and daughters of these laborers will be glad to do better work and live happier lives on farms." The NRS, however, ultimately determined that "too few refugees were fit to be farmers, or wanted to be."[9]

Others also assisted Jewish refugees, including student organizations. At Alabama Polytechnic Institute, the Omicron Delta Kappa (ODK) honor fraternity offered to sponsor a student refugee at the Auburn campus, while the events of *Kristallnacht* prompted the University of Alabama's Hillel Foundation, a Jewish student organization, to sponsor a German Jewish refugee.[10] Jewish students and members of Jewish fraternities and sororities at the university, including both northern and southern Reform and Orthodox Jews, participated in Hillel. The Hillel Student Council collected contributions from university students to help fund the refugee's education at the university, and included tuition, room, and board. By 1940, the organization sponsored two refugee students. Hillel collaborated with the Jewish Federated Charities of Tuscaloosa, B'nai B'rith, and Tuscaloosa's Reform Temple Emanu-El to raise funds for Jewish relief. Tuscaloosa's Gentiles also supported the fund-raising efforts for persecuted European Jewry, and Bruce Shelton of the *Tuscaloosa News*, who had fanned the flames of outrage at "outsider" Jews in the ILD just five years prior, noted that the city's Jews "have given to our charities in a manner far out of their own proportionate numbers" and that "their cause should arouse the sympathetic understanding of everyone."[11]

Alabama's Jews Respond to the Crisis

Individual Jews also sponsored family members and numerous nonfamilial refugees, often much earlier than 1938. It is unknown, however, just how many people came to Alabama in this fashion during the 1930s, but these efforts, which comprised relatively small numbers when compared to major metropolitan centers such as New York City, unquestionably saved lives. Individuals such as Sol Kahn, Charles Wampold, and Julius Hagedorn, in addition to Joseph Abraham and Herman Loeb, were only a fraction of the Jews in the state who sacrificed much to bring family and friends to the United States. Sol Kahn, who had been brought over from Germany by his uncle many years prior to the Nazi attainment of power, in return brought over his nephew and two nieces from Worms, Germany, in 1934. Kahn owned Kahn Manufacturing Company in Mobile and supposedly signed between one and two hundred affidavits—sworn statements that the visa applicant (immigrant) would not become a public charge—during the 1930s to rescue German Jews from Nazi persecution, so many that a family member jokingly quipped that he "was surprised that Hitler didn't send him an Iron Cross" for removing so many Jews from Germany.[12]

In Opelika, Julius and Amelia Hagedorn sponsored six of their relatives from Westheim, Germany, in 1937. Julius S. Hagedorn, who grew up in the Westphalia region of Germany, had returned to visit his relatives in 1935 and had been appalled at the antisemitism rampant there. After his return to the United States, he told the Opelika Kiwanis Club of the "depression and despair among the people" of Germany.[13] Hagedorn quickly made arrangements for his relatives, his brother and sister, Joseph Hagedorn and Rosalie Hagedorn Israelsohn, as well as Israelsohn's son-in-law and daughter, Arnold and Hedwig Stern, and their children, Heinz and Hannelora, to immigrate to the United States. On June 24, 1937, Hagedorn met them at the dock in New York City.

Upon their arrival in Opelika, the townspeople greeted them at the train station, and Opelika's mayor, John Crossley, presented them with a proclamation welcoming them to the United States and to Opelika. In order to acculturate more quickly, Julius Hagedorn suggested that the children Americanize their names—Heinz became Henry and Hannelora became Lora. The local kindergarten teacher, Louise Tollison, even learned German prior to their arrival in order to communicate with the Stern children and help them learn English. While acculturation came easier for the children—Henry Stern recalled that they experienced "a typical American childhood"—the adults understandably had a more difficult time. Ruth Meadows, a vocational teacher in town, worked with the Sterns, using a Sears Roebuck catalog to help them learn English; Hagedorn and Israelsohn, however, never learned English.[14]

Like other refugees who had been sponsored by friends or relatives, they were assured employment. Just as Kahn had done in Mobile, Hagedorn employed his relatives in his business, the largest department store in Opelika. Yet unlike many of the refugees who made it to the United States, the Sterns, Hagedorn, and Israelsohn had made additional financial arrangements to begin their new life in America. Prior to their departure, they sold their belongings in Germany and subsequently purchased goods and merchandise—linens, jewelry, and silver—which they shipped to Hagedorn's department store in Opelika. After they arrived, they sold the goods to members of the community and used the money to establish themselves, even building a house in town. The warm welcome the Sterns, Hagedorn, and Israelsohn experienced was atypical for most refugees, and it resulted from the goodwill of Opelika's citizens and the prominence of Julius Hagedorn in the community. It certainly made an impression, as Henry Stern observed that their welcome was in sharp contrast to the brutal treatment of Jews by the Nazis.[15]

Some individuals relied heavily upon their representatives to assist them. Alabama's politicians strongly condemned the Nazis' treatment of Jews in Europe and were clearly sympathetic to the plight of the persecuted German Jews, but they nevertheless advocated maintaining the current immigration policy. Their support of these immigration restrictions, however, did not extend to their Jewish constituents' family and friends imperiled in Europe whom they assisted by removing the obstacles to obtaining American visas. For instance, US senator Lister Hill used his political influence in Washington to rescue numerous European Jews and assisted many in Montgomery's Jewish community and throughout Alabama in matters both great and mundane. Charles Wampold in Montgomery, a member of Temple Beth-Or and the Montgomery Jewish Federation, used his influence with Hill to get his wife's parents, Bertha and Moritz Manasse, out of Germany. Initially, Moritz Manasse resisted leaving Germany, believing that the persecution "would pass, in time," but after Nazis ransacked their house during *Kristallnacht* the Manasses finally fled, arriving in Montgomery in February 1939, with "nothing but the clothes on their back."[16] Hill also helped Herman Loeb Sr. bring between thirty-five and forty relatives from Bavaria to the United States in 1937, and, on behalf of Etz Ahayem in Montgomery, he secured the visa of Rabbi Moses Albagli, who assumed a position with the Sephardic congregation in 1939.[17] While Hill's sympathy for his Jewish constituents and friends existed largely because of his mother's German Jewish heritage, a fact that he concealed from the public, his actions on behalf of the persecuted European Jews emanated from his humanitarian concern for them and his outrage at Nazi brutality. Indeed, throughout his long political career, Hill unselfishly assisted numerous people, both publicly and privately, who came to him in need.[18] He never made public his actions on behalf of the Jews, nor did other Alabama politicians who helped their Jewish constituents, but he worried that his Jewish heritage, rumored in the community, might hurt him in elections. Hill had actually been raised as a Catholic, but because he was extremely conscious of his public image, he renounced his Catholicism when he sought public office in 1923.

US representative John Sparkman also became a "veteran at writing letters in connection with immigration matters" and helped numerous constituents bring their families into the country. In one case, Sparkman worked for almost two years to secure visas for many family members of Joseph Abraham, a friend and former Huntsville constituent.[19] Abraham's aunts, Elsa and Sofie Loew, had been removed from their homes in Germany and interned at Camp de Gurs, Basses Pyrenees, in Vichy France, in late 1940.[20] Sparkman's attempts to secure passage and visas for the two sisters met with resistance at the State Department, which advised him that it did not "invite aliens to the Consular Offices, and especially those aliens in concentration camps," to negotiate for immigration visas. The State Department determined that the German government had "complete control" over their release from the concentration camp and their transportation from the internment camp to Marseilles.[21] For over a year, the Loew case met with postponement after postponement, much to the dismay of the Abraham family. A day after the Japanese attack on Pearl Harbor, Joseph Abraham despondently wrote to Sparkman "that the war has, or soon will, put a definite end to all immigration for the present, and our only hope now is that my aunts can survive in France." The Loew sisters did not perish. After considerable delay, Elsa and Sofie arrived in America in mid-1942. Abraham credited the determined efforts of Sparkman for their survival.[22]

Jewish Communities Organize

Where individuals and student organizations such as Hillel and ODK had selflessly sponsored refugees, Alabama's Jewish community organizations had not. In 1938, however, Jewish organizations throughout the state began signing affidavits that made them responsible for refugees, so the refugees did not become a financial burden to the general community. Strictly speaking, organizations could not sign affidavits, only individuals could do so. To circumvent this hurdle, individuals within the Jewish community signed the affidavit, with the promised financial backing of the organization. The visa application process, including the information and forms the State Department required in the 1930s and 1940s, was both onerous and extensive.

Those applying to immigrate to the United States had to provide the State Department the following: "(1.) Visa Application (five copies); (2.) Birth Certificate (two copies; quotas were assigned by country of birth); (3.) The Quota Number must have been reached (This established the person's place on the waiting list to enter the United States.); (4.) A Certificate of Good Conduct from German police authorities, including two copies respectively of the following: Police dossier; Prison record; Military record; Other government records about the individual: 1. Affidavits of Good Conduct (required after September 1940); 2. Proof that the applicant passed a Physical Examination at the U.S. Consulate; 3. Proof of Permission To Leave Germany (imposed September 30, 1939); 4. Proof that the prospective immigrant had Booked Passage to the Western Hemisphere (required after September 1939); 5. Two Sponsors ('affiants'); close relatives of prospective immigrants were preferred." The sponsors of these immigrants, whether family or not, had to be "American citizens or have had permanent resident status, and they must have filled out an Affidavit of Support and Sponsorship (six copies notarized), as well as provided: Certified copy of their most recent Federal tax return; Affidavit from a bank regarding their accounts; Affidavit from any other responsible person regarding other assets (an affidavit from the sponsor's employer or a statement of commercial rating)."[23] Paper Walls indeed.

The organizations that sponsored refugees provided housing, job training, employment, and some even offered start-up loans. Such support for the newly arrived refugees may have varied according to the specific community, but resettlement generally proceeded in a similar fashion throughout the United States. According to William Haber, the executive director of the NRS, the resettlement "apparatus begins to function for the refugee family when it reaches the community. A committee, usually composed of local housewives, takes charge of the housing problem—finding an adequate room or apartment for the family and supplying minor deficiencies in household equipment. . . . Normally the refugee committee has some sort of an adjustment program: provision for entertaining the refugees at local homes, parties at Jewish centers, social activities for younger people."[24] The sponsorship of refugees, however, did not replace contributions, fund-raising, or lobbying as the primary methods that organizations employed to aid Jews in Europe, and local groups continued to contribute directly to Jewish welfare and host lectures for fund-raising campaigns "to alleviate suffering and aid escape of Jews trapped by anti-Semitic aggressors in European countries." For instance, Mobile's Jews sponsored a lecture on Austrian Jews at the Jewish Progressive Club in June 1939, while the Mobile section of the National Council of Jewish Women (NCJW) sent generous gifts to "homeless refugees interned in friendly concentration camps in Canada" and began the first Red Cross serving room in the city.[25]

In April 1938, Beatrice Kaufman, who had been appointed as a delegate to the National Council of Jewish Women's Conference in Nashville, urged the Montgomery Jewish Federation to "accept the obligation of caring for refugee families from Germany," as the increasing number of refugees in New York had placed great strain on the resources of the New York Jewish community. Kaufman had been inspired at the Nashville conference by representatives from the National Coordinating Committee for Aid to Refugees Coming from Germany (NCC), which encouraged southern communities to sponsor more refugees. Samuel C. Kohs, the director of the Resettlement Division of the NCC, suggested much the same when he met with members of Birmingham's United Jewish Fund, arguing that "it is easier for [refugees] to adjust to smaller and friendlier communities," although such claims did not always prove to be true. By May 1938, the Montgomery federation had named Henry Weil to chair a local coordinating committee to resettle refugee families in Montgomery.[26]

The NCC originated in 1934 in order to coordinate the activities of approximately twenty Jewish relief and aid organizations in the United States, drawing most of its funding from the American Jewish JDC and the United Jewish Appeal (UJA), two organizations to which Alabama's Jews prominently contributed.[27] The NCC made no serious effort to resettle refugees from Nazi Germany until 1936, "when the flow of refugees . . . began to assume considerable proportions." That same year it created a Resettlement Division to address the problems associated with growing numbers of émigrés and determined to resettle the refugees throughout the country for three reasons. The first reason was to prevent the concentration of the newly arrived refugees in their port of entry, in this case, New York City, a development that would have crippled the support structure of the local Jewish community if left unchecked. The second was for fear of an antisemitic reaction in New York City. The NCC based its third reason on the assumption "that many of the new arrivals could make a better adjustment in the outlying communities where economic opportunities were better and where the Americanization process might be more rapid."[28] To fulfill its mission, the Resettlement Division contacted sponsors, arranged housing, and found employment for refugees. Its work with approximately nine hundred cooperating communities throughout the United States consumed the bulk of its time and energy. As Jewish immigration peaked in 1939, the newly created National Refugee Service succeeded the NCC in caring for the recently arrived refugees, focusing solely on the resettlement and integration of the refugees into American life.[29]

Jewish federations and organizations throughout Alabama worked with the NCC/NRS to help those who had escaped Nazi Germany, with the Birmingham and Montgomery communities taking the lead in accepting refugees and coordinating resettlement into smaller towns in the surrounding areas. By the end of 1938, Birmingham's United Jewish Fund had joined Montgomery's federation in creating a refugee settlement program. Lee B. Weil, the president of Evansville Packing Company and a prominent and respected leader in the Jewish community, chaired Birmingham's Refugee Committee.[30] Walter Lobman, the president of the Montgomery federation, expressed the sentiments of many Jews and Jewish organizations throughout the state when he claimed that it was their great responsibility "to render maximum service to our oppressed people of Europe. . . . So much has the problems of our people increased since 1933 because of events in Germany . . . and other European lands that responsibilities must be shared by every Jew in every community of the United States, for European Jewry is 'Calling America.'"[31]

The first major hurdle both local organizations and the NRS faced centered on the willingness and preparation of refugees to resettle in Alabama. After having been forced from their homes and making a long, arduous journey to the United States, psychologically many refugees found it extremely difficult, if not impossible, to leave the safety and security of New York, with its refugee organizations, large Jewish population, and the economic opportunity the city offered, for an unknown location elsewhere in the country. The problems the NRS and local Alabama communities faced, however, were not new. Similar resettlement of immigrant Jews had been attempted, with some success, by Jewish organizations in the early twentieth century, as immigration from Eastern Europe had increased dramatically after 1881. The Industrial Removal Office (IRO) and the Galveston movement both intended to resettle Jewish immigrants into the heartland of the United States. The IRO operated from 1901 to 1922 resettling unemployed Jewish immigrants from New York to other towns and cities throughout the nation, including Alabama. In fact, between 1901 and 1913, the years when immigration from Eastern Europe was heaviest, the IRO resettled 834 Jewish immigrants in Alabama, the majority being Russian Jews who settled in Birmingham.[32] The IRO, like the NRS later, wanted to speed the process of assimilation and avoid the creation of more Jewish ghettoes in the northeast, generally perceived to be overpopulated slums that festered with disease and crime, which Jewish officials believed contributed to antisemitism among non-Jews. Conversely, the Galveston movement, which flourished from 1907 to 1914, encouraged European Jews to disembark in Galveston, Texas, rather than at ports on the East Coast, such as Ellis Island in New York. Once at Galveston, the Jewish Immigrants' Information Bureau directed them to places west of the Mississippi River. Where the IRO and the Galveston movement worked through B'nai B'rith lodges, the NRS worked through local Jewish federations. Like the NRS, too, in regard to the refugee crisis, both the Galveston movement and the IRO's attempts to resettle immigrant Jews into the nation's interior made barely a dent in the total numbers of Jewish immigrants who had flooded into New York and other northeastern cities.[33]

The NRS tried to avoid some of the problems that plagued these earlier resettlement efforts. Through its Social and Cultural Adjustment Division, the NRS attempted to acquaint refugees with American life and culture prior to their resettlement. This included education about American history, civics, American customs, and the English language, with which many, if not most, of the refugees had difficulty. In fact, the NRS advocated rapid social adjustment for those being resettled in order that it should deprive "anti-alien and anti-Semitic elements [from using] anti-refugee arguments," a preventive measure that benefited both the refugee and Jewish community.[34]

Representatives from the various coordinating committees in the state met in Montgomery in December 1938 for "the purpose of formulating plans and devising ways and means of handling the refugees [throughout] the State of Alabama." They elected Lucien Loeb of Montgomery as the state chairman and organized the state into multiple regions to coordinate the influx of refugees more efficiently, while Birmingham and Montgomery functionally served as the two centers of refugee activity and coordination in the state. Loeb supplied each regional coordinating committee with essential information concerning refugee resettlement and worked directly with the Resettlement Division of the NCC and, after mid-1939, the NRS. Each coordinating committee had three active subcommittees to handle placement, social services, and affidavits. The local coordinating committees pledged to accept "a certain number of refugees on a yearly quota basis," with each community determining its own quota and accepting full responsibility for their welfare.[35] The direction and decisions concerning the refugees' resettlement, however, rested solely with the coordinating committee within each region.

In many ways the lack of social welfare agencies in Alabama at both the state and local levels and the guidance that they could have provided contributed to the initial uncertainty and confusion of refugee committees and added another organizational hurdle that the state committee and local committees had to overcome. Field representatives from the NRS traveled throughout the state meeting with coordinating committees and community leaders to discuss how best to organize themselves. Jewish communities varied throughout the state, with some thoroughly organized to handle the influx of émigrés and others just preparing to organize. Once organized, these committees had to have a source of funding to support the refugees at least until they became self-supporting. Moreover, they had to determine a realistic standard of how to treat refugees once they arrived in greater numbers, as communities at first lavished an inordinate amount of attention on individual émigrés. In one case the Mobile Refugee Committee hired a maid for a newly arrived family, and, in another, a refugee "was 'wined and dined' to such an extent that the refugee indicated that he might have come down for a social visit rather [than] for making a living."[36]

While Gentiles in the press, including Grover Hall in Montgomery and Bruce Shelton in Tuscaloosa, offered encouragement to these Jewish efforts, other Gentiles proposed more material assistance to help resettle refugees by offering to donate tracts of land in Florence, Montgomery, and Autaugaville.[37] The most generous offer came from Prattville merchant E. H. Pearson, who contacted Lucien Loeb in mid-1939 about a plan to resettle "fifty to one hundred Jewish families . . . in the Autaugaville Community," only twenty-five miles west of Montgomery. Pearson, a manufacturer of mops and brooms, offered to sell 4,500 acres of land and his factory and mills, which included twenty-two existing houses, in order to "work out a real home for hundreds of Jewish people who are now homeless." Pearson's proposal called for the creation of a cooperative rather than a privately owned operation and detailed the expansion of the factories and mills, and the clearing of one thousand acres for farms and pastures to facilitate the gradual addition of refugee families to the settlement. In addition to offering to work for the cooperative for "one year without pay so that the business can be firmly established and on a paying basis," Pearson asked Loeb to "select some one whom you have confidence in to set up a system of bookkeeping and open a bank account," in order that the enterprise be above board and that the Jewish community play a central role in its operation.[38]

Pearson had garnered the support of Autauga County officials; the Baptist and Methodist churches in the community; the local bank; and the probate judge, J. F. Posey, not an inconsequential figure in local and county politics. As a member of the Autauga County school board, Pearson also promised educational support for the refugees.[39] As he explained to Loeb, not only do the refugees "need a home and would agree to any reasonable terms" to enter the United States, but also that "we need these people. . . . Our section needs these people. We have land that needs to be cleared and worked. Wooded sections that need to be protected from forest fires, so that a supply of timber will always be available . . . ensuring our section a supply of lumber for years to come." Moreover, he explained, "this set-up would work in harmony with the people of this section, as our people have already expressed themselves as being glad to do all in their power to make the plan a success."[40]

Walter Lobman, Max Baum, and Henry Weil, all members of the Montgomery Jewish Federation, visited Autaugaville to examine Pearson's project and came away convinced of the feasibility of the plan. Because the $50,000 purchase price Pearson suggested went far beyond anything the local Jewish communities could afford, they encouraged Loeb to take the proposal to the NRS, "since the money has to come from New York."[41] In New York, NRS officials rejected the plan. William Haber, the executive director of the NRS, explained that they directed their limited resources toward industrial projects for refugees rather than agricultural projects. He told Loeb that a "relatively small percentage of refugees have had agricultural training," leading most refugees to seek urban areas for resettlement. Even for those who have had agricultural training, Haber continued, "we have found it very difficult to persuade refugees to go into Southern agricultural projects," largely due to the isolation of rural southern communities.[42]

Such reticence on the part of numerous refugees to resettle in the South often produced friction between the NRS and Jewish leaders in Alabama. Many of Alabama's Jewish communities initially requested refugees with certain skills to fill specific jobs, requests the NRS could scarcely fulfill. This caused delays and, in some cases cancellations, in sending refugees to these communities, producing frustration at the state and local level as well as with representatives of the NRS. In July 1940, the NRS could not find refugees for two Alabama communities "simply because of very definite restrictions imposed on the kind of individual to be sent." It also failed to find a family to resettle in Jasper, a small town northwest of Birmingham with a small Jewish population. This caused Birmingham investment banker Mervyn Sterne, a member of the state committee, to express his dismay to Loeb about such delays: "It seems perfectly silly to consider taking up your time and that of others who help you, to get small communities to agree to take refugees and then have no refugees sent them."[43] Loeb subsequently arranged for a refugee family already in Montgomery to resettle in Jasper, although the family returned to Montgomery soon after because it found life in Jasper "very unsatisfactory." An NRS official hoped that the family's return to Montgomery would "impress on both Mr. Sterne and Mr. Loeb the problem of getting families to leave New York for certain of these small towns."[44]

Sterne, one of the most influential men in the Birmingham community, led the United Jewish Fund's initial efforts to aid the persecuted Jews of Europe, and his support for such endeavors never waned. Yet Sterne's antipathy toward northern organizations and his "expressed distrust of professional social workers" produced a deep suspicion of the NRS that frequently prevented the state committee from working smoothly with representatives of the NRS. Both Sterne and Birmingham merchant Isadore Pizitz thought the resettlement of refugees to be a "New York" problem, with which Alabama's Jews were willing to help, rather than the responsibility of all American Jews. They both supported the effort to distribute refugees across the nation but suggested that the NRS adopt a policy of "resettle or else" for reluctant refugees in order to alleviate overcrowding in New York and blamed the NRS for the "poor preparation" of refugees once they arrived. Despite Sterne's and Pizitz's reservations, the NRS and the state committee agreed to concentrate on Birmingham, Montgomery, and Mobile for "general resettlement opportunities" due to the restrictions and limitations of smaller communities that "made it almost impossible to resettle successfully the types of family units that were available."[45] The Birmingham, Montgomery, and Mobile committees then looked to small surrounding communities for further resettlement opportunities. To help ease the frustration involved in delays and cancellations, the NRS urged communities to receive a certain number of refugees and place them in jobs after their arrival. Once refugee committees began doing this, the numbers of refugees placed in Alabama increased.

Despite organizational problems and delays, state and local committees made significant progress in resettling and integrating refugees into American life. In one instance, the refugee committees throughout the state, under the aegis of the state coordinating committee, sponsored a total of ten male refugees to attend the National Youth Administration's (NYA) training facility in Gadsden. The Roosevelt administration created the NYA in 1935 to provide part-time work-study opportunities for high school and college students and vocational education and apprentice training to unemployed youths in order to help them earn a living. The associate director of the Works Progress Administration (WPA), the liberal Alabamian Aubrey Williams, directed the NYA as it attempted to give millions of unemployed young Americans "socially useful and constructive work so that they can become assets rather than liabilities to society."[46] The refugees Alabama's Jewish organizations sponsored attended the trade school in Gadsden until June 1942 when the federal government converted it to a Civil Service training school and limited participation to citizens.[47]

Enemy Aliens

Nazi aggression in the late 1930s and the rapid conquest of Western Europe after war began in September 1939 prompted an increase in American defense preparation. This accelerated both the economy and Americans' fears of Nazi spies and saboteurs in the United States. As historian Arnold Krammer explains, "foreigners in any country have always been viewed with some suspicion, especially during times of international tension. The situation in America was no different. . . . Now, the [European] war confirmed America's worst fears. The sudden appearance of Fifth Columns in Poland, Norway, Belgium, Holland, and France were significant to Hitler's successes. German citizens and Nazi sympathizers, living quietly among the population, cast off their sheepskins when Hitler signaled, revealing themselves as enemy wolves."[48] President Roosevelt voiced such fears of a Fifth Column in a June 1940 press conference when he warned that "the refugees has [*sic*] got to be checked because unfortunately, among the refugees there are some spies, as has been found in other countries. And not all of them are voluntary spies—it is rather a horrible story but in some of the other countries that refugees out of Germany have gone to, especially Jewish refugees; they have found a number of definitely proven spies . . . it is something we have got to watch."[49] On June 28, 1940, Congress approved the Alien Registration Act that required all immigrants, including refugees, over the age of fourteen to be registered and fingerprinted at their local post office, a process that met with overwhelming approval from the American public. According to a Gallup poll conducted on June 10, 1940, 95 percent of respondents replied "yes" when asked the question, "Should all people who are not United States citizens be required to register with the Government?"[50] Within four months, almost five million aliens had registered with the government.

Once the United States entered the war against Germany, the Jews who had fled from Nazi Germany became "enemy aliens." Roosevelt quickly issued Presidential Proclamation 2526, which gave the government the authority to detain, arrest, and deport citizens of Germany who had not become naturalized citizens of the United States. The Federal Bureau of Investigation (FBI) undertook the investigation and surveillance of enemy aliens—the FBI's investigations of potential threats actually began in 1936—and such scrutiny did not spare Jews who had fled Nazi persecution, as Roosevelt's warning made clear.[51] Some within the FBI reasoned that Jewish refugees who had family still in Germany could be forced to aid the Nazis, lest their relatives be killed, and this "unreasonable suspicion of Jewish immigrants and exiles" helped to promote antialien and antirefugee sentiment within the larger population that went hand in hand with the growth of antisemitism in the United States, forcing these refugees to "toe the mark."[52] The United States did not, and indeed could not, intern or relocate Germans or Italians the way it had the Japanese on the West Coast, but the mass evacuations of the Japanese created immense trepidation on the part of Alabama's Jewish refugees that they, too, might be evacuated and interned. While German and Italian émigrés avoided internment, the hastily created Enemy Alien Internment Program imprisoned 31,275 enemy aliens deemed a threat to national security between 1941 and 1946. In Birmingham, the FBI arrested twenty-eight German enemy aliens during the war, although none were Jewish refugees.[53] Nevertheless, this suspicion, as well as the forced evacuation of the Japanese on the West Coast, produced significant consternation among Alabama's Jewish refugees who showed "a genuine desire to do what was expected of them."[54] On February 20, 1942, however, Roosevelt's Executive Order 9106 relaxed the restrictions on both German and Italian enemy aliens and encouraged them to become American citizens.

By 1941 events in Europe transpired that severely limited the ability of Jews to emigrate from wartime Europe and left their fate in the hands of the Nazis. On June 22, 1941, Nazi Germany implemented Operation Barbarossa, a surprise attack on the Soviet Union. Almost immediately, Heinrich Himmler deployed the *Einsatzgruppen*, mobile killing squads that identified and executed Jews, or anyone deemed a threat to the Nazi state in occupied Soviet territory. The invasion of the Soviet Union and the access to the millions of Jews in Eastern Europe set in motion the plans for the extermination of the Jews in Europe. On July 31, 1941, Hermann Göring ordered Reinhard Heydrich to create an "overall plan of the preliminary organizational, practical and financial measures for the execution of the intended final solution of the Jewish question." By October 1941, the Nazi policy of forced emigration and the expulsion of Jews from the Greater German Reich came to a halt as Hitler forbade any further Jewish emigration. This essentially ended the outflux of Jews from Nazi-dominated territories. On January 20, 1942, at a conference at Wannsee outside of Berlin, Heydrich unveiled to Nazi officials the Final Solution of the "Jewish question," the diabolical plan to exterminate systematically all of the Jews remaining in Europe. The Nazis had concentrated Jews in ghettos and detainment camps in Germany and occupied Europe since the beginning of the war in 1939, making deportation of the Jews to the rapidly constructed—in some cases previously constructed—killing centers in Poland and Eastern Europe easier to accomplish. The implementation of the Final Solution ended in the murder of approximately six million Jews.

The NRS resettled over fourteen thousand refugees throughout the United States, a task made infinitely more difficult because, according to the NRS, the refugee who arrived in New York in 1941 was "older, less employable, has practically no means of his own, and has health problems generally associated with higher age groups of the population. In other words, the refugee of 1941 is less resettleable in spite of the fact that communities are now willing to accept refugees for resettlement who are older and less employable than the refugees who came in the years 1937 to 1939."[55] As the number of Jewish refugees entering the United States declined precipitously by the end of 1941, so too did the numbers being resettled. By 1942, with the United States having entered the war, immigration ground to a halt and resettlement of refugees effectively came to an end.

The Birmingham Region

One of the first refugees a community organization sponsored in Birmingham arrived through the auspices of the German-Jewish Children's Aid (GJCA), supported by Birmingham's section of the NCJW. The GJCA began in 1934 in order to save German Jewish children threatened by the growing antisemitic persecution of the Nazi regime. In 1938, the NCJW assumed responsibility for the GJCA and negotiated with the federal government for immigration visas. Women in the local section of the NCJW secured funds and found homes for the children, although they made it clear that "the children were not to be legally adopted, since the parents hoped to be reunited with them, either in Germany or in some other country at some future time."[56] This was nothing new for the NCJW, as the organization had been involved in social reform efforts since it had been founded in 1893. In fact, the establishment of the NCJW marked a new direction for Jewish women as they moved from "denominational concerns to civic uplift and politics, and changed from society ladies to club women."[57] Indeed, local sections of the NCJW had developed programs to aid immigrants in the organization's first few years, and a national program of immigrant aid work had been established by 1903. The GJCA was but an extension of that earlier effort.[58]

Tragically, Henry Birnbrey, who arrived in Birmingham in 1938 through the GJCA, was never reunited with his parents, as both mother and father perished in Germany. Thrown into a concentration camp and severely beaten after *Kristallnacht*, Birnbrey's father, Edmund Birnbrey, died a month later from his injuries. His mother, Jenny Birnbrey, died not long after. No other children came to Alabama through the GJCA. Birnbrey, who was fourteen at the time, stayed in foster homes in Birmingham for nine months before moving to Atlanta. On Sundays he "made the church circuit, speaking to churches about what was going on in Germany." In June 1943, he joined the US Army and served in the 30th Infantry Division, even participating in the D-Day landings at Normandy in 1944.[59] Birnbrey comprised one of the seventy-four children who arrived in the United States from Germany and Austria in 1938. By the end of the war in 1945, approximately 1,200 Jewish children had been rescued by the United States from Nazi-dominated Europe, a shockingly small number when compared to the unfulfilled immigration quotas from Germany and Austria.[60]

After the United Jewish Fund established its Refugee Committee in late 1938, the committee initially requested refugees to fill specific jobs. The inability of the NRS to fill these specific requests forced the Birmingham committee to reevaluate its approach, and some members complained that they had "fallen down on [their] part of that job." Subsequently, their requirements became less specific and the numbers of refugees in Birmingham increased.[61] For 1939, the Refugee Committee set its quota at eighteen refugees. The local Jewish fraternity, Pi Tau Pi, assisted the committee by finding employment opportunities for refugees in adjoining cities. The fund assumed responsibility for the refugees sent first by the NCC, and then the NRS, but often had to use discretion when assisting other émigrés in the city. As one member warned, the Refugee Committee needed "to be careful about refusing to help individuals coming to the city thru [*sic*] their families, since these very families were contributors to the United Jewish Fund, and might expect a certain amount of help from the Fund." At no time, however, did Birmingham's Jewish community refuse to aid anyone in need, including resettled refugees who requested that members of the fund sign affidavits and assume responsibility for their family members incarcerated in Nazi concentration camps.[62] As refugees arrived in Birmingham, committee members secured their employment and advanced funds in the form of loans to provide them a fresh start, including funds to purchase apprenticeships, but expected that "at some time in the future, when they had been at work for some time and acclimatized themselves to the community, they would try to repay the Committee in some way—if not in full, in part." Jewish doctors in the city provided medical attention on a volunteer basis, and the Women's Division of the Refugee Committee addressed housing, placing most of the refugees in private homes, and coordinated cultural activities, such as offering English lessons and sponsoring social mixers designed to make their adjustment to American society easier, a pattern replicated in Jewish community efforts throughout the United States.[63]

Although steel, mining, and other heavy industrial production formed the backbone of Birmingham's economy and gave the city the nickname "the Pittsburgh of the South," Jews had prospered in retail and light manufacturing, and the refugees who arrived generally found employment in those fields. Within a short time, a majority of the refugees became self-supporting. In some cases, the loans the United Jewish Fund provided allowed refugees to establish businesses, including retailing coal, rolling cigarettes, and a boardinghouse and tea shop. Otto Bloom, for instance, established a photography business and "became self-supporting almost immediately."[64] Although a small number of refugees continued to rely on the fund's assistance to support themselves, none accepted, or could accept, public relief. Only an affidavit that guaranteed that they at no time would be a public burden secured their entry into the United States. Indeed, if a refugee applied for public assistance, he or she became subject to deportation. By 1941 the NRS reported that "so well has the American Jewish community met its responsibilities that . . . not a single refugee has been deported as having become a public charge."[65]

Much of the success that the Birmingham committee had in placing refugees in the city was due to Dora Roth, the executive secretary of the United Jewish Fund, who actually directed the day-to-day operation of the committee and tirelessly served as the caseworker for the refugees. Dora Landau Roth was born in Louisville, Kentucky, in 1904. While in Louisville, she received an education at Louisville's Talmud Torah and met Benjamin A. Roth, a graduate of the University of Louisville Law School and a member of the Kentucky legislature. After their marriage in 1928, Dora moved to Birmingham where Benjamin served as the executive director of the YMHA. Upon the creation of the United Jewish Fund in 1936, Dora became its executive secretary, a position she held until her retirement in 1965.[66]

Described by Isadore Pizitz as the "whole works" of the organization, Roth made "practically all the decisions and policies" regarding the resettlement program in Birmingham. Dora Roth's forceful personality frequently rubbed some the wrong way, including on many occasions representatives of the NRS.[67] William P. Engel, perhaps the most influential member of Birmingham's Jewish community and head of the United Jewish Fund, believed that Roth did too much on her own, but he thought better of interfering in areas where she had staked a claim. As the number of refugees in Birmingham grew, problems arose concomitant with their arrival, overwhelming Roth. Convinced that Birmingham needed a full-time caseworker for the influx of refugees into the city to provide "stability and ensure confidence," both Roth and her husband exerted considerable influence on the fund to hire Marjorie Solomon to assume those duties in June 1940.[68]

Birmingham exceeded its 1939 quota of eighteen refugee families by seven units. The NRS tracked refugees by family "units," which varied in size. The twenty-five units resettled in 1939 comprised thirty-two refugees.[69] By the end of 1940, thirty-five family units, comprising some sixty-five to seventy refugees, had been resettled in the city courtesy of the NRS. Of that number, twenty-five units had become self-supporting, with only one man unemployed. Overall, according to Mark Elovitz in his history of the Birmingham Jewish community, Birmingham's Jews, "accepted, resettled, retrained and made over 87 units (125 people) of refugees self-sustaining from 1938 to 1940," largely through the efforts of Dora Roth.[70]

Despite the apparent success in resettling the refugees, Birmingham, more so than any other Alabama city, experienced numerous coordination and communication problems with the NRS, and the Refugee Committee blamed the problems on "an utter lack of cooperation on the part of the NRS." This, in turn, led to resentment and complaints from Roth and people such as Mervyn Sterne and Isadore Pizitz on the State Coordinating Committee. The lack of timely communication, or in some cases "unsatisfactory replies," between the NRS and the Birmingham committee were chief among the complaints. In a couple of cases, the NRS sent mentally unstable refugees, one of whom had to be sent to the state mental hospital in Tuscaloosa while another had a "psychopathic personality" and hence was unemployable. The last individual had to be financially supported by the United Jewish Fund.[71] The delays and cancellations by refugees, in addition to the problems associated with unemployable refugees, caused some prospective employers and committee members to drop out of the program. As a result, Dora Roth warned the NRS that Birmingham "had become somewhat callous to the refugee problem," due to the communication problems and the "unfortunate experiences" that several employers had with refugee employees.[72] Generally, however, Birmingham's Jewish community supported the efforts to resettle the recently arrived émigrés.

Although some hurdles existed in regard to recently arrived refugees, such as little information about a refugee's handicap or disability and the lack of an Employment Committee "to explore the economic resources of the community for intelligent job placement," a more insidious problem emerged in Birmingham in 1940: increasing antisemitism. A "Nazi-inspired campaign" against Jewish department stores, started by what was referred to as the "local Bund"—local bigots and extremists—began to spread rumors that non-

Jewish employees had been fired to make room for the newly arrived Jewish refugees, as well as insinuating that Nazi refugees operated in the city.[73] The increase in antisemitism also extended beyond such "whispering campaigns," as someone painted "a swastika about two feet in height" on a pillar of Temple Emanu-El in 1940, although this was kept out of the press. The following year, in one of Birmingham's upscale neighborhoods, "there was a huge arrow with the word 'Jew' underneath it painted on the street in front of, and pointing to the homes of, about twenty-five or thirty" Jewish citizens.[74] Ultimately, these incidents proved to be nothing more than a nuisance for the community, the rekindling of old suspicions and hate directed at "outsiders" by an intolerant and faceless minority. Yet "several large Jewish employers" in the city, in light of such antisemitism, refused to hire refugees for fear of a backlash directed against them. The largest Jewish department stores, Pizitz, Parisian, and Berger-Phillips, all employed refugees in their stores.[75]

By 1941 the numbers of refugees arriving in the city, and indeed throughout the United States, decreased significantly, ironically at the same time that more jobs became available. Defense preparation had increased production in almost all industrial areas, and employees left good paying jobs in the private sector for even better paying jobs with the government. Consequently, openings for employment abounded, but with few new arrivals to take advantage of the opportunity. The decrease in the numbers of refugees also forced the United Jewish Fund to merge all welfare committees into one, "to handle transient, non-refugee and refugee cases."[76] At the same time, the cultural fissures within the Birmingham community, largely kept at bay during the 1930s by the cooperation to aid suffering European Jews, opened once again as Zionism became an increasingly important issue. Frank Abelson, who was scheduled to assume the chairmanship of the United Jewish Fund by the end of the 1941, pledged his support for the NRS and promised aid to any refugee who came to the city, but he made it clear that he did not approve of the "preferential treatment which some members of his community gave to refugees just 'because they had degrees' or other cultural assets," a pointed criticism of the acculturated Reform Jews who had directed the fund in the preceding years. Abelson had immigrated to the US from Russia in the 1890s and helped establish Birmingham's first Zionist organization. He described himself as a "'Nationalist and Zionist by birth' [whose] heart and soul is with the 'Jewish Homeland'" and one who recognized the need to "alleviate Jewish suffering anywhere."Abelson's shot across the bow resumed a long-standing cultural skirmish that continued to divide much of Birmingham's Jewish community, at least until the establishment of the state of Israel in 1948.[77]

Other Jewish communities worked with both the Birmingham Refugee Committee and the State Coordinating Committee to care for and assist resettled refugees. One such example is Gadsden, whose most significant contribution to the refugee crisis was its oversight and care of the young refugees attending the Alabama School of Trades, part of the NYA's attempt to provide vocational training for America's youth. Between 1938 and 1942, the State Coordinating Committee sponsored a total of ten refugees who attended the Alabama School of Trades. The school, which had approximately two hundred students at any given time, offered training primarily in mechanical vocations: printing, auto repair, painting, welding, carpentry, and electrical work. It also had courses in architecture and a complete farm school. Although students ultimately selected their own vocation, school officials counseled students as to the most appropriate course of study. When John Newberger, a refugee recommended for the school by Dora Roth in Birmingham, wanted to study welding, officials tried to dissuade him, citing the "limited possibilities for employment of a Jew in this field."[78] The majority of the refugee students studied either architectural drafting or printing and found employment immediately after graduation. Some took jobs in Gadsden and nearby Attala, while others moved back to Birmingham, Montgomery, or other places in the state, or joined the armed services.

Gadsden, a town of approximately forty-seven thousand, provided an ideal location for the trade school due to its economy, which depended on steel, coal, rubber, and textiles, and its proximity to Birmingham, the largest industrial center in the South, located sixty miles to the southwest. Moreover, the local Jewish community, particularly the Refugee Committee chairman, provided substantial support for the refugee students from their arrival at the trade school until their graduation. The fifty Jewish families in Gadsden, numbering roughly 175 people, fully embraced the students. Gadsden's Jews largely worked in retail. They owned numerous small shops and the largest department stores on Broad Street, the town's main thoroughfare.[79] The State Coordinating Committee sent monthly allowances for the students to the chairman of Gadsden's Refugee Committee—Ben Kahn, and then his successor, Eugene Weil—who then distributed the funds to the students. They became rapidly acclimatized to the school and community, getting along well with students and faculty at the school. Kahn and Weil kept a close watch over the students, which included providing them weekend jobs and introducing them to Gadsden families who frequently took them into their homes. In fact, they considered Weil's home "an open house for all of them." A couple of the refugees taught Sunday School at the local Reform Temple Beth Israel, and one lectured to public schools in the surrounding area.[80] All in all, they made a good impression on everyone concerned.

After the United States entered the war, the welcoming atmosphere for the refugees at the school began to change. Eugene Weil, who had been a staunch supporter of the students, wanted to remove them from school and return them to New York because "Gadsden is a small community and it is common knowledge that several German-Jewish aliens are at the school." Weil worried that any sabotage that should occur at any of the Gadsden plants and factories could endanger the students and the Jewish community. Local pressure had been brought to bear on Reynolds Fletcher Jarvis, the director of the school, to remove the refugees and "replace them with Alabama boys," something Jarvis managed to avoid until the federal government took over the school in June 1942. Weil tried to minimize the students' profile in the community by warning them to avoid public places at night, travel in groups, and refrain from discussing the war, but he could not remove the students as he desired, as it would have violated the travel restrictions that had been placed on enemy aliens. Nevertheless, Weil wanted to be relieved of his responsibility for them, suggesting that the Birmingham Refugee Committee assume that duty.[81] When the federal government turned the Alabama School of Trades into a Civil Service training school, it stipulated that only American citizens could attend. All but two refugee students had completed their courses and had been employed in their field of choice or had enlisted in the army. The two who did not finish found work in the factories of Attala and Anniston. With the full support of the State Coordinating Committee and the Gadsden community, "most of the refugee enrollees stayed in the state and obtained work in the fields for which they prepared," leading the NRS to declare that the NYA program had been "a success from practically every angle," fulfilling the very obligations with which it had been charged.[82]

Situated approximately fifty miles east of Birmingham, Anniston became another wartime boomtown. Highly industrialized and the largest textile center in Alabama, Anniston grew quickly due to the expansion of industry and the development of Fort McClellan located only five miles away. By mid-1940, Fort McClellan had eighteen thousand soldiers stationed on base, with more on the way. The growth in industrial jobs and the increase in military personnel created "extra purchasing power [that] has caused the retail shops to hum with activity," in turn creating the need for experienced salesmen. Leon A. Sterne, Mortimer C. Sterne, and Carrie Sterne, the brothers and sister of Birmingham's influential Mervyn Sterne, as well as Lee Freibaum, spearheaded Anniston's efforts to resettle Jewish refugees. The local Jewish community had only twenty-two families, but the influx of Jewish soldiers at McClellan helped to fill Reform Temple Beth-El to capacity on Friday evenings and holidays. Although the community had no full-time rabbi, a Jewish chaplain with the Jewish Welfare Board and USO, Abba M. Fineberg, conducted Friday evening services for the Reform civilians and mostly Orthodox soldiers who attended. With the support of the community, Jewish leaders expressed their willingness to accept two units, either experienced in sales or in textiles, with minimal notice. Like other boomtowns, Anniston experienced an acute housing shortage that necessitated the NRS to send only childless couples or single men.[83]

Prior to any organized effort by the community to sponsor refugees, ten had settled in Anniston by late 1940. Nine had been sponsored by their relative, Lee Freibaum, the co-owner of Classe Ribbon Works, who brought his relatives to Anniston, found them employment, and was "mainly responsible for their satisfactory adjustment." Freibaum also employed Joseph Gruneberg, a refugee who came to Anniston through the NRS. While still in Germany, Gruneberg had been arrested after *Kristallnacht* and placed in a concentration camp. After his release, he went to England, forced to leave his wife and son behind in Hagen, Germany. After Harry Hernfeld of Alexander City, Alabama, signed his affidavit, Gruneberg arrived in the United States and then made his way to Alabama. The US consul in Stuttgart, however, rejected the affidavit for Gruneberg's wife because Hernfeld had sponsored too many refugees.[84]

Those refugees who came to Anniston quickly became integrated into the community. By the time the United States entered the war, the refugees living in Anniston had become self-sufficient and their status as enemy aliens only affected those who worked at Fort McClellan, where the base commander, Colonel John Jenkins, ordered all enemy aliens not in uniform to be prohibited from entering. Henry Brill, for instance, had been employed by the post tailor, but had to give up his job. Freibaum then hired him at his ribbon works factory.[85]

The Montgomery Region

After organizing its Coordinating Committee under Henry Weil in May 1938, Montgomery's Jewish Federation successfully integrated numerous refugees into the community. By January 1939, it had sponsored five refugees. The annual quota for refugees, however, increased only slightly to eight per year, as Montgomery, economically oriented toward farming and agriculture, could not provide the level of support that a larger industrial community such as Birmingham could. Yet like Birmingham, Montgomery leaders also complained about communication problems with New York and placed the blame for these problems squarely on the shoulders of the NRS. Henry Weil believed them to be "slow in answering local requests" and found it extremely difficult to recruit refugees for agricultural projects in the region.[86]

As a result of the ever-greater demands placed upon it, the federation faced continual challenges in regard to fund-raising for relief efforts and social services. Walter Lobman, the federation president, surmised that some of Montgomery's Jews needed "much stimulation" to support the continuation of vital programs such as relief work and observed that the city "remained removed from the center of [refugee and relief] activity."[87] In spite of this, the Montgomery Jewish Federation met all needs that became apparent. Like other communities that sponsored refugees, Montgomery's Coordinating Committee often failed to secure employment prior to the refugee's arrival, and the periods of unemployment placed a severe strain on the federation's budget.

The influence of Jews in Montgomery's economic and civic structure helped to alleviate any long-term problems as the federation worked with the Montgomery community at large to help find jobs for those under their care, including sending letters into the community "advertising the services of the refugees" and organizing work projects for the unemployed women. Grover Hall of the *Montgomery Advertiser* helped promote the federation's efforts and appealed to his readers to support a federation-sponsored fund-raising drive to aid persecuted Jews and refugees. As Hall explained, "the Jews of this town tend to keep their sorrows and burdens to themselves." "They never solicit charity funds for their kind among Gentiles," he continued, gently prodding Gentiles as was his wont, "whereas Gentiles gladly prey upon Jews at all times for all good causes." The *Advertiser*, Hall declared, "as a community newspaper, submits that Gentiles (except 'Aryans!') should account it a privilege to lend a hand . . . to their Jewish neighbors and friends, in the struggle of the Jewish Federation to raise its quota for the benefit of Jewish refugees from the tyranny of old-world beasts."[88] Although Hall made a great effort to bridge the divide between Jew and Gentile and had earned respect and admiration from Jews across the state, his editorial nevertheless emphasized the Jews' "otherness" in southern society, an unwelcome reference for Montgomery's Jews.

After the *Montgomery Advertiser* published a short article in April 1940 about a "surprising number of Austrian, German, and Polish refugees" who filled the casinos in Nice, France, the Montgomery Jewish Federation sought to minimize the publicity surrounding their campaign to aid refugees, lest such unsavory connotations be applied to their efforts.[89] Indeed, federation leaders had already had to address the anxiety of "a good many individuals [who] have raised the question whether too many [refugees] are being brought over here."[90] Reform Jews dominated federation leadership positions, and the federation's caution in regard to publicity coincided with the Reform desire to keep out of the public eye. As an observer noted, Montgomery's Jews "prefer to having *no* newspaper story in which the word Jew is mentioned even to having a favorable newspaper story. They hesitate to undertake any efforts toward community education on inter-group relations in which they would appear as a Jewish body."[91] Such a restrained approach by federation leaders often infuriated the Orthodox and Sephardic minority who thought "Jews should be more noisy about protesting the persecutions of their coreligionists."[92] Despite the reticence of a few Gentiles in Montgomery, the federation pressed ahead with its campaign to aid the persecuted Jews abroad and resettle refugees in the River Region. The Montgomery federation's willingness to aid those in need, moreover, extended beyond the persecuted European Jews. At the end of July 1940, it offered to assist in placing English children sent to the United States to escape the expected German invasion of the British Isles.[93]

From 1938 to 1942, twenty-five refugees resettled in Montgomery. The refugees living in Montgomery "adjusted nicely" and quickly became "integrated into local life and affairs."[94] By 1945, however, only seven refugees remained in Montgomery. That so few remained, Rabbi Eugene Blachschleger of Temple Beth-Or believed, was due to the lack of attention given to the refugees' adjustment. The Jewish community helped "to place newcomers in homes and on jobs, but [went] no further," causing many to leave when a better opportunity presented itself. The Refugee Committee had ceased to function by 1944, leaving those remaining with limited resources and guidance. As Jewish soldiers assigned to Maxwell and Gunter Fields arrived in Montgomery prior to and during the war, the community's attention "centered around making things as comfortable and pleasant for them as possible," and was "not at all concerned with newcomers or what the future may bring with regard to any situation which may arise in relation to post-war immigration."[95]

Montgomery also served as the gateway for refugees for central Alabama. Selma, a town of about twenty thousand, with a Jewish population of around three hundred, worked with Montgomery, the state committee, and the NRS to resettle more refugees than any other small town in the region.[96] Sponsorship of refugees in smaller towns like Selma often served to fill the needs of the community, but small communities also faced a threefold problem in attracting refugees: location, the lack of Jewish culture and life, and few employment opportunities. Located fifty miles west of Montgomery, Selma had only one synagogue, the Reform Temple Mishkan Israel, to which Reform, Conservative, and Orthodox Jews in the community belonged, but the congregation had little to attract or to support Jewish refugees.[97] In the heart of the Black Belt, the town and the region relied heavily on cotton. It had an abundance of farms and warehouses to store the cotton, but no industries. Employment opportunities for refugees, limited mainly to retail, increased only slightly after the army established Craig Field nearby in 1941. Despite the addition of the military base, economic conditions remained poor, including successive crop failures, and that limited the Jewish community's ability to attract and resettle more refugees. In two cases, refugees had been unable to find work after arriving. One refugee "walked the streets for three months, looking for work with the aid of the committee, but was unsuccessful." He eventually left Selma for opportunities outside of the state. When Selma's Refugee Committee requested a refugee to be sent, it specified the "type" of refugee that would best fit into their community: "a young, single man, English speaking, non-Sabbath observer, non-foreign type." In other words, someone who could acculturate quickly and easily and whose Jewishness would not be conspicuous. The committee quickly filled its quota of two refugees for 1939 and 1940, and, by the end of that year, had resettled seven refugees in total; the additions had been sponsored by their families.[98]

For some refugees, adjustment and socialization did not come easy. Hermann and Frieda Berger, who had immigrated to New York from Germany in March 1938, had been sent by the NRS and sponsored by Mishkan Israel. After a Jewish tailor died in Selma, the congregation agreed to sponsor Berger, a tailor by trade, and they helped to establish Berger's shop after he arrived in September 1938, allowing him to build his business for the first year. In just a little over two years, Berger had repaid the congregation in full for the loan on his business.[99] At first the Bergers found it difficult to adjust to small-town life in Alabama. They had only been married a few months prior to relocating to Selma, and Frieda had not wanted to leave relatives in New York. As they tried to acclimate to Selma, they became active in the congregation, Hermann joined B'nai B'rith, and they had a daughter, Hanna, who became the "first native born to a refugee in Selma." They had apparently made such strides that the NRS field representative described them as being "exceptionally well adjusted."[100] Yet according to their daughter they felt "quite lonely, and quite isolated" in the beginning. During their early years in Selma "they were struggling very hard just to make do and learn [English], and deal with the fact that their parents were dead, and [they] were finding out about that, sort of in 1942 and '43 . . . they felt different." In addition to their parents, Frieda lost three siblings, while two of Hermann's brothers perished in Nazi death camps.[101]

Having grown up in a more traditional fashion in small towns in Germany, the Bergers also struggled to overcome the cultural differences in the "very Reform" Selma congregation. As Hanna Berger remembered, they could not keep kosher in Selma, "that would have been about impossible . . . they didn't do things they had done in Germany. They still probably kept more traditions than most of the families did here. Not with a Christmas tree. Most of the Jewish kids in town had Christmas trees; not all of them, but most."[102] They even sponsored surviving relatives to join them in Selma. Frieda's brother Julius Kahn, her sister Dora Lewy, and brother-in-law Ludwig Lewy had immigrated to Shanghai, China, in 1939. After the war ended, the Bergers brought them to Selma. Despite the trauma they faced in going forward after the loss of so many family members in the Holocaust and the hurdles of acculturation into an alien and less-than-traditional culture, the Bergers and their extended family happily remained in Selma for the rest of their lives.

The Mobile Region

The Mobile JDC, which had been created in 1933 to address the persecution of the Jews in Germany, tangentially assumed responsibility for refugee resettlement in the port city and in south Alabama, with members of both Sha'arai Shomayim and Ahavas Chesed, as well as representatives of the Mobile section of the NCJW, comprising the committee. Reform Jews, like elsewhere in the state, played the leading roles. The lack of cohesion and leadership in the Jewish community, however, led to a woefully inadequate organizational structure that prevented the Mobile JDC from successfully resettling refugees in numbers corresponding to its resources from 1938 until late 1941. By that time the numbers of refugees entering the United States had declined precipitously. Despite this temporary vacuum of leadership with resettlement efforts, the Mobile Jewish Federation, the Mobile JDC, and the NCJW sponsored highly successful community drives to benefit refugees already in the United States. The close relationship between Mobile's Jews and Gentiles—a visitor from New York wrote in 1940 that "the Jews of Mobile are thoroughly integrated into the Community"—led Mobile mayor Charles A. Baumhauer, in January 1939, to proclaim "Golden Rule Day" in the city. He urged everyone in the Mobile area "to come forward and assist as far as they are able in giving some relief in this urgent situation, designed to relieve suffering humanity regardless of race or creed."[103] In addition, the Beth-Zur B'nai B'rith lodge also assumed a limited responsibility for refugee families in the aftermath of *Kristallnacht*, where the members attempted "to secure employment for them and aid them in every way."[104]

The disarray the Mobile JDC experienced seems to have been precipitated by the turmoil surrounding Sha'arai Shomayim and its rabbi. By the late 1930s, the mental illness that plagued Rabbi Alfred G. Moses since the beginning of his tenure reemerged and caused him to say "things that cause chagrin and unhappiness for the Jews." The increasing instability of Moses prompted the board of trustees to make him Rabbi Emeritus at a relatively young age of sixty-two, a decision that caused "dissension" within the congregation.[105] Abe Pearson, the president of the Reform congregation, "lamented that [such] dissension and controversy were rife in the congregation, much of it attributed to 'certain remarks' made by Rabbi and Mrs. Moses." Robert Zietz, in his history of Sha'arai Shomayim, notes that "some members refused to attend services until matters were corrected."[106] By late 1940, Sidney Berkowitz had replaced Moses as full-time rabbi.

Where local Reform Jews such as Leon Schwarz and James G. Adler had taken the lead in raising awareness and money for the persecuted Jews abroad, curiously they did not in regard to the resettlement of refugees. In their stead, the Mobile section of the NCJW spearheaded the effort, with little direction and even less coordination. The NCJW had members from both the Orthodox Ahavas Chesed and the Reform Sha'arai Shomayim, but it still experienced the cultural divide between the two subcommunities. The ladies of Ahavas Chesed, who had organized Hadassah, joined Reform members in the NCJW, but the women of Sha'arai Shomayim, who had founded the Mobile NCJW, refused to join Hadassah. Such cultural "snobbery" existed among many, if not most, of the acculturated Reform Jews in Alabama and played out in numerous and varied ways. In spite of the social and cultural differences within its organization, the NCJW worked to help resettle Jewish refugees in the city. The Mobile JDC's newly created Mobile Resettlement Agency spent "a good deal of time, energy, and money" on the first two units sent to Mobile, a banker and an attorney, to try "to keep [them] in the manner in which they had been accustomed." This included renting an apartment, hiring a maid, and providing a telephone. The NCJW "found a number of jobs for these two, but the jobs did not pay sufficient for them." They continued assisting the refugees although the banker still had a significant amount of personal funds remaining and did not need the assistance.[107]

Reba Mitchell, the president of the Ahavas Chesed Ladies Aid Society, assumed the chair of the Resettlement Agency but demonstrated little effective leadership.[108] The NRS field representative, Monte Kandel, observed that the NCJW conducted refugee work "with anybody and everybody delegating authority and interest to herself. . . . There has been little or no organization, rampant overlapping of functional responsibilities and serious differences of opinion in the handling of cases." If this was not bad enough, Kandel observed, the section made it "a common practice to air a client's difficulties at [their] general meeting[s]."[109] Nationally, the NCJW's benevolent efforts had developed to become more professional in nature. As Mark Bauman explains, the NCJW's "policy shifted from discussing applicants for aid by name at the meetings to one in which only the officers would investigate on a more individual basis."[110] The Mobile section's approach had not yet developed to that extent. The Mobile section differed, too, from the majority of NCJW's sections whose assumed responsibilities had expanded women's roles in the Jewish community.[111] Mitchell had not wanted to accept leadership of the committee—she thought it "a man's job"—but no one stepped forward to take responsibility for the refugee work, with many adopting a let-someone-else-do-it attitude, causing immense frustration for the NRS. The Birmingham and Montgomery refugee committees also bore the brunt of resettlement work in Alabama as Mobile rarely communicated with the State Coordinating Committee. As a result of the dysfunction the Mobile Resettlement Agency experienced, only three units, numbering eleven refugees, resettled in Mobile between 1938 and 1940, with only six of the refugees coming through the NRS.[112]

The Resettlement Agency reorganized in early 1941. Paul May, the son-in-law of Sol Kahn, and partner with Kahn in Kahn Manufacturing, became co-chair of the committee at the same time that he worked to get his parents out of Nazi-occupied Holland.[113] The NRS lauded May's participation and leadership as he quickly created a placement subcommittee. They viewed him as "a substantial individual and potential employer" in the Mobile region. Under his guidance, the resettlement efforts "had been removed from the 'floor of NCJW meetings' and placed in the hands of a committee of ten chosen from the different Jewish organizations" in the city, and the agency also began to work more smoothly with the State Coordinating Committee. As a result, both May and Mitchell thought the agency could "accept more difficult cases, particularly those requiring retraining or capital loan assistance." Along with May, Sha'arai Shomayim's president, Bernard Eichold, pledged his support for the reorganization of the agency, and Rabbi Sidney Berkowitz embraced resettlement as "a vehicle for revitalizing the community and making them feel that they are part of something big and important to the Jews."[114] The newly appointed rabbi brought an energy to the congregation and to the Jewish community as a whole—he had a good working relationship with the Orthodox congregation—that had been missing since the early tenure of Rabbi Moses. Berkowitz threw himself into both Temple and community affairs, where he frequently spoke to organizations throughout Mobile and led fund-raising drives for suffering Jews abroad. He also became the leading figure in Mobile's resettlement activity, creating a "continuing educational program" for refugees in Mobile and the surrounding communities. By September 1941, he had become the chairman of the Resettlement Agency.[115]

Berkowitz, who had grown up in Terre Haute, Indiana, had been ordained as a rabbi in 1936 after graduating from Hebrew Union College in Cincinnati. He earned his PhD from Cambridge University in England in 1939. Upon returning from England that year, he went back to Hebrew Union College where he had been promised a teaching position. By 1940, Julian Morgenstern, the president of the college, replaced him with a refugee scholar from Germany. According to Berkowitz's wife, Pauline Berkowitz, Morgenstern told him that "someone like you—you're an American boy, and you're young—won't have any trouble finding a pulpit anywhere."[116] True to Morgenstern's word, Berkowitz found a position almost immediately with the Sha'arai Shomayim congregation, his first pulpit as a rabbi.

Under the leadership of May and then Berkowitz, the Resettlement Agency began to convince leaders of the Reform community who had previously been lukewarm in their support of refugee resettlement to embrace the cause more fully. After meeting with Berkowitz and the NRS's Monte Kandel, Ben May, by far the largest philanthropic donor in Mobile's Jewish community, if not in all of Mobile, pledged his support for the resettlement program. He recognized the resettlement of refugees as "an American problem," and he had recently "taken a personal interest in refugees," employing a number of them in his businesses. Securing May's support for resettlement went far beyond his employment capability. He had extensive business contacts within the Mobile business community, and the Jewish Federation often "delegated" him to contact and work with Mobile's Gentiles. Moreover, he exerted a powerful influence over the federation's distribution of funds. Berney L. Strauss, the owner of Hammel's Department Store, also had recently begun to view refugees in a new light. Strauss had previously refused to hire any refugees for his department store "for 'public relations' reasons." His wife, however, had "placed" a refugee girl in one of his departments as a salesperson. Strauss had been so impressed by her work that he threw his support behind the agency, admitting that Mobile had not done enough concerning resettlement. He urged the agency to "tackle some of the difficult cases, especially the 'schlemiels,'" although he would not commit to hiring them in his store. "Send them down," he said, "we'll find something for them."[117]

By mid-1940, Mobile and the surrounding area began to experience intense economic growth generated by defense preparation that not only produced rapid expansion of established industries such as shipbuilding, airplane repair, steel, and textiles but also by the construction of new military bases, such as Brookley Field in Mobile and Keesler Field in nearby Biloxi, Mississippi. Thousands of people who had suffered economically during the Depression flocked to Mobile, causing the population to expand from roughly 80,000 to 112,000 by early 1941. By 1944, Mobile County's population totaled 233,000, an increase of 64 percent since 1940. The dramatic population increase made Mobile a wartime boomtown and "the most congested urban area in the United States." Such rapid expansion created tremendous employment opportunities, in both manufacturing and retail sales, but produced an acute housing shortage in the port city that extended throughout the area, creating hastily thrown-together shanty towns, trailer parks, and boardinghouses that included the renting of "hot beds" that workers rented for an eight-hour shift. As the writer John Dos Passos explained, "Men work in three shifts. Why shouldn't they sleep in three shifts?"[118] Because of this economic prosperity, the refugees residing in Mobile all became self-supporting. The Mobile Resettlement Agency even committed to accepting an "older aged unit" for resettlement, something refugee committees generally avoided because of their limited employability.[119]

Enemy alien status, however, complicated refugees' lives. Because of Mobile's importance to American aircraft and shipbuilding production, Jewish leaders worried that Mobile would be declared a restricted area, removing employment opportunities essential for resettlement. Sabotage had been found at some Mobile plants, and Berkowitz and other members of the agency thought that it might create "anti-alien sentiment" in the region. Indeed, some Mobile residents viewed aliens with the utmost suspicion. As one Mobile resident asked of President Roosevelt, "How many aliens know more of this country than many Americans? They know where our arsenals, munitions manufacturing and shipbuilding plants are located. They know everything about us of any importance that would be of benefit to Hitler or any coalition of powers that would attack us. . . . As to all these aliens and foreigners who don't like our country—send them out—we don't need them."[120] As a precautionary measure, the agency advised the refugees "to keep away from the docks and waterfront around Mobile," despite the fact that no law prevented the hiring of enemy aliens, even in defense industries. Hans Proskauer, a refugee living in Mobile, had been inducted into the army but had been immediately discharged due to his enemy alien status.[121] It is unclear why Proskauer was discharged, as the Selective Training and Service Act of 1940 allowed noncitizens to serve. In fact, the armed services drafted over four thousand enemy aliens and quickly naturalized as many as they could "to resolve the question of too many aliens in the armed forces." They only separated those aliens considered "especially troublesome," although there is no evidence to suggest Proskauer fit that description.[122]

As resettlement dwindled after the United States entered the war, the agency had little to do apart from addressing the occasional needs of refugees already in the community. Of the twelve refugee families that remained in Mobile in 1944—there had been twenty-five families, many of whom left because of other employment opportunities—all had become self-supporting and integrated into Mobile society, taking English classes the NCJW offered, joining organizations such as Hadassah, and even volunteering for war work at the Red Cross or the United Service Organization (USO).[123] By late 1944, Sha'arai Shomayim filled its pulpit with a refugee after its previous two rabbis, Berkowitz and Bertram Wallace Korn, joined the service. Sha'arai Shomayim's new rabbi, Joshua O. Haberman, fled Austria for the United States after the *Anschluss* in 1938. After he arrived in the United States, he attended Hebrew Union College in Cincinnati, Ohio, and was ordained as a rabbi in 1945.[124]

The refugees who remained in Alabama, such as the Bergers of Selma, became part of the fabric of their community. After the number of refugees coming into Alabama decreased in 1941, Alabama's Jewish organizations consequently budgeted less money for refugee resettlement. Instead, local federations increased their contributions to the Organization for Rehabilitation and Training (ORT) and the United Jewish Appeal (UJA), two organizations with the express purpose of aiding suffering Jewry in Europe. ORT, created in Russia in the late nineteenth century, worked with the JDC to offer vocational education to Jews throughout the world, including refugees and Jews in Nazi-occupied Europe. ORT, which had secured the approval of Nazi officials, even conducted training for Jews in the Warsaw Ghetto until its liquidation in 1942.[125] In response to *Kristallnacht*, the American JDC had joined with the United Palestine Appeal (UPA) and the NCC to form the UJA in January 1939 to boost fund-raising efforts for Jewish relief and rescue, a great success as donations to the UJA increased significantly at both the national and local level. This became an increasingly controversial issue within Jewish organizations during the war, however, as Eastern

European Jews and Jews of Central European descent disagreed over the allocation of funds to the non-Zionist JDC and the Zionist UPA. With the revelation of the mass killings in Nazi-occupied Europe in late 1942, Zionism became an increasingly contentious issue among Alabama's Jews. The drive to create a Jewish state in Palestine, however, reopened old divisions between Central and Eastern European Jews. Despite their differences, they worked with one another in an attempt to aid the persecuted Jews of Europe.

3
Zionism in Alabama, 1933–45

The modern Zionist movement began when Theodore Herzl published *Der Judenstaat* in 1896 and the First Zionist Congress convened in Basel, Switzerland, in August 1897. It gained further impetus after Great Britain conquered much of the territories that comprised Palestine from the Ottoman Empire in 1917–18. On November 2, 1917, the British foreign secretary, Lord Arthur James Balfour, issued a declaration in a letter to Lord Lionel Walter Rothschild that promised a "national home for Jewish people" in Palestine, whereby the British government would "use their best endeavours to facilitate the achievement of this objective." Neither Balfour nor the British government, however, provided any timetable for the creation of the Jewish state.[1] Nevertheless, the Balfour Declaration contributed greatly to the Zionist movement.

The Eastern European Jews who immigrated to the United States in the late nineteenth and the early twentieth centuries brought with them a strong adherence to Jewish tradition and the vivid memories of past persecution and pogroms upon which Zionism firmly rested. As Melvin Urofsky notes, among European Jews, "messianic hopes for redemption had always existed in the midst of Jewish misery."[2] Indeed, Zionist organizations had existed among a portion of Alabama's Eastern European Jews since shortly after the Basel conference, but Hitler's assumption of power and the Nazi persecution of the Jews energized the movement among Eastern European Jews and even attracted some new supporters from the Reform community. In Birmingham, Montgomery, and Mobile, Zionists actively organized and campaigned not only to aid and rescue persecuted European Jews but also to build support for the establishment of a Jewish state in Palestine, lobbying local and state politicians to support their agenda. In fact, where it concerned the establishment of a Jewish state, Alabama's Zionists had an easier time gaining support from Gentiles than from Reform Jews.

The wealthier, acculturated Reform Jews of Alabama did not embrace Zionism. Most Reform Jews supported the position of the Central Conference of American Rabbis (CCAR), which, until 1937, opposed the establishment of a Jewish state. According to the Pittsburgh Platform adopted by the CCAR in 1885, "We consider ourselves no longer a nation, but a religious community, and therefore expect neither a return to Palestine, nor a sacrificial worship under the sons of Aaron, nor the restoration of any of the laws concerning the Jewish state."[3] Many of Alabama's Reform Jews agreed with the CCAR's position and did not consider Judaism a nationality. They saw themselves as Americans, adhered to the Classical Reform position that saw acculturation into the larger American culture as the key to success, and worried that any support for the Zionist cause would single them out as incompatible, or even conflicting, with accepted cultural norms and local traditions. As a result they did not believe in drawing attention to themselves, and they were uncomfortable with Jews being in the public eye in connection with such a movement. This attitude cannot be attributed solely to the South or to southern Jews, but the rigid conformity inherent in southern society reinforced it and suggested to them that anything less than 100 percent commitment to American or southern ideals could arouse suspicion. Support for another political state, such as a Jewish state in Palestine, they believed, could easily raise the issue of dual loyalty. To emphasize the point, Myron Silverman, Emanu-El's assistant rabbi, told the Birmingham Rotary Club in August 1939 that Christianity and Judaism "stood unalterably opposed to fascism and communism," and the Nazis' persecutions were shortsighted because "the German Jew is as much a German as any German citizen . . . just as an American Jew is an American. Every contribution they make to the culture of the country in which they live is made as a native of that country, not as a Jew. They are loyal to their adopted countries."[4] Indeed, the nativist sentiment that produced waves of prejudice across the United States in the 1920s and into 1930s—most notably anti-Catholicism and antisemitism, rooted in questions about communism, subversion, and immigrants' loyalties—confirmed many Reform Jews' belief that Zionists were too particular about their Jewishness, determined to cling to their Eastern European culture, and less willing to acculturate to the larger Gentile society in which they lived. As Theodore Lowi observes, support for Zionism "would define the Jew by his ethnicity."[5]

The anxiety that many Reform Jews experienced over Zionism, however, proved to be unwarranted as the Protestant fundamentalist culture of the South did not object to the creation of a Jewish state; in fact, such a culture fervently supported it. Protestant fundamentalists that dominated the South often emphasized millennialism, the belief that the return of Jews to the Promised Land and a resurrected Israel fulfilled biblical prophecy of the Second Coming of Christ. The necessity of a Jewish state to fundamentalist Protestant culture, however, did not mean the cessation or eradication of antisemitism, even among the devout. Indeed, antisemitism endured throughout the South long after the Klan-dominated 1920s.

Southern Baptists, the largest Christian denomination in the state, greatly influenced, if not dominated, all aspects of life in Alabama during the late nineteenth and most of the twentieth centuries. As historian Wayne Flynt notes, Jews, and especially Catholics, bore the brunt of Baptist prejudice prior to the war, even more so than African Americans.[6] In fact, a post–World War II study revealed Southern Baptists to be "the single most antisemitic religious group in the nation." Eighty percent of Southern Baptists believed that "Jews can never be forgiven for what they did to Jesus until they accept Him as the True Savior," compared to only 33 percent of other Protestants nationally who agreed with this statement.[7] In regard to Zionism, a specialist on Jewish evangelism warned the Alabama Southern Baptist Convention in the 1920s that "Zionism made it harder to evangelize Jews."[8] Zionism was not the issue—indeed, it was essential to fulfill prophecy—Jews themselves were the problem. As L. L. Gwaltney wrote in the *Alabama Baptist* in 1933, "the Gentiles do not want to get rid of the Jews. The Gentiles need to be subdued by the Spirit of the Christ that the Jews may see in them the genuineness of their profession and the power of their conviction, and thus be led to accept the Messiah whom they mistakenly and ignobly rejected."[9] To that end, the Southern Baptist Convention maintained a department devoted to Jewish evangelism, while at the same time Baptists like Gwaltney characterized Jews as greedy financiers, purveyors of Hollywood smut, and dangerous radicals, while others sometimes condemned Jews as Christ-killers.[10] This antisemitism, however, did not interfere with Christian support for Zionism. Because the establishment of a new Israel was essential to fulfill biblical prophecy, antisemitism and Zionism, at least for evangelical Christians, could coexist comfortably and without contradiction.

Zionists in Alabama were most active in Birmingham, which had the state's largest population of Eastern European Jews. Both Mobile and Montgomery, on the other hand, also had a significant population of Eastern European Jews, but the Zionist organizations in those cities remained relatively weak, even throughout the war years. The Birmingham Zion Association emerged out of the Federation of American Zionists, founded in 1898, a year after the First Zionist Congress in Basel, by Russian émigrés Frank and Ike Abelson. The association lasted only four years (1898–1901), although supporters attempted to revive it by changing its name to Tikwath Zion. In addition to Tikwath Zion, Young Judaean clubs formed between 1910 and

1912, and a Hadassah chapter, established in 1915, helped keep Zionism alive in Birmingham until the Nazi persecutions fueled the growth of the movement during the 1930s.[11]

Birmingham attorney and Zionist leader Abe Berkowitz admitted that Zionism "was not generally a major concern on the agenda of the Jewish community in Birmingham" from 1923 to 1932, and "the Reform group had nothing whatever to do with Zionism . . . it is fair to say that, maybe with a mere exception, they generally viewed Zionism as synonymous with Russian or Polish Jews." Because of the Nazi persecutions in the 1930s, however, Zionism became more attractive and acceptable to Jews in the city, even a small minority of Reform Jews. From 1933 to 1936, the Birmingham Zionist Organization, a part of the Zionist Organization of America (ZOA), grew to six hundred members, and, according to Berkowitz, "the local Zionist organization was the most well attended organization in the city."[12] Even so, many of the city's prominent Reform congregants remained firmly opposed to Zionism.

Montgomery's first prominent Zionist was the Reform rabbi Bernard C. Ehrenreich of Temple Beth-Or. Ehrenreich, a founding member of the Federation of American Zionists, assumed the pulpit of the Reform Temple Beth-Or in 1906. Like Birmingham's Morris Newfield, Ehrenreich was born in Hungary and married into a prominent German Reform family. Historian Byron L. Sherwin argues that as a Zionist, Ehrenreich made "new inroads for Zionism among the Reform Jewish anti-Zionist congregations of the South. He literally brought Zionism to many Southern communities. His persuasive, magnetizing speaking abilities 'converted' many Southern Jews, from Arkansas to Louisiana."[13] Ehrenreich may have made inroads throughout the South, but he failed to create interest in Zionism within his own congregation, or apparently among Reform Jews anywhere in Alabama. In 1915, Ehrenreich established a youth camp, Camp Kawaga, on Lake Kawaguesaga in Wisconsin. He left Montgomery in 1921 to run the camp full time, although he maintained a close working relationship with his old congregants in Montgomery. By the 1930s any Zionist zeal that Ehrenreich may have engendered had all but vanished within Beth-Or. Beth-Or member Leo Drum, who attended Ehrenreich's Camp Kawaga during the 1920s, "knew nothing about [Ehrenreich's] Zionistic principles" until well after World War II. Drum recalled that Zionism by the 1930s "was just a foreign subject to people in Montgomery."[14] Rabbi Eugene Blachschleger, who served as Beth-Or's rabbi from 1933 until his death in 1965, adamantly rejected Zionism and was a charter member of the anti-Zionist American Council for Judaism (ACJ). He adhered to the traditional Reform practice of acculturation and taught his congregants that "I'm a Caucasian by race, I'm an American by nationality, and my faith is Judaism."[15] Although Reform Jews in Montgomery rejected Zionism, the Eastern European Jews and Sephardim at Agudath Israel and Etz Ahayem did not. They formed a Zionist organization in the city sometime in the 1930s. What the Reform congregation and the Eastern European and Sephardic congregations could agree upon, and indeed what they worked toward in the Jewish Federation, was to open Palestine for the persecuted European Jews.

Jewish Efforts to Open Palestine

After the Nazis assumed power in Germany, Jewish immigration to Palestine increased significantly. Between 1933 and 1939, 204,076 Jews immigrated to Palestine, but the number fell off dramatically after 1939.[16] Because of American intransigence toward loosening its immigration and refugee policy, Palestine offered the best hope for persecuted European Jews. Alabama's Jews responded by working together to keep Palestine open as a haven for those Jews suffering under Nazi persecution. Where Zionists worked to establish a permanent Jewish state in Palestine, non-Zionists accepted Palestine as a logical refuge for Jews fleeing Nazi persecution but rejected the creation of a Jewish state. Anti-Zionists, on the other hand, argued that Judaism was solely a religion and pointedly rejected the idea of it as an ethnic or even a national identity, at least for American Jews. Such a divergence of views allowed for cooperation to aid European Jews but produced tremendous tension and increasing conflict when it came to Palestine. Within Birmingham's United Jewish Fund, for instance, Zionists consistently sought greater funding for Jewish endeavors in Palestine, often with only grudging acceptance by non-Zionist members. It met with outright hostility from anti-Zionists. By late September 1938, with the British threatening to close Palestine to Jewish immigration, Frank Abelson convinced the fund to contribute additional funds to the UPA for emergency relief, only one instance that produced greater collaboration between the subcommunities, as they worked together to keep the doors to Palestine open for fleeing German and Austrian Jews.[17]

The concept of mandates had been invented in the aftermath of World War I to address the dissolution of the Ottoman Empire. The British Labour Party had conceived mandates as a means for ensuring "the well-being of the peoples" living in these conquered and occupied territories rather than relying on the traditional forms of colonialism. President Woodrow Wilson, a staunch opponent of colonialism and the champion for the newly created League of Nations, believed mandates a "sacred trust of civilization" and gave the plan his blessing.[18] Subsequently, the Allied Powers gave Great Britain a Mandate for Palestine at the San Remo Conference on April 24, 1920, and the League of Nations confirmed it on July 24, 1922, providing Britain a legal basis on which to rule Palestine. The Mandate also made Britain responsible for implementing the Balfour Declaration to establish a Jewish homeland in Palestine.[19]

On November 9, 1938, Great Britain issued a White Paper that severely restricted the number of Jewish immigrants to Palestine in order to placate unrest among Arabs who strongly and violently opposed increasing Jewish immigration or the establishment of a Jewish state.[20] With approximately four hundred thousand Jews living in Palestine, the British government believed the intent of the Balfour Declaration, to create a Jewish homeland, had been fulfilled. The White Paper clearly stated that the framers of the Mandate "could not have intended that Palestine should be converted into a Jewish State against the will of the Arab population." To limit the growth of the Jewish population, which depended upon immigration, the British Colonial Office severely limited the number of available Jewish visas. British policy would thus allow only seventy-five thousand Jewish immigrants to be permitted between 1939 and 1944, after which additional immigration would be entirely dependent upon Arab permission.[21] Despite the rapid increase of illegal immigration into Palestine, the restrictions the British White Paper placed on Jewish immigration proved to be a death sentence for hundreds of thousands of European Jews. Ultimately, the White Paper pleased no one, the Arabs included.

One month prior to the release of the White Paper, Birmingham's Jewish leaders learned the disturbing news that Britain was considering repudiating the Mandate and closing Palestine to Jewish refugees. William P. Engel, president of the United Jewish Fund, called an emergency meeting on October 9, 1938, to address Britain's intended policy. Rabbi Newfield argued that the United Jewish Fund served as "the spokesman for the Jewish people" in Birmingham and therefore should speak for the community. As a result, a committee of ten, selected by leaders of the fund and evenly divided among Zionists and non-Zionists, organized Birmingham's response. The committee coordinated its actions with the Montgomery Jewish Federation and sent a telegram on behalf of Birmingham's Jews to Secretary of State Cordell Hull asking the American government to use its influence with the British to keep Palestine open to Jewish émigrés. The committee also looked beyond Alabama for support and guidance as it took direction from the ZOA in New York on how best to protest the anticipated British action. The minutes of the emergency meeting indicated that the committee was "to maintain constant contact with New York, and carry out any planned activities . . . [and] authorized to draft any others who might thru influence and position be able to successfully help carry out the work of this committee."[22]

Newfield, who had done so much to build interfaith understanding in his forty-plus years in Birmingham, drafted Christian leaders to protest the British repudiation of the Mandate. They did not disappoint him. Ewart H. Wyle, the pastor of Birmingham's First Christian Church and the president of the Birmingham Pastors Union, petitioned President Roosevelt to try to halt the "threatening elimination of this haven of refuge to persecuted Jews of the world." Episcopalians, Presbyterians, Catholics, and Baptists—including the Birmingham Baptist Association that represented "47,000 Baptists in the city"—all joined the cacophony of Christian voices protesting the closing of Palestine. Newfield also convinced Wyle to introduce a resolution at the International Convention of the Disciples of Christ, held in Denver, Colorado, calling for Palestine to remain a Jewish refuge. In a letter to Solomon Goldman, the president of the ZOA, Newfield argued that in the midst of expected Jewish pleas and concern, that "messages from non-Jewish organizations and representative leaders will do [the] most good."[23]

Newfield also contacted William B. Bankhead, the Speaker of the United States House of Representatives. On October 10, Newfield led a group of Birmingham's Jews, which included Zionists and non-Zionists, to meet privately with Speaker Bankhead and his brother, US senator John H. Bankhead Jr., at the Bankhead family home in Jasper, Alabama. In addition to Newfield, William Engel, Mervyn Sterne, Joseph Loveman, Leo Oberdorfer, Leo Steiner, Dr. Harry P. Shugerman, and "Alabama's Original Zionist," Ike Abelson, comprised the group that met with the Bankheads. The delegation discussed the anticipated British repudiation of the Mandate, presenting a statement, according to William Bankhead, "of what in their opinion would bring cruel and disastrous results if such action were taken, upon the Jews now residing in Palestine." They urged the brothers to use their considerable influence with the State Department to keep Palestine under the British Mandate and open to refugees. After a "protracted and sympathetic conference," the Bankheads did so, and Speaker Bankhead wrote to Secretary of State Cordell Hull the following day. "The news report referred to may be of course without substantial foundation," Bankhead told Hull, "but you can well understand how even the possibility may disturb and frighten our Jewish citizens, who are bound by ties of blood and fraternity with their fellow citizens in Palestine." Hull responded with requisite sympathy and assured Bankhead of the government's "close and careful attention" to American interests in Palestine, but Hull made no mention of the humanitarian crisis that so concerned American Jews.[24]

The Bankheads had long been supportive of Jewish interests and maintained close friendships with Jews throughout the state. Jacob Fies, the father of Birmingham industrialist Milton Fies, had provided material and financial support to John H. Bankhead Sr. when he ran for Congress in 1886, and Fies's support "made a deep impression on [William Bankhead] regarding the value of Jewish friendship."[25] Only a few months prior to his October 10 meeting, William Bankhead spoke to the B'nai B'rith convention in Washington. Broadcast nationally, his speech, "Democracy in a Changing World," drew lavish praise from Jews around the country. Bankhead castigated the totalitarian dictatorships and called the problem of the Jewish people "inextricably bound up with that of freedom-loving peoples everywhere. . . . Wherever democracy yields to dictatorship the Jew is the first to feel the mailed fist of arbitrary power. He is the first to be profaned, proscribed and disinherited. Wherever democracy reigns supreme, the Jew is accorded equal treatment under the law in common with other citizenry in the land." Yet in the same breath he displayed an incredible dissonance concerning African Americans, an attitude common among white southerners: "Were we to sanction in America any of the monstrous acts now being perpetrated on the helpless Jewish people in other lands, it would constitute an assault upon the very foundations of our government." Nevertheless, his stirring conclusion no doubt prompted the many resolutions from Jewish lodges that followed in the wake of the speech: "until the one man nations of the world can produce greater military leaders and strategists than Joshua; until they can point within the circle of their own to men who have stood closer to God than Moses; until some Aryan is wiser than Solomon or a sweeter singer of lyrics than David; until they can produce a greater moral philosopher than Jesus of Nazareth—let them beware of asserting that no good can come out of Palestine—that there is no heroism or genius among the fellow citizens of Isaiah—no heritage of character left to the descendants of the Maccabus [*sic*]."[26]

Jews and Gentiles not only in Alabama but also across the nation praised the speech. The Walker County Lodge of B'nai B'rith, in Bankhead's home town of Jasper, expressed its gratitude for the Speaker's "past, present and continued friendship for the Jewish race," and the Beth-Zur Lodge of B'nai B'rith in Mobile lauded the speech and told Bankhead that his words "will go far toward a proper understanding among the peoples of this country, and will give the right-thinking people of non-democratic countries much 'food for thought.'" Mobile's Leon Schwarz, a close friend of the Speaker and the one who suggested to the B'nai B'rith executive committee that Bankhead speak at the convention, called the speech "especially impressive." Bankhead's speech even drew praise from non-Jews outside of the state. As an Irish-American wrote from Seattle, "I have seen conditions in Germany . . . and your speech should be in the hands of every American."[27]

In addition to the Bankheads, US representative John Sparkman heard from his Jewish constituents in Sheffield who requested that he "telegraph the President . . . expressing your hope that this Government will disapprove any steps leading towards the abandonment of the mandate by Great Britain." Sparkman offered to write Roosevelt directly and agreed that "we should take every reasonable step to assure that England shall not sidestep her responsibility in connection with Palestine."[28] When Rabbi Stephen S. Wise solicited Sparkman's support to keep Palestine open for Jews, Sparkman responded that he had already "signed a statement giving my personal approval to the move for a national home for the Jewish people in Palestine."[29]

Despite the prominence and influence of Alabama's congressional members in Washington, or the Bankheads' great support for Jewish endeavors and desire to aid the Birmingham delegation, their protests on behalf of the Jews had absolutely no effect on British policy, and they failed to dent American immigration policy or influence greater action toward Nazi Germany by the State Department and the Roosevelt administration. In any case, Jewish leaders did not limit themselves to lobbying political leaders. They also contacted Christian leaders and educators, such as Newfield did in the Birmingham area, to petition Roosevelt to use his influence with the British government on this matter, although they had no more success than the politicians.

Zionism in Birmingham

Newfield, who had been president of the CCAR in 1931, had long opposed the Zionists' goal of a Jewish political state. In the face of Nazi persecution, Newfield, like many other Reform Jews across the nation, reexamined his position. According to his biographer, Mark Cowett, Newfield's opposition stemmed from his belief that "an American Jew's allegiance belonged first to the United States. As a Jewish clergyman in a city where conformity to American ideals was expected, he perhaps believed that Jews had constantly to prove their commitment to those ideals." Indeed, Newfield hewed closely to the Pittsburgh Platform during his long tenure at Emanu-El. In regard to the Zionist cause, he referred to himself as a "non-Zionist" rather than an "anti-Zionist," one who saw Palestine as a refuge for persecuted European

Jewry but not as a Jewish political state, a belief many members of Emanu-El shared. By 1938, Cowett argues, the Nazi persecution of Jews in Germany transformed Newfield into a Zionist.[30] While some of Emanu-El's congregants underwent a conversion to Zionism, owing largely to the tragedy of *Kristallnacht*, Newfield's position on Zionism is not entirely clear. He continued to support rescue efforts for the persecuted European Jews and "was clearly distressed" about British policy in Palestine. In the 1920s and 1930s, he had "supported Jewish colonization in Palestine," and, as Cowett observes, this "indicates that his non-Zionist position was never very far from a Zionist stance."[31] Yet he never joined a Zionist organization or worked directly for the establishment of a Jewish state in Palestine. His collaboration with the ZOA's Goldman or his meeting with the Bankheads about the White Paper in October 1938 does not necessarily mean, as Cowett argues, that Newfield became a Zionist. It does mean, however, that he and other non-Zionist members of the emergency committee desired to keep Palestine available as a refuge for persecuted Jews, working with and even taking instruction from the Zionist organization. Even Newfield's son, Mayer Newfield, said his father "was not a Zionist. He was not anti-Zionist. . . . He believed the idea of a homeland for the Jews was contrary to the concept that the world will experience universal brotherhood when the Messiah eventually comes. Were he alive today, he would certainly be pro-Israel and pro-Zionist, but at the time he was not."[32] As Cyrus Arfa observes, even when Reform rabbis vehemently opposed a Jewish state in Palestine, they were "willing to do whatever was possible within their power to restore the biblical land as a Jewish cultural center and provide a homeland for those Jews who needed it or desired it as a haven."[33] Moreover, Newfield's association with Zionism failed to influence the older, staid members of Emanu-El who so revered him. Indeed, this issue drove a wedge between some of them and Milton Grafman, Newfield's successor and an active Zionist. Yet Newfield's embrace of Zionism, if it can be considered an embrace, provided a greater awareness for the Zionist cause among Birmingham's Gentile leaders and the press.

In Birmingham, the local district of the ZOA and Hadassah, the women's Zionist organization, energetically promoted Zionism through organized community projects, fund-raising drives, and sponsoring lectures by prominent speakers to rally support for the cause. Eastern European Jews who attended Temple Beth-El and K'nesseth Israel comprised the vast majority of the Birmingham Zionist organization, headquartered in a second-floor office of Frank and Ike Abelson's Alabama Novelty Company. The Abelson brothers, both born in Russia in the 1880s, immigrated to the United

States in the mid-1890s. They resided in the "Jewish ghetto" of Birmingham's north side in the early twentieth century where many Eastern European Jews were concentrated and where "oldtime Jewish ghetto personalities" such as the Abelsons formed Zionist groups such as the Birmingham Zion Association, Tikwath Zion, and Hadassah. By the 1930s, the Jewish community had moved to the south side of the city, and the Zionist organizations grew in number, especially after Hitler and the Nazis assumed power in Germany in 1933. Birmingham's chapter of the ZOA grew to six hundred members by 1936, and Hadassah, which had been formed in 1915 by Annie Abelson, the wife of Frank Abelson, had reached a membership of 350 women in 1937. Hadassah promoted many endeavors in Birmingham, ranging from health care to education. Its central role, however, remained in promoting health care and hygiene in Palestine. In 1934, Hadassah spearheaded a vital new project, Youth Aliyah, which brought Jewish "children into Palestine from Germany—giving them hope and security and a chance to be unafraid once again."[34]

In addition to sponsoring programs such as Youth Aliyah or the Young Judaean Club, Zionists also promoted the movement by regularly offering lectures by figures of national and international renown usually held at the YMHA or Temple Beth-El. The author Ludwig Lewisohn, a German-born Jew, spoke in Birmingham on a number of occasions. In March 1940, he appeared at the YMHA and urged the audience to support the Zionist movement. Calling Jews "a people in exile," Lewisohn argued that "everywhere there is a Jewish problem." Although the United States might become a utopia for Jews, where "Jews might be 100 per cent American and still a Jew," he doubted such a development because "Jews are a people, striving to maintain their ways of life." In a pointed critique of the Reform position, he stated that Jews "cannot be reduced merely to a religious sect. Assimilation and the melting pot are not the answer to the Jewish problem. . . . The answer is a Jewish homeland, where Jews may be really emancipated to develop their own lives."[35] That same month, a pivotal moment in the growth of Zionism in Birmingham occurred when Dr. Solomon Goldman, the national president of the ZOA, addressed a packed crowd at the YMHA. Goldman came to Birmingham "to help swell the ranks of those inspired Jews who sincerely believe that in Palestine lies the Jewish salvation . . . [and] to enlist new members in the Zionist movement."[36] He tried to alleviate the fears of many Reform Jews by explaining that "great men of America have seen no conflict between Zionism and national patriotism"—referring to Supreme Court justice Louis Brandeis—and expressed "sympathy for any Jew who wonders if he is guilty of 'dual allegiance.'" Yet like Lewisohn, Goldman forcefully argued that "every people must have a soil of its own where its genius can have complete and unhampered expression," and declared that whatever is built in Palestine "will be achieved by the Jews."[37]

According to Mark Elovitz, not all Eastern European Jews in Birmingham had "fully committed" to Zionism at that point, but Goldman's appearance convinced almost all of them to embrace the cause.[38] Joe Radoms responded to the Zionist "call to arms" and credited much of his "awakening" to Goldman's honesty in admitting that "we cannot guarantee that the Zionist movement can permanently solve the Jewish problem, but my conscience dictates that such a course is the honest one to follow."[39] The local press reacted favorably to the event, and Charles Feidelson of the *Age-Herald* described Goldman as a powerful "voice of faith," but he noted that "the implication was plain that the preservation of identity as a people and the growth of a great racial tradition were embraced in the Zionist dream." The need to maintain identity, religion, culture, and tradition "are deeply understandable and natural human urges that command general support among tolerant, liberal peoples everywhere," but despite Goldman's attempts to allay the fears of dual loyalty, Feidelson asked "how far should there be emphasis on racial separateness in countries other than the homeland?"[40] This was a question that no doubt made many Reform Jews uneasy.

Two months after Goldman's appearance in Birmingham, Newfield died. Newfield had been ill for some time, and his effort on behalf of Palestine in 1938 had taken its toll.[41] Although the rabbi had worked hand in hand with Solomon Goldman and the Zionist movement, few members of Emanu-El spoke in its favor. As before, the Jews of Beth-El and K'nesseth Israel played the leading roles in the Zionist movement in Birmingham. Prominent members of Emanu-El headed the United Jewish Fund, their desire to alleviate Jewish suffering abroad continued unabated. As Fannie Newman Goldberg, a member of K'nesseth Israel, explained, the Reform Jews "were interested not in Zionism as we were interested in Zionism, but in saving the lives during the time of Hitler."[42] Until the revelations of the mass killings of Jews in Nazi-occupied Europe in late 1942, support for Zionism rested almost exclusively with the Eastern European Jews and Sephardim in the state.

The Milton Grafman Era Begins

December 8, 1941, ushered in a new era for Birmingham's Temple Emanu-El as Milton Grafman arrived in the city the day after the Japanese attacked Pearl Harbor. Installed as the temple's rabbi a few days later, the thirty-four-year-old Grafman led the congregation until his retirement in 1975, and he remained active in the community until his death twenty years later. His dynamic personality and effusive enthusiasm provided a striking contrast to the staid Morris Newfield, who had been the congregation's rabbi since 1895. Born in Washington, DC, in 1907 and raised in Pittsburgh, Pennsylvania, Grafman attended the University of Cincinnati and Hebrew Union College, where he was ordained in 1933. He served as rabbi of Adath Israel in Lexington, Kentucky, from 1933 to 1941, working with Hillel groups at the University of Kentucky and Transylvania College. Grafman quickly connected with the youth at Emanu-El after arriving in Birmingham, and this connection came at a momentous time as Emanu-El's young men went off to war. As one soldier wrote to Grafman during the war, "My father was very fond of Dr. Newfield. I thought him a lovable, understanding man, too. Yet there was something I didn't cleave to. To me you are the very best of modern Jewry."[43] Another Emanu-El soldier, also writing from the battlefield, confided to Grafman, "you're really the first one we've ever had that I could turn to."[44]

Grafman's service to Emanu-El, and to the Jewish community at large, came at a time when Jews faced the greatest peril in their long history. Unlike most American Jews, Grafman had witnessed Nazi persecution and brutality firsthand, and the knowledge gained from the experience fueled his zeal to combat such inhumanity and injustice. Between June and August 1938, while he was still serving in Lexington, Grafman toured thirteen European countries, including Nazi Germany, under the auspices of the American Seminar, affiliated with the International YMCA. George Sherwood Eddy created the American Seminar in 1921 as a study tour designed to observe European conditions and help combat American isolationism. As a member of the American Seminar, Grafman held the title "lecturer" rather than rabbi and carried a State Department letter introducing him as "Mr. Milton Grafman," omitting any reference to his Jewishness. In fact, he was one of two rabbis on the tour. During his three-month sojourn, Grafman kept a diary of his experiences. As the seminar neared Germany, the anxiety and trepidation expressed in his entries became palpable. Eddy had been barred by the Nazis from entering Germany, leading Grafman and the other rabbi in the American Seminar, Alfred Minda of Minneapolis, Minnesota, to question the wisdom of their entering the country as well. Eddy told the two rabbis that they "owed it to their people" to see firsthand the tragedy unfolding in Nazi Germany. Consequently, both Grafman and Minda continued on the tour.[45]

When the group arrived in Berlin, Grafman saw little antisemitic persecution, only storefronts with Jewish names. The tragedy and horror of the Jews' plight became clear after he made contact with Berlin's Jewish community, visited synagogues, Jewish homes, and restaurants. "All I can say is that my experiences in Berlin for six days were the most harrowing and crushing I have ever had," Grafman wrote, "I saw with my own eyes a beaten and crushed people, a whole people in the throes of death, uttering their last dying gasp. In a few more years those gasps will be nothing more than a death rattle. The persecution is proceeding with greater and still greater vigor. There is and there will be no let up—until the last Jew has died or left the country. And then the scapegoat will be the Christian non-Aryan. Then, perhaps, the Christian world will awaken. . . . No hand of mercy will be extended. No Nazi will help them and no German, no matter how sympathetic, will dare to help them. . . . These poor souls will literally starve to death—and no one will lift a finger for them!"[46]

What followed next probably concerned him more than anything else he witnessed on the tour, and it was something that bothered him even after he moved to Birmingham in 1941: "But, perhaps, my greatest disappointment, my most intense aggravation, came from the fact that there is absolutely no hope whatsoever—particularly from the non-Jew. That the Jew is doomed in Germany I know now for a certainty. But I always felt that the non-Jew outside of Germany would feel our problem more deeply, particularly if he visited Germany. But I'm afraid this is not so. As I pointed out, externally Germany gives a good impression. It took me two days to get a glimpse of the tragedy here. The average tourist can very easily leave here and honestly say he saw little or no persecution. He is impressed with the cleanliness and orderliness of Germans, forgetting that Germany always was neat, clean, and with the exception of the distressing post-war era—orderly. He is impressed with the emphasis on health and body building, forgetting that the intellect is being sacrificed, that the humaneness of a whole people is being submerged in a philosophy based upon hatred, and bound to eventuate in war!" Moreover, Grafman despaired when he talked to Americans living in Germany—they did not know he was Jewish—who had "absorbed" Nazi antisemitic propaganda that the Jews had brought the persecution on themselves. One American woman with whom he spoke thought that while the Nazis should have been more "subtle" about their discrimination against her Jewish friends, she still did not associate with them any longer to avoid "being classed as Jew-lover, and besides, they all had the same story to tell and she got tired of having them weep on her shoulder." This attitude on the part of Americans in Germany, and even in the American Seminar group, he wrote, "gave me sleepless nights and restless days during my visit to Germany. If this was all the understanding we could get, then what hope was there for the Jew in Germany, or elsewhere?"[47] In a letter to a friend, he confided, "I'm afraid that no one will believe my story when I return. All I can say for now, is that you can believe anything you hear or read about Nazi treatment of Jews. Their cruelty is beyond description and nothing they would do would come as a surprise. . . . But perhaps worse than anything, this antisemitism is spreading like a poison. You can see it everywhere you go."[48] This intimate exposure to the harsh realities of Nazi antisemitism and the enormous threat it posed to Jews everywhere, together with his acute sense of social responsibility and staunch Zionism, helps to explain Grafman's zeal for the many relief and rescue efforts on behalf of European Jews.

Grafman's early years in Birmingham proved to be extremely productive for himself and for Emanu-El. In 1943 he helped to establish a Birmingham chapter of the National Conference on Christians and Jews as well as offering an Institute on Judaism that brought together Birmingham's Christian clergy and "religious educators" in order to "cultivate a better understanding of Judaism in its relationship to Christianity through a study of their common historical roots and religious traditions."[49] Such interfaith work continued the efforts of his predecessor Morris Newfield, who had forged close friendships with a number of Christian clergy. Birmingham had "well trained and highly educated ministers," but it also had many minsters "whose academic background [left] much to be desired and therefore tend[ed] to be on the narrow side as far as Judaism [was] concerned," and even with Christian denominations other than their own. Grafman's desire to educate Christian leaders in the city can clearly be seen as a manifestation of the disappointment and dismay he experienced with Christians in Nazi Germany. In 1946, Grafman's Institute on Judaism for Christian Clergy became an annual event that continued throughout his tenure as Emanu-El's rabbi. Grafman thought it had "done more to improve intergroup relations than any other interfaith activity that's taken place in the city of Birmingham."[50]

Unlike Newfield, however, Grafman vocally supported Zionism and attracted a number of Eastern European Jews to Emanu-El from nearby Beth-El. Grafman appealed to those traditional Jews who felt uncomfortable with Classical Reform services by reviving some traditions that Newfield had abandoned. Coupled with the transitions at Temple Beth-El, this resulted in dramatic membership growth for the Reform congregation—from 350 families to 560 families by 1952. As Fannie Newman Goldberg recalled, only after the "outflux of Jews from Temple Beth-El that went into Emanu-El and under Rabbi Grafman," did the Jews of Emanu-El become "more interested in Zionism."[51]

At Beth-El there had been a growing unease throughout the 1930s over how many of the old traditions should be retained or discarded among the acculturating immigrant generation, and especially among their children. In contrast to Emanu-El, Beth-El had a Hebrew school, held no Friday evening services, and observed two days of Rosh Hashanah instead of only one. In 1938, Beth-El's board of trustees quarreled over whether women could become members in their own right. Mark Elovitz, who was a former rabbi at Beth-El in the 1970s, observes that even with "all the bluster and fanfare aside, Temple Beth-El was, in spite of its protestations to modernity and progressivism, still 'definitely an Orthodox house of worship' in 1939."[52] The quiet, scholarly Abraham Mesch, who arrived in 1935 and led the congregation until his death in 1962, presided over the transition of Beth-El from Orthodoxy to Conservatism, formally identifying with the Conservative movement in 1944.

Mesch, who had immigrated to the United States from Poland in 1923, had studied at Chicago's Hebrew Theological College and had been ordained at the Hebron Yeshiva in Palestine in 1934. He also received a PhD from the Illinois College of Law and a ThD from the Central School of Religion.[53] After arriving at Beth-El in 1935, Mesch began to implement changes at the synagogue, including reenergizing the Sisterhood, organizing a Junior Congregation, and, in 1938, starting the Beth-El Forum, a discussion program that "attracted Friday evening crowds of 300–500 people." When Harold Altschukl of the American ORT Federation spoke about "The Rehabilitation and Retraining of the Jews in Central and Eastern Europe" in 1939, over five hundred attended, many of them from Emanu-El and K'nesseth Israel. With this process of change, Mesch significantly increased the congregation's membership from 305 families in 1937 to 500 families by 1944, even as some members moved to Emanu-El. By 1949, Beth-El had grown to 636 families and became the largest Jewish congregation in the state.[54]

While the attraction of Reform Judaism, the social status associated with the Reform Temple, and Grafman's dynamic personality encouraged many families to move from Beth-El to Emanu-El, the transition from Orthodoxy to Conservatism under Mesch likewise encouraged immense growth at Beth-El. After US immigration doors closed in the 1920s, Eastern European Jews and their children acculturated and moved into the middle class, at the same time that Conservative synagogues began to flourish. The social and religious transitions that occurred at Beth-El under Mesch only lessened differences with German Reform Jews and reflected trends occurring nationally. Two other factors should also be considered when discussing the growth at Beth-El under Mesch. First, Mesch was an ardent, committed

Zionist who believed that "there is no place in the world where the Jew feels so much at home, so free, as in the Holy Land. . . . Palestine is the place for Jews who are interested in what is 'typically culturally Jewish.'"[55] Second, Mesch is the only Orthodox/Conservative rabbi in Alabama who served his congregation for any significant length of time. At Agudath Israel in Montgomery or Ahavas Chesed in Mobile, the other Orthodox synagogues in the state, the congregations had only intermittent rabbinic leadership, often heavily relying on lay leaders or local Reform rabbis. Mesch's personality, intellect, and commitment no doubt drove Beth-El's growth, but without such consistent rabbinic leadership, something Beth-El had not had in the past, it is doubtful the congregation would have experienced such dramatic increases.

Grafman entered the rabbinate at a time when Reform Judaism underwent significant change, especially regarding Zionism. Cyrus Arfa has argued that since 1895 Reform Judaism has experienced a "gradual but relentless self-transformation" toward a pro-Zionist position, accepting it in the CCAR's approval of the Columbus Platform of 1937, which stated that "the obligation of all Jewry [is] to aid in [Palestine's] upbuilding as a Jewish homeland by endeavoring to make it not only a haven of refuge for the oppressed but also a center of Jewish culture and spiritual life."[56] Many children of Eastern European immigrants had received their education at Hebrew Union College and had become Reform rabbis, including Grafman, whose parents had emigrated from Lithuania and present-day Poland. Yet this embrace of the Reform tradition did not mean abandoning older cultural traditions such as Zionism. Indeed, the Columbus Platform resulted because "many of the younger rabbis were more self-assured than the older classical Reformers such as Newfield, and could more easily accept notions of cultural pluralism, or more specifically ideas of 'dual' loyalties without fearing adverse Christian responses."[57] Grafman, who attended the CCAR meeting in 1937, almost certainly voted in favor of the Columbus Platform, and he definitely can be characterized as a self-assured young rabbi who fervently embraced the pro-Zionist position well before his appointment to Emanu-El.[58]

Despite the lack of outspoken support for Zionism among Emanu-El's members prior to Grafman's arrival, the congregation enthusiastically welcomed him as rabbi, and his pro-Zionist stance at that point aroused no noticeable resistance or controversy. A number of congregants remained ardent anti-Zionists, but Zionism did not become a central issue at Emanu-El until after the revelations of the mass killings in late 1942. The safety and well-being of the large number of its members who actively participated in the war effort was of far greater concern and significance to the congregation than Zionism. Nevertheless, Grafman played a leading role in Birmingham's Zionist cause. Indeed, his prominence as Reform rabbi further added to the city's dynamic and politically connected Zionist leadership, by far the most vibrant and influential in the state.

Zionism and the Holocaust

Historian Thomas A. Kolsky has observed that "the extraordinary intensification of Zionist activities in the United States after the outbreak of the war in Europe in 1939 provoked an American Jewish anti-Zionist reaction."[59] This can clearly be seen in Alabama, as Zionism became a more divisive issue by 1942 as a number of Reform Jews began to push back against the Zionist movement. When the CCAR adopted the Columbus Platform in 1937, acknowledging Palestine as *a* center of Jewish life, but not *the* center of Jewish life, the Reform movement had effectively declared its neutrality regarding Zionism, yet at the same time it had moved closer to the Zionist position than it had ever been under the Pittsburgh Platform. That "neutrality" did not mollify the intense emotions within Reform Judaism surrounding the idea of a Jewish state. The CCAR's resolution on February 27, 1942, stating that Jews in Palestine "be given the privilege of establishing a military force which will fight under its own banner on the side of the democracies, under allied command, to defend its own land and the Near East to the end that the victory of the democracies may be hastened everywhere," brought the Zionist controversy within the Reform movement to a head.[60]

On June 1–2, 1942, thirty-six dissident Reform rabbis crafted a statement at an Atlantic City meeting responding to CCAR's support for a distinctly Jewish fighting unit. Ninety Reform rabbis ultimately signed the statement, although none were from Alabama. The rabbis professed their belief in "the universalism of Judaism's ethical and spiritual values and teachings," recognized that Palestine had a role to play in "relieving the pressing problems of our distressed people," and offered to "render unstinted aid" to Jews residing there. "In the light of our universalistic interpretation of Jewish history and destiny, and also because of our concern for the welfare and status of Jewish people living in other parts of the world," the dissidents proclaimed, "we are unable to subscribe to or support the political emphasis now paramount in the Zionistic program. We cannot but believe that Jewish nationalism tends to confuse our fellow men about our place and function in society and also diverts our attention from our historical role to live as a religious community wherever we may dwell. Such spiritual role is especially voiced by (Reform) Judaism in its emphasis upon the eternal prophetic principles of life and thought."[61] This declaration by the dissatisfied Reform rabbis acted as a mission statement of the American Council for Judaism (ACJ), founded December 7, 1942, as the first anti-Zionist organization in the United States. The establishment of the ACJ only two weeks after the State Department confirmed the mass killings of Jews in Eastern Europe made the ACJ extremely unpopular among numerous American Jews. As Monty Noam Penkower explains, "in short order, the anti-Zionist rabbis were not merely beleaguered but reviled, castigated as traitors in their people's most anguished hour. . . . The fires of the Holocaust seared the young Reform rabbinical wing, as it did their fellow American Jews, converting them to a visceral understanding of the indissoluble link that existed between Jewish catastrophe and Jewish sovereignty."[62]

The tension and conflict in Alabama over Zionism became particularly acute in Birmingham, with its large population of Eastern European Jews and strong Zionist organizations. The revelations of the mass killings drove some Reform members toward Zionism, and newly appointed Milton Grafman attracted a number of Eastern European Jews to Emanu-El, strengthening the Zionist forces in the Reform congregation. Even so, many non-Zionist and anti-Zionists remained. As Mark Elovitz writes, the "unrelenting" attacks and disparagement of the Reform stance by the city's "indomitable Zionists" created "a small, though sometimes bitter, minority of local Jews" who never embraced Zionism.[63] Prominent Reform Jews such as the investment banker Mervyn Sterne, attorney Leo Oberdorfer, industrialist Milton Fies, merchant Joseph Loveman, and Rabbi Newfield's son, Dr. Seymon Newfield, all joined the ACJ. Sterne, who had been elected the first president of Birmingham's United Jewish Fund and who actively supported relief and rescue operations for European Jews, adamantly opposed Zionism. Sterne later said that he faced more antisemitism and discrimination from other Jews—"Jews with extreme views"—than from Gentiles because he was the "wrong kind of Jew."[64] Sterne, however, commanded the respect of all of Birmingham's Jews and Gentiles, and he worked closely with Zionists to rescue and provide relief to persecuted European Jews on behalf of the United Jewish Fund, but he had a thin skin concerning the frequent, and often harsh, criticism of his position on Zionism. Ironically, many of those who favored the position of the ACJ, with its insistence upon a religious definition of Judaism, were often noted for "their failure to attend religious services."[65] Nevertheless, despite the contentious disagreements over Zionism, the Nazi persecutions in Europe drove many Reform Jews, not just in Birmingham but statewide, toward a greater concern for Jews worldwide, if not outright acceptance of the creation of a Jewish state, a trend observed among Reform Jews throughout the United States.[66]

Both Emanu-El's Grafman and Beth-El's Mesch joined with 757 rabbis across the nation in signing a statement rebuking the ninety Reform rabbis of the ACJ. The rabbis regarded "Zionism not only as fully consistent with Judaism but as a logical expression and implementation of it. . . . Zionism is not a secular movement. It has its origins and roots in the authoritative religious texts of Judaism. Scripture and rabbinical literature alike are replete with the promise of the restoration of Israel to its ancestral home. Anti-Zionism, not Zionism, is a departure from the Jewish religion." The statement also addressed the idea of dual loyalty that so many Reform Jews feared: "Every fair-minded American knows that American Jews have only one political allegiance—and that is to America. There is nothing in Zionism to impair this loyalty." Five of the rabbis who signed the declaration were from Alabama. Rabbi Samson H. Levey of Mishkan Israel in Selma, Rabbi Luitpold Wallach of B'nai Israel in Florence, and Rabbi Samuel Teitelbaum, stationed at Fort McClellan, joined Birmingham's Grafman and Mesch in signing the declaration.[67]

Grafman had, since his appointment to Emanu-El's pulpit, warned his congregation of the danger that Hitler's Germany posed to Jews everywhere and had quickly joined the local Zionist organization, much to the consternation of some of his constituents.[68] Some months after the revelation of the mass killings in Europe, Grafman and Mesch organized a prayer and protest meeting at the YMHA. In urging his congregants to attend, Grafman wrote:

> Israel's hour of testing is at hand. Unspeakable tragedy has overwhelmed our people. Two million European Jews lie dead—victims of Hitler's horrible sadism! The remaining few million Jews on the European continent are threatened with annihilation within the coming months! Is there nothing to stay the evil decree? Is there no one to plead our cause? Is there nothing that can be done? There is much to be done—NOW! Millions of Jews, perhaps, will die before Hitler is defeated. But MILLIONS can be saved! . . . BUT NOTHING WILL BE DONE UNLESS WE JEWS WHO STILL LIVE IN SECURITY RAISE OUR VOICES IN PRAYER AND PROTEST. If we are not outraged by this terrifying tragedy, IF WE DO NOT SPEAK UP—WHO SHALL? True, only an aroused Christian conscious can save us—but the conscience of the Jew lies dormant. . . . Will this meeting accomplish anything? I don't know.

> I do know, though, that doing nothing, saying nothing, will accomplish nothing. I do know that I must pray for those who have been martyred. I do know that I must raise my voice in protest against the Nazi decree of death. I do know that sincere prayers can move mountains! I do know that the voice of a united Israel will not go unheeded. I do know that every Jew with a shred of sympathy in his being for his fellow Jews will want to join all of us in prayer.[69]

A few weeks later, on April 8, 1943, the rabbis organized the Jewish community to participate in the International Day of Prayer for the Jews in Palestine, which included Jews and Gentiles around the world.[70]

Zionist leaders in Birmingham used their personal friendships and business connections to garner the support of Gentiles for Zionism. No one did more in this regard than attorney Abe Berkowitz, whose connections with local politicians frequently resulted in public support for Jewish and Zionist endeavors, either through civic proclamations or telegrams of support. After the American government confirmed the mass killings of European Jews in November 1942, Berkowitz began lobbying his state representatives to endorse Zionism. He convinced Birmingham's members of the Alabama legislature, Representative Sid Smyer and Senator James A. Simpson, to sponsor a resolution in May 1943 that stated the "policy of the Axis powers to exterminate the Jews of Europe through mass murder cries out for action by the United Nations representing the civilized world." Because of this, the Alabama legislature, in a joint resolution, called for the "establishment of a Jewish homeland in Palestine" because of the mass murder of European Jews. This was the first resolution of this type passed in the United States.[71]

That same week, Zionists held a memorial for murdered European Jews at the YMHA and brought national Zionist leader Ludwig Lewisohn to speak at the memorial where he praised Alabama for endorsing a homeland for the Jews. Lewisohn later spoke to a crowd at the Tutwiler Hotel where he told them that "Germany . . . is already insane," and had "physically exterminated 2,000,000 Jews and quarter of a million Poles." Of the severe immigration restrictions that hampered Jewish rescue, he said, "if the free nations don't want us, they don't have to have us. But, give us Palestine."[72] The *Birmingham News*, no doubt with the great influence of editor and columnist Charles Feidelson, published an editorial following Lewisohn's appearance endorsing Zionism: "What is not to be lost sight of is that this war began 10 years ago when Hitler launched his campaign of Jewish extirpation. The nations now fighting the Axis did not at the time grasp the significance of this explosion of barbarism. They shut their eyes and ears, and then they appeased, until the monster was upon them. It is a profound irony that, at this stage of the game, when so much blood and sacrifice have been given to the defense of civilization, an adequate measure of decency, justice and freedom should be withheld from a people which embodies the tragedy and the hope of the struggle." Feidelson had always stressed the need to open Palestine to Jewish refugees, but the horror of the Holocaust, by 1943, seems to have swayed Feidelson toward the acceptance of Zionism. He did not become a Zionist, however. He understood the compelling desire for a Jewish homeland, but considered Zionism ultimately "untenable."[73]

The British White Paper of 1939, which had severely limited Jewish immigration to Palestine, also stipulated that after March 1944 all Jewish immigration would be contingent upon Arab permission. Britain's military weakness in the Middle East and its desire to prevent Arabs from joining the Axis convinced British leaders of the necessity of appeasement. To combat this, in late 1943 Birmingham's Jews formed the Birmingham Emergency Committee for Palestine to "mobilize all energies and resources of Jews in the city 'to prevent this miscarriage of justice and repudiation of the sanctity of covenants.'" The committee quickly gained endorsements from the Christian community. Milton Grafman chaired the committee, but it included Mesch of Beth-El and Rabbi Joseph Goldberg of K'nesseth Israel as well as prominent members of all congregations, including non-Zionists from Emanu-El. As had occurred with the Alabama legislature, Jewish leaders lobbied local politicians on both the Jefferson County Commission and Birmingham City Commission to pass similar resolutions supporting a homeland for the Jews. The Jefferson County Commission resolved that "the establishment of a Jewish homeland in Palestine . . . be commended to the considered judgement of the United Nations, not only as an act of justice to the Jewish people and the righting of an ancient wrong, but as an integral part of the new democratic world order in which every people shall have the right to self-government and self-determination in accordance with the principles for which now are waging war." These resolutions were a part of a national drive the American Zionist Emergency Council coordinated to get Congress to approve such a resolution in order to pressure Britain into opening Palestine for Jewish refugees and, ultimately, for the creation of a Jewish homeland.[74]

As 1944 approached and with the Final Solution reaching its apex, protests against British policy came from the pulpits, the press, politicians, and even from organized labor across Alabama. Grafman told his congregation that three million Jews had already been murdered in Europe, and closing the doors of Palestine via the White Paper meant not only "selling out" the hopes and aspirations of the Jews but also a death sentence to the five million remaining Jews in Europe. Only by speaking as one voice can American Jewry make a difference, Grafman warned. To that end, he declared that "now is the time for every Jew not in [the] ZOA to join immediately." He even appealed to Christians, calling the impending crisis the "greatest challenge" to the conscience of the Christian world, quoting Matthew 25:40: "Even as Ye have done unto the least of these, My children, Ye have done this unto Me."[75] In the press, one of the state's most influential papers, the *Montgomery Advertiser*, argued that opening Palestine would save "thousands who will otherwise be massacred" and blamed "the dead hand of Chamberlain's appeasement politics [for] keeping the door of Palestine shut against the Jews of Europe." By opening the "Gates of Hope," Britain could save the Jews from "perhaps the worst Captivity in their long and tragic history."[76] By late 1943, the *Birmingham News* acknowledged that the issue "is dear to all Jews, non-Zionists as well as Zionists . . . two or three million European Jews have now been liquidated. The five million still alive would be facing a future bitter enough, if no White Paper were casting a shadow on them." To shut the remaining Jews out of Palestine "is in effect to clinch a Hitler victory, whatever happens on the battlefield." As the date drew nearer, the *News* remarked that the British policy "smacks of Nazi tenderness toward the Jews."[77] Syndicated columnist John Temple Graves also weighed in: "They say that 2,000,000 Jews have been murdered in Europe. Certainly the Jewish people in Axis-held lands have suffered as they nor any other people have ever suffered before. And all over the earth as they seek refuge they find quotas and immigration restrictions shutting them out. If the civilized world in whose name we make war is to prove its right to the name, something generous and brave must be done for the persecuted Jewish people. If the America in whose democratic and humanitarian sign we are defeating Hitler is worth its victory, something heartfelt and loud must go from here to England in protest against the cruelty and cowardice of the White Paper."[78]

In January 1944, Rabbi Stephen Wise, a prominent Reform rabbi from New York and cochairman of the American Zionist Emergency Council, toured Alabama, lecturing to civic and religious groups where he urged Alabamians to "do all they can to prevent the enforcement of the document." In Mobile, he spoke at the Government Street Temple. Sha'arai Shomayim's new rabbi, Bertram W. Korn, also spoke throughout the region to both Jewish and Gentile groups on the injustice of the White Paper and the necessity of public support against British policy. Jews in Mobile had condemned the White Paper as "legally, morally, and humanly indefensible," and subsequently, both B'nai B'rith and the Sha'arai Shomayim Congregation passed resolutions that urged the British to abandon their immigration policy. B'nai B'rith called the repudiation of the mandate "a morally indefensible act," while the Reform congregation proclaimed, in part, that "by excluding Jews, as Jews, from the right of entry into Palestine, and restricting Jews, as Jews, from the acquisition of land, [the White Paper] does violence to the fundamental concept of democracy . . . and thus to the very purposes and ideals . . . of the United Nations."[79] Although Wise did not visit with Montgomery's Jewish community, the Montgomery Jewish Federation also passed a resolution calling on Montgomery's representatives to support the abrogation of the British White Paper.[80]

Politicians and labor unions also sent telegrams and letters to the White House calling for action. Mobile's Jews lobbied their friends in labor and government. Mobile's representative in the US House of Representatives, Frank Boykin, had long been sympathetic to Jewish concerns, and the Mobile Central Trades Council, part of the American Federation of Labor (AFL), adopted a resolution that described the British policy as dealing "a severe blow to the Jewish victims of Nazi bestiality, seeking escape from extermination at the hands of Hitler henchmen." The council demanded "the abrogation of the White Paper . . . [or] any action which restricts the rights of Jews to immigrate into Palestine."[81] In Birmingham, Abe Berkowitz convinced Cooper Green, president of the Birmingham City Commission, to contact Alabama's representatives in Washington and urge them to condemn the British policy. A number of Alabama politicians, including Senator Lister Hill and Representative John Sparkman, had been staunch supporters of Jewish interests in Washington, and on this issue they did not let their Jewish constituents down.[82] Indeed, Jewish leaders in Birmingham, such as Berkowitz, Abelson, and Grafman, relied heavily upon these representatives as their voices in Washington.

One of those politicians, Representative John Newsome of Birmingham, actively supported attempts to sway British policy on Palestine. Newsome received hundreds of letters and telegrams urging him to support the Gillette-Rogers Resolution that called on the British government to open Palestine for increased Jewish immigration, which he then submitted to the House Foreign Affairs Committee for their "information and guidance."[83] When Representative Pete Jarman of Alabama, who served on the House Foreign Affairs Committee, appeared to have reservations about the resolution creating a "rift" between the United States and Great Britain, both Berkowitz and Grafman contacted Jarman to clear up any confusion about the resolution. Berkowitz also warned anyone from the American Zionist Emergency Council to refrain from approaching Jarman to lobby his support. "Like it or not," Berkowitz told the national Zionist organization, "men like Jarman are sectionalists, [and] want to hear from their own folks and understand the language of their own folks only. I do not claim that I have the ability to persuade him to do anything that I want him to do but there are some people in Tuscaloosa who he respects and whose views he will listen to." According to Charles Feidelson, who met with Jarman in Washington, the congressman expressed his support for the resolution.[84]

Zionists also organized a luncheon for Birmingham's religious and civic leaders to lobby their support for the Gillette-Rogers Resolution. As a result, Ike Abelson reported that "there will be about 500 telegrams sent from Birmingham to President Roosevelt" to support their cause.[85] Lobbying efforts such as these included both Zionists and non-Zionists, but while the Jews in Alabama worked together to influence British policy on Palestine, they remained divided over whether Palestine should be only a haven for European Jews, as non-Zionists advocated, or become a permanent Jewish homeland, as Zionists desired.

The concerted effort by Alabama's Jewish community to pressure the British to rescind the White Paper and open Palestine failed, but it demonstrated the influence of the well-coordinated Zionist movement on local politicians, as well as on religious and civic organizations. The campaign also demonstrated that Americans overwhelmingly supported the attempts to rescue European Jews by opening the doors of British Palestine. When it involved opening the doors of the United States to save the same Jewish lives, despite the lamentations of politicians and the press—the *Birmingham News*, perhaps the loudest voice in the state on this issue, argued that "most Americans" viewed saving the remaining Jews as "primarily an issue of elementary humanity and justice"—no one, including those politicians who so vigorously aided Birmingham's Zionists, endorsed changing American immigration policy.[86]

The plight of the Hungarian Jews vividly illustrated the reluctance of Alabamians to welcome Jewish refugees into the United States. In March 1944, German troops occupied Hungary and began to deport Hungarian Jews to the extermination camp at Auschwitz, with the Hungarian government's collaboration. The War Refugee Board (WRB), which President Roosevelt established in January 1944 to rescue European Jews and offer relief to concentration camp inmates, began a campaign designed to pressure Hungary to stop the deportations. Many prominent individuals and influential groups joined the campaign. Alfred E. Smith, former governor of New York and one-time Democratic presidential candidate, crafted his own statement of support for the Hungarian Jews and urged that the United States offer "all available facilities to save nearly one million Jews facing extermination in Hitler occupied Hungary and . . . [establish] refugee havens in this country and allied countries as means of encouraging marked victims to escape from Nazi-ridden countries . . . as evidence of our good faith."[87] Seventy-one "prominent Christians, including nearly a score of governors and four Nobel Prize winners," signed Smith's statement. When contacted for support, Alabama governor Chauncey Sparks "heartily" embraced the idea, but only if refugees were "subject to repatriation after the war if immigration quota is exceeded."[88]

Many Alabamians missed Sparks's caveat of repatriation and quota limits. Birmingham attorney Joseph Mudd feared that the increased immigration would exacerbate "class antagonisms." He pointed out that Albert Einstein, a Jew, had earlier fled from Nazi persecution but now sponsored anti-poll-tax legislation, an anathema to southern white supremacists, and argued that "this is a sample of what will come from the other refugees." Mudd's anti-semitism and xenophobia were readily apparent. As he further explained, "there is no such thing as 'temporary refuge.' Once they are admitted to this country there will be every reason on earth why they should remain here permanently. They will argue loudly that there is no other place to go; to oust them would be inhumane." The irony of inhumanity was lost on Mudd. He echoed so many others who fought increased immigration: "the refugees can certainly escape the persecution of Hitler short of traveling thirty-five hundred miles. There must be many places of safety within a radius of a thousand or two thousand miles of Hitler dominated territory."[89] Mudd gave no clue as to where those locations might have been.

Community Dissension

By 1945 Zionism became a defining issue in the Birmingham Jewish community. In March the internationally renowned author and Zionist Pierre Van Paassen lectured in the city and harshly condemned the British for their policy on Jewish immigration to Palestine. Soon after, the *Birmingham News* published an article on Arab claims to Palestine, which suggested that "Jewish leaders will have to find territories other than Palestine to accommodate their fraternity." This prompted the president of the Birmingham District of the ZOA, Abe Berkowitz, to respond in his typical unrestrained fashion with a fiery letter printed a week later. "There are a considerable number of Arabs in this country who would support this statement," Berkowitz wrote, and "they may be found in prisoner of war camps wearing the uniform of Rommel's Afrika Nazi Corps. . . . They are a lovable crew, inclined towards peace and amity but they have experienced a little difficulty in washing their hands stained with the blood of American sons and the sons of our Allies." Berkowitz continued by denigrating the Arabs—decrying their lack of religiosity, their incivility and ignorance, as well as their lack of productivity, hygiene, and sanitation—and explained that Palestine had a measure of civilization only because of the Jews who lived there. The agitation by "Nazi Arabs" in the Middle East, he warned, was "fed with foreign money and ceaselessly inflamed by Nazi and Fascist propaganda."[90]

A few days later, the *News* responded with an editorial "to comment on recent attacks on the Arabs and the British which have had a local circulation as official Zionist propaganda." In the editorial, the *News* warned Zionists that "one-sided zealotry" would not aid their cause, specifically citing both Van Paassen's lectures and Berkowitz's letter. In addressing Van Paassen's condemnation of Britain, the *News* wondered what good it would do to so pointedly criticize Britain's shortcomings, noting that such accusations were "bound to stir resentment among those who cannot forget that England is our ally in the war." Additionally, while it recognized a "soft answer" to the Arab point of view unrealistic to expect, the *News* characterized Berkowitz's letter as "so extreme, we thought, as to be self-defeating." "Zionism will not win supporters outside the Jewish community," the editorial cautioned, "if its affirmative, positive values are subordinated to contention and name-calling. Zionism will not wax stronger if it comes to rely on rancor, on an extreme nationalism." The *News*, which had been sympathetic to the Zionist cause, counseled Zionists to take a more moderate tone.[91]

The editorial response of the *News* had no apparent effect on Zionists in Birmingham. The editors, including contributing editor and columnist Charles Feidelson, clearly underestimated the passions surrounding the issue, passions that made compromise virtually impossible. The *News*'s characterization of Berkowitz's letter as too extreme also failed to acknowledge that Berkowitz was indeed correct in his description of Nazi Arabs in POW camps, Fascist propaganda throughout the Middle East, and the Jewish contributions to Palestinian infrastructure and burgeoning prosperity.[92] With the full realization of the fate of European Jewry, Zionists thought moderation, not extremism, to be self-defeating.

At Emanu-El, the *News*'s editorial brought the festering unrest over Zionism to a head and revealed the deep schism within the congregation. Rabbi Grafman and Feidelson clashed over the tenor of the editorial. Feidelson was not anti-Zionist, like some others at Emanu-El. He, most likely, was a non-Zionist who fully supported the need to open Palestine for Jewish refugees. Grafman thought Feidelson responsible for the editorial, but Feidelson maintained that it reflected the newspaper's position and not the individual writer's opinion. A heated conflict between the two resulted in Feidelson's resignation from the temple. Although a number of Emanu-El congregants opposed Grafman over his "pronounced Zionist tendencies," a majority at Emanu-El supported him. A large number of those supporters came from Zionists whom he had attracted to Emanu-El since his installment as rabbi in late 1941.[93] The resulting congregational split at Emanu-El reflected the divide within the larger Jewish community, as the antagonism between Zionists and the Reform Jews associated with the ACJ led a visitor to remark that the community "is seething with under the surface turmoil," a turmoil that continued until 1948.[94]

Zionism did not create the level of dissension within Mobile's or Montgomery's Jewish communities as it did in Birmingham. Mobile could be described as "mainly Zionistic," with an active district of the ZOA, Hadassah, and a Young Judaean Club. Zionist leadership centered on members of Ahavas Chesed, including Joseph Bear, Sam Weingarten, Morris Stern, and Sam Ripps, but prominent and respected Reform Jews also embraced Zionism. Attorney Leo M. Brown, who had been president of Sha'arai Shomayim and one of the most respected men in the Jewish community, was a devoted Zionist. Primarily because of participation of Reform members such as Brown, there had been "no serious conflicts" or "violent opinions expressed" between Zionists and the small group of anti-Zionists in the city. Other members of the Reform congregation, such as Paul May, the son-in-law of fervent Zionist Sol Kahn, donated to the local Zionist organization although he did not consider himself a Zionist.[95] By 1943 the Reform congregation had even employed a rabbi who was Zionist.

In January 1943, Sha'arai Shomayim appointed Bertram Wallace Korn as rabbi after Sidney Berkowitz joined the army. Bernard Eichold, the president of Sha'arai Shomayim, had known Korn since 1940 when Korn was a student at Hebrew Union College. Eichold had suggested him as Berkowitz's replacement. Korn arrived in Mobile three days after his ordination. Like Grafman in Birmingham, Korn was a young and energetic Zionist. Five days after his arrival in Mobile, he lectured on Zionism at the fifth anniversary celebration of the Jewish Progressive Club where members of Ahavas Chesed received him warmly. Over the course of his short tenure in Mobile he spoke to numerous civic groups in the city and in the surrounding area about the necessity of a Jewish homeland, and his efforts on behalf of Zionism caused Eichold to remark that "he has devoted so much of his time and energy in gaining a hearing for that movement which has never had a spokesman like him in Mobile before. In numerous sermons he has clarified the meaning of Zionism for many who misunderstood its meaning; in personal conversations he has done his best to convince people of its rightness." Although Korn served the Reform congregation less than a year before becoming a chaplain in the military, he established an outspoken Zionist presence at the Government Street Temple and forged strong friendships with Zionists at Ahavas Chesed. Joe Bear, one of the leaders of the Ahavas Chesed congregation, even organized a farewell celebration for Korn prior to his induction into the army.[96] The strength of the Zionist movement in Mobile, driven primarily by Eastern European Jews from Ahavas Chesed, coupled with the prestige and influence of Reform Jews such as Leo Brown and the tireless, though limited, efforts of Korn, allowed Mobile's Jewish community to avoid the often rancorous tensions that plagued Birmingham in the postwar years. Although anti-Zionists remained among the Reform congregation, most at Sha'arai Shomayim had ambivalently—or perhaps passively—accepted Zionism.

Conversely, the Reform-dominated community in Montgomery remained firmly non-Zionist, and, to a certain extent, anti-Zionist in its orientation, and the ACJ held great sway among the congregants at Beth-Or. Montgomery's most outspoken critic of Zionism, the highly influential Adolph Weil Sr., provided "substantial financial support" to the ACJ and considered Zionism "the greatest enemy of the Jews." He even refused to contribute to the Montgomery Jewish Federation because he believed it allocated too much of its funds to organizations such as the UPA. Weil and the small group of anti-Zionists that coalesced around him remained "on the alert to attack Zionism whenever an opportunity is presented." Beth-Or's Rabbi Eugene Blachschleger, however, provided a moderating influence to Weil's extremism and prevented Zionism from becoming a more divisive issue within the community during the war. Blachschleger, although a charter member of the ACJ, maintained an active relationship with Agudath Israel's rabbi, Samuel S. Lerer, who himself was Palestinian and an "enthusiastic" Zionist.[97]

The Zionist organizations that existed in Montgomery centered largely on congregations Agudath Israel and Etz Ahayem. Only by the late 1930s and early 1940s did these Zionist organizations develop and grow. By 1941 a representative from the Montgomery chapter of the ZOA had been included on the board of the federation, and by 1944 Rabbi Lerer had been successful in reviving Hadassah, the only Zionist organization that included a Reform contingent. It is doubtful that the Reform members of Hadassah had any Zionistic tendencies. They only wanted "to support the work Hadassah has done in Palestine."[98] Despite the work by Lerer, who tried to develop enthusiasm for Zionism in Montgomery, the entrenched non-Zionist and anti-Zionist leadership in the dominant Reform community meant Zionism had little influence outside of the small and often insular Orthodox and Sephardic communities.

The campaign to keep Palestine open as a refuge for the persecuted Jews in Europe exacerbated the tensions between the Eastern European Jews who had accepted Zionism and the smaller, influential, and vocal group of Reform Jews who largely worked to open the British-controlled territory as the most obvious haven for those fleeing Nazi terror. The Nazi persecutions confirmed and reinforced Alabama's Eastern European Jews' adherence to Zionism, and they remained the driving force behind the Zionist movement. The persecution and atrocities, moreover, contributed greatly to the growth of Zionism among the state's Reform Jews and prompted many who had emphatically rejected the idea prior to the rise of Nazism to view the Zionist cause as a viable, even necessary option. It was, however, a controversial issue upon which not all Reform Jews agreed. Although Alabama's Zionists were unable to influence British policy on Palestine, America's immigration quota system, or Roosevelt's positions regarding European Jewry, national Jewish organizations were also unsuccessful. Yet the Zionist campaign in Alabama clearly demonstrated the influence Jews, both Reform and Eastern European, had on the press, local politicians, and civic and religious organizations in the state.

A number of Reform rabbis also played a pivotal role in the movement and in how the public came to perceive this crusade. Eli Evans describes Birmingham's Milton Grafman as one of "the new breed of Reform rabbis, the men who had served in World War II and replaced the generation of rabbis who had been at their temples for four or five decades . . . all came to realize that identification with Israel was the only hope for the American Jewish community."[99] Grafman never served in the war, only as "a chaplain behind the lines" in Birmingham, but he and other young Reform rabbis in Alabama, such as Bertram Korn in Mobile, who did serve in World War II, became articulate advocates for Zionism in congregations that traditionally had shunned the movement. The older generation of rabbis that Evans describes also played an important, although indirect, role in the growth of Zionism. Part of Rabbi Newfield's legacy at Birmingham's Emanu-El was to serve as an "ambassador to the Gentiles," to shape the Gentile population's perception that he spoke for the entire Jewish community. Indeed, one could say the same for Eugene Blachschleger in Montgomery, Alfred Moses in Mobile, and many other long-serving Reform rabbis throughout the United States. Despite the differences between Birmingham's Newfield and Grafman in both style and substance, Newfield's reputation and public prominence proved extremely beneficial as he provided an established platform for Grafman to speak to a wider audience when he began his ministry in 1941.

4
The Alabama Press, Nazi Antisemitism, and the Holocaust

Alabamians, whether Jewish or non-Jewish, black or white, received most of their information about Nazism, Nazi antisemitism, and the Holocaust in roughly the same fashion: through the press, most commonly from newspapers. Newspapers in the state had no dedicated correspondents abroad; like many others around the country, they relied on Associated Press (AP) and United Press (UP) reports and often took their cue from influential national newspapers such as the *New York Times*. But Alabama newspaper editors and journalists did not rely solely on these reports. Instead, they interpreted these events for their readers through editorials and commentary. In doing so, the press in Alabama—in Birmingham, Montgomery, and Mobile particularly—covered the persecution of the Jews extensively and exhibited greater sympathy for the plight of the European Jews than did the national press. For instance, many of Birmingham's Jews believed they had "a friendly press" in the city, an attitude confirmed after close examination of Birmingham's newspapers. Such an attitude can be found in Montgomery's and Mobile's newspapers as well, the cities that had the largest and most significant Jewish populations in the state.[1] Birmingham's Jews, additionally, may have influenced the friendly attitude of the press by virtue of the fact that they held positions of prominence in civic affairs greater than their numbers would suggest. Similarly, historian Robert Drake argues that North Carolina newspapers, when compared to papers from other states throughout the nation, were more sympathetic to the plight of European Jews during *Kristallnacht*. Drake's conclusions, in conjunction with the attitude of the Alabama press, suggest that the southern press generally was more sympathetic to the Jews suffering under Nazi persecution than the press outside of the South.[2] Because of this friendly attitude, in Alabama at least, the press's sympathetic coverage of Nazi persecution of Jews and the Holocaust frequently translated into advocacy for greater measures to be taken on behalf of the suffering European Jews. Despite this apparent sympathy, however, Alabama's editors and journalists, like other editors and journalists throughout the United States, failed to comprehend the extent or to grasp the ramifications of the mass murder of the Jews.

Two significant and influential studies, Deborah Lipstadt's *Beyond Belief: The American Press and the Coming of the Holocaust, 1933–1945*, and Laurel Leff's *Buried by the Times*, have explored the American press's crucial role in shaping Americans' perception of the Nazi persecution of the Jews. Both scholars note the tendency of the press to downplay or bury reports of antisemitic brutality and Nazi atrocities.[3] As Lipstadt and Leff have shown, the press played a crucial role in shaping how the public understood the events that transpired in Europe during the 1930s and 1940s. Lipstadt has argued that "the press became part of the historical process by virtue of the role it played as conduit of information."[4] Indeed, the way the press tells a story helps to shape public opinion and reaction.

While the most read section of a newspaper typically is the front page, emphasizing what is immediately essential or important, editorial content is vital in shaping a newspaper's "voice," a critical component in how the press tells the story. The editorial page has been referred to as "the soul of the paper," where the editor can comment on the ideals, problems, and lives that affect the community. As Neil O. Davis, the editor of the *Lee County Bulletin*, pointed out, it is the only way that "the real opinions and thoughts of the editor reach the reader."[5] In a series of 1943 articles on the various functions of the press, the *Birmingham News* observed that the editor is central to the operation of a newspaper because he "decides what is fit to print and what is not fit to print. It is he who differentiates between news and propaganda. It is he who can if he will, give the leadership that every energetic community must have."[6] Such a position carries with it power, influence, and no small measure of responsibility. But editors do not function in a vacuum; the press is less a "neutral or passive observer" of contemporary history than it is a historical actor. Editorial opinion frequently influenced what the public thought and most certainly helped to mold community opinion. Grover C. Hall Sr., the editor of the *Montgomery Advertiser*, could be considered a "crusading editor" who not only shaped the newspaper's outlook and voice but also used the editorial page to campaign for or against issues he deemed important, as he did when he won a Pulitzer Prize in 1928 for his editorials condemning Ku Klux Klan violence. In that instance, Hall helped to shift public opinion against the Klan, which in the late 1920s gradually lost power and influence in Alabama. Moreover, as one reader of the *Birmingham Age-Herald* noted, "most of your readers are people who like for somebody else to form their opinion."[7]

Both Lipstadt and Leff are concerned only with the national press—in Leff's case the hugely influential *New York Times*. While Lipstadt's study provides a comprehensive analysis of the national press, it pays scant attention to the American South beyond the *Atlanta Constitution*. Many white southern journalists and editors, however, faced a challenge unique to the South: how to criticize Nazism as brutal, undemocratic, and "abhorrent to every instinct of decency and justice" without simultaneously condemning the Jim Crow system. That system, the very basis of southern society, was itself inherently incompatible with and contradictory to American democratic ideals. Members of the press certainly understood the central role that racism played in the Nazi system, as they condemned and ridiculed the Nazi claims of Aryan racial superiority; however, white editors and journalists retained their own sense of racial superiority in regard to blacks without any apparent sense of irony.[8] This inconsistency produced an incredible cognitive dissonance among the vast majority of white editors and journalists when it came to confronting the similarities between Nazi and southern racial thought.

Alabama's black press, conversely, made the connection between Nazi and southern racism easily, pointing to the claims of Aryan superiority, antisemitic persecution, and later the mass killings of Jews to illustrate the threat the idea of racial superiority posed and to expose the hypocrisy of the Jim Crow South. The black press frequently used the terms *Nazism* and *Hitlerism* to condemn racist injustice, such as lynching, poll taxes, or discrimination in hiring practices. In fact, blacks condemned white hypocrisy more forcefully than they did the Nazis' persecution of the Jews. Although this chapter will contrast how the white press and the black press in Alabama covered and interpreted the events of the Holocaust, a future study will more fully examine how Nazism, Nazi racism, and the Holocaust affected African Americans and their struggle for civil rights.

Initial Reactions to Nazi Persecution

The March 1933 outbreak of violence against the Jews in Germany, coming shortly after President Paul von Hindenburg appointed Hitler chancellor, provoked protests throughout the Alabama press. Editorials described the riots as "unwarranted and inhuman," and referred to its instigators as "clowns [who] have taken charge of Germany." AP reports about the violence appeared on the front pages in many daily newspapers. Nazi-directed persecution prompted the editors of the *Birmingham Age-Herald* to express support for the Jews, stating that "the Jewish race has done more to further the common good of humanity than all other races combined. . . . The measure of our obligation to the Jews is unpayable."[9] Owned by Victor Hanson, the *Age-Herald*, and its sister paper the *Birmingham News*, consistently provided a friendly venue for Jewish viewpoints in Birmingham. Hanson employed a team of editors that included Charles N. Feidelson Sr., an outspoken and opinionated member of the Reform Temple Emanu-El, who brought a Jewish perspective to the editorial board.

In *Buried by the Times*, Laurel Leff explains that Arthur Hays Sulzberger, the Jewish publisher of the *New York Times*, believed that "being Jewish was solely a religious, not a racial or ethnic orientation . . . that carried with it no special obligation to help fellow Jews. . . . In fact, American Jews who helped other Jews because they were Jews threatened to undercut their position as Americans." Leff argues that Sulzberger's fear that he could be charged with dual loyalty was the source of his opposition to "emphasizing the unique plight of the Jews in occupied Europe." As a result of this opposition, the *New York Times* tended to "submerge" information and minimize the fate of the Jews in Europe.[10] Most of Alabama's Jews—and most Jews in New York for that matter—saw no danger in publicizing the Nazis' antisemitic atrocities, either prior to or during the war, or in publicly advocating a stronger American policy of intervention and rescue. This was true of a majority of Reform Jews, although they generally shared with Sulzberger the classical Reform position that acculturation into American society was the key to success.[11] Indeed, the prominence and influence of Alabama's Reform Jews in both the civic and economic life of the state, their significant degree of acculturation, and the interfaith outreach of the Reform rabbis, against the background of a recurring streak of philosemitism in the South, influenced non-Jews' perception of events in Europe. Most white southerners identified the persecuted German Jews with the South's own acculturated Reform Jews. The persecuted German Jews were not, to be sure, the "loud" Eastern European Jews many southerners viewed as unsavory radicals and agitators.

Alabama's journalists and editors wrote extensively on various aspects of Nazism. Initially, they focused on the Nazi government's repressive nature and persecutory tendencies, and, by the mid-1930s, its aggressive foreign policy. They underlined the incompatibility of Nazism with the ideals of American democracy: the unpopularity of Nazism in the United States, the *Birmingham Age-Herald* suggested in mid-1934, had more to do with the antidemocratic nature of the Hitler regime than with its persecutions. While the papers called the persecution of the Jews "abhorrent to every instinct of decency and justice," the condemnation of Nazi Germany, the *Age-Herald* opined, was "the product not only of sympathy for a hounded minority in

Germany, but of a profound resentment directed against the whole savage course pursued by the 'New Germany' in rooting out every evidence of democracy, in suppressing freedom of opinion, and in emphasizing preparation for war as the only panacea for German ills."[12] The press viewed the antisemitic persecution of the Jews as an aspect of the repression, brutality, and aggression that constituted the vicious modus operandi of the Nazis. It produced an intensely negative view of the Nazis, magnified by the increasingly harsh antisemitic persecution in the 1930s and later the murderous atrocities of the Holocaust, that colored journalists' and the public's reaction to Germany that endured even in the postwar period.

Criticism of the Nazis continued throughout the mid-1930s as the violent antisemitic persecutions in Germany persisted. Editorials often blamed Hitler or Nazi leadership for the violence, but at times they suggested that events had moved beyond the control of party leaders. An AP article picked up in the *Age-Herald* in mid-1935 reported that "Nazi hot-heads, deaf to party orders banning 'direct action' against Jew and Catholic 'state enemies,' hindered Reichsfuehrer Adolf Hitler's efforts to curb extremist tactics in the Third Reich's anti-reactionary drive."[13] A common editorial response to German antisemitic violence appeared in the *Mobile Register*, which warned that should the persecution of the Jews in Germany continue, the United States "might have to alter [its] attitude toward Germany. . . . If Hitlerism is going to mean a series of outrages perpetrated against the Jewish citizens, the stripping of these citizens their rights, and the enforcement of policies and the permission of practices intended to degrade them, Germany will lose both the sympathetic interest and the respect of civilized peoples everywhere in the world."[14]

Although the *Mobile Register* condemned the Nazis, its editors appeared oblivious to any correspondence between the policies and practices that degraded Jews and stripped them of their rights in Germany and the policies and practices that did the same to blacks in the South. The state's white press saw attacks by "Nazi hot-heads" as similar only to attacks on blacks carried out by extremist groups such as the Klan; indeed, the press frequently compared the Nazis to the Klan. When, for example, the *Birmingham Age-Herald* called for "moral condemnation" of Germany for its "official and avowed policy of the government to deny to a whole class of its people their equal rights as citizens on account of their Jewish decent," but acknowledged only those "inexcusable manifestations" of prejudice and violence in America committed by Klan elements, it either ignored or failed to grasp the fundamental similarities between Nazi and southern racism.[15] Whether Hitler or other Nazi leaders officially authorized or explicitly ordered such attacks, the antisemitism Nazi rule perpetuated was "a deep-seated ideology" that condoned a culture of violence toward Jews and others minorities in Germany.[16] The deep-seated ideology of racial superiority that permeated the Jim Crow South also condoned, or at least ambivalently accepted, similar atrocities against blacks. Was it not "official" state policy to deny blacks as a "whole class" their equal rights as citizens on account of their descent? Many white southerners either did not understand this or refused to accept it.

In September 1935, an editorial in Birmingham's *Southern Jewish Times* noted that "anti-Semitism, prejudice, discrimination and inter-racial ill-will are still rampant," even spreading beyond Germany and "infecting other countries," particularly those in Eastern Europe. As a result, the editorial went on, American Jews were "far better off than the rest of world Jewry." The editors argued that "we have a government that will not tolerate any second-hand treatment to its racial minorities and to its citizens of religious minorities. We do not know the feeling of traveling—politically speaking—second-class."[17] Much like the editorials in the *Mobile Register* and the *Birmingham Age-Herald*, the *Southern Jewish Times*, too, saw no contradiction when it deplored Nazi antisemitism but dismissed the idea of the "second-hand treatment" of racial minorities. In this sense, it took a very "southern" position in regard to injustice and discrimination.

It would have been surprising had the editors at the *Southern Jewish Times* compared the treatment of southern blacks with persecuted German Jews since southern Jews generally reflected southern white attitudes rather than "minority" attitudes. The discrimination against African Americans generally did not affect southern Jews, either physically or economically, and the level of acculturation into southern society played an important role in this identification with white attitudes. Moreover, Jews largely did not compete with non-Jews in regard to employment, and those Jews whom non-Jewish businesses employed usually were in upper management. Thus their economic well-being was secure. Indeed, an anti-discriminatory federal agency such as the Fair Employment Practices Committee (FEPC) meant "nothing to them as a matter of their own welfare . . . and few of them are excluded from the pleasures of life by reason of lack of money or their Jewishness." Although some observers noted an "inner conflict" among southern Jews in regard to black civil rights, most firmly believed that they were in no position to advocate for African Americans. The memory of Scottsboro and the example of Rabbi Benjamin Goldstein still resonated.[18]

The passage of the Nuremberg Laws in September 1935 provided observers in the press the best opportunity not only to examine the evolving Nazi policy toward the Jews but also to compare the situation of Jews in Germany with that of blacks in the American South. With the Nuremberg Laws, the Reichstag forbade marriage and miscegenation between Jews and Aryans, and reserved citizenship for those of "Aryan blood," thereby excluding Jews from citizenship. Jews in Germany had already been barred from public service and admission to the universities and had been expelled from the medical and law professions. The Nazis continually amended the Nuremberg Laws, further limiting opportunities for Jews to earn a living and even forbidding them to use or enjoy public amenities such as parks, zoos, public benches, or public transportation.[19]

Such restrictions, when compared to the Jim Crow laws in the South, are startlingly similar. Southern racialism touted the white race, with its Protestant Anglo-Saxon heritage, as the superior race in the American South, with "inferior" blacks to be controlled through fear and segregation. White supremacy in the American South served as both a political philosophy and a racial ideology. Miscegenation concerned white southerners as much as it did Nazis. The southern Jim Crow laws that had emerged in the decades after Reconstruction to control the newly freed southern blacks circumscribed the opportunities and civil rights of African Americans just as the Nuremberg Laws affected German Jews; indeed, both racial systems were based upon the idea of racial superiority. Such similarities were hard to miss, but miss them white southerners did. Although the idea of a superior race found significant support throughout the United States and across Europe, no other Western culture had created a racial-caste society that matched Nazi Germany or the Jim Crow South. Even South Africa's system of apartheid had not fully developed by this time. Only after the Nazis began murdering the Jews, first by the *Einsatzgruppen* and then through the systematized killings in the death camps, did the two systems diverge.

It might seem that Hitler's emphasis on racial purity and racial supremacy should have found a receptive audience in Alabama and the American South, yet it did not. On the contrary, white Alabamians, indeed most white southerners, rejected the idea of Aryan racial supremacy despite their widespread support for southern white supremacy and the segregation of the races. White Alabamians based their criticism of the Nazi claims of racial superiority largely on their distaste for the Nazis' brutality and aggressive foreign policy, not on an explicit rejection of the idea of racial superiority. Most southern whites, as adamant defenders of Jim Crow, exhibited a cognitive dissonance when it came to Nazi claims of Aryan racial supremacy. For example, when the Nazis further amended the Nuremberg Laws in late 1938, the *Birmingham Age-Herald* recounted how "streets and whole areas have been banned in Berlin for Jews. . . . Their living quarters have been restricted and throughout Germany they have been forbidden to own or operate automobiles and motorcycles." The editorial noted that "this kind of mass treatment of a whole people" fell short of the outward violence of *Kristallnacht* but went on to say that these "outrages . . . are, in some respects, even harder to believe and continue a program that for sheer cruelty becomes more and more astounding." This segregation of Jews in Germany, the paper argued, was "the negation of everything that [had] been achieved since barbarism to recognize and protect the dignity and worth of the individual and to assure justice to all men."[20] An editorial published in the *Age-Herald* only a few days earlier had observed that such decrees were "more far-reaching and destructive" than violence against the Jews.[21] Yet it seems the *Age-Herald*'s editors, generally regarded as progressive or liberal, did not regard the Jim Crow restrictions on residence or civil liberties as an injustice or even an indignity for African Americans.

"The Egregious Gentile"

The persecution of the Jews in Germany, combined with the increase of antisemitism in the United States, prompted perhaps the most outspoken critic of Hitler and the Nazis, Grover C. Hall, the editor of the *Montgomery Advertiser*, to publish an editorial titled "The Egregious Gentile Called to Account: Clinical Notes on His Lack of Gallantry and Sportsmanship, His Bad Mental Habits, His Tactlessness, His Lack of Imagination, His Poor Discernment, His Faults as Citizen and Neighbor, His Gullibility and Arrogance." Hall wrote "The Egregious Gentile" in 1936 but did not publish it immediately because he feared the reaction of the conservative white community in Montgomery. He printed it only on December 4, 1938, shortly after *Kristallnacht*.[22]

In "The Egregious Gentile," Hall took non-Jews to task for the double standard they applied to Jews. Critical of what he saw as the typical non-Jew's "pettiness, his arrogance, his snobbishness, his bogus humanitarianism," Hall marveled at the non-Jew's escape from accountability, unlike the Jew whom non-Jews tended to think of and discuss "first as a Jew and then as whatever else he may be. We attribute virtues to him as a class that are characteristic only of individuals; we attribute vices and frailties to him as a class that any man of sense should know are peculiar only to individuals, whether Jews or non-Jews." He explained that as a non-Jew, he could commit crimes or indecencies and be punished as an individual, and "in no circumstances would I hear the taunting phrase: 'Gentile! Catch Him!'" By placing southerners' attitudes and double standards under such scrutiny, Hall hoped to increase their tolerance, not only toward the Jews but also toward other minorities as well.[23]

Hall also saw the similarities in American and German antisemitic thought. The idea that "the Jew is at once the evil genius of Communism and the designing, sinister pillar of Capitalism—at once the money-lending Marxist and the money-lending Shylock," appeared in literature in both the United States and Germany at the time. Hall believed that Nazi-styled pogroms in the United States were not an impossibility, and argued that had Henry Ford's antisemitic campaigns come after October 1929 instead of during the prosperous Harding-Coolidge years, it "might have led to physical, economic and political persecution of Jews unparalleled in the history of American fanaticism." The allusion to Nazi antisemitism was obvious, and, much like other southern editors when it came to the Nazis, Hall called on the specter of Ku Kluxism when addressing the issue. The American mob, he wrote, "is as violent, as cruel and as blindly unreasoning as the mob of any other country. We have only to stir its passions to the bottom. . . . The American Jew today is fortunate that no Nordic scalawag and demagogue with the wit and boldness to release a pestilence has risen to identify in the minds of the dispossessed and the despairing the Jew and the devil as one and the same. . . . Put the American mob in rags and feed it on the crumbs that fall from the table of the man who still has an income, convince it that Israel's hosts are at its gate and it will pick up its flaming torch and march."[24]

Hall's concern with both national and international affairs no doubt made him aware of the increasing antisemitism abroad and in other parts of the United States, and this affected Hall's perspective in Montgomery as he wrote in 1936. It certainly influenced his decision to publish the article after *Kristallnacht*. He commented later that had "such an article been printed [before Hitler came to power] it would have been read by a few people and regarded by them as a curious academic discourse."[25] Yet as antisemitic sentiment mounted in the United States, in many ways a derivative of the events transpiring in Europe, Hall's observations were particularly acute. H. L. Mencken, the acerbic Baltimore writer and a close friend of Hall, acknowledged Hall's perception of the possibility of a violent antisemitic movement in the United States and noted, "if we go into a European war and got painfully burned, the boobs will lay all the blame on the Jews. The more intelligent Jews are well aware of this danger and all those I know are very uneasy."[26]

Intended to be a "critical examination of . . . this troublesome question of race and religion," Hall's "compassionate tongue-lashing" of non-Jews received an overwhelmingly positive response from readers across the nation.

The praise for the editorial surprised Hall and convinced him that "our people are sound and ready for battle in defense of our democratic institutions."[27] Alabama senator Lister Hill read the entire article into the *Congressional Record* in January 1939, and Alabama's Jewish community universally lauded the article. Montgomery's Agudath Israel congregation praised the article and unabashedly declared, "it is becoming increasingly evident that the very existence of the Jew today is due, in no small measure, to the fact that Gentiles of your high caliber and great humanitarian sympathies lived in the past as well as today."[28] The article was such an overwhelming success that the *Advertiser* filled around thirteen thousand orders of extra copies of the article before allowing the US Government Printing Office to handle the orders, including one for ten thousand copies.[29] Hall's contemporary, John Temple Graves of the *Birmingham Age-Herald*, explained to his readers that while "The Egregious Gentile" had been "quoted and reprinted in two hemispheres and has been translated into several languages," it had not received the same exposure in the American South. The extraordinary length of the editorial, Graves surmised, "is why [it] has not been reproduced in the South as it should have been."[30]

According to his biographer Daniel Hollis, Hall "gained a greater satisfaction from the essay than anything he had ever done in his life."[31] After his untimely death in early 1941, the Jewish community in Alabama lamented the loss of a friend, and none more so than Montgomery's Jews. In a resolution commending the life of Hall, the Reform Temple Beth-Or declared that he "was free of bigotry, racial prejudicies [*sic*] and hatreds, and gave to every man the same right that he reserved for himself, to think, speak and worship as he pleased."[32] The B'nai B'rith Hillel Foundation at the University of Alabama in Tuscaloosa established a Grover Cleveland Hall Memorial Award "in memory of one of the noblest spirits of the South—a crusader for justice and tolerance." The award went to the junior student who had done the most "to improve inter-group relations" at the University of Alabama.[33] Yet even as Hall recognized the similarities in antisemitic thought, he apparently failed to see the similarities between Nazi and southern racial thought. Hall, a political moderate and racial paternalist, would have undoubtedly rejected such a comparison. His idea of tolerance toward a minority such as African Americans did not preclude the ideas of white supremacy and African Americans' supposed innate inferiority. As Hollis explains, "it probably never occurred to him that he could validly use the same arguments to assail the white majority's prejudice toward the black minority."[34] Nevertheless, "The Egregious Gentile" was a capstone to Hall's brilliant journalistic career.

The Religious Press

With the exception of editorial outbursts in the rural press against "outside agitators" or "New York Jews," the secular press in Alabama largely condemned antisemitism, both domestic and foreign, and supported cooperation between the Christian and Jewish faiths. This favorable attitude was in large part due to the efforts of Reform rabbis in Birmingham, Montgomery, and Mobile. Nonetheless, the prejudices of which "The Egregious Gentile" disapproved found expression in the religious press. Both the *Alabama Baptist* and the *Catholic Week*, while not rabidly antisemitic perpetuated the stereotype of the Jew as the radical and the "money-lending Shylock." Religion, not race, lay at the heart of this antisemitism. The *Catholic Week* opined that for the Jews "the higher and nobler quest of life, spiritual aspiration, has been lost in commercial and financial ambition" and that "the Jewish religion has ceased to be the religion of God, since it refused to accept Jesus." The Catholic paper also criticized Judaism as an empty religion because of the inroad of rationalism, attributed especially to the "Reform Jew." The paper did, however, reserve a measure of respect for the piety of Orthodox Jews.[35]

L. L. Gwaltney, the editor of the *Alabama Baptist*, the newspaper of Alabama's Southern Baptist Convention, wrote in May 1933 that Hitler persecuted the Jews because the Jewish capitalists had been responsible for Germany's defeat in 1918, to silence Jewish Communists influenced by Russian propaganda, and to erase the influence of Karl Marx, "who was a German Jew and a Socialist." While criticizing Hitler's treatment of the Jews, Gwaltney argued that Jews "are the sons of Jacob and many of them, to this day, out Jacob Jacob in hypocracy [*sic*], deceit, and a love of money . . . the Gentiles do not want to get rid of the Jews. The Gentiles need to be subdued by the Spirit of the Christ that the Jews may see in them the genuineness of their profession and the power of their conviction, and thus be led to accept the Messiah whom they mistakenly and ignobly rejected."[36] In July, Gwaltney argued that certain elements in the German government commanded "the strongest support of Baptists," although he quickly condemned the Nazi attempt to make churches more subservient to the state. Throughout the early 1930s, such stark and stereotypical descriptions flowed from Gwaltney's pen. Only as the Nazi antisemitic persecutions intensified did his sympathy toward the Jews increase, driven by his disgust with the Nazis' brutal measures, not by any modification of his religious views.[37]

Prior to 1936, Baptists, especially those who visited Germany in the early years of Hitler's regime, generally refrained from condemning the Nazis. In August 1934, Berlin hosted the Fifth Baptist World Congress, which a number of Alabamians attended. Alabama's prominent Southern Baptists had largely reserved their opinion on events in Germany, and the Baptist World Congress convinced many of those in attendance that Hitler and the Nazis had been unduly criticized in the American press. Reverend Charles F. Leek, pastor of the Highland Avenue Baptist Church in Montgomery and a columnist for the *Alabama Baptist*, attended the World Congress and afterward promoted "A New View of Hitlerism." Some "Baptists outside Germany" initially had wanted the congress moved out of Berlin because of the Nazi excesses, but, Leek exclaimed, "Thank God this was never done." He described in benign terms the Nazi "Baptist 'brown-shirts'" who participated in the congress and reported that his experience in Berlin had convinced him that Hitlerism was "for Germany a safe step in the right direction." Leek apparently saw no conflict between the Baptist faith and Nazism: "Evangelical New Testament Christianity transcends all political and social systems and finds its own manner of expression regardless. Without compromising precepts and principles it may accommodate its means and methods to shifting conditions."[38] Leek stood out in Montgomery as a fire-breathing preacher of the Word and impressed even Grover Hall, the uncompromising editor of the *Advertiser* and the bane of fundamentalists in the capital city. Hall considered Montgomery's pastors "uniformly meek," with the lone exception of Leek. That was as far as Hall's admiration went. According to Hall, Leek had a "likeness to a horse's arse. In Montgomery he is held in contempt," especially by progressives.[39]

The experience of the Baptist World Congress convinced Baptist leaders such as Leek and Gwaltney that the secular press had distorted the truth about Hitler and Nazism. Gwaltney, who had not attended the conference, praised its success, concluding that the Baptist delegates in Berlin had "all the freedom they needed"; neither had Baptists been "repressed in their activities in Germany, nor are they proscribed by the German authorities." These reports of religious freedom in Germany, along with the success of the congress in Berlin, convinced Gwaltney that stories of evangelical persecution by the Nazis had been blown out of proportion. If these reports were true, he wrote sympathetically, then "Hitlerism has been greatly misrepresented on this side of the water."[40]

The Baptists held their World Congress before the Nazis' terrorism and boycotts of the Jews were renewed in March 1935, and both Gwaltney and Leek gave more consideration to the "glowing reports brought back from Berlin by Southern Baptists" than to the "foreign dispatches" that described the dissension in German religious life. Moreover, during the first years of the Nazi regime, Gwaltney and Leek saw the Nazis as a bulwark against

Bolshevism. Gwaltney's antisemitism and his fear of Communism, both evident in the editorial pages of the *Alabama Baptist*, led him to characterize most Jews as "greedy radicals" or outright Communists. Despite this, he later promoted aiding Jews who suffered from Nazi persecution. By 1936, both Gwaltney and Leek had partly changed their minds about Hitler and condemned Nazism as simply an "alternative [form] of totalitarianism." A year later Gwaltney determined that "the whole Hitler system is a menace to the welfare of the world," and that Americans absolutely could not countenance dictatorship, a decision at the time that had little to do with the treatment of the German Jews.[41]

Kristallnacht prompted Baptists to examine more closely the plight of Jews in Germany. Charles Leek commented that "everyone outside of the Berlin-Rome Axis criticizes Germany but no one seems willing to have the mistreated Jews as their guests or neighbors. That makes one wonder if the criticisms are sincere." Gwaltney added that "these outbreaks against Jews in Germany . . . are done on a miserable pretext" and urged readers to remember that "our own tolerance of other races and religions is often not what is should be. . . . Can we check these evils in ourselves and in others? After all, it is a matter of religion."[42] The brutality of *Kristallnacht* convinced Gwaltney, a pacifist, reluctantly to support American military preparedness because "not to face reality would be disastrous to German Jews, Rumanian Baptists, and other victims of Nazi pogroms."[43]

Kristallnacht

In Alabama, the secular press and the public responded to *Kristallnacht* by forcefully condemning the Nazis and their attacks on the Jews. Throughout much of November and into December, editorials throughout the state, as well as letters from readers, addressed events in Germany. The *Birmingham News*, the *Birmingham Age-Herald*, and the *Mobile Register* consistently produced front-page headlines and in-depth editorials on these events. Yet only the *Montgomery Advertiser*, with its publication of Hall's "The Egregious Gentile," conducted a serious self-examination of America's attitudes toward the Jews. Most of the editorials characterized the attacks as "going to new extremes" or "Nazi madness."[44]

A *Clarke County Democrat* editorial followed a common pattern of castigating "the Germans for their brutal, inhuman and unjustified persecution of the Jews" and suggested an inexact parallel to the Klan with "enough similarity in them to cause all self respecting Americans to hang their heads in shame that this country ever harbored such an organization or encouraged such sentiment." The *Aliceville Times*, on the other hand, bitterly condemned the "heathenism" of the Nazis, whose "reign of terror" had allowed Jews "fewer privileges than the Alabama Negro." But while the *Times* acknowledged that southern blacks enjoyed few rights, it pointedly rejected any comparison of the Jews in Germany with blacks in the South. In late November 1938, the Southern Conference for Human Welfare (SCHW), an interracial civil rights organization, met in Birmingham and in the course of its meeting condemned segregation and the Jim Crow system. Only a week after it had condemned the Nazi brutality of *Kristallnacht*, the *Aliceville Times* opined: "there are members of the [SCHW] who could readily draw a comparison between the manner in which the Nazis were treating the Jews and the manner in which Southerners are treating Negroes. Heated Hitlerites butcher helpless Jews while heady Southerners lynch helpless Blacks. But they failed to follow through with their logic and see that Negroes had never atained [*sic*] a proportionate social status of the Jews in Germany, and furthermore, they failed to see the most important fact that Southern Negroes are satisfied with their status, and that their living conditions are more or less what they themselves make them."[45]

After *Kristallnacht*, some observers suggested that the Nazis were "letting up" on the Jewish persecutions. As Deborah Lipstadt has shown, the press expressed optimism that *Kristallnacht* perhaps "marked the end of the terrorist campaign against the Jews."[46] No one could imagine the horrors that would lie ahead. Yet some in the press, although hopeful of a "mitigation of the recent horrible antisemitic brutality," recognized the danger that remained for Jews in Germany and Austria. In February 1939, the *Birmingham Age-Herald* observed that "so long as the narrow, hateful intolerance of Nazi doctrine dominates Nazi leadership, there can be no return to fundamental human decency in the treatment of German minorities." At the same time, the *Aliceville Times* argued that Nazi terror had not abated and that "it seems to be a certainty that outbursts of terrorism are bound to break out at any time . . . which will bring about incredible incidents and more tales of horror."[47] After Germany occupied Czechoslovakia in March 1939, the *Birmingham News* noted that "the plight of the Jews in Europe grows more serious . . . [adding] between 300,000 and 400,000 more Jews to the list of those who are being driven and persecuted."[48] These comments suggest that by early 1939 the press had begun to recognize that antisemitism was integral to Nazi policy.

The distaste for Nazi duplicity and intrigue extended well into American society, and popular culture reflected such sentiment. In May 1939, the motion picture *Confessions of a Nazi Spy* opened in Alabama theaters. The film starred Edward G. Robinson as a Federal Bureau of Investigation (FBI) agent who foils a Nazi espionage operation, replete with stock characterizations of the Gestapo and Nazi leadership as well as newsreel footage of Nazi rallies and marching German troops. *Confessions* was based upon the serialized articles of Leon G. Turrou, a former FBI agent who had investigated active Nazi spy rings in the United States during the mid-1930s. Warner Brothers' Studio, which had previously made a number of anti-Fascist films, produced *Confessions* despite pressure from the Production Code Administration (PCA) and the German Consul General in Los Angeles. The film received enthusiastic support from critics and moviegoers, more for its political condemnation of Nazism than anything else. Yet critics of the film labeled its message as the propaganda of Hollywood Jews. In fact, the PCA had forbidden Warner Brothers to mention the Nazis' persecution of the Jews.[49]

In Tuscaloosa, some moviegoers saw the film as a believable depiction of the Nazi menace, but others reacted in a manner that exposed the antisemitism within the community, prompting an acrimonious exchange in the pages of the *Tuscaloosa News*. One reader, Elmer Barke, asked editor Bruce Shelton why he had not used his "crusading zeal" to denounce the "patent attempt to influence Tuscaloosa audiences against the German people, many of whom have been the objects of ridicule and scorn since the picture showed in town." The star of the film, he pointed out, "was E. G. Robinson, an alias for his real Jewish name." (Robinson's name had been Emanuel Goldenberg). Barke wondered if Shelton had lost his zeal "for some thirty pieces of silver," and questioned why no anti-Communist film had been shown, since it opposed "all forms of Christianity as much as Naziism."[50]

Shelton did not respond to Barke's letter, but others did. One reader viewed the film as educational rather than propaganda, due to the "obvious Nazi threat to democracy," and wrote that "screaming Jew at Edward G. Robinson is a means of getting our minds off realities."[51] Another reader, Paul Locust, supported Barke's suggestion of a Jewish conspiracy, calling the film "the latest explosion of Jewish propaganda and agitation against the Germans in America. Not only are the Jews spreading corruption over the German people by this picture, but are also padding their pockets with cash from the theater admissions lured from the American public. This picture fans a flaming fire of racial hatred and prejudice." In addition to reiterating Robinson's Jewish heritage, Locust explained that the film "was touched throughout by Jewish hands. Freedom of speech is taken advantage of by the Jews to make freedom of speech intolerable for the Germans." Locust also described an incident where "an intelligent group" of University of Alabama students "yelled out thunderously 'Jewish propaganda' when the picture ended."[52]

Whether or not university students actually yelled "Jewish propaganda" at the conclusion of the film cannot be ascertained, but these letters indicate that antisemitism existed openly in Tuscaloosa, which was a hotbed of racism and intolerance despite the existence of a university in its midst. The *Tuscaloosa News* and its editor, Bruce Shelton, can only be described as politically and racially reactionary, and the *News* helped contribute to the climate of racism and intolerance in the area. In fact, only six years had passed since the *Tuscaloosa News* had stirred up antisemitic feeling in the community by condemning the ILD's attempt to defend three African Americans accused of raping a white woman. After ILD lawyers had been escorted out of town by the National Guard, a lynch mob murdered two of the three accused. As Glenn Feldman notes in his study of the Klan in Alabama, "local anti-Semitism was a function of the Klan's broader hatred of Jews in the 1930s, largely stemming from Jewish influence in Hollywood and its relation to race."[53] Moreover, Barke and Locust fit the profile that Hall described in "The Egregious Gentile," and their views paralleled those of Gwaltney, who wrote of the Jews' love of money and control of the movie industry. In this context, the establishment of the Grover Hall Award by the Hillel Society was not surprising; Jewish students in Tuscaloosa had something to fear.

After the war began in September 1939, the press devoted much of its attention to the military effort and less to the persecution of the Jews. Lipstadt correctly observes that over time, as the persecutions "became a familiar topic, many papers increasingly tended to place it within the inner recesses of the paper, treating it as well-known or 'old' news." It is equally true, though, that editorials had an effect—often a profound one—on public opinion, especially when they came from a respected editor such as Grover Hall or an influential newspaper such as the *Birmingham News*.[54] These papers continued to editorialize on the suffering of the Jews in Europe, although the *Montgomery Advertiser*'s editorials became much less pointed and crusading after Hall's death in early 1941. In general, however, all papers spent noticeably less time on the suffering of European Jewry.

In February 1940, the *Birmingham Age-Herald* commented on the "terrible reports" coming out of Poland that "Germany is seeking to exterminate the Polish race in occupied regions." The editorial did not specify the Jews as the target in this case, and it suggested caution in accepting such reports: "it is difficult . . . to get at the exact truth. There is, inevitably, a tendency to exaggerate such conditions." Nevertheless, the *Age-Herald* recognized that "there can be no doubt whatever that a fearful terror does exist, that a horrible persecution has been taking place."[55] After the fall of France in mid-1940, the *Birmingham News* finally recognized that "hatred of the Jews and a determination to force them out of all participation in German affairs are cardinal points in Hitler's ideology," and described Hitler as "the most relentless persecutor of the Jews that the world has ever known."[56]

As Nazi Germany continued its eastward expansion with the invasion of the Soviet Union in June 1941, additional mass killings of Jews followed. As before, the Birmingham papers covered the plight of the Jews in occupied Europe, although they did not always differentiate between the Jewish and non-Jewish victims of Nazi atrocities. By November 1941 the *Birmingham News* commented on "more than 100,000 persons" who the Nazis had executed, calling such atrocities the product of "a barbaric system" and "savagery." One reader called the reports "beyond one's comprehension" and asked, "how long can one go undisturbed by present world events? Is it possible that Americans are so callous that nothing, no matter how shocking disturbs them?"[57]

The persecution of European Jews, according to Lipstadt, had become a familiar topic to news editors and the American public. But when the mass killings began, readers did not fully grasp the news. Birmingham editor and columnist Charles Feidelson noted as much in early 1942 when, describing antisemitic outrages, he commented that "it is questionable whether even American Jews are as responsive to such disclosures as they once were. They, too, have grown used to the monster."[58]

The Jim Crow of All the Ages

The Nazis considered blacks, too, an inferior race—a point not lost on the African American press. The black press often compared Nazi racism to southern racism; it began to address the issue of Nazi negrophobia in 1932, even before Hitler became chancellor. Northern newspapers such as the *Pittsburgh Courier* and the *Chicago Defender* reached into almost all black communities throughout the state, exposing black Alabamians to views more radical than the ones published in local black newspapers.[59] While no circulation figures exist, it seems likely that the *Courier* and the *Defender* reached more people throughout Alabama than any of the black papers published in the state. Readers of the black press were thus familiar with Nazi negrophobia and its striking similarities to the Jim Crow racism whose existence many southern white journalists vehemently denied.[60]

Hitler's racial policies did not involve the extermination of blacks—a fact that can be traced to the insignificant number of blacks in Germany and the Nazis' plans for a colonial empire. The Nazis considered the segregation of blacks—specifically those in overseas colonies—to be an acceptable and nonthreatening measure to ensure the purity of Aryans. Africans represented, in their view, "a pliable source of unskilled labour," which stood in sharp contrast to their view of the Jews as a "huge threat" and as a force "bent on the subversion and enslavement" of Germany—politically, economically, and racially.[61] The Nazis' view of blacks differed little from that of southern whites. White southerners had put racist ideas into practice long before the Nazi Party had come into existence, and southern white society, too, used segregated blacks as a plentiful and "pliable" source of labor.

By the beginning of 1941, both leading African American newspapers in Alabama, the *Birmingham World* and the *Weekly Review*, had published editorials condemning Hitler and warning their readers of the threat Nazism posed to blacks.[62] Discrimination and degradation had produced in many African Americans an apathy toward the national defense effort. The *Weekly Review*'s Robert Durr reminded his readers frequently that Nazism thrived on race hatred, pointing out that in *Mein Kampf* Hitler had characterized blacks as subhuman. In an attempt to combat apathy on the part of African Americans, Durr argued: "If I were a white man I would have little or no fears for a future that brought even Hitlerism. But with Negroes it is different. . . . In the persecution of the Jews, the Negro has been given a pattern of his estate under Hitlerism. May God have mercy on the misguided Negro who does not see the unveiled threat of great tribulation with the passing of democracy. It is true that under democracy Negroes are circumscribed; under Hitlerism it is conceivable that they may be exterminated."[63] The *Birmingham World* also noted that a Nazi victory would be a "dark day for the Negro," and any implementation of Hitler's racial vision would make American slavery seem tame by comparison. The *World* criticized the poor treatment of blacks under American democracy but advised "all sane Negroes" to support America in its stand against Nazism, arguing that "in a Hitlerized U.S.A. we would have no rights for anybody else to violate."[64]

After Emory O. Jackson became editor in July 1941, the *Birmingham World* became a stronger voice for civil rights. The *World* frequently compared Nazi ideas of Aryan supremacy with American ideas of white supremacy. Robert Durr and the *Weekly Review*, on the other hand, took a more accommodating approach, comparing only lynchings and other extreme violence to Nazi actions, an approach similar to that of white journalists. Durr had been an employee at the *Birmingham World* until 1935, when he left the paper to establish the *Weekly Review*. Birmingham industrialist Charles DeBardeleben, owner of Alabama Fuel and Iron Company, financed the paper. Not surprisingly, Durr consistently railed against organized labor—particularly the Congress of Industrial Organizations (CIO)—and portrayed white company owners in a favorable light.[65]

In February 1943, both black Birmingham newspapers ran a syndicated article describing registration procedures for Negroes in German territory. The *Weekly Review*'s sensational headline proclaimed "Hitler Out to Get Negro Scalps: Awful Fate of Jews Awaits Them." The article explained that Heinrich Himmler had ordered all "Negroes, Negresses, Mulattoes and quadroons" in Reich territory to register with the Office of the Chief of Reich Security. By this time the mass killings of the Jews in Europe had become public knowledge; the article stated plainly that "there can be no doubt what will happen after their registration, as Negroes are treated as [are] all 'inferior races.'"[66] Despite the article's ominous warning, no evidence exists that the Nazis included blacks in their plan for mass killing, and the paper did not mention the registration again.

Perhaps because of the implicit threat that raising the issue represented to the social and political hierarchy, only a few white journalists chose to address Nazi negrophobia. Most, however, either ignored or rejected the idea. Only as the United States moved closer to war did certain white journalists, such as Birmingham's John Temple Graves, address Nazi negrophobia, and they may have done so largely out of concern about "black lethargy" toward the coming conflict.[67] Graves, whose syndicated column appeared throughout the South, had long championed greater rights and opportunities for southern blacks. Like other southern liberals of the time, however, he never questioned the necessity of segregation.[68] He recognized the discrepancy between the claims of a democratic society and its practice in the South, but like many white southerners who struggled intellectually with the contradictions, Graves downplayed the fundamental similarities between the Jim Crow system and Nazi racial ideology. When the NAACP's *Crisis* asked "whether there is a difference between the code for Negroes under Hitler and the code for Negroes under the United States," Graves pointed to the harsh treatment of blacks in occupied France. He wrote that black leaders should understand "that even though the Negro may not have received all he thinks he should under the Stars and Stripes, he is infinitely better off under that banner than under the dreadful sign of the Swastika." He addressed his column to Robert Durr, the editor of the *Weekly Review*—whom he considered a "good" black leader—urging him to inform those "less enlightened" of the truth about Hitler and his treatment of blacks.[69] Graves consistently advocated for maintaining the status quo in regard to social reform during the war and had little patience with those arguing for social change. Only after the war, Graves counseled, could the South gradually move toward racial justice. His emphasis on Nazi negrophobia and his description of Hitler as "the Jim Crow of all the ages" and the "greatest race-hater in history" came out of his desire to end black agitation for equal opportunity. Such agitation, he believed, would chip away at the façade of better understanding between the races that southern liberals had so carefully crafted.[70] For many years southern liberals such as Graves had promoted the idea that a "delicate balance" existed in race relations in the South, and that problems of inequality could be worked out satisfactorily only by southerners themselves, without the interference of northern liberals and the federal government. Graves aggressively promoted himself as one who not only understood the problems of southern blacks, but who also knew what was best for them. Demands for greater civil rights threatened this perceived balance and moved the issue beyond the paternalistic approach of southern liberals.

Some African Americans took offense at Graves's assertion. The *Birmingham World* responded that "America, and the South in particular, cannot be excused for not treating the Negro better because the Nazi treats him worse. . . . For [the Negro] to surrender his fight for the best that democracy has for the sake of the approval of his friends would be no more sane [than] for America to cease her fight for democracy for the smiles of Hitler." The editorial pointedly criticized Graves's position on social reform by stating that "the status quo doctrine plays into the hands of Hitler."[71] The *World*, and later its crusading editor, Emory O. Jackson, never fit into the mold of what Graves considered good or responsible race leadership. Conversely, Jackson never considered Graves a true liberal, referring to him on numerous occasions as a "white supremacy" southern liberal. Jackson referred to Graves as a "southern friend" of the Negro "on faith rather than . . . by deeds and favorable action"; it seems clear that Jackson never considered him a true friend of African Americans.[72] In contrast, Robert Durr, whom Graves apparently viewed as an acceptable black spokesman, argued only a few days later that "this is certainly no time for the Negro to take advantage of the national crisis to the disadvantage of the country, but it is no time for the country to nurse and cultivate the things here at home that create Hitlers."[73] The difference between the more activist editors at the *World* and the accommodationist Durr of the *Weekly Review* could not have been more clear. In any case, by the end of the war, Graves, like many other self-styled "southern liberals," abandoned his tenuous position on race and became an ardent champion of white supremacy in the South.[74]

The Final Solution

Nazi savagery reached its peak after Nazi officials laid out plans for the Final Solution at the Wannsee Conference on January 20, 1942. With the creation of more death camps in occupied Eastern Europe—some camps had been constructed prior to Wannsee—the Nazis began the systematic extermination of European Jewry. Even so, war news continued to overshadow the stories and editorials concerning the mass murder of the Jews in Europe. Although the larger daily newspapers, such as those in Birmingham, Montgomery, and Dothan, provided editorial comment on the events, the rural, weekly press used its limited space to cover news that had a more direct bearing on their readers' lives and rarely commented on the annihilation of the Jews. Nevertheless, Alabamians generally could not be considered uninformed in regard to the extermination of European Jews.

News of the mass extermination reached leaders in the United States in August 1942. In late November 1942, Rabbi Stephen S. Wise publicly announced that mass murder of the Jews in Europe had already claimed over two million Jewish lives. Shortly after Wise's revelation, the *Birmingham News* characterized the events as "sufficient to condemn the Nazis for all time." The *News* predicted further atrocities if German military setbacks persisted. "If there were no other reason for a determination to defeat the Axis," its editorial concluded, "ample justification would lie in the persecution of the Jews. For there can be no peace in a world where nations of military power have so little consideration for the feelings and just aspirations of minority elements in their population."[75] After Wise's announcement, the larger daily newspapers in Alabama reported more frequently on the mass killings, though not on a regular basis. The vehemence of editors' and readers' comments suggests that they believed the incredible stories of mass murder, although it is doubtful that they grasped the enormity of the Nazis' crimes.

Condemnation of Nazi atrocities went hand in hand with appeals for aid to European Jews. Usually these appeals consisted of urging the British to open Palestine as a haven for the Jews, an effort that had changed little since the mid-1930s. Rarely did editors raise the question of American culpability in barring Jewish immigration. In one of the few instances, the *Birmingham News* suggested that American outrage at the mass killings was simply "hollow expressions of sympathy" that would do little to change immigration policy.[76] When the AP reported in August 1943 that "more than three million Jews have been 'liquidated' since 1939 by planned starvation, forced labor, deportation, pogroms and methodical murder," the *Birmingham News* argued that "non-Jewish Americans have an inescapable responsibility" to aid in the rescue of Jews dying by the millions in Nazi-occupied Europe. "Confronted with such bloody statistics, with a tale of ruthlessness that has no precedent in human history," the editorial continued, "are non-Jews to say that this is something outside their field of constructive pity? Never again must such a holocaust sear mankind. . . . It is not too much to say that by her tangible response to this unspeakable heartlessness will America prove whether she has learned the lesson of this war."[77] What the American Christian response should be, the *News* never stated. With the exception of the *Birmingham News*, there had been little to no public acknowledgment that opposition to Jewish immigration to the United States had contributed to the crisis.

More commonly, editors and readers focused on British Mandate Palestine. One reader suggested to the *Montgomery Advertiser* that the United States persuade the British to open Palestine to the remaining Jews in Europe, as it "is the nearest and most practical haven. . . . Only its doors need be open[ed] for masses of Jews to save themselves."[78] Many groups, both Jewish and non-Jewish, urged the British government through petitions, condemnation, and resolutions to open Palestine. As Germany neared defeat by the beginning of 1945, the press published reports of Nazi atrocities, but usually without editorial comment. The opening of the camps in April 1945, however, forced the press and the American public to confront the full measure of Nazi depravity.

War Crimes

The liberation of the camps offered an opportunity to verify firsthand the enormity of Nazi crimes, and those who visited the camps were profoundly shocked by the experience. Demands for justice appeared immediately in the press. Yet when the press recounted the Nazis' crimes, it rarely mentioned the Jews as the special victims of the Nazis. The *Dothan Eagle*, long antagonistic toward the Nazis, wrote: "everywhere liberating American armies turn they find German bestiality on every hand, and enormous, amazing and sickening amount of it. Some of the victims are still alive and most of them will be able to tell under oath how they have been mistreated. And there are authenticated photographs, bushels and bushels of them, to preserve German horrors." The *Eagle* made note of how American POWs had been "abused, murdered and systematically starved" by the Nazis, and described the incinerators and mass graves of the "women, children and helpless French,

Belgian, Dutch and Russian slave laborers." The editorial, however, did not mention the Jews.[79]

Other newspapers followed the same pattern. James Coleman, editor of the *Greene County Democrat*, recounted the crimes of the Germans—"the atrocities of their invasions, their slaughters, their prison camps, their slavery, their destruction of cities in other lands"—and recalled the story of Sodom and Gomorrah. Like Abraham searching for fifty righteous men, "if the allies cannot find many good Germans . . . [Germany] must be dismembered." While Coleman prominently used the Hebrew story in his editorial on the search for justice, he failed utterly to mention the Jews when recounting Germany's crimes.[80] In the *Alabama Baptist*, Gwaltney marveled at the barbarity of the Nazis: "emaciated bodies of Nazi victims stacked like cordwood, men were hung on spikes—like sides of beef until they died. And . . . chared [*sic*] bodies by the hundreds which were burned in furnaces." Gwaltney mentioned specifically only the suffering of American prisoners, however, not that of the Jews.[81] Even the *Birmingham News* and *Birmingham Age-Herald*, the newspapers perhaps most sensitive to Jewish concerns, did not characterize Nazi atrocities as a seminal Jewish tragedy. The *News* placed the blame of "war crimes" on "Prussian militarists," and for "crimes against humanity" on "the men in charge of the concentration camps who permitted their prisoners to starve, for the Gestapo members who tortured the innocent, for the SS troops who shot Allied soldiers they had captured."[82] Charles Feidelson, too, discussed "the Belsen concentration camp" and the Nazi "philosophy of arrogance, plunder and extermination" without mentioning the destruction of the Jews.[83]

Historian Peter Novick notes that the majority of those liberated from camps in Germany, such as Bergen-Belsen, Buchenwald, or Dachau, by American or British troops largely were not Jews, unlike camps in the East that were liberated by the Soviets. In fact, he estimates that Jews comprised only about one-fifth of those liberated in German camps. "If Jews did not figure prominently in contemporary accounts of . . . camps liberated in the spring of 1945," Novick explains, "it was not because of malice or insensitivity, but because they did not figure that prominently among those liberated." Moreover, he suggests that correspondents did not maliciously downplay the presence of Jews in the camps when they described French Jews as Frenchmen rather than as Jews. To do so "seemed to be buying into Hitler's categories. It was the Nazis who denied that a French Jew could be a real Frenchman, etc. American correspondents' usage was 'anti-facist.'"[84]

Although the American correspondents' failure to mention the Jews can be plausibly explained, it is more difficult to do so for the many Alabama journalists and editorial writers—Feidelson included—who had condemned the Nazis' antisemitic persecutions since 1933 and had expressed sincere sympathy for the Jews after the mass killings had been confirmed in late 1942, few of whom characterized what had transpired as a Jewish tragedy. Perhaps journalists such as Feidelson thought the reading public would assume the Jewish nature of the atrocities in the light of the front-page stories that had vividly described the Jewish suffering and destruction in Europe. Or perhaps Laurel Leff is correct in her assertion that the *New York Times*, "the newspaper of record," shaped press coverage of the Final Solution to the point that there was a conscious or unconscious lack of attention to the Jews.[85] Nevertheless, in 1945 editorials on Nazi atrocities stressed the maltreatment of American soldiers first and indiscriminate German aggression second. In the euphoric aftermath of Germany's defeat and the somber exposure of widespread Nazi atrocities, the press either ignored or overlooked the extermination of the Jews.

Among Jews and African Americans, the mass murder of European Jews had a profound impact. The effect on Alabama's Jews was, of course, palpable. The revelation of the mass killings for African Americans' influenced their perception of the war and of the idea of racial supremacy. For African Americans, the barbarity of the Nazis, especially toward the Jews, provided a platform from which to denounce the concept of racial supremacy. The black press condemned the mass killings perpetrated by the Nazis as a way to warn Americans against the dangers of racism in the United States. When the *Birmingham World*'s headline proclaimed the murder of seven hundred thousand Jews in Eastern Europe in January 1945, it used the terms "lynched" and "segregated Jewish concentration camp" to convey the horror in a way that resonated with its readers. The article also urged its readers to change "the color of these victims to black or brown and you will have and [*sic*] idea of what Africa or the American Black Belt would resemble under fascist rule."[86] The *World* continued to use the example of Nazism and Nazi atrocities to condemn racism in the United States, most brazenly perhaps with a cartoon that showed southern white politicians murdering members of the Fair Employment Practices Committee—a federal agency created specifically to ensure racial equality in national defense industries—in the same fashion that Nazis murdered Jews in the camps. In May the *World* published a piece by the syndicated columnist William A. Fowlkes, who called the mass murders "horrible," but noted that "the crimes of the Germans, who under Hitler were declaring themselves the master Nordic superior race and who hooted down all men of foreign color and strain everywhere, should serve to take some of the wind out of the sails of Christianity-teaching white men everywhere."[87] Unlike the *World*'s January article, which had provided some detail on the mass murders, Fowlkes's column did not mention the Jews but used the German atrocities to illustrate the arrogance and evils of racial supremacy in general.

Conversely, white Alabamians who rejected the idea that southern white supremacy resembled Nazi racism often pointed to the mass exterminations of the Jews as evidence. As one *Birmingham News* reader asked, "where are the gas chambers in which we have destroyed millions of Negroes? . . . Where are the concentration camps in which we have starved thousands of Negroes to death?"[88] Comparing Jim Crow to the Final Solution, however, ignored the fact that Nazi policy toward the Jews, which had consisted of oppression, persecution, exclusion, and the expulsion of the Jews from German life and society, had developed into the systematic extermination of all European Jewry by early 1942. White oppression of blacks in the American South, including the extralegal violence such as rape and lynching, never evolved into a systematic program of mass killing. Any comparison of Jim Crow and the Holocaust was thus untenable. White conservatives used such comparisons to illustrate the supposedly benign and paternalistic treatment of blacks in the South, in this way contributing to and reinforcing the cognitive dissonance white southerners experienced when confronted by the similarities between Nazi and southern racial thought. Most white Alabamians, however, simply avoided comparing the two.

When the remaining leaders of the Nazi regime faced final judgment at Nuremberg in October 1946, few white Alabama newspapers commented. The black press, on the other hand, continued to use the examples of Nazism and Nazi atrocities to condemn racism in the United States. The *Birmingham World* published a cartoon that linked Klan elements to the executed Nazi leaders. Another William Fowlkes column made the connection between the Nazis and white supremacy. The pictures of the executed Nazi leaders, he wrote, "should serve as a psychological blow . . . to those perpetrators against human equality, opportunity and freedom—those rank espousers of racial supremacy. Somehow, I hope the warning is thorough and sufficient to strike for peace around the globe. All Nazis are not dead."[89] Robert Durr's *Weekly Review* also noted that those executed at Nuremberg "were all antisemitic [and] likewise anti-human. The two always go together." Durr's piece did not compare Nazism and white supremacy as Fowlkes did but condemned antisemitism as "a particularly vicious form of human depravity. . . . Whoever persecutes Jews is on the road which leads to the persecution of everybody and the end of freedom for everybody."[90]

Of the few white newspapers to comment on the Nuremberg verdicts, the

Clarke County Democrat cautioned against sympathy for the condemned, arguing: "we can't forget the hundreds of thousands of Jews who were brutally murdered, tortured or starved to death; the innocent women and children, the old and the weak, who were killed because they served no useful purpose for the Nazis."[91] Unlike many of the editorials published shortly after April 1945, the *Democrat* mentioned Jewish suffering, but it did so only after mentioning other groups who had suffered at the hands of the Nazis. When the *Democrat* numbered the Jewish deaths at "hundreds of thousands," it reflected a common view that Jewish suffering during the war, while tragic, was simply the best indicator among many measures of Nazi depravity. It also reflected the perception that the Final Solution was only tangential to the war. Indeed, such thinking helped to diminish the recognition of the Holocaust as a central event of World War II until years after the war's end.

Given the coverage of and commentary on the Final Solution, no literate person in Alabama could have been ignorant of the events of the Holocaust. Even so, understanding of its ramifications eluded most, and the enormity of the destruction and the suffering of untold millions the war caused overshadowed the millions of Jewish deaths at the hands of the Nazis and their allies. Alabama's editors and journalists had been integral in informing the public in the state of the Nazi persecution of the Jews, but they, too, when they placed the Jews among other groups persecuted and murdered by the Nazis and not as the primary group targeted for annihilation, demonstrated limited insight and understanding. As Lipstadt has argued, the American press's coverage of the mass killings in this manner "clouded the public's perceptions of the Nazi war against the Jews. The Final Solution was in and of itself difficult to accept. The skeptical and ambiguous treatment of it by the Allies and the inability of the press to break with this pattern served to reinforce public confusion, doubt, and disinterest."[92] The Alabama press, too, though it condemned the barbarity of the Nazis' antisemitic policy from the beginning, expressed sympathy for the persecuted Jews, and reported and commented on the stories of the mass murders, failed in the end to explain the particularly Jewish nature of the Holocaust. Equally striking in the context of the Jim Crow South was the white-run press's failure to draw lessons from the Nazi example about the racism in its own backyard.

5
The War

The Japanese attack on Pearl Harbor on December 7, 1941, brought the United States into the Second World War. Despite Japanese aggression, Hitler and Nazi Germany, not surprisingly, figured critically in how Alabama's Jews responded to the war, whether they supported servicemen on the home front or those who served in the military. Hitler and the Nazis presented a tangible threat to Jews everywhere, made explicit to American Jews with the public revelation of the mass murders in late 1942. Even Alabama's press presented Nazi Germany as the primary enemy of the United States, and the news stories and commentary on the European theater far outweighed those on the Pacific war. The war created significant challenges for Alabama's Jewish community, not the least being the many Jews who departed in the service of their country. Many of the young men who grew up in the 1930s quickly became aware of the danger Nazism posed. Sam Kayser of Mobile exemplified such a person. Kayser, who fought in the European theater during the war, remembered that as a teenager growing up in the 1930s, the adults "didn't talk around the kids that much. But, I just hoped we were going to defeat Hitler before he got over here and got some of us. I didn't have any deep thoughts at age thirteen to fourteen. By the time I got to high school, we were thinking we were getting ready to go to war. We didn't like the Germans period. I mean, all of us were united in the way we felt. It had nothing to do with religion, [but] the Jews felt it more acutely."[1]

Jews responded, as did other religious groups across the nation. Not only did the local Jewish congregations and organizations prove to be vital components of the local and state war effort, but individual members of the Jewish community also joined civilian defense groups, volunteered for the Red Cross and the United Service Organization (USO), and participated in various other programs and service groups in their community. Jewish organizations throughout the state, large and small, supported the war effort in an energetic fashion, whether through keeping in contact with their members in the armed forces, holding special patriotic services, or opening their doors to

Jewish servicemen stationed in their area. In Anniston, for instance, the local Jewish community worked closely with the Jewish Welfare Board (JWB) and USO to entertain Jewish soldiers stationed at nearby Fort McClellan. In Dothan, the community did the same for Camp Rucker. Jews throughout the state gave freely of their time, effort, and resources, and in many cases their family members, to the service of their country.

The national Jewish Welfare Board (JWB), which had been founded in 1917 to recruit and train Jewish chaplains for the armed services, played the central role in organizing local Jewish communities to serve the troops stationed nearby, supporting the development of community programs for the men or allowing the continuation of existing programs, work that would have physically and financially overwhelmed the communities otherwise. In February 1941, on the national level, the JWB joined with five other civilian agencies—the Young Men's Christian Association (YMCA), the Young Women's Christian Association (YWCA), the Salvation Army, the National Catholic Community Service (NCCS), and the National Travelers Aid Association—to form the USO in order to boost morale and provide recreation for American servicemen.[2] Numerous Jewish communities throughout Alabama organized JWB committees to serve the soldiers stationed at nearby military bases or, in the case of Birmingham, to serve the numerous soldiers who frequently visited the city for rest and recreation. The JWB, like the other USO agencies, served soldiers of all faiths, but especially emphasized the men of Jewish faith, providing not only recreational activities but also spiritual guidance, home hospitality, and the management of war records in addition to ensuring the general welfare of the men under their care. Unlike the other USO agencies, only the JWB activities could be considered "community get-togethers," as such events included, and indeed relied upon, nearly every member of the local Jewish community.[3]

Local rabbis also played a central role in the JWB operations, lending their credibility as the most visible and respected leaders in the Jewish community and providing for the spiritual welfare of soldiers stationed in Alabama. Since the army rarely had enough Jewish chaplains to go around, rabbis from the local congregations either worked with the JWB or took it upon themselves to minister to the Jewish servicemen in nearby camps. Due to the dominance of the Reform movement in the South and the dearth of Orthodox rabbis in small-town Alabama, Reform rabbis such as Montgomery's Eugene Blachschleger or Dothan's Alfred Wolf frequently became the only rabbi that the overwhelmingly northern Jewish soldiers stationed in the state would see. Such an arrangement sometimes led to discontent among some Orthodox servicemen over religious services or *kashrut*, but such conflict occurred less frequently than one might imagine. Nonetheless, the servicemen appreciated the efforts of the local communities and the rabbis on their behalf.

Approximately 550,000 American Jews served in World War II, between 11 and 12 percent of the Jewish population in the United States, roughly the same proportion for the total population.[4] Alabama's Jews, like Sam Kayser, responded to their nation's call, as did Jews throughout the nation, serving in every branch of the US armed forces. Those Jews who served in the military during World War II conveyed a deep sense of their own identity as Jews, something described in Deborah Dash Moore's *GI Jews* as "an imposing and powerful force."[5] Just as their sense of identity emanated from their letters or recollections, so too did their strong feelings of accomplishment and victory. Although Moore examines men from the northeast in her study of Jewish soldiers during the Second World War, their experiences closely correspond to their Alabama counterparts.

Anniston

Located five miles from Anniston, Fort McClellan experienced significant growth in early 1941 thanks to the Selective Training and Service Act of 1940. Home to the Basic Immaterial Replacement Training Center, McClellan grew from eighteen thousand in mid-1940 to approximately twenty-seven thousand in early 1942, including five thousand African American soldiers of the 92nd Division. In 1943, McClellan became home to the Infantry Replacement Training Center, which provided basic combat training for the army, in addition to housing three thousand POWs in a Prisoner Internment Camp. By the end of World War II, approximately five hundred thousand soldiers had received their training at Fort McClellan.[6]

Initially, Rabbi Abba M. Fineberg served as the JWB's field director for the Anniston and Fort McClellan area. A native of Niagara Falls, New York, Fineberg arrived in Anniston in mid-1940, where he offered spiritual support for Jewish soldiers at McClellan until the army appointed a full-time Jewish chaplain in March 1941. He also served as the de facto rabbi of Temple Beth-El, as the Reform congregation had no full-time rabbi. Fineberg established a JWB Service Club and created and administered programs for the morale of the Jewish soldiers stationed at McClellan prior to the organization of the USO, coordinating the support of the Jewish communities in Anniston, Birmingham, Gadsden, and Atlanta for JWB-USO efforts. Although Fineberg transferred to Camp Shelby, Mississippi, in June 1941, he established a successful JWB-USO program and a strong working relationship with local Jewish leaders that continued to benefit the soldiers at McClellan throughout the war.

The Anniston Army and Navy Committee, led by Mortimer C. Sterne, made great effort to support the JWB-USO programs, although numerous problems arose in dealing with the ever-increasing numbers of men, problems that almost every small Jewish community adjacent to a southern military installation faced. In early January 1941, McClellan had approximately seven hundred Jewish soldiers, a number that increased substantially when the bulk of the New York National Guard's 27th Infantry Division arrived some six thousand strong later that month, with reinforcements arriving regularly. By February, Fineberg estimated the number had grown to twelve hundred Jewish soldiers; by April it reached approximately two thousand.[7] No agency that comprised the USO in Anniston had adequate facilities for the large number of men aggregating at McClellan, and certainly not the tiny Jewish community, which numbered only twenty-two families. Services at Temple Beth-El filled to overflowing, even before the influx of men from the 27th Division, and the temple building proved to be too small to hold recreational activities. The overcrowding and the cost associated with hosting such a large number of men caused some at Beth-El to argue that "these are New York boys, and New York should take care of them," not an uncommon sentiment, as members of the State Coordinating Committee had made similar arguments in regard to the refugee problem only a year earlier. Nevertheless, the Anniston Jewish community entertained the soldiers every Sunday, although they looked to the JWB and the Birmingham and Atlanta communities for significant financial contributions. Even in Birmingham, many thought that "since the JWB received a great deal of money from the USO," that the national office of the JWB should be responsible for all expenditures.[8] This parsimonious attitude did not extend to hosting Jewish soldiers in private homes on the weekends. Most Jewish families in Anniston and many in Birmingham had two to three soldiers for Sunday dinner every week, although it was not nearly enough to care for every Jewish soldier at McClellan. In some cases, Gentile families hosted Jewish soldiers for dinner, providing personal contact and attention for soldiers away from home.[9]

In order to host any recreational activities, the JWB had to rent dance halls or theaters, often at exorbitant prices. The poor condition of Anniston's existing facilities prompted Anniston's JWB leadership, first Fineberg then Morris D. Kronenfeld, to press for either constructing or purchasing their own building, an endeavor the local Jewish community wholeheartedly supported as long as the JWB paid for it. Indeed, the entire Anniston community, not just the JWB, needed quality recreational facilities. A confidential YWCA report concluded that Anniston had almost no community recreation and only "three very dirty, dingy dance halls." "Children from twelve to sixteen make up one quarter of the audience in a cheap entertainment hall," the report read. "Soldiers, couples and prostitutes make up the rest. This provides the only evening recreation for groups, other than soldiers, or women of the professional sort." Margaret Klein, the welfare director of Calhoun County, agreed with that assessment but observed that "our problem is not professional prostitutes . . . but juvenile delinquents—girls 14 and 15 years of age who are attracted here by uniforms, the excitement and the prospect of a good time. If soldiers had a center where they could take these girls or where they could meet other girls, many of them would spend their time in healthful recreation. They have no place to go, and have turned to less innocent relationships."[10] Throughout 1941, the JWB, as well as other USO agencies, arranged for temporary accommodations for their programs and events, although these arrangements proved wholly unsatisfactory. By May 1942, the Federal Recreation Center, which the city commission had previously occupied, became the main USO center in Anniston. Almost all of the USO agencies contributed to the function of the new facility, but due to the JWB's efficiency and previous work in the community, in addition to the influence and standing of the Sterne family, Mayor W. S. Coleman and Anniston's leading citizens demanded that the JWB operate the center. The JWB relied heavily on donations from the surrounding communities to outfit the center. Books and shelves, furniture, and recreation equipment arrived courtesy of those in Anniston, Birmingham, and Atlanta. In one instance, the Workmen's Circle in Birmingham, a Jewish socialist fraternal organization, generously donated two ping-pong tables to the center.[11]

Despite the opening of the new USO center, the USO in Anniston experienced tremendous dysfunction. Nathaniel Nason, the regional representative of the JWB-USO, noted that "Anniston has been a headache of long duration to USO," with the individual agencies competing with one another rather than working together in the interest of the soldiers. Coleman had demanded that the JWB assume the responsibility for running the USO center in the federal building not only because of JWB efficiency but also to prevent it from being operated by the unpopular NCCS. In fact, Nason stated that the NCCS "is so unpopular with many southern communities of which Anniston is but one example." He later quipped that the NCCS workers were "as out of place in Anniston as Father Coughlin would be."[12] The Anniston Jewish community, however, did not want the JWB to manage the USO center "because of a strong desire to avoid friction" in the community, but such strong pressure from community leaders forced them to acquiesce.[13]

The JWB hosted numerous activities for soldiers, including movies, lectures, dances, and other entertainment where the local Jewish community provided food and distributed cigarettes. At one Mother's Day dance, they held a drawing for fifty free telegrams for the soldiers. Dances proved to be the most popular events by far, usually held once a month, and usually on Saturday evenings since dancing was not allowed in Anniston on Sundays and Jewish Sabbath observance precluded Friday nights. Their success relied heavily on Benjamin Roth of the YMHA and Birmingham's Jewish community, which organized the transportation of young women to the JWB-USO center. Often the JWB had to advertise by word of mouth to the Jewish men in camp or else the dance would attract overwhelming numbers of non-Jews. "Of course we shall turn no one away," JWB's Fineberg explained in early 1941, "but since we are bringing up Jewish girls from Birmingham we prefer to have the Jewish soldiers." Anywhere from sixty to ninety young women traveled to Anniston for the Saturday dances, which attracted bulging crowds of Jewish and non-Jewish soldiers, so many that they outnumbered the women five to one.[14] In the first dance the JWB held in the new USO building in May 1942, over fifty women came from Birmingham, yet they were outnumbered by GIs eight to one. Funding the transportation between Birmingham and Anniston so women could attend dances and other activities became difficult for the JWB and the YMHA. In many cases the women paid their own way to Anniston, particularly after the United States entered the war. Their presence greatly pleased the Jewish soldiers at McClellan who "were overjoyed at the prospect of meeting Jewish girls." Such gatherings, including picnics at Oxford Lake or a barn dance hosted by Atlanta's Junior Hadassah, often led to invitations to visit Birmingham or Atlanta, where many soldiers enjoyed the hospitality of Jewish families on the weekend or for holidays. In order to ensure that these extremely popular dances continued even without the regular visits of Birmingham's young women, Kronenfeld visited the nearby Jacksonville State Teachers College to inquire about their female students attending dances, but Clarence W. Daugette, the president of the college, did not want his students to mingle with soldiers because of "unfavorable experiences" he had during World War I.[15]

The Anniston YMCA, for their part, organized a group known as the "V" (Victory) Girls in mid-1941 who pledged "to meet the social needs of the men in Service by providing the boys with activities and their presence at the USO centers." Initially, the "V" Girls served only the YMCA center, but they quickly became a fixture at almost all of the USO centers in Anniston, including, in many instances, the JWB-USO center. The "V" Girls numbered around fifty, and membership was restricted to Anniston's "socially acceptable females," but not the "average working girl." Although they provided entertainment at the USO centers, the girls had a reputation for being "snobbish." Soldiers frequently complained that the girls only danced with them as a "patriotic duty" and did not "have dates with them or accept them into their homes." Interestingly, Jeanette Rund, the daughter of Samuel Isaac Rund, a member of the JWB, led the predominately non-Jewish "V" Girls organization. Samuel Rund had married Margaret Alabama Bond, a Gentile, and in the Protestant-dominated small town of Anniston, the younger Rund no doubt felt "more at home with the YMCA than the JWB." Nevertheless, Nathaniel Nason, the JWB regional representative, observed that "this is an outstanding achievement for a Jewish girl in Anniston."[16] After the creation of the main USO center at the federal building and with the cooperation of the various USO agencies, dances for the soldiers occurred on a regular basis, with young women coming from Gadsden, Talladega, Jacksonville, and other surrounding towns, in addition to the local "V" Girls and the Jewish girls from Birmingham.[17]

Ensuring that the men had a place to observe important holidays such as Passover and the High Holy Days frequently presented numerous headaches for the JWB and the local community. On such days Anniston's Jews opened their doors to McClellan's servicemen, but they could not hope to accommodate every Jewish soldier stationed at the camp. Anniston had neither the facilities to hold such a large gathering nor the ability to provide kosher meals. The JWB contacted the communities in Birmingham and Atlanta and requested them, and in some cases pleaded with them, to welcome men into their homes. For the camp's first Passover in 1941, the JWB made provisions for 753 Jewish servicemen to observe the holiday in private homes in these cities, and roughly 150 more made their own arrangements in Birmingham and Atlanta. Hundreds more remained on base. Special furloughs for soldiers to travel to Birmingham and Atlanta on Friday morning had to be arranged, although not all regimental commanders, it seems, received orders about the furloughs. JWB's Fineberg made "a last minute appeal, personally, to several regimental commanders," including calling one at 11:45 p.m. on Thursday evening. He was ultimately successful in securing leave for the soldiers, but in doing so he ran afoul of the division chaplain for his "considerable annoyance [and] by his lack of manners," leading to an uneasy relationship between the JWB and the division chaplain. Moreover,

Anniston had little room to accommodate the large number of families that visited during the holidays. The growth of defense industries had brought thousands of people to the Anniston area seeking work, causing the population to expand from an estimated 25,477 to approximately 40,000. Coupled with the lack of residential construction, Anniston, like other wartime boomtowns, experienced a serious housing shortage, forcing the Army and Navy Committee and the JWB to scour the town for lodging for these families, often with little success.[18]

The difficulties of supporting such large numbers of men went beyond logistics. Prior to the war, most of the Jewish soldiers belonged to the 27th Division and hailed from New York City. Even after the New York 27th Division shipped out after Pearl Harbor, the vast majority of Jewish servicemen at McClellan came from the large population centers in the north. Once at McClellan, they experienced stark cultural differences, which the JWB tried to ameliorate. Anniston's Jewish life centered on the Reform Temple Beth-El, and the JWB's Abba Fineberg, and later the Jewish chaplains, Rabbis Joseph H. Lief and Samuel Teitelbaum, all belonged to the Reform movement. Most of the soldiers who passed through McClellan came from Orthodox communities in New York, although many of these men could be considered only nominally Orthodox. Any semblance of Orthodox observance could scarcely be found in Anniston, and Fineberg explained that he wanted to do all they could for the "Orthodox element" but thought his options to be "limited by the capabilities of the men—over 75% of whom cannot read Hebrew." Moreover, he observed that if given a choice between a Reform seder or an Orthodox seder, "an overwhelming number chose the reform seder, altho [*sic*] the great majority of the men are orthodox."[19] Temple Beth-El offered no options for an Orthodox observance either. Sherry Blanton, in her history of the temple, notes that even in 1946 the Reform congregants had been scandalized by a "student rabbi" from McClellan who "had quite loudly conducted a High Holy Days service completely in Hebrew with the building's windows wide open." The board of trustees, fearful of the opinion of their Gentile neighbors about the Hebrew chanting, made it clear to succeeding student rabbis that they conduct only a Reform service.[20]

The JWB also faced tremendous problems concerning the observance of *kashrut*. In such a small Reform-dominated town, keeping kosher proved to be virtually impossible. Fineberg, who ministered to McClellan's Jewish soldiers prior to the appointment of a full-time Jewish chaplain, received harsh criticism from the National Council for Young Israel, an Orthodox agency, not only for his Reform services but also for his lax regard for *kashrut* when he granted "rabbinic dispensation to the Jewish boys to eat pork and other trefa foods."[21] Fineberg had few alternatives since he could not make McClellan's mess hall serve kosher food, nor did Anniston have a *shochet* or a kosher restaurant. Indeed, what Jewish soldiers faced while at McClellan was no different from what Jewish soldiers faced at military installations throughout the United States. As Deborah Dash Moore explains in *GI Jews*, "If reveille awoke young American men to the reality of military service, army food alerted many Jewish men to the fact of their difference. 'Eating ham for Uncle Sam' challenged identities absorbed in their mother's kitchens. Forcing down *treyf* food like ham and pork was only the beginning of the problem. If one habitually or ritually observed the prohibition against the mixing of meat and dairy dishes or various kosher strictures, the complications multiplied."[22] Such was life for Jewish soldiers at McClellan.

While the hospitality committee served kosher sandwiches at JWB-sponsored events, the closest Anniston could come to a proper kosher restaurant was at Henry Harris's Delicatessen, which the JWB convinced to provide "kosher-style" meals.[23] The JWB, with the help of Mortimer Sterne, eventually established a kosher kitchen in mid-1941. The JWB had previously discussed opening a facility under the direction of a refugee family but instead brought in Anna Grude, who had experience running kosher kitchens in Atlanta and New York. The Grude Kosher Kitchen, however, closed within a few months due to lack of sufficient business. The unfortunate timing of her opening coincided with summer maneuvers that all but emptied McClellan. The local Jewish community also did not patronize her kitchen. The JWB had worried that the thoroughly acculturated Reform community might harbor some "negative feeling" toward a strictly kosher establishment. Whether any negative feeling toward Grude's kitchen existed among the community is unknown, but Grude certainly believed that she did not have the support of those in Anniston.[24] The JWB later tried to construct a kosher kitchen at the JWB-USO center, but that too proved unsuccessful without a *shochet* or a place to purchase kosher foods and meats in town. Shipping such commodities from Cincinnati or New York was entirely too expensive, and without proper storage facilities, even the purchase of kosher food from Birmingham or Atlanta could not be undertaken.

Anniston's Jews seemed oblivious to such inconveniences. The JWB's Kronenfeld observed that "the local Jewish community is disinterested in this problem, and as a matter of fact, see no reason why the dietary laws should be observed."[25] The attitude the Anniston Jewish community exhibited toward *kashrut* reflected similar attitudes of many Jews throughout the South, especially among Reform congregations. As Marcie Cohen Ferris explains in her study of southern Jewish foodways, as Central European Jews settled in the South in the mid- to late nineteenth century, they gradually "shaped an identity that focused on ethical principles more than Jewish ritual and ceremonial practices. It was important to fit into the larger society and in many homes, Jewish dietary laws were dropped because of the community's small numbers and the difficulty of obtaining kosher foods."[26]

The JWB had an overwhelmingly positive influence on Anniston's Jewish community. Despite the reservations the Jewish community had with the JWB managing the largest USO center in Anniston—the community initially had "a strong desire to avoid friction"—the JWB's competent leadership reflected well on the Jewish community as a whole. Because Anniston's entire Jewish community could scarcely provide the manpower needed to organize and staff many JWB events, they relied on "the enthusiastic support and practical help" of many non-Jewish volunteers, even for religious functions. As the JWB-USO center closed in May 1947, the JWB noted that "at our mass Sedarim . . . during the war years and after, when so much volunteer help was needed, we found that our non-Jewish volunteers actually outnumbered the Jewish ones."[27] In addition to fostering amity with Anniston's Gentiles, the JWB served to unify the Jewish community in a way few things had in the past. "Every function of a specifically Jewish character," the JWB noted after the war, "whether religious, cultural or social . . . involved practically the entire Jewish Community."[28]

Gadsden

In Gadsden, an industrial city thirty miles to the north of Anniston, the JWB had limited opportunity to serve the soldiers stationed at nearby Camp Sibert. Established in the summer of 1942, although not completed until the spring of 1943, Camp Sibert was home to the army's chemical warfare training facility.[29] The city of Gadsden performed all services for the troops through a Soldier Service Center sponsored by the Federal Security Agency (FSA) and administered and staffed by Works Progress Administration (WPA) personnel. The FSA became "the chief [federal] agency coordinating recreational interests in defense areas" after it had been tasked to do so in December 1940 in order to mitigate many of the problems associated with rapid community growth. Gadsden had attracted thousands of new workers with the expansion of its industries, including the construction of the Gadsden Ordinance Plant in 1941. The addition of Camp Sibert meant the influx of thousands more into the area. Gadsden's population swelled even further on the weekends as hundreds of soldiers from Fort McClellan flooded the bars and nightclubs to purchase liquor, something they could not do in "dry" Calhoun County.[30]

The recreation Gadsden's Soldier Service Center provided for soldiers left much to be desired. Murray Rosenberg, the assistant to the Jewish chaplain at Camp Sibert, lamented that "the morale down here is unfortunately quite low. There are no planned social or recreational activities to speak of. The nearest sizable town to camp is Gadsden which has nothing to offer the men except possibly a meal in a restaurant, usually at exorbitant prices . . . there is nothing for the service man to do except walk the streets, which they usually do until it's time to return to camp." Rosenberg, along with many other soldiers at Sibert, wanted a USO center in Gadsden. The USO, however, could not operate in Gadsden because of an agreement with the FSA, and the Gadsden community only allowed USO services for African American troops at Sibert and the establishment of a Travelers Aid Troop Transit Lounge. This USO-FSA agreement did not apply to the JWB, which, for its part, tried to cover Camp Sibert from Anniston and subsequently established a somewhat ambivalent relationship with Gadsden's Jewish community.[31]

The members of Gadsden's Temple Beth Israel entertained the soldiers of Camp Sibert as best they could, opening their doors to them for Friday evening services and hosting socials and parties in the temple's vestry on Sunday afternoons. Due to the strict camp regulations on weekday passes, almost all recreational events took place on the weekends. Gadsden's Jewish community resisted assistance from the JWB; they did not want to be identified with it because they feared that if Gadsden's Gentiles learned they had received "professional assistance" from a national organization such as the JWB, then "these church organizations will brand them as being different and furthermore [it would be] an admittance that the work now being carried out by the [Jewish] community is not effective." The JWB's regional representative, Nathaniel Nason noted in late 1942 that other communities in the South responded to the JWB in similar fashion and characterized it as a "perfectly natural reaction." One year later, Nason confided to Louis Kraft, the JWB's executive director, that while the community's hostility toward the JWB had eased somewhat, Gadsden remained "medieval in [their] thinking."[32] The leader of the Gadsden Jewish community, Merlin Hagedorn, adamantly resisted overtures to create an Army and Navy Committee, even in the face of lobbying by his friends Leon and Mortimer Sterne and Lee Freibaum, a Gadsden native who had settled in Anniston. Hagedorn had no objections to the JWB's visits to Camp Sibert, which by March 1943 had approximately three to four hundred Jewish soldiers, far more than Beth Israel could hold for Friday evening services. Kronenfeld arranged for Rabbis Mesch and Grafman in Birmingham to conduct services at Sibert until the army appointed a Jewish chaplain to the camp, which it did in mid-1943. By September 1943, Hagedorn had relented in his opposition to the JWB, and Beth Israel hosted its first JWB-sponsored Home Hospitality luncheon. Despite this apparent thaw between Hagedorn and the JWB, the Jewish soldiers at Sibert, especially the newly appointed Jewish chaplain, received little in the way of cooperation from the Gadsden community. Rosenberg observed that "they seem a little standoffish" to the Jewish men and officers at Sibert and "could stand a good job of community organization."[33]

In mid-1943, the army appointed Orthodox rabbi Louis Engelberg to Camp Sibert as its Jewish chaplain. John B. Isom, a fellow chaplain who roomed with Engelberg at Sibert, recalled the rabbi's strict observance of the Sabbath, when he "could not turn on or off a light, build a fire, answer the phone, ride in any vehicle, nor smoke his pipe. When I was not there it must have been miserable for him when it was cold. He could not start a fire but he could sit by those I built and use the lights I turned on." "In the shank of the Sabbath afternoon," Isom continued, "he would pace the floor waiting for the sun to go down so he could light up his pipe." Even after the rabbi married and moved off base, "he would leave his Buick in front of the chapel after the Jewish service on Friday evenings, and walk the three or four miles home in rain, sleet or snow," a far cry from the relaxed observance of the Reform Jews in Anniston or Gadsden.[34]

Even with an observant Orthodox rabbi as chaplain, Camp Sibert's Jews faced the same difficulties in observance of *kashrut* as did those at Fort McClellan. For Passover in 1943, however, Engelberg convinced his superiors at Sibert to maintain a kosher mess hall, which they did for all eight days, even providing new pots, pans, and cutlery. The wives of officers and enlisted men contributed, and the women of Beth Israel assisted the rabbi in the preparation of the seder. The Ladies Auxiliary of the Jewish War Veterans in Birmingham donated food, and the newly established Women's Committee of the JWB distributed kosher food packages to the men on duty or in the hospital who wanted to participate. Almost 150 Jewish men from Sibert traveled to Birmingham to observe Passover in private homes. The Orthodox rabbi had such an excellent relationship with Birmingham's Jewish community that he secured their "wholehearted cooperation" with activities at Camp Sibert. Such cooperation allowed Engelberg to serve an estimated 825 meals during the week of Passover.[35]

Montgomery

During World War I, Montgomery's Jewish community had worked with the newly established JWB to support the servicemen stationed at nearby Camp Sheridan and Taylor Field. Temple Beth-Or's rabbi, Bernard C. Ehrenreich, served as the first JWB representative for Montgomery and the unofficial Jewish chaplain at Sheridan and Taylor. The well-established Reform Jews of Beth-Or, more so than the Eastern European and Sephardic Jews of Agudath Israel and Etz Ahayem, played the leading roles in providing comfort and recreation to the troops stationed in Montgomery, opening the temple and the Standard Club to soldiers for entertainment and services. The JWB, thanks to Ehrenreich's entreaties, also built a Jewish Welfare Home at Camp Sheridan.[36] While the contributions of the Orthodox and Sephardim of Agudath Israel and Etz Ahayem had been minimal during the First World War, largely due to their lack of financial and social standing in the community, their contributions would not be so slight during the second.

Much had changed in Montgomery by 1940. Camp Sheridan closed soon after the end of World War I, and the property was sold to the city of Montgomery. Taylor Field remained but served only as a small auxiliary airfield. Montgomery still had two military posts, one established, the other newly created. Maxwell Army Air Field had been a repair depot during World War I, but thanks to Montgomery congressman Lister Hill, it grew significantly, becoming the center of all Army Air operational training in the eastern United States in 1939. In 1940, the army leased the city's municipal airport to create the Municipal Basic Flying Field, a training center for cadets, renamed Gunter Field after Montgomery's recently deceased mayor, William A. Gunter.[37] In the months following Pearl Harbor, approximately eleven thousand troops were stationed at Maxwell, while roughly three thousand served at Gunter.[38]

Much like Ehrenreich in the First World War, Beth-Or's rabbi, Eugene Blachschleger, ministered to the Jewish troops stationed in the Montgomery area, conducting services, visiting the sick, and facilitating the correspondence between soldiers and their parents. Blachschleger served not only Beth-Or but also as the initial JWB representative in Montgomery and the de facto Jewish chaplain at Maxwell and Gunter. By March 1941, he led weekly services at Maxwell and Gunter Fields where, as a soldier described, Blachschleger's "ardent fervor . . . has spiritually strengthened all cadets of the Jewish faith." He distributed prayer books and scripture readings that "each Jewish cadet will be able to use throughout his military service and treasure thereafter," and wrote to parents "at a time when these cadets had little opportunity to write home themselves." Much like the Jewish troops stationed throughout Alabama, most of those at Maxwell and Gunter came from the Orthodox tradition. As Blachschleger noted of those who attended services or parties at Beth-Or, "many of them had never before been inside a Reform Temple." Despite the differences between Blachschleger and the men, the Jewish soldiers extended a warm thanks to the rabbi and the Jewish community for "the hospitality we have received at Maxwell Field [that] shall be remembered always." Blachschleger ministered to the Jewish servicemen on Maxwell and Gunter until March 1943, when the army finally assigned a Jewish chaplain to Maxwell.[39]

In 1941 the Montgomery Jewish Federation created a JWB Council to coordinate activities and address concerns associated with the servicemen and to help alleviate the heavy burden placed on Blachschleger. Just as the federation operated largely within the confines of Beth-Or, Blachschleger conducted JWB business through the temple offices. When groups such as Hadassah, the Council of Jewish Women, the Hebrew Ladies Benevolent Society, or B'nai B'rith planned their own functions for servicemen, the activities had to be "cleared through Rabbi Blachschleger's office." Because of this, organizations in Montgomery closely identified the JWB with Beth-Or. Blachschleger's leadership of the Reform congregation and his interfaith work within the larger community had won the confidence and admiration of the most important segments of Montgomery society, bestowing instant legitimacy on JWB's work in the city, including with other USO agencies in Montgomery who saw nothing wrong with the JWB working out of the Beth-Or offices. Members of Agudath Israel and Etz Ahayem, however, expressed their dissatisfaction with the arrangement. Unlike the First World War, the JWB Council and its committees now included members of the Orthodox and Sephardic synagogues who had been largely marginalized in 1917–18. With the JWB operating out of Beth-Or, marginalization occurred once again, despite the moderating and conciliatory influence of Blachschleger. For his part, Blachschleger did not seek to solely direct JWB affairs or exclude others from meaningful participation, but the lack of consistent rabbinical leadership at both Agudath Israel and Etz Ahayem and his role as the rabbi of the most prominent Jewish congregation in the city meant that both Jews and Gentile turned to him for community leadership above and beyond his ministerial obligations. In fact, the president of the Jewish federation, Myron Rothschild, pleaded with the JWB to send a full-time representative because Blachschleger's "facilities are over taxed and he is really having a difficult time to keep up with the work in addition to his rabbinical duties." To mitigate the pressure placed upon Blachschleger and to coordinate the efforts of "the entire Jewish community," the national

JWB appointed a full-time representative to Montgomery in May 1942, a decision with which the overworked rabbi wholeheartedly agreed.[40]

Before a representative could be appointed, the JWB had to address the concerns of prominent Reform members of the council who wanted "no separate JWB operation" in Montgomery, whose activities had to be "conducted jointly with other agencies or through one of the Jewish institutions." The chairman of the Montgomery JWB Council, Myron Lobman, as well as Blachschleger, Henry Weil, and several others on the council, argued that the JWB "should not in any way disturb the USO scene by giving even the slightest indication of segregation—namely, that our worker when and as he arrives on the scene should be placed in the present USO facility operated by the YMCA." The YMCA-USO Soldiers Center on Commerce Street operated as the main USO center in Montgomery, but the NCCS had opened its own USO center on Lee Street, upsetting numerous organizations and adding to an already strong anti-Catholic sentiment in Protestant-dominated Montgomery.[41] In order to avoid any community backlash, or be singled out as Catholics had been when they opened their separate USO center, Lobman demanded that the JWB operations be integrated into the current YMCA-USO center, and that the new JWB representative, Maxwell H. Tasgal, be interviewed before coming to Montgomery to determine if he would fit in with the conservative southern community. Lobman convinced Irving Engel, who had relocated to New York from Birmingham in the 1920s and knew "very well the conditions in Montgomery," to interview Tasgal in New York to ensure he did not have a personality that would "grate upon the general public" and embarrass or endanger the Jewish community.[42]

Tasgal, who apparently passed the hastily arranged interview with Engel, arrived in Montgomery in May 1942. Working out of the YMCA-USO center on Commerce Street as the Montgomery JWB Council demanded, Tasgal began a vigorous JWB program that included parties and dances at Temple Beth-Or, Agudath Israel, and the Standard Club; "watermelon cuttings" at Oak Park in the summer months that featured swimming and dancing; and weekly "At Homes," where local families hosted servicemen every Sunday afternoon. The Montgomery JWB Council had contacted all of the Jewish families in Montgomery to urge them "to attend social functions, meet the boys and invite them to their homes," generating large turnouts for JWB functions and great enthusiasm for the home hospitality program. Indeed, the community considered it their "patriotic duty to boost our soldiers' morale." When Orthodox soldiers requested kosher meals, the JWB "extended to the boys home hospitality on Friday evening and Sunday noon in homes observing the dietary laws" because Montgomery had no kosher restaurant. The JWB, however, received few such requests. During the holidays, Montgomery families not only hosted servicemen from Maxwell and Gunter but also took in Jewish servicemen from Craig Field in Selma and Camp Rucker in Dothan. Moreover, many of these families opened their doors to Gentile soldiers who accompanied their Jewish friends to the "At Homes." A soldier stationed at Gunter Field observed that this "permitted the Gentile fellows who were sorely in the need of social contact to get a glimpse and an impression of Jewish life, which otherwise may not have been afforded them. I know all too well that lasting impressions are made by soldiers in the Army, and any kindness shown them leaves a lasting imprint on their impressionable minds." The JWB, in fact, operated on a nonsectarian basis and encouraged inviting Gentile soldiers into Jewish homes, a practice that Montgomery's Jews embraced.[43]

The success of many of the USO programs, whether the JWB's programs, the NCCS's, or the YMCA's, relied heavily upon organizing and recruiting girls to attend, as male-only events drew significantly fewer soldiers. The JWB maintained a mailing list of all the Jewish girls in Montgomery and the surrounding area, and Tasgal "sent a weekly card containing the activities scheduled for the following week." He also tried to organize the approximately fifty Jewish girls in Montgomery under one organization in order "to have a suitable representation at all [USO] functions." Such organization, however, proved difficult to accomplish as the social and cultural rift between the Jewish subcommunities prevented such cooperation. Instead, Junior Hadassah organized a Soldiers Service Squad, while girls at the Reform-dominated Standard Club formed the Standard Sorority "to care for the religious, social and recreational needs of Jewish officers." Both organizations sponsored dances that became the most well-attended events the Jewish community hosted. Events of any size, however, often took place at the Standard Club because the Jewish community lacked any other place to host large gatherings, such as a dedicated JWB center. Although this offered a larger venue for such occasions—the Standard Club allowed the JWB to host bimonthly dances at the clubhouse—the men preferred dances held at either Agudath Israel or Temple Beth-Or. These buildings could hold only about fifty to sixty soldiers, but the smaller number meant a more evenly distributed male-female ratio where the men could "dance without having someone cut in." Other female organizations contributed to the JWB effort as well, such as the Tau Gamma Nu sorority, from which a small number of members created an active Hospital Visitation Committee.[44] The Jewish soldiers appreciated the girls' efforts. In December 1942, they hosted a Girls Appreciation dance at Temple Beth-Or in honor of those who had been "active in all JWB activities."[45]

Not everyone was pleased by the abundance of activities. The chairman of the JWB council, Myron Lobman, had "heard comments to the effect that the JWB is giving too many affairs, which keeps girls from attending the dances given at the USO club." The YMCA-USO center served the majority of white servicemen in the Montgomery area, and female presence was in great demand; however, not just anyone could attend the events at the USO club. Girls had to have two recommendations in order to be "accredited" by the USO club hostess and receive passes to the events. As more Jewish soldiers began to frequent the center, the director requested more Jewish girls attend the events. As a result, Lobman advised Tasgal that "every effort should be made to have a good representation of Jewish girls at the USO dances." Lobman had long opposed purely Jewish social activities and wanted the JWB to incorporate their activities with the YMCA. He worried that the numerous JWB events "are bound to cause prejudice" toward the Jewish community. Most Jewish girls did not frequent the YMCA-USO center, and Tasgal noted the difficulty in trying to convince the Jewish girls to attend the USO dances. Doing away with popular JWB socials, he reasoned, would not increase Jewish participation at the USO club.[46]

There is no evidence of the prejudice that Lobman feared, but his concern that the JWB avoid being seen as too Jewish, or his concern over Tasgal's lack of familiarity with southern racial customs, led to a contentious relationship between the two. Tasgal had voiced his opinion that the USO board should have an African American representative, due to the existence of a black USO center in Montgomery, and Lobman worried that Tasgal would create problems for the Jewish community if he became too outspoken on racial issues. Moreover, Lobman believed that Tasgal, who was Orthodox, favored the group from Agudath Israel and Etz Ahayem in the JWB activities. More likely, Tasgal's energetic and ambitious program ran counter to the tentative approach Lobman and many other Reform members favored, and created a less-than-sympathetic attitude on the part of Tasgal toward the Reform group, although no evidence of favoritism exists. A visiting NJWB official noted the poor relationship between Tasgal and Lobman and observed that the "proverbial 'Orthodox-Reform' problem still exists. The former doing the work and the latter giving good lip service." After Tasgal's induction into the navy in late October 1943, Lobman again wanted to "look over" his replacement, even suggesting that Bernard C. Ehrenreich, the retired former rabbi of Beth-Or, become the new JWB representative. After Tasgal's departure, Lena Schulwolf directed all of the JWB activities in Montgomery until a new JWB representative could be found.[47]

As the war progressed, and without an efficacious JWB representative, community enthusiasm for such an energetic program lagged, as it did throughout the nation, leading to a reduced effectiveness in the JWB program. Each community experienced its own particular difficulties that contributed to this lack of effectiveness, whether through community dysfunction or the loss of an effective JWB director to the service. Moreover, simple fatigue from continually hosting and participating in social functions contributed greatly to the lack of enthusiasm for JWB programming, and more than likely adversely affected other USO programs as well. These smaller Jewish communities in Montgomery, Dothan, Anniston, or elsewhere across the nation, had fewer members and resources to rely upon, but correspondingly greater responsibility because no other USO agency could provide to Jewish servicemen what the JWB program offered, and the JWB was unable to function properly without the support and contribution of the local Jewish community.

To generate renewed enthusiasm, the Montgomery section NCJW "adopted" as their special project the home hospitality program that had fallen into decline. Even so, Montgomery continued to experience difficulties that hampered its ability to function as a community. Paul W. Aron replaced Tasgal as JWB representative in late 1943 and immediately commented on the Orthodox-Reform divide. Aron observed that JWB "activities follow along the lines of this divergence, respective committees handling the two main affairs, the Sunday Social and the Wednesday night dance . . . it will take some time to bridge the gap between theory and practice."[48] A national JWB official characterized Montgomery's Jewish community as not "enterprising or cooperative" despite their willingness to serve the troops. Aron and a subsequent JWB representative, however, failed to carry on an organized and effective program. By the end of the war, there was not enough work in Montgomery for a full-time JWB director as both Maxwell and Gunter had only approximately four hundred Jewish men.[49]

Selma

Fifty miles to the west of Montgomery, the community of Selma played host to the men of the newly established Craig Army Air Field. The city council created a Selma–Dallas County Defense Recreation Committee in the summer of 1941 to provide recreational opportunities for the men stationed at Craig. A Soldiers Club had been on the second and third floors of the YMCA building downtown, which the WPA operated from August 1941 until July 1942, when the USO assumed responsibility for the recreational program.[50] Just as Blachschleger led the initial JWB operations in Montgomery, Rabbi

Samson H. Levey of the Reform Temple Mishkan Israel directed the Jewish community's efforts in Selma. In fact, city leaders tapped Levey to serve as the campaign chairman for the USO fund-raising drive even before the JWB had been organized in Selma. Levey ministered to the Jewish men at Craig Field, the number of which fluctuated between 200 and 250 throughout the war. Selma's NCJW also assisted Levey, with members frequently serving as hostesses at the socials sponsored by Mishkan Israel. Selma had a Jewish Club, but the club had no recreational facilities. The temple's community center only held about one hundred, so the small Reform congregation used the YMCA building when it had too many men to accommodate, such as during the High Holy Days.[51]

By May 1942, the JWB had established a presence in Selma. Maxwell Tasgal oversaw the JWB activities from his office in Montgomery, but he relied heavily on Levey and the newly formed Army and Navy Committee to organize the recreational events and conduct the home hospitality program. They utilized the temple's community center and also hosted socials at the YMCA Soldiers Center once a month. The size of the JWB program in Selma paled in comparison to programs in either Montgomery or Anniston, but the Selma JWB committee made every effort to meet the needs of the Jewish servicemen in their care. They faced two significant, but not uncommon, problems carrying out their program, however. The first problem, which numerous JWB committees experienced, resulted from the lack of Jewish girls in Selma. Although Jewish servicemen at Craig attended dances and socials at the YMCA-USO center in Selma, no purely Jewish coed dance could be offered by the JWB, as they frequently were in Montgomery. As a result, the Army and Navy Committee tried to arrange for young women from Birmingham to travel to Selma. When this proved unworkable, they instead took the men from Craig Field to dances at the Standard Club in Montgomery. Different religious traditions between the majority of Orthodox servicemen at Craig and the Reform Rabbi Levey constituted the second problem. Since Craig Field had no Jewish chaplain, Levey held services on base every Friday evening. A number of the Orthodox men expressed their dissatisfaction with the services the rabbi conducted, although Levey tried to offer "compromise" services that appealed to both the Reform and Orthodox tradition. As a concession to the observant Orthodox soldiers, Levey allowed them to use the temple every Friday evening where they conducted their own service, prompting one of the concerned soldiers to "write to his mother, who is extremely orthodox, to tell her things are coming along fine." Despite these problems, Selma's Jewish community contributed significantly to the welfare of the Jewish men at Craig Field. In fact, Tasgal commended them on doing an "excellent job" and frequently held up the Selma JWB committee as a "fine example" to the often discordant Montgomery JWB Council.[52]

Mobile

One element of Mobile's rapid growth during the war years was the establishment of Brookley Army Air Field. The Army Air Corp purchased the Bates Field municipal airport in 1938, renamed it Brookley Field, and used it as a maintenance base and an Air Material Command that supplied air bases around the nation. During World War II, the army had eight thousand men stationed at Brookley, including three thousand African American soldiers. In addition to the soldiers, Brookley employed approximately seventeen thousand civilians, making it Mobile's largest single employer.[53] Both the Orthodox Ahavas Chesed and the Reform Congregation Sha'arai Shomayim attempted to meet the needs of the approximately one to two hundred Jewish soldiers at Brookley. The Orthodox congregation entertained soldiers at the Jewish Progressive Club while the Reform members hosted socials at the expansive Government Street Temple. Both synagogues provided services and *oneg shabbat* to the men. Yet their unwillingness to work together ultimately harmed the effectiveness of their respective programs, such as when soldiers failed to appear for community events planned for Passover in 1942. The failure of the events led to severe disappointment among the community members, but Sha'arai Shomayim's rabbi, Sidney Berkowitz, admitted later that a lack of communication between the Jewish community and Brookley Field was to blame as "no letter had been written to the Post Commandant in relation to the holidays." Moreover, a soldier at Brookley observed that both the Orthodox and Reform groups "are very inactive as far as a planned program goes. They may have a periodic spree but this is shortlived because they do not plan ahead or work in a very organized fashion. If they get lectured they feel ashamed and respond but this is not the way the things should be run. . . . What they need are people who are willing to work, ideas, and a little initiative. New blood might do the trick."[54]

While "new blood" in Mobile's Jewish leadership was not in the offing, Sha'arai Shomayim experienced significant turnover during the war. Rabbi Berkowitz, who had arrived in Mobile in mid-1940, volunteered for the army as a chaplain, causing great consternation among the congregation's leaders. Bernard Eichold, the congregation president, worried what the rabbi's departure would do to the congregation. Previous to Berkowitz's arrival, Sha'arai Shomayim "had almost disintegrated from apathy and factional quarrels,"

Eichold told the CCAR's Committee of Chaplains. "During the two years that this Rabbi has been the leader of this congregation, he has welded the membership together and infused new enthusiasm and vigor into the religious life of the Jewish community. Should he leave now, the entire structure might collapse. Would the US Army still want him to volunteer under these circumstances?" Bernard Brickner of the CCAR remarked that "if we lose this war, no congregation will be stabilized and integrated. The morale of our men in the army is of infinitely greater importance than that of maintaining one or two congregations."[55] After Berkowitz departed, Bertram Wallace Korn assumed the pulpit at Sha'arai Shomayim in January 1943, until he, too, departed for the army after less than a year in Mobile. Although the departures caused a certain dislocation within the Reform community, both Berkowitz and Korn provided such energetic leadership at the temple that Sha'arai Shomayim did not collapse as Eichold had feared.

In predominantly Catholic Mobile, the NCCS had established two recreation centers, the USO Club for Soldiers and the USO Women's Club. In fact, Mobile had no USO advisory council, only the NCCS. Jewish servicemen stationed at Brookley numbered too few to warrant a full-time JWB director. Instead, Milton D. Kulick oversaw operations in Mobile from his JWB office in Biloxi, Mississippi. He thought it imperative "to organize the community efforts so that the cleavage between the Orthodox and Reform groups could be reduced." Due to Kulick's advice, the Orthodox and Reform groups formed a Mobile JWB Army and Navy Committee in November 1942. Kulick strongly urged the national JWB to support this endeavor: "It cannot be over-emphasized that one of the most important by-products of the Mobile Army and Navy Committee, if it transpires will be the unification of this community and to this end, as much assistance as we can render is indicated." The Army and Navy Committee did indeed work together, increasing communication not only between the Jewish community and the authorities at Brookley but also within the Jewish community itself. In lieu of a dedicated JWB facility, the committee began using a large room on the second floor of the Government Street Temple as a day room for the servicemen, agreeing that it would serve as "common ground" for both the Orthodox and Reform members. The Jewish Progressive Club even donated a Sefer Torah to Brookley Field in the name of the JWB Army and Navy Committee. The committee also agreed that "all publicity and all activities . . . would be issued in the name of the Mobile Jewish Welfare Board Army and Navy Committee," a positive indication, Kulick observed, "that the ties will draw the dissident factors closer together. . . . In the process of working together, I am sure that much in common will develop and reunion will eventually result." The cooperation did not unify the community as Kulick had hoped, but despite the divide that remained between the Reform and Orthodox congregations they worked together through the Mobile JWB Army and Navy Committee and willingly aided those servicemen stationed in the area.[56]

Dothan

One month after the bombing of Pearl Harbor, the US Army began construction on the Ozark Triangular Division Camp, later named Camp Rucker, located between the Wiregrass towns of Ozark, Dothan, and Enterprise. One wit described the southeastern Alabama installation as being "about 1400 miles south of Wrightstown [New Jersey] and 3 miles north of hell."[57] Originally built to serve thirty-five thousand men, the camp grew rapidly after it officially opened in May 1942, surpassing its planned capacity by the end of the year. The three thousand airmen at Napier Army Air Field in Dothan seemed almost insignificant compared to the large number of servicemen stationed at Rucker.[58]

The small number of Jewish families in the Dothan area limited the effectiveness of the community's efforts to provide adequate recreational opportunities for approximately seventeen hundred Jewish soldiers stationed at Napier Field and Camp Rucker by late 1942. Jews never resided in the region in great numbers and had only established themselves in the Dothan area in 1890. After roughly forty years of unorganized worship in private homes, Dothan's Jews formed Temple Emanu-El in 1929. A number of families moved away during the Depression, causing the congregation to become inactive. By 1938, Jews in the Dothan region began to reorganize because "Hitler and the rising wave of persecution in Europe aroused new consciousness of their religion," which led to the reactivation of the congregation in December 1938. By 1941, Emanu-El's congregants had completed a new synagogue and hired Alfred Wolf as their first full-time rabbi.[59]

Emanu-El served as the home congregation for all thirty-three Jewish families in the area, including eleven families in Marianna and Panama City, Florida, who had similar responsibilities pertaining to the Marianna Army Air Field and Tyndall Army Air Field, respectively. The temple opened its doors to those in uniform, and Rabbi Wolf traveled to the various bases in the region, including Marianna and Tyndall Fields, to conduct weekly services and visit the infirm. Such effort came at significant expense as Wolf expended his time and congregational funds to do so. Wolf's friend, Rabbi Louis I. Egelson of the Union of American Hebrew Congregations, observed that "it is too great a burden on a Jewish community of forty or fifty members to provide the funds necessary for the regular entertainment of Jewish soldiers in the vicinity of the community."[60]

At Wolf's behest, the Jewish community formed the Dothan Army and Navy Committee in January 1942 to prepare for the large number of men expected at Camp Rucker, despite the fact that the JWB had not yet been established in Dothan. Because Wolf had been doing JWB work without any formal recognition, Emanu-El's president, Ike Rimson, petitioned the JWB to grant Wolf an honorarium above his expenses, explaining that "the small salary which this young congregation is paying the Rabbi is hardly adequate for the regular work which he is doing for us." Numerous congregations asked the JWB for an honorarium for their rabbi, but the policies of the National JWB Committee on Army and Navy Religious Activities prevented any subsidy beyond expenses incurred in JWB work from being granted, explaining that "rabbis with congregations and annual salaries should only receive expenses in connection with services on behalf of men in the armed forces."[61] However much the JWB wanted to assist Wolf and Emanu-El, they too were stretched thin in both resources and manpower, and financial assistance to rabbis across the nation, above and beyond reimbursements for expenses, was far more than they could afford to do. Because of this, the JWB considered rabbinical work with the troops, whether by Wolf in Dothan or Blachschleger in Montgomery, to be done on a volunteer basis only. Wolf and the congregation pressed on, even when their responsibilities to the Jewish servicemen seemed too much for such a tiny community.[62]

Wolf played a central role in how Dothan's Jews responded to the challenges presented during the war, explaining to the JWB that "in this small Jewish community everybody works together. . . . Since the community is young and inexperienced in Jewish organizational work they usually rely on their rabbi to assign specific tasks to them."[63] While the congregation may have been young and inexperienced, so too was Wolf, who had accepted the position at Emanu-El just after his ordination at Hebrew Union College in 1941. Wolf had been born in Eberbach, Germany, in 1915, and had attended Berlin's Institute for Jewish Studies before taking part in an exchange program with Hebrew Union College in 1935. At the time, he did not recognize that the exchange program "was the first organized attempt to get Jewish people trained in religion out of Germany," but Wolf later credited the program and Hebrew Union College's president, Julian Morgenstern, with saving his life.[64] What Wolf and Emanu-El lacked in experience, they made up for with enthusiasm, hosting the troops at the temple for Friday evening services and receptions, organizing community seders, and opening their homes to the men on weekends, although their small numbers made it impossible to conduct a home hospitality program for everyone but a select few servicemen.[65]

For the first few months of 1942, Dothan's Jewish community, and particularly Wolf, had to proceed without the assistance of the JWB. The FSA, not the USO, directed recreational activities in the Dothan area, which included Ozark and Enterprise, and the WPA operated the Soldiers Center in Ozark and the Dothan Recreational Center, two facilities wholly unsuited to deal with the tens of thousands of men flooding into Rucker monthly. The USO could not enter a community except when that community could not cope with the recreational problems the increasing soldier population brought about, nor could the USO "impose [itself] on a community if it desires to operate its soldiers center." Without the agreement of the FSA and the formal request of community leaders, the USO was barred from Dothan, a situation that greatly affected the Jewish community as they could only receive JWB professional and monetary assistance if Dothan requested USO services. Initially, leaders in Ozark and Dothan strongly opposed the USO because they feared the loss of federal funds in connection with the FSA. After being assured that this would not occur and with pressure applied by state politicians, Ozark's mayor and Dothan's city commission voted unanimously to extend an invitation to the USO to begin operations in the area.[66]

Despite the acceptance of the USO by local politicians in Dothan, who really had little choice since the sheer numbers of men at Camp Rucker threatened to overwhelm the small community of twenty thousand, two organizations maintained an "aggressive opposition" to the USO. The WPA, which continued to operate its Soldiers Centers in Ozark and Dothan, feared that once the USO established its presence, that "their Center will be closed off, and so they are doing everything possible to undermine the position of the USO in the community." The local ministerial alliance also voiced its opposition because two minority agencies, the NCCS and JWB, had been selected to jointly administer the USO center that had been planned for Dothan. The criticism by this "narrow Protestant group," as Wolf referred to them, contributed to a growing community resentment against the USO, as rumors circulated that "the Catholics and Jews are going to open the Center and make a profit out of running the Center." Even with the anti-semitic implication in such a rumor, this resentment targeted the Catholics more so than the Jews. Throughout Alabama, with the exception of the city of Mobile, local officials, churches, and even other USO agencies detested working with the dogmatic and uncooperative NCCS.[67] This antipathy toward working with the NCCS seems to have been caused by the intransigence of the Catholic agency rather than any explicit anti-Catholicism, although certainly anti-Catholic prejudice cannot be discounted. Moreover, neither JWB officials' and Jewish community leaders' responses, nor the sources, suggest that bigotry colored Jewish attitudes toward the NCCS. On the contrary, Jews frequently had to contend with antisemitism on the part of Catholic leaders and NCCS representatives, especially the virulent antisemite Father Arthur Terminiello who directed the NCCS in Anniston after his transfer in 1945.[68]

Even after the USO had been invited into the Dothan area in July 1942, it took more than six months for a USO center to be constructed, causing community leaders and army authorities to become impatient with their lack of progress. By October 1942, Rucker's commander limited the men's access to Dothan, attributing his decision to the city's inability to assimilate such a large number of men, although an "abnormal increase in venereal disease" among the soldiers also contributed to the decision.[69] The army only lifted the restrictions when the USO center and the American Legion canteen and dorms had been completed in January 1943. Until the center opened, the NCCS's Alexander Hogarty, the director of the USO in Dothan, refused to create any recreation programs for the men, increasing community resentment toward the USO. Moreover, he did not want to cooperate with the new JWB representative, Saul S. Elgart, and refused to participate in a joint program with the JWB unless the NCCS explicitly directed him to do so. Hogarty's reluctance to offer anything resembling a USO program meant only the JWB offered any sort of USO program for the area's servicemen, but with extremely limited resources. This situation meant that the JWB became the face of the USO, putting Dothan's Jewish community "in the position of acting as buffers between the general community and the USO," a position they certainly did not relish.[70] Hogarty's lack of leadership, and the resulting strain between the NCCS and the JWB, caused the Jewish community to lose interest in the USO, although not in the JWB.

When Elgart arrived in Dothan in September 1942 as the new JWB representative, he served not only the Dothan area but also Marianna, Panama City, and Tallahassee, Florida. The main focus of his efforts, however, remained in Dothan, working with the local community and the growing number of Jewish servicemen at Camp Rucker. The Dothan JWB Army and Navy Committee had functioned ineffectively since its creation, but Elgart and Wolf reorganized it and gave it "a definite program to follow." In fact, Elgart noted that the community "is anxious to cooperate and do the job but has simply needed direction," something Wolf noted months earlier. The

Army and Navy Committee in other cities normally carried out the bulk of JWB work, but in Dothan it served "only as a planning body. Whenever any work has to be done, you call on the entire Jewish community of 19 families to aid you."[71]

Providing recreation for the Jewish soldiers at Rucker and Napier, even in the best of times, could be daunting given the limited resources available. For the soldiers themselves, the lack of recreational opportunities, in addition to being in rural southeast Alabama, was even more frustrating. Corporal Herbert Kahn's company, which consisted of numerous northern Jews largely from New York, found great difficulty in adjusting to the climate and culture in southeast Alabama. Kahn observed that "all these boys down here are from the north, over a thousand miles from their homes and their past environments. They're new to the army. . . . My first months were spent near home, with people not totally different from those to whom I had been accustomed. Down here the problem is entirely different. Not only must these rookies accustom themselves to the army itself—but to the country, the climate—the natives!"[72] The "natives" at Temple Emanu-El, in conjunction with Elgart's JWB program, attempted to make the adjustment easier for the men. Events included Sunday open house at the temple, continued home hospitality for the men, and socials following the Friday evening services at Emanu-El. The JWB used the temple's facilities for events, but Emanu-El's congregation imposed severe restrictions on those events, forbidding dancing, piano playing, "or any other type of social activity not in keeping with good Baptist rules."[73] Dothan's Jewish community had no young women to attend the socials, nor were any Jewish girls located within one hundred miles of Dothan, limiting the JWB program out of necessity. That did, however, solve the problem of dancing at the temple. The city of Dothan did not prohibit dancing per se, but the Protestant fundamentalist culture prevalent in the region certainly did not condone it. Instead, Elgart and Wolf frequently hosted events such as record concerts, amateur movie nights, talent shows, and Simchas Torah Parties, events that averaged about 125 in attendance. In a memorable April 1944 event, Emanu-El and the JWB sponsored a Passover seder at Camp Rucker in which approximately one thousand people from Rucker, Napier, and Emanu-El attended. The event was so large that German prisoners of war from the adjacent POW camp were pressed into service. As a member of Emanu-El commented, "it was, perhaps, poetic justice that German prisoners of war were placed at their disposal for the celebration of our Festival of Freedom."[74] The events that Emanu-El offered in conjunction with the JWB were run as USO events, and therefore open to anybody, although Jewish servicemen constituted the majority of participants.

After the opening of the USO center in January 1943, larger socials and dances could be held, although the lack of girls—not just Jewish girls, but any girls—made the success of such events more difficult. The longer-established WPA Dothan Recreation Center had a stranglehold on girls in the vicinity; it had organized them as the Victory Belles, further adding to the USO's difficulty. Elgart lamented that the "scarcity of girls as dancing partners and the primitiveness of the communities surrounding Camp Rucker make the holding of a mass dance an almost impossible objective. What in a large city would be an ordinary dance, in this area becomes a tremendous undertaking."[75] Even as the JWB and the NCCS worked together at the USO center, the two operated in an entirely different fashion. The JWB worked closely with the Jewish community and Emanu-El's Wolf, creating a distinctive program of numerous Jewish-only events, in addition to the jointly operated USO events. The NCCS, on the other hand, operated solely as the USO, with no agency commitment whatsoever. It did not offer Catholic-only events such as a Communion Breakfast. It is difficult to determine why this was the case concerning the NCCS and the Catholic community in Dothan, but it is most certainly the case that Rabbi Wolf's leadership and the Jewish community's desire to serve the men in uniform contributed to an enthusiastic, albeit limited, JWB program.

By far the most successful JWB-USO event occurred on June 26, 1944, when Molly Picon visited Camp Rucker on a USO tour. Picon, the "Darling of the Yiddish theater," had earned international acclaim for her performances in film, radio, and on stage.[76] Between fifteen hundred and two thousand men attended the concert, the largest group to attend an event at Camp Rucker. Israel H. Mistovsky, who succeeded Elgart as Dothan JWB director, estimated that "nearly every Jewish boy who was off that evening attended the performance," in addition to the approximately seven hundred non-Jews in attendance. Although Mistovsky raved about the popularity of the concert, not everything went as planned. "The songs that Miss Picon sang certainly could not be considered as part of a Jewish educational program," he complained, adding that "some of her numbers belonged in burlesque," not a surprising complaint given Picon's theatrical background. Mistovsky warned the JWB that her act definitely should not appear "in a program sponsored by a Servicemen's Religious Council that sought cooperation from the chaplain's office. . . . Some of the chaplains present were definitely offended, and with good reason. One need not be a Puritan to have felt as so many people did." While Mistovsky and the chaplains might have been offended—there is no record of Rabbi Wolf's response—it is apparent that the men were not, as Picon said that they were "the most receptive group of people before whom she appeared."[77]

Birmingham

Birmingham's Jews responded like other communities around the country, contributing their time, energy, and money to support the morale and material interests of the men and women in the service of their country. Birmingham's United Jewish Fund, besides acting as the organization coordinating aid to Jews in Europe, helped community members locate missing relatives, advised people how to ship goods overseas, and kept track of the city's Jews who served in the armed forces. Birmingham's Jewish community opened the YMHA to the soldiers, and the center served as the main recreational facility for Jewish servicemen from nearby Fort McClellan, Camp Sibert, and even Maxwell and Gunter Fields in Montgomery, who came to the city on weekend leave. The Ladies Auxiliary of K'nesseth Israel, the Jewish War Veterans Auxiliary, Junior Hadassah and Senior Hadassah, the Birmingham section NCJW, Temple Beth-El Sisterhood, Temple Emanu-El Sisterhood, and Bessemer's Temple Beth-El Sisterhood alternated sponsoring weekly socials for the men at the YMHA on the weekends. The Jewish War Veterans Auxiliary, for instance, had over two hundred members who volunteered, visiting hospitals from Tuscaloosa to Anniston to minister to the recovering servicemen.[78] At Camp Sibert they served refreshments after Emanu-El's Rabbi Grafman or Beth-El's Rabbi Mesch offered services on base. Birmingham's Jewish War Veterans and the Council of Jewish Women hosted numerous programs at Fort McClellan, young girls traveled to Anniston for JWB dances, and even the Jewish socialist fraternal organization, the Workmen's Circle, donated clothes to war refugees in Eastern Europe.[79] Indeed, the three congregations, and virtually every Jewish organization in the city, lent support to one wartime endeavor or another.

Benjamin Roth, the director of Birmingham's YMHA, played a key role in the coordination of all of the recreational efforts for the men and women in uniform, working with JWB directors and supporting activities throughout the state and directing Birmingham's home hospitality program. The YMHA also served as the JWB headquarters in the city. In 1917 the YMHA and the Young Women's Hebrew Association (YWHA) had combined their resources to form the JWB to support Jewish military personnel in World War I. After the war, the JWB continued its operations and in 1921 became the governing body for all of the Jewish community centers, including the YMHA and YWHA. Because of this, Roth and the Birmingham YMHA remained heavily involved in serving the Jewish servicemen in the city and in surrounding towns, even before the involvement of the USO. Only in mid-1942 did the city of Birmingham request the USO to step in as the central organization for soldier morale and recreation to replace its badly run city operation. Birmingham had close to five thousand soldiers stationed at the Birmingham Air Base, and hundreds, if not thousands, of soldiers visiting on the weekends, but JWB-USO officials thought that "there is no serious need for [the] USO in a city the size of Birmingham which can absorb a large number of soldiers" if not for the small and inefficient operation already in existence. Although the YMCA became the central operating agency, JWB continued to operate out of the YMHA.[80]

At Temple Emanu-El, Rabbi Grafman began a newsletter called the *Serviceman* in 1943 to keep in contact with his parishioners in the military and boost their morale. He used the bimonthly, four-page newsletter as a "clearing house for news of Emanu-El service men" and a "medium of contact between our boys and [the] congregation."[81] Grafman later said that those "boys [in the service] . . . are the congregation of tomorrow. If they were in town they'd be in the Temple but I can send my services to them abroad and make any foxhole a bit of Birmingham." By doing this, Grafman became what he described as a "chaplain behind the lines, a rabbi [who] would dedicate 24 hours of every 24 to the war front at home."[82] The *Serviceman* became Grafman's and Emanu-El's most direct contribution to supporting the troops. His extensive experience with the Hillel groups in Kentucky certainly helped to foster a strong bond with the young men of Emanu-El, but Grafman also took seriously his responsibilities as the leader of his congregation, and he had, even at his young age, a well-developed sense of moral and civic duty. The *Serviceman* was but a manifestation of this duty.

Initially, Grafman intended the *Serviceman* to be for those in the armed forces, but the first few issues had such a wealth of information about the men that all of the families at Emanu-El as well as friends began requesting copies. Shortly after its initial appearance, other congregations throughout the United States requested copies and sought advice on starting a similar newsletter for their members.[83] Not surprisingly, those in the service enjoyed it the most. Almost all the letters from Emanu-El soldiers in Grafman's files express their appreciation for, and their anticipation of, receiving the newsletter. By late 1944 the circulation of the *Serviceman* had reached over seven hundred, with 170 of them going to the men and the one woman in the service.

The news about the various Emanu-El men in the service came from soldiers' letters sent either to Grafman or their families, who then shared the news with Grafman. In most issues, the content focused on the soldiers: their whereabouts, exploits, or views about the war, and it also reported the sad news about those killed or missing in action. Frequently, information concerning someone's whereabouts led to a reunion of old friends, whether stationed overseas or stateside. The *Serviceman* also included news about the home front. The Birmingham newspapers allowed Grafman to use their articles in the newsletter, and popular items such as sports columns frequently appeared within its pages. Every issue described the weddings, births, and services that took place in Birmingham since the last issue, including how Emanu-El members contributed to the war effort, such as those training to be registered nurses or the campaign to collect books and magazines for soldiers overseas. In addition to the *Serviceman*, the Sisterhood put together care packages for the men at Grafman's suggestion, and he made sure that they received them, especially on important days such as Hanukkah. The soldiers stationed overseas and stateside, as well as the entire congregation, appreciated the efforts of Grafman and the Emanu-El Sisterhood.

Keeping a record of the Jewish boys in the service fell to Dora Roth, as so many thankless tasks often did. Just as Roth spearheaded Birmingham's refugee work, she also maintained the detailed records of Birmingham's servicemen, which she shared with the JWB's Bureau of War Records (BWR). Roth relied heavily on the three congregations and all of the women's groups for accurate information, and the detailed, time-consuming compilation of information suited her meticulous nature. The importance of the enterprise also made her justifiably proud of her work. After being questioned by BWR officials about the accuracy of her work, she snapped, "I bet there aren't three Jewish men living in Birmingham who have been omitted from my files. If they have, you find them, and I'll eat them. But I am not going to sit down with a city directory listing three hundred and seventy-five thousand individuals just to see if I have missed anybody." Many Jewish communities never knew how many of their members served, despite the concerted efforts of the BWR. Not so for Birmingham, from which 516 members of the Jewish community served in the armed forces. Fourteen of those were killed in action, thirty-nine were wounded, and fifty-eight received awards for meritorious service.[84]

In the Army Now

Jews throughout the state clearly recognized the threat that Nazism posed to Jews worldwide. Moreover, where the revelations of the Nazi mass murders in Europe shocked and dismayed all Jews—indeed, it shocked and dismayed non-Jews as well—it profoundly influenced the perception of their identity as Jews. Rarely had the vulnerability of the Jews to antisemitism been so starkly exposed. Many in Alabama's Jewish community had lost contact with relatives and friends in Europe, and the press's ample coverage of the mass murder of European Jews left little doubt as to the fate of those relatives and friends. To illustrate the stakes the war against Nazi Germany had for Jews, and how Jews should respond to the threat, Rabbi Milton Grafman wrote in the *Serviceman* about a former Emanu-El member in the service, Henry Birnbrey, who had emigrated from Germany in 1938 as part of the GJCA through the sponsorship of the Birmingham section of the NCJW, and he resided in the city for nine months. According to Grafman, Birnbrey went from being a "Hitler victim to American soldier in the cause of freedom," and had "a very personal stake" in the war as his "father and mother died in Germany from the persecution suffered in Hitler's concentration camps."[85]

Prior to and during their service, many of Alabama's Jewish soldiers believed that the war against Nazi Germany had greater meaning, much like Henry Birnbrey. Arthur Prince of Mobile recalled that even "with our limited knowledge about how beastly [the Nazis] were, it still made us hate them. . . . We hated Germany a little more than the average soldier, because again the difference in perspectives by being a Jew, you understood German Jews a little more than somebody of some other background. You knew that those people were suffering simply because they were Jews, like you are."[86] Bill Kirsch, who had arrived in the United States as a refugee in 1940, resettled in Montgomery before joining the army and becoming an American citizen. As he wrote to Edith Weil in 1942, "Since ten o'clock this morning I am a U.S. citizen and mighty proud of it. I never dreamt this would happen to me after only sixteen months in the country. Now I don't mind being sent across [the Atlantic]. In fact I hope that I'll have a chance to send some of the Nazi louses to Valhalla."[87] Norman Niren, a member of Birmingham's Temple Beth-El, served as a radio operator in the Army Air Corps and flew on bombing missions into Germany in 1945. After learning of the murder of millions of Jews, the war became very personal to Niren, who had wanted "to get back at Hitler so bad." On a bombing mission over Berlin, he got his revenge, symbolically at least: "I had to take a number two the worst, and we had some open boxes. . . . I did it in a box and when they opened the bomb bay doors and dropped the bombs, I had on there 'For Hitler Only.'"[88]

Grafman received many letters from Emanu-El's members in the military that not only illustrated this belief as they confronted the horrors of Nazi antisemitism firsthand but also reinforced their identity as Jews. Toward the end of the war, as Harry Boblasky moved through Germany with his company, he and five other Jewish soldiers held a seder the first night of Passover in a small German village with gefilte fish that one had received in a care package from home, matzo rations, and two bottles of wine, which they had "liberated" from the Wehrmacht a few days before. The following evening, Boblasky and his comrades entered Rheydt, the birthplace of Joseph Goebbels, where they held services and another seder with other Jewish troops in the area. Although he described the seder in that location as "an ironic pleasure," Boblasky wrote that he had not seen any synagogues in his trek through France, Belgium, Holland, or Germany, "but before this war is over it is my sincere desire and wish to attend services in one of our Temples in Germany, if only the pillars are left."[89] Another Emanu-El member, Malvin Mayer, also described how the Nazis had destroyed the Jewish population in Europe. He recalled his surprise at seeing a burned-out synagogue upon entering a small German town, and he later learned that over three hundred local Jews had perished. Only one "disabled, beaten seventy-six year old man" remained. Mayer and the twenty-five other Jewish soldiers in his battalion repaired the synagogue and held Friday evening services, although they could not help but notice that "all that remains . . . of its past glory is a broken tablet honoring all those who died fighting for the kaiser." "Ironic, you say," he wrote to his family, "[it is] all too common in this lovely but accursed land."[90] Sam Kayser of Mobile served with the 88th Infantry Division in Italy during the war, and as the only Jew in his outfit, had no opportunity to practice his religion in the field. He became close to three Irish Catholics, and before they went into combat they had "this little Catholic priest who would come [and] set up a little altar and we'd take our hats off. I didn't like taking my steel helmet off and praying, but I sneaked and kind of edged up, thinking it wouldn't hurt." His friends reassured him that it wouldn't "take because I wasn't Catholic." Nor did his Jewishness cause any problems or arouse any resentment. In fact, Kayser only discovered they knew he was Jewish when he overheard others mention it in platoon headquarters. As he recalled, "we'd just come back from some patrol, [and] somebody said, 'Kayser has a lot of guts. Did you know he was Jewish?' And they said, 'No, I didn't know that.' And that was it. It didn't affect me one way or the other. I wasn't going to try to be the only Jew, or Super Jew, or anything."[91]

Both Mayer and Kayser, moreover, were exposed to the horrors of the Holocaust, albeit in a secondhand fashion. Even so, the experience shook both of the men. Mayer's outfit assisted four liberated Polish Jews who related their horrific treatment at the hands of the Nazis. These accounts so impressed him that he described them as "stories that the world should know and yet I hesitate to say them to my own family; they are so horrible."[92] Although Kayser served in Italy for the duration of the war, a member of his platoon visited Mauthausen Concentration Camp in the days after the war ended, and his description of the survivors in the camp left a lasting impression on the Mobilian. "That guy had been in combat a year and a half and he was so shaken," Kayser recalled, "he said he saw these walking skeletons and he couldn't describe it. He was so horrified. That was my brush with the Holocaust."[93]

Yet for Kayser, the revelations of Nazi depravity certainly colored his attitude toward Germans and Germany, an antipathy he described as natural. "All the times we've been to Europe," Kayser said, "I mean it's several times, I've never stepped foot in Germany. I have no desire. Even today, I have an aversion to a German accent." Despite his feelings regarding the Nazis or their persecution of the Jews, Kayser never considered fighting the Germans personal, and he explained that while in combat no one had time for such feelings or thoughts: "When you're up there that long, and you're under those circumstances, you're so tired, you just want to stay alive. . . . You didn't sit around thinking about how much you hated the Germans, you just wanted to be sure one of them didn't kill you. . . . If you got a chance to shoot one of them, [you did]. It's a mentality you get from being in combat for a while. And it doesn't take long. A week or ten days, you're pretty much a veteran, or you're pretty well killed."[94]

Other Jews in Alabama confronted the horror of the Holocaust firsthand. Milton Klein, a member of Sha'arai Shomayim in Mobile, witnessed the aftermath of the Final Solution, arriving at Buchenwald after it had been liberated. "I saw the gas chamber. All of that did exist," he remembered, "it was just about the worst thing I'd ever seen and there was no excuse for it. But they put Jews and Gypsies and anybody else who was opposed to the government, no matter what they were, they all went to concentration camps and they really were death camps. That's what they were. They weren't living camps. They starved them to death or gassed them."[95] Arthur Prince, whose father immigrated to the United States from Romania, attended the Orthodox Ahavas Chesed prior to serving in the army. As Prince's company moved quickly through Germany, he saw no synagogues and no Jews, save for the displaced persons who came to their camp near the French border. As his division fed those in need, Prince was able to communicate with one survivor in Yiddish. After hearing his tragic story of Dachau, Prince gave him his mezuzah.[96] Herman "Dick" Loeb of Montgomery's Temple Beth-Or helped to liberate the work camp at Ludwigslust, near the Elbe River in Germany. Working with the 82nd Airborne, Loeb arrived after the Nazis had vacated the camp, "leaving 250-odd, a few more perhaps, bodies that they didn't have time to bury." Loeb witnessed the barbaric conditions in which the victims had been forced to live and die, a "sickening" experience. His company made the German townspeople gather at the camp where the "chaplain told them it was their fault, they knew about it, and they dug the graves and buried the people."[97]

Roger N. Blum of Birmingham had little contact with the horrors of the Holocaust during his service. He did, however, right an injustice that was all too common during the war, an experience that produced profound satisfaction for his family and himself. Blum grew up in Brumath, France, a small town in the Alsace region. As Europe inched closer to war, his parents urged him to emigrate. In fact, Blum applied for an American visa the day after the Munich Conference ended. By 1939 he had settled in Birmingham, living with his aunt and uncle, Jimmy and Jeanette Hirsh, where he attended Temple Emanu-El. Like many other immigrants, Blum found himself in the army after the United States entered the war in 1941. By 1944, Blum was back in France with General George S. Patton's 3rd Army, an outfit with which he served until shipping back to the United States in late 1945.[98]

During the war, Blum's family, who had not emigrated, avoided deportation to the camps by fleeing Brumath for Vichy, France, living quietly in Nyons for the duration of the war. When they returned to their home in Brumath after the war ended, they discovered that a Nazi official who had been stationed in Brumath had stolen their furniture and most of their possessions. In November 1945, just before returning to the United States, Roger Blum visited his parents in Brumath on a two-week furlough when he learned of the theft. Blum quickly discovered where the man lived and set out to recover his parent's property. "All I had with me was the heavy winter uniform I wore, my tooth brush, comb, and I carried my pistol," Blum recounted. After making his way to the small German village where the man lived, Blum took a local police officer with him as a witness. "The moment I walked in the man's house I recognized the furniture and the good dishes that belonged to us," Blum said, "I walked from room to room and everything I knew was ours I told him 'this does not belong to you, etc.' He wanted to know how I knew, and I told him that all the items belong to my parents and I am confiscating them." Blum's family could not simply enter the American zone in Occupied Germany to retrieve their property without proper clearance, so Jimmy Hirsh contacted Senator Lister Hill who ultimately cleared the way for the Blum's property to be returned.[99]

The revelations of mass killings, and their exposure to the horrific manifestations of Nazi antisemitism and barbarity profoundly affected these Jewish servicemen. Dick Loeb's presence at Ludwigslust and his "horrible experience" in caring for survivors in the days and weeks that followed created a "deep-down dislike, bordering on hatred of the Germans," a common refrain by many of the Jews surveyed in this study.[100] Marks "Bubba" Marcus, also from Temple Beth-Or in Montgomery, knew of the persecution of the Jews prior to the war, but remembers "as a young kid, you didn't pay a lot of attention to it." As a soldier in the Signal Corps during the waning days of the war, Marcus met hundreds of displaced persons and survivors who shuttled through a nearby American hospital and used the opportunity to learn about their experiences: "Some were from Belsen. Some from Auschwitz. . . . It was so sad. You'd try not to hear so many horrible stories . . . you couldn't listen to all of them, you know." The encounters with survivors deeply impressed Marcus and made him much more aware of his Jewish heritage, and much more concerned that it continue. He immediately sent his paychecks to the Montgomery Jewish Federation, the first time he had ever given to the organization. "It probably renewed my interest in being Jewish," he said. "If we are 'the chosen people,' you'd hate to see that tremendous influence of the Jews throughout history end. . . . But as far as God, you wonder sometimes."[101]

Harold Marlowe of Birmingham's Emanu-El experienced Nazi brutality firsthand, not as a liberator, however, but as one of the liberated. After his plane had been shot down while on a bombing run over Italy in mid-1943, Marlowe had been imprisoned in Naples, where he and other members of the crew spent a month in the hospital recovering from their various wounds. Italian authorities paraded the prisoners in front of civilians who jeered and ridiculed them, and then forced them to witness the destruction Allied bombs had caused. If the Italians intended to provoke a sense of guilt in the airmen by showing them the destruction of the raids, they misjudged badly, as Marlowe observed that "we sure did a swell job on it." Transferred to a camp in central Italy, Marlowe eventually escaped and spent over a month evading German troops, staying with numerous friendly Italian families, even helping harvest grapes in appreciation for their assistance. After being wounded trying to cross to American lines, he was finally recaptured, sent to Austria where he received medical aid, and transferred to Stalag Luft IV in Poland where he suffered severe maltreatment at the hands of the Nazi guards.[102]

By February 1945, the Germans forced over eight thousand prisoners to march west to escape the oncoming Soviet army. Marching approximately fifteen to twenty miles each day in freezing conditions, with little to eat or keep them warm, many prisoners perished on the 550-mile trek. Finally liberated by British troops in May, Marlowe had lost sixty pounds after his horrendous ordeal. Recuperating in Germany after the war, Marlowe's observations of the German people dismayed him. His treatment while a prisoner, Marlowe said in June 1945, "did not make me bitter. I expected what I got. It is what I have seen since my liberation that embitters me." The "Hitler spirit," he thought, still resided within the German people, especially the youth. "They are 'civilized' barbarians, and our cigarettes and chocolate bars will not win their gratitude and kindness." This "soft handling" of the German people, Marlowe declared, "is breeding another war."[103] Although Marlowe endured more than most who served, his attitude toward Germans and Germany is consistent with many Jews who held, and in some cases continue to hold, antipathy toward anything German. The myriad of reactions examined in this study mirror the findings of Deborah Dash Moore's *GI Jews* but can also be compared, specifically in regard to the liberation of the camps, to the responses of non-Jews as well.[104]

The soldiers who returned from the war brought back with them experiences that profoundly shaped their outlook and desire to become involved in community affairs. The American Jewish Committee's (AJC) Isaiah Terman observed in early 1946 that young veterans, such as Birmingham's Edward M. Friend Jr., Jerome "Buddy" Cooper, Alfred Swedlaw, and Leroy Monsky, lacked the "influence and prestige" necessary to assume an immediate leadership role but nonetheless had an active interest in community affairs. "Their Jewish consciousness was evidently heightened by recent experiences," Terman remarked, "and they are all eager to make a contribution to the Jewish community. Perhaps, they are also motivated by an urge to assume leadership roles such as they enjoyed in the service."[105] These veterans, whom Grafman referred to as the "congregation of tomorrow," began to assume leadership roles in the postwar period, within the Jewish community and within the larger society.

The Jewish communities in the state had also been profoundly affected by the war and the revelations of the Nazi atrocities. The tragic events in Europe had convinced many in the Reform community that a Jewish state in Palestine was needed, even necessary, but the rift between the German Reform and Eastern European Jews over Zionism did not disappear overnight. It was the leadership of these veterans, whether in Birmingham, Montgomery, Mobile, or smaller towns throughout the state, that helped to usher in changes to their respective communities and eventually mend the rift that remained between the Reform and Orthodox communities.

1. Cartoon by Wilbert Holloway, published in the *Pittsburgh Courier*, November 25, 1933.

2. Anti-Nazi stamps.

3. Cartoon by Hubert Harper, published in the *Birmingham Age-Herald*, September 9, 1938.

4. Cartoon by Hubert Harper, published in the *Birmingham Age-Herald*, March 31, 1933.

5. Cartoon by Henry Brown, published in the *Birmingham World*, January 16, 1945.

6. Cartoon by Jay Jackson, published in the *Birmingham World*, August 7, 1945.

7. Judge Charles S. Feidelson, editor and columnist of the *Birmingham Age-Herald* and *Birmingham News*, courtesy of Birmingham, Alabama, Public Library Archives, Portrait Collection.

8. Rabbi Milton L. Grafman. Grafman became the rabbi of Birmingham's Temple Emanu-El on December 8, 1941, and led the congregation until his retirement in 1975. Courtesy of Stephen W. Grafman, Potomac, Maryland.

9. Hermann and Frieda Berger standing in front of Bendersky's department store in Selma, Alabama, in 1939. The Bergers resettled in Selma in 1938 through the auspices of the National Refugee Service. Photograph courtesy of Hanna Berger, Selma, Alabama.

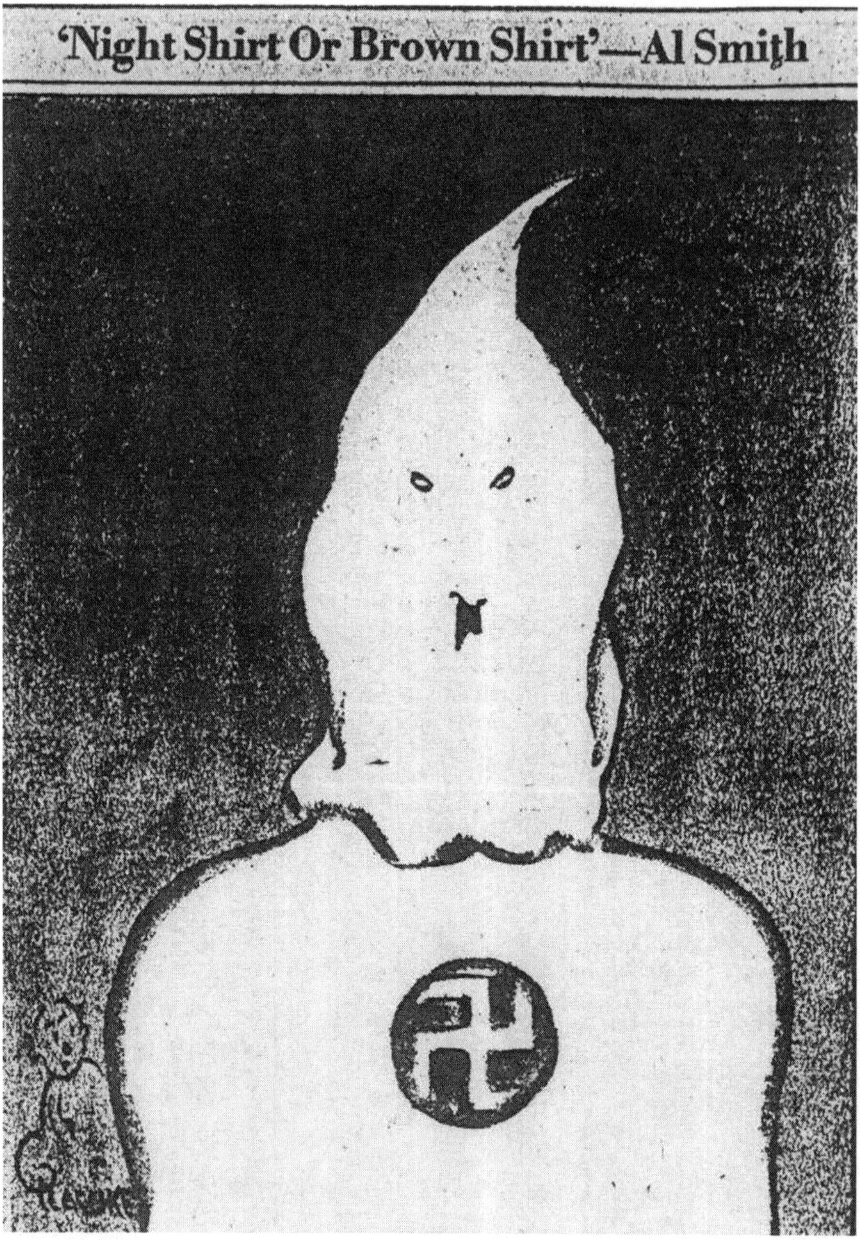

10. Cartoon by Paul Plaschke, published in the *Mobile Register*, April 8, 1933.

11. Rabbi Eugene Blachschleger (center) of Montgomery's Temple Beth-Or with the young ladies of Montgomery's Jewish community and the Jewish airmen from Maxwell and Gunter Fields. Courtesy of the Jacob Rader Marcus Center of the American Jewish Archives, Cincinnati, Ohio. *americanjewisharchives.org.*

12. A "watermelon cutting" for the men of Maxwell and Gunter Fields, sponsored by the Montgomery Jewish Welfare Board. Courtesy of the Jacob Rader Marcus Center of the American Jewish Archives, Cincinnati, Ohio. *americanjewisharchives.org.*

13. Religious service held at Temple Beth-Or, Montgomery, Alabama. Courtesy of the Jacob Rader Marcus Center of the American Jewish Archives, Cincinnati, Ohio. *americanjewisharchives.org*.

14. A day of swimming and relaxation at Montgomery's Oak Park for the men of Maxwell and Gunter Fields. Courtesy of the Jacob Rader Marcus Center of the American Jewish Archives, Cincinnati, Ohio. *americanjewisharchives.org*.

15. Leon Schwarz, member of Congregation Sha'arai Shomayim in Mobile. Courtesy of the Springhill Avenue Temple Archives, Mobile, Alabama.

16. Rabbis Sidney Berkowitz, Stephen S. Wise, and Bertram W. Korn at the Centenary Celebration of Congregation Sha'arai Shomayim, January 23, 1944. Courtesy of the Springhill Avenue Temple Archives, Mobile, Alabama.

17. Benjamin and Dora Roth. Benjamin Roth directed Birmingham's Young Men's Hebrew Association and Dora Roth served as the executive secretary of Birmingham's United Jewish Fund. Courtesy of Mary Kimerling, Birmingham, Alabama.

18. Abe Berkowitz, attorney and Zionist leader in Birmingham. Courtesy of Mary Kimerling, Birmingham, Alabama.

19. Cartoon by Hubert Harper, published in the *Birmingham Age-Herald*, November 18, 1938.

20. Mary Louise and Bert Rosenbush with the Holocaust Memorial in the Demopolis Jewish Cemetery, Demopolis, Alabama. Bert Rosenbush erected the monument at his own expense. Except for inscriptions at Birmingham's Temple Emanu-El and Temple Beth-El, it is the only Holocaust monument in Alabama.

21. Isaac Abelson. Known throughout Birmingham's Jewish community as "Uncle Ike," Abelson, along with his brother Frank, established the first Zionist organization in Alabama in 1898. He was considered "Alabama's original Zionist." Courtesy of Rosalyn Siegal, Birmingham, Alabama.

6
Antisemitism and Racism during the War

Antisemitism had increased noticeably in Alabama during the years preceding the war, driven by the participation of northern Jews in the Scottsboro trials and the antisemitic rhetoric emanating from Nazi Germany, and such bigotry increased after the war began, especially after the American entry. The ongoing racial activism by dissatisfied African Americans, federal antidiscriminatory agencies such as the Fair Employment Practices Committee (FEPC), and anxiety over the war exacerbated both racial suspicion and antisemitism in the state and throughout the South as racial reactionaries quickly pointed to connections between Jews and blacks in either civil rights agitation or interracial endeavors. Moreover, as the Nazi persecution of the Jews increased, transforming into a policy of mass murder by 1941, so too did the awareness of antisemitism in the United States. Although Leonard Dinnerstein notes in his seminal work on American antisemitism, "outbursts of antisemitism were less frequent in the South during the 1940s than they were elsewhere in the country," such bigotry persisted. Because of this, Dinnerstein observes, "southern Jews watched themselves carefully."[1] Such was the case in Alabama where not only did Jews have to worry about local antisemitic activity, which included a Holocaust-denying Catholic priest, but also about the reactions of white racists to African American protests against discrimination.

Birmingham syndicated columnist John Temple Graves, like Grover Hall in Montgomery, worried over the spread of antisemitism, especially when he believed that it had increased in Alabama and his beloved Southland. In January 1939 he wrote that "lately this writer has been shocked to hear several men who look upon themselves as leading citizens and highly civilized human beings express an unblushing antipathy to certain other men for the sole reason they are Jews." Graves wrote in his daily column that these men "are unashamed of their bigotry, their stupidity, their un-Americanism. Consciously or not, they have surrendered to Adolf Hitler."[2] In late 1940 Graves spoke to the Layman's League at St. Mary's Episcopal Church and made similar comments: "how strange that some of those who are considering themselves most patriotic today and associating that patriotism with a new venting of their hatred of the Jewish people, as if the country about which they are being patriotic was not the United States but Germany."[3] By early 1941 Graves noted that "news that Jew-baiting and Jew-hating is on the increase in some parts of the South, including this one, must be making Adolf Hitler very, very happy." He called the "Jew-baiting" in the South "more un-American than anywhere else because there are fewer members of the Jewish race here to make a race problem."[4]

Like many white southerners, Graves was vitally concerned with race and race relations. After it became apparent that the United States was moving toward war, Graves began to argue more strenuously against domestic crusades during a time of crisis, an argument directed specifically against African American demands for civil rights. After a reader suggested that Graves's criticism of "Jew-baiters" amounted to a crusade against antisemitism and called on him to cease discussing the matter, Graves responded by declaring, "Reason totters! That a suggestion for a 'moratorium' on domestic crusades should call for a halt to standing up for the first principles of America is beyond sense," apparently not regarding African American demands for civil rights as "standing up for the first principles of America."[5] Reasoning and American principles, in fact, had little to do with Graves's, and most white southerners', stance toward African Americans. Graves's response simply reflected the willful and intellectually bankrupt disregard that white southerners had for African American aspirations and rights. Moreover, his use of "race" to describe Jews not only demonstrated the confused incoherence of southern racial ideology but also southerners' lazy thinking regarding the subject, much like their dissonance concerning Nazi and southern racism.

Despite Graves's criticism of domestic crusades, there was no coordinated, indigenous movement at the time—either locally or regionally—to promote greater civil rights for African Americans, and apart from the Communists no black leader in the state actively advocated social equality or desegregation prior to the war. White southern liberals like Graves, including a number of Jews who fit into this category, argued for only a gradual extension of civil rights, although not social equality, to worthy blacks. In advocating such ideas, however, they pledged their unwavering support for racial segregation since this idea of Gradualism accepted the belief in the inherent inferiority of blacks and advocated against the application of the Fourteenth and Fifteenth Amendments. Those who went beyond this, such as Rabbi Benjamin Goldstein or white liberal activists Virginia and Clifford

Durr, were either ostracized from polite southern society or forced from the South.

Making the connection between Jews, radicalism, and racial integration came easily to southern white reactionaries who had never forgotten Scottsboro, nor forgiven the defendants' Jewish attorneys for their attempts to overturn the racial status quo. One such individual, Augustus Brenners, a Birmingham attorney and columnist for the white-supremacist *Southern Watchman*, targeted Charles Feidelson, the liberal Jewish editor and columnist for the *Birmingham News* and *Age-Herald*, as part of a "Communistic program" that opposed things such as the poll tax. Brenners characterized Feidelson as part of a group who "cannot pronounce the word 'America' but who lustily sing their anthem about God blessing it, are 'adopted' citizens of this country and are very anxious to become its foster parent. They never had a country of their own, but are full of expedients as to how this one should be run."[6] Although his parents had emigrated from Russia, Feidelson had actually been born in the United States and raised in Georgia. He attended the University of Georgia in Athens, was admitted to the Georgia Bar, and worked as a journalist in North Carolina and Virginia before moving to Alabama in the 1920s.[7] Such details, however, mattered little to people such as Brenners due to Feidelson's liberal leanings, and Brenners's description of Feidelson as a radical or outside agitator was typical of the southern reactionary obsession over race and the maintenance of white supremacy.

Reactionaries such as Brenners often brought tremendous pressure to bear on public officials at the state and local levels, and such demagoguery produced, if not direct results, a *Sturm und Drang* that increased racial and religious tension. This atmosphere, understandably, gave pause to many Jews before supporting issues or enterprises that might suggest agitation against or subversion of the status quo. Jews in Alabama, however, did not advocate black equality, at least not openly. A few rabbis, such as Morris Newfield in Birmingham, openly chastised extremist organizations and advocated that greater educational and economic opportunities be provided for African Americans, but such a position did not challenge the Jim Crow system. Indeed, the example of Goldstein in Montgomery still resonated among the state's Jews, serving as a cautionary example to rabbis who might criticize racial injustice. The majority of Alabama's Jews, like other Jews through the South, remained ambivalent and silent regarding black civil rights.

In Talladega, the close proximity of refugee German and Austrian Jews to African Americans caused the local white community to view the refugee Jewish scholars at Talladega College with tremendous suspicion. Many refugee Jewish scholars, unable to find employment at white universities because of antisemitic hiring practices, found employment at black colleges and universities throughout the South. The three German Jewish refugee scholars in Talladega—five in total, but only three during the war—brought to the college under the auspices of the Committee on Displaced German Scholars, discovered the same discrimination and oppression they had fled in the 1930s, except that in Alabama, blacks, not themselves, comprised the oppressed minority. The immersion of these Jews both physically and intellectually in the culture of the black college community allowed white reactionaries to see that which they wanted to see, particularly after refugee scholar Donald Rasmussen and his wife, Laura, ran afoul of segregation laws by dining with Louis Burnham, a member of the Communist Southern Negro Youth Congress, at an African American restaurant in Birmingham in 1942.[8] The most prominent black school in the state, Tuskegee Institute, did not hire any refugees. When the NRS approached Tuskegee about the placement of Jewish refugee scholars, President Frederick D. Patterson refused on the basis that the school's "unwritten policy since the founding of our work has been that only members of the Negro race should be employed on our staff."[9]

Limited evidence is available concerning African American views of Jews in Alabama during this period because most of Alabama's African American newspapers published during the 1930s are no longer extant. A glimpse into the relationship between the two groups in the state came after the NAACP's *Crisis* published an article on "Jew Hatred among Negroes" in its February 1936 issue. The author claimed that a "by-product" of Nazism "seems to be a great increase in anti-Semitism among Negroes. When one considers that the Nazis have no more, or possibly even less regard for the Negro than the Jew, this becomes a somewhat ironical state of affairs."[10] Mobile resident J. E. Malone, an African American, suggested that the letter's author might be correct about the relationship in the northeast, but not in the South where "the Jew is the Negro's best friend." He also noted that Jews regularly paid black domestic workers well above what whites paid, an assertion many Jewish employers supported.[11] Malone argued that "in the Southland it is the white man who hates the Jew," which he attributed to the "prejudice which exists in the hearts of the southern whites on account of the Jew's economic position here in the South. . . . I feel that the anti-Jewish feeling that exists among my people is small and insignificant and therefore not alarming."[12] Even Ralph Bunche, who visited Alabama and the South frequently in the late 1930s and early 1940s interviewing African Americans for the Carnegie Corporation's study of race relations in the United States, noted the lack of black antisemitism in the Alabama communities he visited.

The affinity between blacks and Jews, of which Malone describes, did not prevent African Americans from requesting from Jewish merchants the same considerations white customers enjoyed. In late 1938 the Mobile NAACP pressed the Jewish-owned Hammel Department Store to include restrooms for its black customers. When Hammel refused to do so, citing the fact that southern department stores did not provide such facilities for blacks, John L. LeFlore, the head of the Mobile NAACP, replied that "even if such were true in many instances it certainly cannot justify an identical attitude. . . . Two wrongs cannot make right." LeFlore pointed out that Hammel enjoyed "a more lucrative colored patronage than the average department store," and providing such facilities would only increase African American patronage. But LeFlore also appealed to the commonalities that he perceived between southern blacks and Jews when he addressed Hammel's owner, Berney L. Strauss: "Anti-Semitic waves of oppression are spreading extensively in other parts of the world. We have been sympathetic toward the Jewish people in their struggles to combat such intolerance and bigotry. Thousands of thoughtful colored people throughout the United States have contributed to efforts aimed to alleviate the plight of Jewry. We are bewildered that a member of one oppressed group, because of favorable geographical and other conditions, would be unsympathetic and recalcitrant in regard to the rights of another persecuted minority."[13] Although LeFlore indicated in his letter that the NAACP would advocate boycotting the store unless restroom facilities were built for black customers, this does not appear to be motivated by antisemitism. Conversely, his appeal to Strauss suggests, at least for LeFlore, a common bond between blacks and Jews that should unite the two groups rather than set them apart.

The state's black press wrote little about the Jews, and when it did mention them, it often was in connection with the antisemitic persecutions and racial worldview of the Nazis. The only example of black anti-Jewish sentiment in the state's black press can be found in the *Birmingham World* in early 1941. The *World* published a guest editorial from the *Cincinnati Independent*, which wrote: "Under Hitler, no Jew may obtain the economic status of the poorest 'Aryans.' This is no brief for the Jews, many of whom are responsible for some part of our oppressions. But would Hitler be less harsh on a race which he considers even lower than the Jews?"[14] While it is arguable that this does not represent southern black antisemitism, as it originated from an Ohio black newspaper, it nonetheless did appear on the editorial page of the *Birmingham World*.

During the war years, the charged racial atmosphere made even influential, acculturated Jews extremely wary of how they and their community could be perceived. For instance, as the debate over immigration, refugees, and the White Paper raged in 1944, Milton Fies, vice president of DeBardeleben Coal Company and a member of Birmingham's Temple Emanu-El, refused to endorse Tuskegee's United Negro College Fund (UNCF) campaign, despite his previous support for African American education. Fies told Tuskegee's President Patterson that there were already a "sufficient number of men of Hebraic religious affiliation on [the] committee," referring to Joseph Loveman and Louis Pizitz, both successful Birmingham merchants who served on the UNCF committee. Fies, one of the most prominent Jews in Alabama's business community, clearly understood that too much Jewish support for African American endeavors, or any interracial group for that matter, would only confirm southern Gentiles' perception of Jews as agitators. Indeed, any action or stance that might emphasize the Jews' "otherness" in a land of rigid conformity, or call into question the Jew's already-suspect loyalty to the status quo, caused tremendous anxiety for prosperous Jews in the South. Fies also cited the "considerable anti-Semitic feeling in the United States and particularly in the South," as a reason for his reluctance to support the endeavor.

Harry M. Ayers, the publisher and editor of the *Anniston Star*, noted as much in May 1944: "there seems to have been somewhat of an upsurge of prejudice [antisemitism] during the last year or so . . . there may be a renascence of Ku Kluxism, which in years past was responsible for the ruination of the businesses of several good Jewish merchants in this city, not to mention brutality of the worst sort."[15] Even Rabbi Stephen Wise could not help but be aware of the tensions surrounding the influx of refugees when he visited Alabama in early 1944. At his lecture at the YMHA in Birmingham, he "violently denied" that he supported unlimited immigration into the United States when questioned.[16] This sort of antisemitism, by no means uncommon and by no means confined to southern reactionaries, helps to explain why the United States faltered when faced with the greatest moral and humanitarian crisis in modern history.

The Father Coughlin of the South

Perhaps no one in the state did more to promote and spread vicious antisemitic propaganda than Catholic priest Arthur W. Terminiello. Originally from Boston, Terminiello had been appointed to the Central Missions of Alabama during the early days of the Depression where he ran a mission for black sharecroppers in St. Teresa's Village in the community of Bolling, located approximately fifty miles south of Montgomery. Terminiello also led "motor missions" throughout the state, teaching "the truth about the Catholic Church, and to clear it of the false charges made against it" in an exceedingly anti-Catholic part of the country.[17] The fiery priest warned his Catholic brethren that the church would have to launch "a counter-offensive, a blitzkrieg, if necessary," to combat the "decadence [of] non-Catholic denominations" in the South and "their doctrine of hate and indifference" against Catholic doctrine. "This means," Terminiello declared, "a Catholic offensive—a Catholic panzer Division" to spread the Catholic word.[18] Such itinerant preaching from the back of a "trailer chapel" was a common practice among Evangelical Protestants, but extremely unusual for Catholic priests. Even more unusual, Terminiello sang Protestant hymns and used the King James Bible for his services in order to connect with his southern audiences. By the early 1940s, Terminiello began publishing a paper called *Rural Justice* in Troy, Alabama, modeled after Father Coughlin's *Social Justice*, that bashed the New Deal and President Roosevelt, frequently tying the administration and the war effort to Jewish interests.

Terminiello received national attention when the liberal New York periodical *PM Magazine* described *Rural Justice* as an intolerant Coughlinite paper and criticized its circulation in New York City. Terminiello called such criticism "the wrath of a well-organized international Zionism." Referring to leading American Jews as modern-day "Pharisees," Terminiello told *PM*'s William Wiener that "your leaders object to Hitler's treatment of your race because they are a minority with very definite rights; but they do not object to the same persecution of Christians and Jews in other countries. No one can deny that these modern Pharisees of America are today running our Government for their own selfish and hypocritical designs. The vast majority of Jews are just as much slaves to their leaders as Germans are slaves to Hitler."[19] Pressure from Bishop Thomas J. Toolen of the Mobile Diocese eventually halted the publication of *Rural Justice* in June 1943, just as Terminiello claimed a circulation of twenty thousand. By October, Terminiello had been transferred—or as he viewed it, demoted—to Huntsville, where he led the Church of the Visitation.

In June 1944, Terminiello began broadcasting his sermons on the Huntsville radio station WBHP, but later extended the radio program to the North Alabama Network, giving his antisemitic and subversive diatribes a wider audience. He broadcast his most controversial sermon, "The Cross of War: Is It Due to Stupidity or Cupidity?," on October 22, 1944, where much of the Tennessee Valley heard Terminiello accuse Roosevelt of sacrificing Pearl Harbor to the Japanese—he called it the "Pearl Harbor massacre"—in order to drag the United States into war for the "sordid" reason of profit. In a Christmas

Eve 1944 sermon titled "Santa Claus or Christ: The Call for a Christian Crusade," Terminiello condemned the war as "a cause which is becoming more UNJUST every day" and called for the immediate end to the war as well as a crusade to demand justice for American soldiers abroad who "must not be the victims of the crooked cross of Nazism or of the DOUBLE CROSS of our Allies." Sermons such as this went far beyond Alabama as hate groups such as the antisemitic Gerald L. K. Smith's America First Party disseminated them through their pamphlets and journals. Such propaganda prompted Smith to dub Terminiello "the Father Coughlin of the South." Smith, whom Terminiello joined on a speaking tour in 1946, considered Terminiello "the best, if not the only, substitute that can be found [for Father Coughlin] in the United States."[20] Critics of Terminiello, however, called him a "paid propagandist for fascism . . . what a swell Quisling he would have made for that low Goebbels!" Such reaction led Bishop Toolen once again to transfer Terminiello in May 1945, this time to Anniston's Sacred Heart Church, where he served only six months.[21]

After being transferred to Anniston, Terminiello opened an office in Birmingham, sixty miles to the west, for his Union of Christian Crusaders, which he had formed in October 1944. He began publishing a newsletter called *The Crusader* by the thousands.[22] Terminiello's antisemitic diatribes increased in both volume and vitriol. He called for a "death march" on Washington to bring to justice members of a Zionist "invisible world empire" that included the Jewish syndicated columnist Walter Winchell and Harry Monsky, the head of the national B'nai B'rith. In a letter to his followers, Terminiello described how "B'nai B'rith is now conducting a campaign to raise $4,000,000 to carry on their anti-Christian plot to exterminate those who oppose their plans for world domination and the rape of the Holy Land. They are going to call it 'exterminating anti-Semites.' How we succeed against these millions will depend upon the loyalty, the unity of purpose, the courage and generosity of Crusaders who will not allow Christianity to be exterminated." This plot also relied upon "un-Christian Hollywood morality"—traditional antisemitic propaganda considered Hollywood to be controlled by Jews—to undermine the basic foundations of Christian society, while "Masonry and Zionist propaganda" would shatter religious unity.[23] Such a conspiracy theory might have seemed far-fetched to Gentiles, but Jews immediately recognized it as a variation of the forged *Protocols of the Elders of Zion*. In November 1945, Toolen removed Terminiello from his pulpit because he refused "to obey the orders of his bishop to cease sending out literature which we feel is detrimental to the church and the unity of our country." As a result, the Catholic Church declared that Terminiello "is no longer considered a priest in good standing." Toolen's actions, Charles Feidelson observed, meant "Terminiello is in effect unfrocked and is now merely a fomenter of hate."[24]

After the press in Birmingham ran a series of articles about Terminiello's Christian Crusade and his ties to nationalist, right-wing organizations, the defrocked priest blamed the Anti-Defamation League (ADL) "and its stooges and cohorts," and he specifically named the *News*'s Feidelson for attempting to intimidate and libel him. He also criticized the Birmingham chapter of the National Conference of Christians and Jews (NCCJ), primarily Temple Emanu-El's Rabbi Milton Grafman, for his attempts to promote a "neo-Judeo-Christian nondescript quasi-religion called 'Tolerance'" in the city's churches and schools. Terminiello constantly criticized the idea of tolerance and unity because he thought it a sinister method for promoting a "plot for world empire and revolution."[25] Conversely, Birmingham's Jews cooperated wholeheartedly with the NCCJ and had concentrated their community relations efforts on the interfaith group.

Resistance to such interfaith cooperation came from more than just Terminiello, as the NCCJ had difficulty in gaining support from both fundamentalist Protestants and Catholics, including the Catholic bishop T. J. Toolen, certainly no friend or supporter of Terminiello. While Toolen allowed priests under his jurisdiction to participate in the NCCJ, he made it clear that their participation did not have his blessing. At no time, however, did Toolen resort to crass and vicious antisemitic rhetoric to criticize the NCCJ as did Terminiello.[26]

Terminiello also harbored an incredible animosity toward Zionism, going as far as to propose an amendment to the US Constitution that would ban the movement. He thought "Zionism means the inducing of American citizens to leave the United States to form a Super State which will directly or indirectly control the destinies, the morals, the liberties and finances of this nation" and branded it as one of the most "menacing" movements in the world at the time, "calculated to do Jews as well as the rest of the world more harm than any other one influence." He claimed to have never encouraged "intolerance because of race," but his outlandish remarks, either in person or in print, often seemed to be calculated to inflict ever-greater offense. In one instance, he claimed that Julius Streicher, the Jew-baiting editor of the Nazi newspaper *Der Stürmer*, had been a Zionist, and in another he published a short article relating how Zionists planted fabricated stories about Nazi atrocities in order to establish a Palestinian homeland. In the April 1946 issue of *The Crusader*, he printed an absurd article titled "Hebrew American Confesses Jews Ruling Europe," that stated, "politically, Jews in Europe never had less reason for complaint than now. . . . In fact, in some countries their political position is almost too good and it may eventually result in harm to the Jews." In the face of six million Jewish deaths at the hands of the Nazis, Terminiello's malice is staggering: "Officially and unofficially, there are no discriminations made against the Jews; anti-Semitic propaganda, the bane of Jewish life in pre-war Europe, is extinct. Politically, the European continent has gone Left further than ever in its history, AND THIS REFLECTS FAVORABLY ON THE POSITION OF THE JEWS."[27] Indeed, in many of the issues of *The Crusader*, Terminiello intimated that the extent of the mass murder of Jews had been grossly inflated.

By late 1945, Terminiello had become friends with Gerald L. K. Smith, perhaps the most prominent antisemite in the United States. Early in 1946, Terminiello became the chaplain for Smith's Christian Veterans of America and joined him on a tour of northeastern cities, speaking in Philadelphia, Cleveland, Pittsburgh, Detroit, and Chicago.[28] Protestors and picketers met them at every stop. In Cleveland, outside of the auditorium, Terminiello punched a protester, and in Chicago the meeting had to be halted when protestors rioted as Terminiello railed against Eleanor Roosevelt, New Deal liberals, "Communistic Zionistic Jews," and the ill-treatment of Germans for "the real and imputed crimes of Hitler."[29] Chicago police arrested Terminiello and Smith and charged them with inciting the crowd, disorderly conduct, and disturbing the peace. After Terminiello's conviction, two Illinois higher courts upheld the verdict before he appealed to the US Supreme Court. He contended that the Chicago ordinance violated his First Amendment right to free speech. On May 16, 1949, the Supreme Court issued a 5–4 decision overturning the Chicago verdict. The landmark *Terminiello v. Chicago* decision upheld free speech rights, although dissenting Justice Robert H. Jackson, who had prosecuted Nazi leaders at the postwar Nuremberg Trials, thought "Terminiello's language too close to that of the fascists, whose defeat was considered important enough to justify going to war." In his dissent, Jackson wrote, "This Court has gone far toward accepting the doctrine that civil liberty means the removal of all restraints from these crowds and that all local attempts to maintain order are impairments of the liberty of the citizen. . . . There is danger that, if the Court does not temper its doctrinaire logic with a little practical wisdom, it will convert the constitutional Bill of Rights into a suicide pact."[30] *Terminiello v. Chicago* has had a monumental impact on First Amendment rights. Its influence has extended well beyond protecting the hate speech of a bigoted, antisemitic Alabama priest.

The scurrilous attacks on Jews by Terminiello, whether through his paper *Rural Justice*, his radio broadcasts, or his Union of Christian Crusaders, concerned Alabama's Jews who worried over the rise of "Christian fascists." In Montgomery, the distribution of *Rural Justice* throughout the region alarmed the Jewish community. Protests to Bishop Toolen by Simon Wampold, the president of the Montgomery Jewish Federation and the head of B'nai B'rith, fell on deaf ears, and even the local ADL failed to halt the publication of the paper. While Montgomery's Jews had experienced only isolated antisemitic incidents, Terminiello's influence made them much more conscious of the increasing antisemitism in both the state and nation, particularly when additional antisemitic propaganda appeared in the state. For instance, a weekly newspaper published in Clanton, the *Southern Outlook*, appeared in 1945 that regularly published some of the same antisemitic and reactionary writers that Terminiello's *Rural Justice* and *The Crusader* relied upon. Terminiello even contributed to the *Southern Outlook*. The ADL estimated that the weekly paper reached approximately forty thousand throughout the central Alabama region spreading pernicious propaganda about Jews and blacks. The *Montgomery Advertiser* called the *Outlook* "one of the most viciously unfair and contemptible distortions of truth . . . ever to come from the typewriter of any man save the late Adolf Hitler."[31] Subsequently, Wampold initiated a Public Relations Committee in Montgomery to combat antisemitism and to mitigate the effects of such entities as the *Southern Outlook* or demagogues like Terminiello. This effort, however, met with little success. As one observer noted only a month after the European war ended, "only several year ago, the Jews of Montgomery felt assured of their secure status. Today, that situation is changed."[32] Over the next two decades, Montgomery's Jews, as well as Jews throughout the state, remained uneasy over their status as racial turmoil and antisemitism roiled the state during the civil rights era of the 1950s and 1960s. Terminiello belonged to the vanguard of southern demagogues who increasingly exploited antisemitism to further their political and social agenda. The most prominent in Alabama was navy rear admiral John G. Crommelin, who in 1950 continued the antisemitic crusade in Alabama, basing his political campaigns firmly upon racism and religious bigotry by claiming that a Communist-Jewish conspiracy sought integration and the "mongrelization" of the white race.[33]

The Anglo-Saxon Federation

Unlike the outspoken Father Terminiello and his Union of Christian Crusaders, a much more insidious antisemitism took the form of the Anglo-Saxon Federation of America, led in Birmingham by "a spell-binding preacher," Trevor P. Mordecai, the former pastor of Birmingham's First Presbyterian

Church. The federation served as an American counterpart to the British-Israelism movement that believed that Anglo-Saxons directly descended from the lost Ten Tribes of Israel. Mordecai, who had immigrated to the United States from Wales, attributed his surname "to Israelitish descent," but not to any Jewish heritage.[34] Originally, the British-Israelism movement had been generally philosemitic rather than antisemitic, regarding Jews "as brother Israelites, the descendants of different but related tribes." As historian Michael Barkun argues, British-Israelism, in its early stages, "emphasized a fraternal, although patronizing, relationship with the Jewish people," at least until William J. Cameron, the former editor of Henry Ford's antisemitic *Dearborn Independent*, became involved with the Anglo-Saxon Federation in 1931, pushing the organization toward an association with right-wing racist and antisemitic organizations that, over time, ultimately produced the Christian Identity movement.[35]

Cameron's influence on the federation was also chronicled by John Roy Carlson, a pseudonym for the journalist Avedis Boghos Derounian, who, in 1943, published *Under Cover*, an account of American fascists and undercover Axis agents. Carlson joined the federation in his clandestine investigation and wrote that Cameron, the federation president, believed that "Anglo-Saxons, not the Jews, were the true sons of Israel" and "promoted anti-Semitism by distributing wholesale editions of the *Protocols* [*of the Elders of Zion*]," in many ways replicating his earlier antisemitic crusade while running the *Dearborn Independent*.[36]

During the 1930s until the end of World War II, the Anglo-Saxon Federation, which at the time was not tightly controlled or coordinated, still "retained significant elements of traditional British-Israelism" while welcoming increasingly vicious racist and antisemitic ideas into the movement. Thus it is impossible to determine to what degree antisemitism pervaded Mordecai's "ministry," since little is known of his teachings beyond that fact that he believed that his "reconciliatory view" of Anglo-Saxons as the descendants of the lost tribes was "the only answer to anti-Semitism."[37] One Jewish newspaper in 1945, however, warned that some "professional hate promoters" were targeting Birmingham and Birmingham's labor leaders through antisemitic organizations such as the Anglo-Saxon Federation. Someone even asked Rabbi Stephen Wise, who was touring the state in January 1944, whether or not Anglo-Saxons were the descendants of the lost tribes, as the Anglo-Saxon Federation claimed. Wise "admitted 'it may be true.' But, he added, 'I don't believe it.'"[38]

Mordecai's teachings caused much more consternation for Lee B. Weil, the president of Birmingham's United Jewish Fund and a former chair of its Refugee Committee. In March 1944, Weil "only recently" realized that antisemitism had "become a serious factor in the life of Birmingham." He had been aware of "latent prejudice, which made itself felt every once in a while," but the "engineered" and "organized" efforts by Mordecai to spread the antisemitic teachings of the Anglo-Saxon Federation convinced him that "the poison of Hitlerism had come to infect American life—even in my own city." The idea of Anglo-Saxons as the true descendants of Israel, Weil said, "sounds harmless enough, but it is another expression of the 'herrenvolk' idea. It stands for racial arrogance, out of which springs so many forms of Jew-baiting." Mordecai's success meant "turning men and women who consider themselves devout Christians and believers in the Bible into critics and enemies" of the Jews, and his efforts on behalf of the Anglo-Saxon Federation followed a disturbing increase in antisemitism in Birmingham that saw whispering campaigns against Jewish merchants and refugees and the defacement of a pillar of Temple Emanu-El, where someone painted "a swastika about two feet in height." In one of Birmingham's upscale neighborhoods the following year, "there was a huge arrow with the word 'Jew' underneath it painted on the street in front of, and pointing to the homes of about twenty-five or thirty" Jewish citizens.[39] Such trends, culminating with Terminiello's Union of Christian Crusaders and the recruiting successes of Mordecai's Anglo-Saxon Federation, gave the impression of "a deep current of active animosity running through every stratum of society." For Weil, the most disquieting aspect was "that so many persons are now unashamedly anti-Semitic" that it had unsettled the friends and "well wishers" of Birmingham's Jews. "It is the same fact," he warned, "which makes me feel that we must look to our defenses."[40]

In response to what he saw as an orchestrated antisemitic campaign, Weil proposed the creation of a local community relations committee devoted not only to addressing ugly instances of antisemitism but also to promote preventive educational measures. While Birmingham had a chapter of the ADL, it had an incredibly weak presence. Weil contended that community defense must come from inside the community, not from any outside, northern organization based in New York or Chicago. He asked, "What can the brightest, the best informed resident of one of the congested centers of Jewish life know about the customs of the South, the business and other relations between Jews and non-Jews, and all the other factors which go to make up the local picture?"[41] By early 1945, Weil had succeeded in creating a Jewish Community Council, attracting close to fifty individuals to the organizational meeting, but it ultimately fell victim to an internal rift in the Jewish community over Zionism. He garnered the support of Zionists in the community although he was a non-Zionist. Weil was "one of the extremely rare non-Zionists" in Birmingham who earned the respect of Zionists, largely for his leadership and enthusiastic support of the United Jewish Fund, but despite his ability to work with Zionists in the city, his committee "functioned ineffectively" because it could not find unity between the Zionists and non-Zionists. The resistance by anti-Zionists, primarily by those who belonged to the American Council for Judaism (ACJ), proved to be the greatest obstacle. Leo Oberdorfer, the "leading anti-Zionist" in Birmingham and a member of the ACJ, strenuously objected to the formation of the community council because it "would serve only to strengthen the Zionists and promote ghettoism." As an outside observer noted of the ACJ, "whatever weight the small chapter of the Council enjoys in the Birmingham community is derived not from activity carried on by it but as a result of its abstention from the affairs of the community."[42] The disunity in the Birmingham community dismayed Weil and eventually led to his disgust and eventual disinterest in the endeavor.

Goldman v. Hicks

Terminiello and, to a lesser extent, Mordecai represented the most flamboyant and dramatic manifestations of antisemitism in Alabama during the 1940s, but most forms of antisemitic discrimination remained institutional in nature, supported by bigoted perceptions that remained rigidly ensconced in American attitudes. Such perceptions could clearly be seen in the case of *Goldman v. Hicks* in January 1941. In August 1939, Madge Hardy Hicks divorced William H. Hicks after he had assaulted her with the intent to injure her. The divorce proceedings provided for joint custody of their three-year-old daughter, Lorraine Hicks. After Madge Hicks married Godfrey Goldman, a Jew, in February 1940, William Hicks sued for exclusive custody of the child on the grounds that the marriage to Goldman rendered the mother unfit to care for the child. During the trial, Hicks's attorney, Horace Wilkinson, articulated the stereotypical attitudes Gentiles usually held of the Jews:

> So far as I have been able to find this is the first case in Alabama where a gentile mother, with a daughter of tender years, put her own preference so high, and the welfare of the child so low, as to enter into a status of this kind. . . . The Jews are outstanding people in some respects. For some reason, which we do not know, God

> Almighty seems to have especially endowed them with commercial instincts. They have the faculty for making money. They like money, and other people do too, for that matter. They place a great deal of emphasis on money. But I like to think there are things in this world above money and particularly in the case of a girl. I like to think the young girls of this country are being raised to value and appreciate character and culture, and all those things worth while in life, and prize them more than anybody's gold. I do not think it to the best interest of the child to be raised in an atmosphere where money is a God. And what has the child gained if it acquires all the money that the Jewish race could bestow upon it and lose its own soul?

Birmingham circuit judge Leigh M. Clark agreed with Wilkinson, and on October 26, 1940, gave full custody of the child to William Hicks, adding that "society has set up a barrier between Jew and Gentile in Alabama."[43]

The Alabama Supreme Court overruled Clark's decision that the marriage to "a man of Jewish race did not create a condition which rendered the wife unfit or unsuitable" to care for the child, since "marriages which are not forbidden by statute, or violative of social morality, can have no effect." Moreover, Justice J. Edwin Livingston, who wrote the decision, found Godfrey Goldman "a man of exemplary habits and splendid character."[44] After the high court overturned the Clark decision, the *Montgomery Advertiser* railed against Wilkinson, calling his courtroom argument "the most vicious and degraded example of bigotry and religious intolerance to offend the spirit of decency in Alabama." The *Advertiser* reminded its readers that Wilkinson had been one of the leaders of the Ku Klux Klan during the 1920s, and, as a member of the Alabama Bar, he could still "present his intolerant filth" to a court of law. The *Advertiser* editorial came only three weeks after the death of its editor, Grover Hall, who had penned the influential "The Egregious Gentile Called to Account," and the paper's position mirrored the position Hall most likely would have taken. Not only had Hall quickly condemned antisemitism, but he had also won a Pulitzer Prize for his opposition to the Klan in 1928. Moreover, Hall had been a staunch supporter and advisor of Wilkinson's political rival, Governor Frank M. Dixon, until Hall's untimely death. The *Advertiser* called for Wilkinson's disbarment since "no man who would transgress a specific guarantee of the Constitution of the United States in his arguments before a court of law—or anywhere else—should be allowed to practice law in the courts of this democratic land."[45]

Wilkinson responded to the *Advertiser* with radio spots denying any antisemitism on his part. Wilkinson, a deacon in the Baptist Church, was a vicious racist and spent much of his life trying to preserve white supremacy, even joining his political rival Frank Dixon to form the Dixiecrat Party in 1948. Wilkinson's ownership of Art-Craft Publishing, the company that produced the *Southern Outlook*, indicates obvious antisemitism, yet an examination of Wilkinson's life and career reveals little open prejudice against Jews.[46] His friend, Mobile's Leon Schwarz, gave him the benefit of the doubt. Schwarz had known Wilkinson for over twenty years and described their relationship as "the friendliest sort." The men had served together on Governor David Bibb Graves's staff during Graves's second term in the mid-1930s. Schwarz remarked that he did not know "what is inside the head of Horace Wilkinson's mind concerning the Jews" and acknowledged that Wilkinson had been a member of the Klan but explained that "so was Gov. Bibb Graves, who named another Israelite and me on his personal military staff, and many others of our faith to public office. I refuse to hold to account in this day men who joined the Klan in its infancy. With many who had political ambition, the Klan was just one more thing to join to get some votes." Wilkinson's relationship with Schwarz clearly fits Jonathan Sarna's definition of "the Jew next door," while Goldman conveniently fills the role of the "mythical Jew." Wilkinson never resorted to the crass antisemitic ranting of a Terminiello or Coughlin, preferring to reserve that particular predilection for African Americans, but he willingly employed the most invective antisemitic claims in order to win a judgment for his client. As Schwarz notes, the Goldman case quickly became a "forgotten incident," even after only a few months, but he added that "if the case had been upheld by the Alabama Supreme Court, I believe Jewish people in Alabama would have seen that it was carried to the U.S. Supreme Court."[47]

The Grand Hotel

Another common form of antisemitism included the exclusionary practices of businesses and social organizations, a practice that had begun in the 1880s, although such discrimination was generally less acute in the South than elsewhere in the United States.[48] The fact that such discrimination was less common did not lessen the sting for Jews. When the Grand Hotel resort in Point Clear, Alabama, refused service to Harold S. Weil of New Orleans in mid-1942, the leaders of the Jewish community in Mobile did not simply accept the slight, they worked to abolish the hotel's antisemitic policy. Such a policy must have come as a shock to the Jews of Mobile who believed that they had "always maintained a relationship of friendship, and mutually-merited respect and consideration of the highest degree" with the Gentile community. The cooperation between Jew and Gentile in Mobile exceeded the cooperation between the Reform and Orthodox congregations. Leo M. Brown, the president of the Mobile Jewish Federation, told the owner of the Grand Hotel, Edward A. Roberts, that the hotel's exclusionary policy had "given offense to the entire Jewish community of Mobile." Not one to mince words, Brown condemned the policy as "alien to the ideals . . . of which America and all good Americans are engaged in the present world-wide struggle." Moreover, Brown refused to acquiesce to such treatment, warning Roberts of "the acrimonious recriminations and the bitter conflicts that will necessarily ensue from a continuation of the policy . . . to say nothing of the more serious and far-reaching repercussions throughout our city and southland that would be certain to result therefrom." Although Brown intimated that local Jewish leaders would not be afraid to publicize the dispute, they worked quietly and behind the scenes to alter the hotel's policy.[49]

Roberts, who in addition to owning the Grand Hotel also served as president of Waterman Steamship Corporation, told Brown that the hotel had adopted such a policy since it catered to "people from far distant points" who were far less tolerant than himself. Roberts had left the decision regarding policy to the hotel manager, Van Cadenhead, who explained that the decision to exclude Jews was "strictly a business proposition" and should not be construed as personal, citing his many friendships with Jews to reinforce the point.[50] E. B. Peebles, the president of the Prichard National Bank, eventually mediated the dispute. For Brown and the Jewish community, the policy of exclusion of "communicants of a particular religion is not only immoral, but it is un-American and in direct conflict with the ideals of justice for the maintenance of which the democratic world is now at war." Brown demanded the cessation of the hotel's antisemitic policy, a statement indicating Roberts's regret for the policy, as well as a letter of apology from Roberts to both Harold Weil and the Jewish community in order to ameliorate any ill will and to "satisfy our Jewish sense of honor." Roberts quickly complied with the demands and issued an apology to the Jewish community for the "embarrassing" situation, which Peebles blamed on a regrettable "misunderstanding" between Roberts and Cadenhead. In the end, Brown doubted "very seriously that Jews will visit the Grand Hotel in the future in any considerable numbers, regardless of the outcome of our efforts. Most right-minded Jews have a very keen sense of their own dignity and honor and would not wish to visit any hotel where they would not feel welcome, either at the hand of the management or of the remaining guests."[51] As the *Goldman v. Hicks* case and the Grand Hotel incident demonstrate, Jews in Alabama did not passively accept maltreatment.

Antisemitism in the Military

Jewish soldiers stationed in Alabama, too, confronted antisemitic attitudes. At Fort McClellan, copies of Father Coughlin's *Social Justice* could be found at recreation halls, and Jewish soldiers reported antisemitic incidents in their regiment, including remarks "by non-Jewish soldiers who felt that the Jewish-European situation was responsible for their being in the army." To combat this, the JWB director in charge of morale for Jewish soldiers, Rabbi Abba Fineberg, thought that programs addressing interfaith relations would "enlighten the non-Jewish men regarding this subject."[52] Similar incidents could also be found at Camp Rucker outside of Dothan. A wife of one of the Jewish officers found an antisemitic poem "lying around" at a service club on base that encapsulated the most pernicious falsehoods pertaining to Jews in wartime.

America's Fighting Jew
A poet wrote a tribute to our country's fighting Jew;
Let's join our friend, the poet and drink to that Jew, too
But where are all his other pals, I mean, Saul, Abe and Moe;
They're making tailored uniforms for those who have to go.
Their patriotic brethren remain at home to buy
Their country's Stamps and War Bonds, financed by those who die.
Remember Jake and Sidney? How bravely did they talk
Of: "How we should get Hitler and bring him to New York."
But Jake is now ensconced in ease in charge of Immigration,
Deploring on the radio his race's segregation;
While Sidney aids in getting funds to care for refugees
Who swarm within our borders with jingoistic pleas.

Don't overlook another Jew that's always in the fight,
He's fearless, brave and dauntless in showing us the light.
He holds a rank of prestige within our Naval Force;
He's heard each Sunday evening engaging in discourse.
No other man could take his place, nor fill this hero's shoes.
In World War I he earned his fame while wearing Navy blues;
An Admiral's receptionist, he bravely carried on,

Arranging dates and schedules from night to early dawn.
His voice comes booming over the air with cunning, sly invective,
Attacking men of proven worth it seems is his objective.
This cunning is per-patriot, I think you all know well,
Our famous Naval hero—Commander Walter Winchell.

Go onward Christian soldiers and fight for freedom's right,
They'll stay at home and help to buy the guns with which you fight.
They'll sell your ma a trinket to honor you while gone,
To wear upon your girl's lapel, to honor you while gone;
They'll make your shoes and raincoats to wear out in the fight;
That's if the contract suits them, and if the price is right.
They'll stand upon the sidewalks and wave Old Glory high
As all the Gentile soldiers go marching proudly by.
A case of forging War Bonds—the first to be disclosed—
Quite justly falls to Israel—the first to be exposed.
In setting up black markets in steel or hoarded food,
You're sure to find a Bornstein or others of his brood.

In practices lascivious they seem to have no fear,
As panderers of lust and vice they have no worthy peer.
Let one expose a member of this mercenary race,
And he's labelled "Anti-Semite," and no longer held in grace.
To fool us simple Christians another name they coin—
A Burkowitz becomes Burke, while Cohen's changed to Coyne.
These famous champs of tolerance don't practice what they preach.
We give them all fair warning—in their great anticipation
Of post-war nations to control with monied domination;
That after Johnny Doughboy had Hitler on the run
He's coming back to get the Jew, the dirty son-of-a-gun.[53]

Numerous examples of such antisemitic poems and literature could be found at military installations across the United States. As historian Leonard Dinnerstein points out, the antisemitic poems and ditties written during the war "reflected deep-seated feelings held by Americans in civilian life that could neither be countered nor controlled by military personnel even when they desired to do so."[54]

The existence of such antisemitic poems or literature at either Fort McClellan or Camp Rucker indicates there was a responsive audience, even if they could scarcely be blamed on the antisemitic attitudes of Alabamians. Nevertheless, the stereotypes present in such literature certainly circulated among the state's Gentile population. In fact, questions over whether Jews received "soft assignments" in the armed forces arose frequently during the war, leaving numerous Jewish leaders, including Rabbi Louis Werfel of Birmingham's K'nesseth Israel, desperate for accurate information to provide to non-Jewish groups.[55] Christian leaders, such as Jeanette Rank of the NCCJ, also needed such information after being confronted by Gentiles who questioned Jewish participation in aviation and other "dangerous combat branches of the service." Such questions, historian Joseph Bendersky argues, "conformed to traditional stereotypes of inherently selfish, weak, and cowardly Jews shying away from anything physically strenuous or dangerous and being antimilitary almost by nature," a notion explicit in the poem found at Camp Rucker.[56] Rank turned to Dora Roth who had compiled such information on behalf of Birmingham's United Jewish Fund. Roth's data dispelled such stereotypes and showed Birmingham's Jews served in a "greater proportion [in army aviation] than would be expected on the basis of [their] proportion in the army as whole." Moreover, the achievements of Birmingham's Jewish servicemen far exceeded the expectations of the officials of the NJWB's Bureau of War Records who kept statistics on American Jewish participation in the armed forces. "Out of 400 men in the service from Birmingham alone," Roth reported, "over one hundred of them are commissioned officers. That is a little higher than the ten percent you have been figuring on. Who says we Southerners are slow?"[57] Rank, who worked closely with the Jewish community in the NCCJ, used Roth's data extensively in her interfaith work to show that "Jews are doing their share and more in the armed forces of our country," dispelling the frequent misapprehension of the Jews' role in wartime.[58]

Such antisemitic attitudes and outrages did not discourage everyone. Emil Carl Hess of Birmingham, a lieutenant in the navy, believed that such antisemitic attitudes would be mitigated once the war ended. "Boys who have been through hell together aren't going to hate," he said. "When the servicemen come home they won't go for anti-semitism. They will have a healthy outlook on life. They are going to remember the friends who fought side by side with them, without giving a thought to difference in creed." Hess thought the experiences of war would alter attitudes in the postwar world. "The trouble-makers, those who would sow discord between Christian and Jew, are the people who are sitting this war out, or just talking about it," Hess stated. "The boys who are doing the fighting have a different slant on things."[59]

In some ways, Hess's evaluation was correct. Nationally, antisemitism decreased in the postwar years. Leonard Dinnerstein explains that "a remarkable metamorphosis occurred in the United States following the end of World War II. After more than half a century of increasing animosity toward Jews, antisemitism in the United States suddenly began to decline." Victory and postwar prosperity offered optimism and opportunities that Americans embraced, rather than the "alleged culpabilities" of minorities. Dinnerstein also notes the returning veterans played a large role in combating antisemitism. "Thousands of veterans had lived with intolerance in the armed forces," he writes, and they "hoped to reform the prejudiced nation that they had left behind. . . . To what extent the knowledge of Hitler's slaughter of six million Jews contributed to the desire to curb bigotry is impossible to state but after 1945 millions of Christian Americans became more cautious in expressing negative reactions to Jews."[60] On the other hand, Alabama does not seem to fit into this national pattern as antisemitism most certainly did not disappear, with Father Terminiello, the reemergence of the Klan, and reactionary papers such as the *Southern Outlook*, the most visible and prominent fomenters of hate and bigotry in the state in the late 1940s. One should not overlook the optimism and opportunity of postwar society, in addition to the attitude of the veterans, as Hess pointed out in 1944, that went a long way to mitigating some of the antisemitic bigotry, but by 1950, ironically, retired rear admiral John G. Crommelin's antisemitic and racist political campaigns helped fuel the bigotry and racism that permeated the state during the civil rights struggles in the 1950s and 1960s.

7
Postwar Alabama

The end of the war did not end disagreements over Zionism, as the conflict between Zionists and anti-Zionists of the ACJ continued to divide the Jewish communities in Birmingham and Montgomery and would continue to do so until the establishment of the state of Israel in 1948. In some instances it endured even longer. The differences between Zionists and anti-Zionists, although significant, did not prevent the Jewish communities from working together once again to assist the displaced persons, most of whom were Holocaust survivors, find a new home in Alabama, recalling the earlier cooperative effort to resettle prewar refugees from Nazi Germany. At the same time, veterans returned to civilian life, trying to begin or to continue their lives interrupted by war. In doing so they began to fill new leadership roles in the Jewish community over the course of the following decade that helped to fill the breach earlier religious and cultural differences created, as well as the festering contention over Zionism.

Controversy and conflict over Zionism could be felt in many of the cities and small towns in the South and elsewhere in America. In Alabama the clash between those associated with the ACJ and the Zionists was most apparent in the larger cities of Birmingham and Montgomery. Throughout the rest of the state, the classical Reform tradition dominated the smaller Jewish congregations, and the lack of sufficient numbers of Eastern European Jews in these small towns prevented any cultural controversies such as Zionism from becoming problematic issues. In Mobile, the younger, more vibrant Eastern European Jews wholeheartedly supported Zionism, while the older Reform congregation maintained a passive, if ambivalent, attitude toward it. Zionism, however, never became a contentious issue in the port city, despite the clear cultural divide, largely due to the support of influential Reform Jews such Leo Brown and Sol Kahn for the Zionist cause.

Nowhere in Alabama was the ACJ more influential than in Montgomery, where one observer noted that "there is a considerable amount of anti-Zionist feeling and strong sentiment in favor of the American Council for Judaism." Although the ACJ purportedly promoted the tenets of classical Reform Judaism, it offered little in the way of a positive program, and local ACJ chapters, such as the one in Montgomery, did little more than oppose local Zionists. Such a situation did little to engender enthusiasm among Reform Jews. As Temple Beth-Or's president, Henry A. Weil, also a member of the ACJ, reported in March 1946, "the lack of Zionism as a burning issue here in Montgomery probably accounts for the attitude of indifference in the Temple and its work."[1] Moreover, because the leadership of the federation was largely from Reform Jews who favored the council, it resisted any efforts it deemed sympathetic to the Zionist program. Ultimately this threatened the ability of the federation to function as an effective body. At the beginning of 1948, federation leaders continually postponed that year's fund-raising drive, apparently being "unwilling to raise money for UPA." As Beatrice Behrman reported, the Zionists finally "formed a committee headed by Nace Cohen—went to the Federation and [said] 'We're going to conduct a campaign—if you want to join, fine—if not, the h[ell] with you.' In other words, they called their bluff. They made arrangements for an opening dinner . . . [and] the Weils and Loebs and Lobmans finally joined the campaign."[2]

This did not mean that members of the federation could not work together, especially when the circumstance warranted. Montgomery's Jews, including the factions associated with the council and Zionism, joined to support European Jews who had survived the war, whether through the resettlement of displaced persons or contributions to relief organizations. For instance, in January 1949, Temple Beth-Or was designated as "a collection depot for the JDC overseas relief supplies collection." Both the NCJW and Hadassah led the collection program, and all of the city's Jewish organizations contributed. "This collection is deemed urgent because of the terrifying winter faced by 1 ½ million of our European brethren and in the hope that we may stay the hand of death which hangs over them through cold, disease and starvation," the notice for contributions read, "through the extra help of this supply collection it will be possible to bolster the diet of long-starved men and women in the former Nazi concentration camps."[3] Despite this collaborative effort to aid suffering Jewry abroad, those associated with the ACJ refused to contribute to any organization or endeavor associated with Palestine, even after the state of Israel had been established.

The Zionist controversy remained more intense in Birmingham, where an outside observer noted that the community remained "violently split" over the Palestine question at the end of the war. Although most Jews in

Birmingham contributed to and worked with the United Jewish Fund, the city's Zionists, comprised mainly of the Eastern European Jews at Temple Beth-El and K'nesseth Israel, dominated most of the Jewish activities in the city. National Jewish organizations in contact with Birmingham's Jewish community, such as the American Jewish Committee (AJC), frequently lamented the division among the city's Jews. The AJC, the oldest Jewish advocacy and self-defense organization in the United States, represented elite German Jews whose attitudes toward Zionism could be considered ambivalent, or even anti-Zionist.[4] The AJC had long attempted to establish a chapter in Birmingham, and many of the Reform Jews in the city should have flocked to it. Yet they did not. In fact, no one in the Birmingham community strongly supported the AJC, despite the fact that Alabamian Irving Engel, brother of William P. Engel, headed the national organization. The loyalty that Birmingham's Jews had to the United Jewish Fund prevented the establishment of an AJC chapter, or the establishment of any other organization that might compete with the fund for community resources. With the exception of the community's "dissident minority"—those belonging to the American Council for Judaism—Birmingham's Jews strongly supported the fund and its emphasis on overseas aid. As the AJC's Lawrence Koch noted, "even community leaders with an anti-Zionist turn of mind work cooperatively in the Fund. . . . [It] receives excellent support from the entire community despite the fact that much controversy over Palestine has prevailed."[5] The fact that Zionists and anti-Zionists cooperated within the fund's framework, albeit with limitations, was somewhat unusual as intracommunity organizations such as this often fell victim to infighting over Zionism.[6] The fund continued to function effectively for Birmingham's Jewish community, and only after the establishment of the state of Israel in 1948 did the Zionist controversy eventually subside.

The AJC looked to the young veterans who had recently returned to Birmingham not only as the best hope to heal the rift over Zionism but also to spearhead a new AJC chapter. "The [Birmingham] community fails to see the forest because of the trees," Koch observed. "It wastes its resources in ideological quibbling and fails to rally to more important questions which involve real threats to community welfare." The young veterans, he said, "have a positive attitude toward Jewish life but have not participated in Jewish community activities."[7] Milton Grafman and Dora Roth, both of whom were longtime friends of Koch, agreed with his assessment that the greatest possibilities for new leadership in the community came from the younger generation who had "shunned the extremes in the Palestine fight."[8]

The Creation of Israel

The news of the mass murder of European Jews had strengthened Zionists' resolve that only a homeland could provide lasting Jewish security, causing an "inability to recognize moderate positions retards the process of bringing the divergent elements together not only in relation to the question of Palestine but with regard to most other matters affecting the Jewish community as a whole."[9] The revelations of the mass killings had also profoundly affected Reform Jews, causing many of them to move closer to, and even embrace, Zionism. Because their background differed considerably from many Eastern European Jews who were imbued with Zionist principles from an early age—most Reform Jews had been raised to acculturate into the Christian-dominated culture—whatever Zionist feelings that they had were bound to be only moderate in contrast to the outspoken, militant Zionists in Birmingham.[10] In fact, William P. Bloom of Tuscaloosa told Maurice Eisendrath, the president of the Union of American Hebrew Congregations, that "the thinking of the Jewish Community of Birmingham would not be representative of that of the rest of the state."[11]

Isaac "Uncle Ike" Abelson, who had worked for Zionist causes almost all of his life, remained the "emotional spirit" of Birmingham's Zionists, but attorney Abe Berkowitz, who had assumed the leadership of the Birmingham Zionist Organization by 1945, played a more dramatic role in making the Jewish state a reality. Henry Montor, the director of the United Jewish Appeal (UJA), selected Berkowitz as one of seventeen American Zionists to be invited to Rudolf G. Sonneborn's New York apartment to hear David Ben-Gurion, the chairman of the Jewish Agency for Palestine, who asked these men to help Jews in Palestine fight for their ancestral homeland. Such materiel aid most commonly took the form of army surplus, including guns and other weaponry, which became readily available after World War II due to demobilization. In fact, the War Assets Administration offered "hundreds of thousands of tons of military equipment, from mess kits to tanks, airplanes, machine guns, artillery, and even warships" for sale as scrap. Although no notes of the Ben-Gurion meeting were taken, and few documents of these endeavors were created, the campaign to gather the resources for the independence and security of Palestinian Jews was chronicled by journalist Leonard Slater in his 1970 book *The Pledge*. According to Slater, the book was "a heroic tribute to the participants."[12] Sonneborn recounted that "we were asked to form ourselves into an . . . American arm of the underground Haganah. We were given no clue as to what we might be called upon to accomplish, when the call might come, or who would call us. We were simply asked to be prepared and to mobilize like-minded Americans."[13] Berkowitz pledged his assistance. The Sonneborn Institute, as the group came to be called, met with members of the Haganah on a regular basis to learn what was needed and to coordinate their activities.

Although it is not known why Montor specifically selected the seventeen men to meet with Sonneborn and Ben-Gurion, Berkowitz clearly had many of the qualities necessary for such a secretive operation: his Zionistic fervor, his business and political connections, and not least his discretion. As Barbara Bonfield argues, "it was clear that the group had to have credibility within their communities, as well as the ability to conduct fund-raising activities and to secure the commitment of members of their communities to the effort. In addition, the founders of the Institute had to overcome fear on the part of American Jews, who were, in some cases, acting clandestinely in defiance of laws of the United States Government."[14] Birmingham's Zionists rallied to the cause. Led by Berkowitz, they began to collect the materiel Ben-Gurion and the Haganah had requested. They raised funds and "collected all manner of goods from truck loads of helmets to a contribution of 3,000 forks from Isadore Mazer." Mark Elovitz notes that "the Kimerling family lent a truck with a driver to the cause. The truck was loaded with tires and the tires' inner-tubes were stuffed with guns and pistols and shipped to New York to see that the 'cargo' would not be apprehended."[15] The head of the FBI, J. Edgar Hoover, was "sympathetic" to Jewish efforts, as long as the arms would not be used in or against the United States. The efforts to collect this surplus on the part of the Sonneborn Institute and the Haganah even reached beyond the United States as corrupt Latin American politicians aided it.[16]

When the United Nations passed a resolution on November 29, 1947, to terminate the British Mandate of Palestine and create a new Jewish state, Zionists rejoiced and held a victory rally at the YMHA. Ike Abelson spoke for many on that occasion when he said, "I feel after a lifetime of interest and anxiety in the movement, that this is the culmination of a dream the Jewish people have had for some 19 centuries. The realization of the dream is particularly necessary since the emergence of a virulent anti-Semitism as practiced by Hitler and his supporters."[17] The anxiety Jews felt in the movement did not end with the UN resolution; indeed, the UN resolution marked the beginning of civil war between Jews and Arabs in Palestine. Zionists continued to gather surplus and materiel for the Haganah and responded to any public criticism of the Jewish state. One such response centered on a letter published in the *Birmingham Age-Herald* in March 1948 that described Jews in Palestine as "a body of invaders" who had "no right to it whatever." In a letter titled "The Arab Case against Zionism," John J. Beshara of Birmingham criticized Zionism as "an expansionist, terroristic, racialist, pagan, aggressive totalitarian movement different only in degree from Nazism." Alex Rittenbaum and Isadore Sperling wrote scathing letters in response. Rittenbaum, the president of the Birmingham Zionist Organization, countered that the grand mufti of Jerusalem, Haj Amin al-Husseini, sponsored Arab violence in Palestine with "criminal bands from other countries." Calling the mufti a "Nazi war criminal," Rittenbaum reminded readers that "only a year ago, at an American prisoner of war camp at Opelika, Ala., there were hundreds of the same Arabs wearing the Nazi swastika, their hands stained with the blood of American boys. You would not have found any Jews in that camp. The Jews in Palestine, 30,000 of them, were fighting with the British, Americans and the Allies—fighting at Tobruk and El Alamein." Creating a Jewish state in Palestine, Rittenbaum concluded, would mean "an island of democracy in a sea of feudalism and fascism."[18]

Roughly three thousand Arabs, captured when the Axis surrendered North Africa in May 1943, had been imprisoned at the Opelika POW camp. Moreover, recently declassified documents from the National Archives reveal that Husseini actively recruited Muslims for the Nazi SS, met personally with Hitler in Berlin, and had been promised a role in the Nazi extermination of Palestinian Jews once the British had been defeated. The extent of his activities and his relationship with Hitler and the Nazis had been kept quiet in the years following the war, according to Richard Breitman and Norman Goda, but "the Allies knew enough about Husseini's wartime activities to consider him a war criminal." Husseini fled to Switzerland after the war but ultimately became a prisoner of the French. In spite of his wartime activities, the French released him in 1946 so as "to avoid offending the Arabs of North Africa."[19] Rittenbaum was correct in pointing out the participation of a criminal element from outside of Palestine, as "a number of . . . former SS and police officials found not only havens, but postwar employment in Middle Eastern countries. There they were able to carry on and transmit to others Nazi racial-ideological anti-Semitism."[20]

Israel's declaration of independence on May 14, 1948, prompted neighboring Arab countries to invade Israel the following day, turning the civil war between Jews and Arabs in Palestine into the 1948 Arab-Israeli War. By the time the Israeli War for Independence ended in June 1949, Israel had increased its amount of land twofold and ensured the existence of a Jewish state in Palestine. In the aftermath of independence, the Caravan of Hope toured Alabama in April 1949 on a "whistle-stop" campaign "to promote the

$250,000,000 national United Jewish Appeal fund" to resettle the refugees still occupying the Displaced Persons camps in Europe. In Mobile, Mayor Ernest Megginson, Rabbi Aaron Shapiro of Ahavas Chesed, and Rabbi Samuel M. Gup of the Government Street Temple as well as other local dignitaries, warmly welcomed the caravan to the port city. The public was invited to tour the traveling exhibit, which displayed the Israeli Declaration of Independence and numerous other cultural items from Israel. When it arrived in Montgomery, Jews sympathetic to Israel raised $250,000 for the UJA. In Birmingham, a similar scene unfolded as Mayor Cooper Green, Rabbis Grafman and Mesch, along with a host of Jewish leaders in the city, greeted the train at the station. The caravan carried with it three members of the Israeli Defense Forces who had distinguished themselves in the war for independence. As Israeli captain Yaakov Wayland told the packed crowd at the Tutwiler Hotel, "We'll make the Negev Desert produce a living. We have won the war. We've made politicians into realists. We know the Egyptians are too frightened to lift guns again. My 17 years of soldering haven't been in vain."[21] For Zionists such as Abe Berkowitz, Ike and Frank Abelson, Alex and Sol Rittenbaum, Dora Roth, and Max and Tillie Kimerling, such testimony validated all of their work and sacrifice for the nascent Jewish state.

Israel has also recognized the commitment of Alabama's Zionists to the creation of the Jewish state in Palestine. When the Jewish National Fund attempted to reforest the many arid parts of Israel in order to make the new nation fertile once again, Israel established an "Uncle Ike" Abelson Forest to honor "Alabama's Original Zionist." In 1967, Israel awarded Abe Berkowitz the Israeli Freedom Medal "because of his services to the ZOA and Israel."[22] In October 1997, Israel honored Alabama and Alabama's Zionists by unveiling a monument to the state at the American Promenade project in Telz-Stone, just outside of Jerusalem. The promenade, designed to "further strengthen US-Israeli relations," was designed for monuments and flags to the fifty individual US states celebrating their ties to Israel. Rabbi Eliot Sherman, who directed the promenade project at the time, said that Alabama's monument "is the largest one" because of the resolution the legislature passed in 1943 calling for the creation of a Jewish state in Palestine. "As far we know," Sherman added, "only Alabama stood up for us in America." Indeed, the entire text of the 1943 resolution is engraved on the monument. That monument, Ehud Olmert said, "will be a constant reminder . . . that Israel has friends in Alabama."[23]

While the establishment of the state of Israel in 1948 did not end the rift over Zionism, it fostered the process of reconciliation, a process that took many years to accomplish and included the intermarriages between Central and Eastern European Jews—and even the Sephardim—that occurred during the war years and in the years that followed. Many Reform Jews who had been either ambivalent or outright antagonistic toward Zionism in the years prior to the war reassessed their position, especially in light of the murder of millions of European Jews. Others simply accepted Zionism as a *fait accompli* after 1948. In Mobile, Reform Jews gathered at the Government Street Temple where Elias Sedlin, a recent graduate of Murphy High School, "appealed for a growing sense of unity and togetherness among all Jews of our community." Others in the congregation, including Rabbi Samuel M. Gup, concurred. Gup "supported this appeal by asserting that there [were] no theological differences among the Jews of Mobile . . . [and] that whatever social differences existed, these were of little consequence" considering the momentous event in Palestine.[24] In Birmingham, William P. Engel, the president of Temple Emanu-El, remarked that "the Jews have established their own nation, and whether we were Zionist or Anti-, enthusiastic or passive, we must admit that this is no longer the question. We can lay aside our likes or dislikes in these directions and hope that this new Nation will be established on the plane of tolerance, peace and understanding; that it will always be the refuge for the displaced and the abused people of the world and that its future history may be so moulded as to make it the beacon for all other Nations of the world to follow. We are no less loyal to America when we hope for these things."[25]

The ACJ, moreover, began to dwindle in number and in relevance, either because members recognized, as Engel did, that the question of a Jewish state had been settled, or they had become "disillusioned by the absence of a positive Council program."[26] Bertha Erlick, a charter member of Birmingham's ACJ, withdrew from the council because she saw no reason for "perpetuating internal Jewish controversy" after the creation of a Jewish state. Others in the ACJ, however, remained adamant in their anti-Zionism and continued to perpetuate the controversy over Zionism, even beyond 1948. Bernard Steiner, for instance, a prominent banker and a member of one of the Jewish community's "first families" in Birmingham, remained an extreme anti-Zionist. An observer noted that Steiner "seems to head the list of assimilationist Jews. He is not active in Jewish affairs, contributes poorly to the UJF and is particularly unsympathetic to its fund raising because of the application [of] some of the proceeds to Palestine needs."[27]

Those who belonged to the council in Birmingham attended Temple Emanu-El, where their clash with Rabbi Milton Grafman over Zionism had begun during the war. Ironically, Grafman's strongest critics were "the very people who were responsible for bringing him to Birmingham."[28] Although the Zionist controversy at Emanu-El eventually subsided, the criticism of Grafman by these dissidents did not. By 1955, a small group of congregants, led by Milton Fies, left Emanu-El to start their own congregation, the Temple for Reform Judaism. The new congregation expected that they would get anywhere from 100 to 150 families to join. By December 1955, only twelve families had resigned from Emanu-El to join the new Reform congregation. Marvin Engel observed that "the people who have joined the Temple for Reform Judaism are by and large couples who are inactive, non-attending members of Temple Emanu-El. I might go a step further and say that they were, for the most part, inactive not only in the Jewish congregation but equally so as far as community activities were concerned." Grafman noted that members of the breakaway congregation were motivated by a "personal vendetta" against him, based largely on his attraction of new members from Beth-El and his Zionism. His critics, he said, were composed of "neither payers nor prayers" who were definitely anti-Zionist. Engel also credited the conflict over Zionism as the major reason why they left Emanu-El, and "are actively being sponsored by the American Council of Judaism. . . . This has never been admitted; in fact, it has been denied."[29]

Displaced Persons

In the aftermath of World War II, tens of millions of Europeans had been left destitute and homeless, but unlike most victims of the war's destruction, Europe's Jews had been uprooted, stripped of their possessions, imprisoned, and specifically targeted by the Nazis for extermination. By 1947, approximately 250,000 survivors of Hitler's Final Solution had been concentrated in Displaced Persons camps in Germany, Austria, and Italy.[30] While some Jews returned to their original hometowns, many of them, primarily Polish Jews, did not have that option due to the violent antisemitism that remained. Instead, these survivors, through the auspices of numerous Jewish aid organizations, immigrated to Palestine, the United States, and other countries willing to accept them. While the majority immigrated to Palestine, approximately 140,000 settled in the United States.

The NRS, which had directed the resettlement of Jewish refugees in the late 1930s and early 1940s, again played a central role in postwar resettlement of Jewish Displaced Persons. In order to meet the new crisis, the NRS merged with the NCJW's Service for the Foreign Born in August 1946 to create the United Service for New Americans (USNA), an organization devoted to assisting Jewish DPs. These Holocaust survivors who resettled in the United

States were not called "survivors" as they would be in the decades that followed. Instead, the USNA used the terms "DP" or "New Americans." As historian Beth Cohen states in her penetrating examination of postwar Jewish refugees, "While—intentionally—there was nothing about its name to suggest it, USNA was strictly a Jewish agency funded by the United Jewish Appeal. Its goal was to work with the American [JDC] in Europe and with local cooperating Jewish communal agencies around the United States . . . to facilitate the refugees' resettlement away from New York City."[31] Much like the prewar refugee crisis, Jews and Jewish organizations in New York worried that the immigrants would remain in the city, overwhelming their resources and creating undesirable Jewish ghettos. While most of the immigrants who arrived in the United States remained in New York City, Jewish agencies placed tremendous pressure on the USNA to resettle the newcomers in other locales.

Unlike the earlier crisis, where only individuals could sign affidavits for refugees, welfare agencies such as the USNA now could provide "corporate affidavits" and assume responsibility for the newcomers. The NRS, prior to its transformation into the USNA, had suggested to President Harry S. Truman that it be granted the "authority to act as sponsors of potential immigrants," a suggestion to which Truman quickly agreed. This change in immigration policy, as Cohen explains, "had a profound impact on the agencies directing the resettlement efforts. Granting the agencies responsibility relieved the US government of the major financial burden of the immigrants."[32]

Jews in Alabama did not form a statewide committee to coordinate resettlement of DPs as they did in 1938. Instead, the USNA worked with and through local Jewish communities and agencies to arrange resettlement. Numerous problems surrounded the resettlement of these newcomers, some of them reminiscent of the prewar efforts. Many of the problems, however, were quite new, generated by the circumstances of the newcomers themselves, who had been profoundly affected by their experiences in the Holocaust; the communities, too, had been affected by the war and the revelations of the Holocaust, and these changes and controversies within the communities reverberated well into the postwar years.

When the USNA visited Montgomery in April 1948 to inquire about the possibility of resettlement for DPs, it found the Jewish community in turmoil. Although the Orthodox and Sephardic congregations became more cohesive in the years following the war, even establishing the Jewish Progress Club in response to their exclusion from the Reform-dominated Standard Club, the community remained riven with cultural differences, primarily concerning Zionism and Israel. As a result, the Jewish federation had not even begun its fund-raising efforts for the year because no one had been willing to assume the chairmanship. The "hard feelings" in the community generated over Zionism caused Beatrice Behrman, who had come to Montgomery on behalf of the USNA, to observe that "with all of this local feuding, there is the lack of cooperative spirit necessary to undertake our program of resettlement."[33] Despite their sharp disagreements over Zionism, Montgomery's Jews recognized the need to resettle DPs and agreed "that their community would be willing to assume the responsibility for participating in a resettlement program," with each subcommunity, Orthodox, Sephardic, and Reform, participating.[34]

By 1949, Montgomery had organized a refugee committee to facilitate the resettlement of DPs and accepted an initial quota of five units. Yet problems inherent within the Jewish community prevented members of the committee from cooperating efficiently, a problem Montgomery's Jewish community faced when it organized its coordinating committee in the late 1930s. For example, those on the case committee remained continually at odds with members of the employment committee as to the types of jobs made available to the newcomers, complaining that they wanted to "push them into a job as soon after they arrived as possible, regardless of the kind of job," leading to frustration on the part of the immigrant and those in the community. The USNA field agent, Albert Meyers, reminded them that a job that "lacked any future, or was of such a nature as to hinder a newcomer's adjustment in the community was pointless and only added unnecessary difficulties to the resettlement process." The lack of sufficient industry in Montgomery, in addition to the generally low wages offered for nonskilled workers in the region, made self-sufficiency difficult to achieve, especially for those immigrants with families to support.[35]

As Edwin Rosenberg, the president of the USNA, observed, the newcomers, because of their experiences in the Holocaust, had little opportunity to learn a trade, fewer cultural opportunities, spoke little English, and "their hardships have caused a variety of defects which require medical treatment. They are, therefore, not as readily employable and consequently a larger proportion requires help."[36] A number of the DPs who had been resettled in Montgomery fit this description, and such circumstances provided a significant but not insurmountable obstacle. Yet the poor resources for newcomers in Montgomery and their lack of economic success made adjustment extremely difficult. Although Montgomerians had been "quite friendly" in their welcome, there remained a substantial difference between the "costly social life" of Montgomery's Jews and what the newcomers could afford. Because the newcomers had not been "absorbed" into the community, Bernard

Lobman remarked, it became "discouraging to the people themselves who are unable to become self-supporting and live an ordinary, normal life."[37]

A member of the refugee committee, Edith Weil, told the USNA that Montgomery's "interest in the resettlement program is being affected by the attitude of the New Americans, their unrest and discontent" and their desire to return to New York. The employment committee, she stated, spent much time arranging jobs for the newcomers, a task made more difficult due to their "language limitations and lack of skill. After prospective employers are persuaded to take the newcomer and train him for a job, he remains just long enough to get to be useful and then decides to leave. The employment committee is losing sympathy and patience. The case committee feels that something is wrong somewhere. Either people are persuaded to come here against their will, or they are not briefed sufficiently to know what to expect of a small southern community as to job possibilities, salaries, and so forth. . . . The whole program seems to have bogged down and we are just about ready to throw up the sponge."[38] Initially, the USNA believed that unskilled, unattached immigrants would be preferable for Montgomery, a small, nonindustrialized city, where they would be able to adjust much more quickly than entire family units. This, however, was not the case, as single men found adjustment much harder than anticipated.

These newcomers, moreover, came face to face with Jim Crow segregation, an uncomfortable reminder of the racism responsible for their suffering at the hands of the Nazis. Those Jewish refugees who fled the Nazis prior to the war or who had survived the camps reacted in a similar fashion after being resettled in the segregated South. Some left the South while others attempted to conform. As Lawrence Powell asks of the DPs and the racial climate in New Orleans, "how far could one let the assimilation process go without sacrificing Jewish identity and diluting Jewish culture?" Apart from leaving the South, the attitude survivors took, Powell notes, was to endure the discomfort as long as they were not persecuted.[39] In this regard survivors in New Orleans differed little from survivors in Alabama cities such as Montgomery. Although the unskilled newcomers often took low-paying manual jobs, they could not take jobs African Americans generally held because it was considered "degrading to the community." This led some newcomers to believe "that they constitute a third class in the southern social structure, just a little higher than the Negro population." In Montgomery they did not have anyone to whom they could turn to discuss these problems, often insisting "that only other DPs can understand them," further increasing their social isolation and their desire to leave.[40]

Much of the community's difficulties stemmed from its lack of professional casework agencies to assist in helping the newcomers adjust to their new life. The refugee committee also did not have anyone who could speak German or Yiddish to mitigate the newcomers' sense of isolation. As a result, the USNA's Saul Travin observed that "the community cannot deal too successfully with difficult cases, older immigrants or those who do not have some knowledge of English." Much of the casework for the immigrants fell to Hannah Simon, the secretary of the Jewish federation. Members of the refugee committee had repeatedly requested a full-time professional caseworker to assist in easing the newcomers' transition to their new life in Montgomery, but had been rebuffed by Joseph Marshuetz, the president of the Jewish federation and a relative of Simon, who preferred to keep Simon in that position. As a result, the Montgomery community could scarcely relate to or assist the newcomers in their adjustment, and the Montgomery section of the NCJW, the organization that directed the resettlement, became "discouraged over the fact that so many of their units want to leave Montgomery which they interpreted as an indication that they had failed." Between 1949 and 1951, Montgomery had resettled thirteen units, although by September 1951 only four units remained.[41]

In the nearby Black Belt town of Selma, only two refugee families remained from the prewar resettlement. Only one of those, the Bergers, had come through the efforts of the NRS. Mishkan Israel's new rabbi, Peter Levinson, was a refugee as well. He came to the United States in 1939 through the NRS to study at Hebrew Union College in Cincinnati, Ohio. Levinson arrived in Selma in mid-1948 and became quickly acclimated to the small, southern community, gaining the acceptance in Selma of both the Jewish and non-Jewish communities. He had even been given time on the local radio station "for general talks on matters of civic interest." When Beatrice Behrman came to Selma in February 1949, she found a community that had successfully resettled a number of refugees. As Behrman presented the problems facing the hundreds of thousands of DPs remaining in Europe, "the deep and warm human interest of these people in the plight of the overseas Jews," she recounted, "was an experience to witness."[42] Selma quickly agreed to participate in the resettlement program and accepted a quota of six family units.

In October 1949, Selma welcomed the Sznur family "with open arms." Originally from Poland, the Sznurs experienced tremendous difficulty in adjusting to their new life. Apparently Clara Sznur had an "irrational jealousy" concerning her husband that led to loud and often public quarrels between the two. She was thoroughly convinced that her husband was having an affair with a Polish woman behind her back; an affair, she insisted, that began prior to the war, persisted throughout the conflict, and was continuing in Selma. Mrs. Sznur had been seen "walking around the [boarding] house at night in the nude looking for someone or something under beds, closets, etc., apparently . . . for this Polish woman." Of course, no Polish woman such as this existed in Selma. Her husband explained that she had been unable to put her experiences during the war behind her and "was physically run down and was nervous and over-wrought as a result of her terrible experience while in hiding from the Germans during the war years." The loud quarrels soon became public knowledge and convinced some in the community that the Sznurs needed to be returned to New York. The disturbing behavior jeopardized the resettlement program in Selma.[43]

The psychological problems Mrs. Sznur suffered were not uncommon in Holocaust survivors. Those immigrants who arrived postwar differed profoundly from those who arrived in the late 1930s and early 1940s. As Beth Cohen argues, "the influence of the Holocaust on survivors was pervasive from the start. As the refugees moved forward, they harbored this trauma in their lives, deeply a part of them but invisible to the outside world. This essential difference, so critical to the survivors' existence after the Holocaust, was what made them unlike other immigrants. And this was lost on those who were there to help them."[44] While the physical and psychological trauma of the Holocaust undoubtedly played a role in how the survivors coped with their new lives, it did not mean that this trauma consigned them to perpetual depression or fear. William B. Helmreich, who examined the lives of hundreds of survivors, suggests that "taking into account their past suffering, the survivors' ability to think rationally about the event and to analyze it in a way that permits them to go on living with themselves and with others is noteworthy. Although they cannot forget the horrors they endured and have been scarred by them, they function well and seem to require less professional counseling and assistance than one would suspect." How survivors coped with their experiences and the success that they have shown in building new lives, Helmreich argues, offers "valuable lessons for all those who suffer through adversity and tragedy."[45]

By 1950 the "deep and warm human interest" toward DPs that Behrman had found in Selma had dissipated, and community leaders found it "impossible to accept any more quotas." They cited the many difficulties they faced in "housing, re-educating, finding jobs, and readjusting these immigrants."[46] Although they did not mention the Sznurs, it was obvious that the problems associated with the readjustment of the newcomers contributed to their decision. Moreover, Rabbi Levinson had decided to return to Germany to take a new position, leaving the Jewish community without any leadership. Seymore Cohn, who served as the congregational president, told the USNA that the various problems, in addition to the lack of leadership in the community, meant that "responsibility or not—the Selma community is definitely not receptive towards accepting any additional displaced families. . . . I honestly feel that the Jewish community of Selma is hardly able to take care of any additional displaced persons and I know the feeling is that we do not *want anymore*."[47]

Members of Birmingham's Displaced Persons committee worked well together, despite serious disagreements over Palestine, and avoided the dysfunction Montgomery's refugee committee experienced. Numerous members of the community contributed to make the resettlement of DPs a success. Dora Roth, as she did in the earlier refugee crisis, effectively directed the program from her position as executive secretary of the United Jewish Fund; Rebecca Blumberg and Tillie Kimerling consistently visited and checked on the newcomers; and Buddy Cooper, who headed the employment committee, made it clear that "the task of job-finding and satisfactory placement is the responsibility of every Jewish person in the community."[48] Jewish doctors and dentists offered free medical treatment, and the United Jewish Fund provided assistance to those newcomers who had yet to become self-supporting. As the Displaced Persons committee reported, "Many of the problems that confront any community working with the resettlement of DPs will begin to disappear once these men become self-sustaining economically, and do not feel the need and indignity of taking supplementation from the DP Committees."[49]

To publicize the UJA's fund-raising campaign to aid DPs in Europe, the United Jewish Fund publicized the experiences of two veterans from Birmingham who had witnessed the horrors of the Final Solution. The *Birmingham News* published two articles in September 1947 that described in vivid detail the suffering of Jews at the hands of the Nazis and the plight of the survivors still residing in DP camps. David Levin, who had been one of the first Americans to enter Buchenwald, said that even after what the prisoners had gone through, they "still wanted to live." But freedom from the camps did not follow liberation, Levin argued. "Still, even now in 1947," he continued, "when the rest of the world has gone about its business, these same distraught people are still shut in camps—DP camps under UN supervision, but camps nonetheless." He thought it Americans' duty to "make good the faith these people had in America and Americans when we came to the gates of Buchenwald" and to give them "their first real chance at freedom and a new life."[50] Two days after Levin's account appeared in the press, Tarrant's Joe Kanter explained in another article that "America has missed its big chance to see justice done for the displaced underdogs of Europe." Kanter had been in charge of DPs in the area of Selb, Germany, and believed that when Germans "saw America was not going to demand that Jews and other DPs get fair treatment, they began to feel that we were weak. There were cases of harsh treatment against DPs all over again. In one town a German official refused to give Jewish DPs any food at all. This official was a definite former Nazi. When the Germans found that we were going to round up DPs and put them in concentration camps, then they regained their old cockiness." Kanter had little faith in the United Nations' administration of the DP problem, or that Jews could remain in Germany outside of DP camps, but he urged the *News*'s readers to contribute to the UJA campaign to assist "these unfortunate people in any case. Having failed to do more it is our duty to do this small thing."[51]

By 1950, Birmingham had resettled eleven units, numbering twenty-seven individuals. Chaim and Chana Schniper, who had escaped from Cherson work camp in the Ukraine in 1945, could be considered representative of those survivors who settled in Birmingham after the war and made a new life for themselves. The Schnipers immigrated to the United States in 1950 through the auspices of the USNA and had been sponsored by the United Jewish Fund upon their arrival in Birmingham. Born in Rowno, Poland, Chaim Schniper had been in medical school when the Nazis invaded. Although Chaim was well educated and spoke several languages, his lack of English limited his opportunities. Like other resettled refugees, he had no driver's license or automobile and thus had to walk or take the bus to work, school, or the market. During the day, he worked at the Alabama Novelty House for the Abelsons and Rittenbaums, while in the evening he took English courses at nearby Phillips High School. At home, Chaim taught what he had learned to Chana and their two sons, Jack and Abe. In 1955, they became US citizens. Through their determination and the assistance of the Jewish community they eventually opened their own business, Schniper's Dry Goods. The Schnipers remained in Birmingham for the rest of their lives.[52] In fact, few DPs in Birmingham experienced any maladjustment. Karl Friedman recalled that "some few who came were angry, belligerent, demanding and unpleasant, all conditions forgivable in light of what they had been subject to in their former homelands. Some never changed and lived out their lives in stress and loneliness." Despite these unfortunate and tragic cases, the resettlement of DPs in Birmingham met with great success.[53] Chaim and Chana Schniper's life and success serve as but one example of the vital work those in the community undertook to resettle Holocaust survivors.

The majority of DPs and Holocaust survivors who immigrated to the

United States remained in New York, surrounded by a vast cultural support network, numerous Jewish welfare agencies, and greater opportunities for employment and success. Small towns such as Selma, or nonindustrialized cities such Montgomery, could provide few, if any, resources or support for the newcomers. This pattern was not found only in the South, but throughout the Midwest and West, with small Jewish communities who, eager to help, lacked the resources or opportunities to assist in the acclimatization of the newcomers to American life. As a result, most of the Holocaust survivors who settled in Alabama did so many years after the war, making the adjustment to American life in places outside of the state.

The deep concern of Jews, as well as many Gentiles, about events transpiring in Europe in the 1930s and 1940s—the antisemitic persecution in Nazi Germany followed by war and the mass murder of the Jews in Nazi-dominated Eastern Europe—clearly altered the outlook of Alabama's Jews. These events compelled them, like Jews throughout the United States, to contribute to relief and rescue efforts on behalf of European Jewry. Their efforts included organizing themselves to support Jewish refugees fleeing Nazi persecution; lobbying of local, state, and national officials; support for the American war effort, either on the home front or the front lines; and by opening their arms to the survivors of Hitler's Final Solution. Despite the religious, cultural, and economic divisions within the community, Alabama's Jews clearly recognized the immense danger Nazism posed to Jews and worked together in numerous common endeavors to alleviate the suffering of European Jews imperiled by Nazism, and they did so successfully within the scope of their influence. Yet no matter how well they organized, lobbied, or formed interreligious coalitions, the limitations imposed by policies, decisions, and events beyond their control meant that the most they could hope to accomplish was to save a small number of individuals.

Simultaneously, Alabama's Jews, like the southern white non-Jewish majority, exhibited a profound cognitive dissonance in regard to the implications of Nazi racism and the Holocaust to racial intolerance in Alabama and the South. African Americans, as the black press demonstrated, empathized with persecuted European Jews because of their own experience with racism, segregation, and racial violence. Jews, however, refused to draw any parallel. Some had openly embraced southern mores; others tacitly accepted them. Moreover, that their racial status could possibly be called into question, despite considering themselves part of the white community, also reinforced such silence. They had learned the lesson of the few Jews who had openly supported black rights, that such an association would not be tolerated within the confines of Jim Crow.

The establishment of Israel did not bring about a resolution to the many divisions and issues surrounding Alabama's Jews—and indeed Judaism itself—but it did lay a substantial foundation for closer relationships between the Jewish subcommunities that members of these communities built upon in the decades following. Central to these efforts were the returning veterans, whose experiences in the service and in the war had profoundly affected their worldview. As Deborah Dash Moore explains in her study of Jewish GIs, "Jews in the service unexpectedly came to appreciate Judaism in a new way in part because the armed forces treated it with respect. As one of the three 'fighting faiths of democracy,' Judaism assumed an American legitimacy unanticipated at the start of the war. Protestantism, Catholicism, and Judaism were deemed to share common values that made them religions of democracy." As Moore points out, "the war would do more than enshrine the Judeo-Christian tradition as America's faith . . . it would subsequently delegitimize those who claimed that the United States was a Christian country and that only Protestants were Christian. Acceptance of the Judeo-Christian tradition in the armed forces would force Protestants to share the Christian label with Catholics and include Jews as equal partners in America."[54]

These veterans, imbued with such experiences, spurred further conciliation within Alabama's Jewish community. Men such as Arthur Prince and Milton Klein in Mobile; Herman "Dick" Loeb in Montgomery; and Edward M. Friend Jr., Jerome "Buddy" Cooper, Emil Hess, and Robert Loeb in Birmingham assumed leadership roles in their respective communities in the following years. In fact, Hess and Loeb spearheaded a Birmingham chapter of the AJC in 1949, the first chapter established in the city. Many veterans also joined other congregations upon their return home rather than attend the one in which they were raised, further breaking down the cultural barriers of the past. Arthur Prince in Mobile, who grew up in the Orthodox Ahavas Chesed, remembered that when "[I] came back from the Army, I had some feelings for Reform Judaism, I liked the service better. I liked, I just liked several things better. I believed more that way. So I told my parents I was enjoying the Temple, this was 1949 after college. And they were just so glad . . . that I was going to be a Jew." When veterans returned, Prince noted, "a lot of them joined the Temple, even a lot of them that had been raised as Orthodox Jews, as had I."[55]

The Nazi persecution of the Jews that began in 1933 and culminated with the slaughter of six million European Jews can be seen not only as the most tragic and horrific period in modern Jewish history but also as a vivid illustration of the interdependent connections between European events and local and regional developments in the United States, more specifically in the American South. For Alabama's Jews, it is the point when they began to put aside their significant cultural differences, working together in common for the welfare of persecuted and suffering European Jews. Differences still existed, to be sure—some controversial and divisive like Zionism, others more ephemeral, such as class and acculturation. The mutual interest Jews of all traditions shared, whether driven to aid Jews abroad, to care for Jewish servicemen stationed in their town, or to assist Holocaust survivors in starting a new life, created common ground that facilitated greater cooperation with the community. With the revelations of the Holocaust, even the most divisive issue began to dissipate as support for Zionism emerged among more of the state's Reform Jews. The establishment of Israel, and the acceptance of the Jewish state by many Reform Jews, further eroded cultural differences. Of course, not all of Alabama's Reform Jews accepted Zionism; some adamantly remained anti-Zionist. Even today, cultural differences remain within the Jewish community, but these lessen with the passing of each generation. Yet in the shadow of Hitler's murderous program, Alabama's Jews began to coalesce, creating the decisive turning point when Alabama's Jewish community began to conceive of themselves as part of a much larger Judaic culture.

Postscript

For most Alabamians and indeed most Americans, life returned to normal in the years following the end of the war. As time passed, Alabamians reflected back on World War II with growing nostalgia, remembered by many, as Studs Terkel brilliantly chronicled, as the "Good War."[1] The murder of six million European Jews during the war was not part of this nostalgia. For the state's non-Jews, the Holocaust, for all intents and purposes, disappeared from public discourse for roughly thirty years, with only a brief interlude of the Adolf Eichmann trial in 1961. Only with the broadcast of the television miniseries *The Holocaust* in 1978 was Alabama's non-Jewish population reintroduced to the Nazi crimes of genocide.

Scholars of American Jewry disagree over whether American Jews remained silent about the Holocaust in the postwar years, at least until the Eichmann trial brought the Nazi crimes back to the fore. Israel's Six-Day War in 1967 and the Yom Kippur War in 1973, for Jews at least, clearly raised the specter of another Jewish Holocaust, this time in the Middle East, not Europe. Many scholars argue that prior to this American Jews generally did not talk about the Holocaust, and only during this period did the Holocaust begin to assume a central place in Jewish discourse and memory. Recent scholarship by historian Hasia Diner has contradicted the idea that Jews remained silent about events of the Holocaust in the postwar years, that they instead continually discussed and memorialized those murdered by the Nazis since the war's end. Given the dearth of research into the postwar Alabama Jewish community, however, it is unclear how Jews in Alabama reacted in the period between the end of the war and the late 1960s. Indeed, much work in this area remains to be done.

Jewish Silence in Postwar America?

Numerous scholars have argued that American Jews said little about the Holocaust in the roughly two decades that followed the end of World War II.

In 1957, sociologist Nathan Glazer remarked that the "murder of six million Jews by Hitler"—Glazer did not use the term Holocaust—and the creation of Israel "had remarkably slight effects on the inner life of American Jewry." Although Glazer noted that "hundreds of thousands who had had little or nothing to do with Jewish life were drawn into Jewish activities . . . not many people responded to these events by joining the synagogue."[2] Beginning early in the 1980s, scholars claimed that American Jews remained silent in regard to the Holocaust in the years following the war.[3] By the early 1990s, Edward S. Shapiro, in *A Time for Healing: American Jewry since World War II*, the final volume of the American Jewish Historical Society's five-volume The Jewish People in America series, observed that American Jews prior to the 1960s were reluctant to talk about the Holocaust, communities had no commemorations, and there existed "little public discussion among Jews regarding the fate of European Jewry." According to Shapiro, this reluctance ended in 1961 with the Adolf Eichmann trial in Jerusalem, in addition to the appearance of some of the first books on the Holocaust, including Elie Wiesel's *Night* (1960) and Raul Hilberg's *The Destruction of the European Jews* (1961). By this time, he continued, survivors were more willing to discuss their experiences, and the Six-Day War in 1967 sparked repressed memories as "Jews had to confront a very real possibility of a second Holocaust."[4]

As Shapiro and others have argued, the Holocaust remained on the fringes of American and American Jewish consciousness until the late 1960s and early 1970s. The most comprehensive and perhaps the most controversial study to articulate this argument is Peter Novick's *The Holocaust in American Life*. Novick contends that the Holocaust barely, if at all, registered among Americans as a singular event prior to the 1970s, after which it proceeded to become firmly entrenched in American life and culture, with both Jews and non-Jews, by the end of the twentieth century, perceiving it to be one of the most important events in history. While hardly doing justice to Novick's complex and nuanced arguments, one can summarize his position as follows. The initial silence prior to the 1960s and 1970s was due to conscious choices American Jews made not to talk about the Holocaust. Conversely, the Holocaust became central to "how American Jews understood themselves and how they represented themselves to others" after the 1970s also because of conscious choices American Jews made.[5]

The reasons behind the silence included geopolitical considerations and those of a more personal nature. In the years immediately following the war, the focus on German crimes interfered with Cold War mobilization of West Germany. The Holocaust, at least in the late 1940s and 1950s, "was the wrong atrocity" for American purposes, especially in regard to the Manichaean Cold War narrative the West created. Communists, including defenders of Ethel and Julius Rosenberg, frequently used Holocaust rhetoric. As a result, American Jews remained silent to avoid being labeled a "Red" or a Communist Jew, a common antisemitic stereotype that had persisted since the Russian Revolution in 1917. Moreover, American Jews did not want to be perceived as victims, especially during the "upbeat and universalist postwar mood" of the country. Because of that, Jews generally avoided the subject of the Holocaust.[6]

The reticence of American Jews to publicly discuss the Holocaust eased with the Eichmann trial. According to Novick, the Eichmann trial marked "the first time that . . . the Holocaust was presented to the American public as an entity in its own right, distinct from Nazi barbarism in general." In doing so, the term "Holocaust" became "firmly attached" to the slaughter of European Jewry.[7] The anxiety that the 1967 Six-Day War produced among American Jews reoriented the agenda of Jewish organizations toward greater support for Israel, but Israel's difficulties in the 1973 Yom Kippur War magnified this anxiety and cemented both Israel and, subsequently, the Holocaust at the center of American Jewish consciousness. Consequently, Israel became the most important focus of organized American Jewry and perhaps the critical identifying factor of American Jews. In fact, Novick argues that thereafter, "the hallmark of the good Jew became the depth of his or her commitment to Israel."[8]

While American Jews had internally and informally discussed the death of "the Six Million" in the years after World War II, this discourse did not make the Holocaust a central part of the American Jewish experience or identity. The "massive investments by Jewish communal organizations in promoting 'Holocaust consciousness'" in order to mobilize support for Israel after the Yom Kippur War began the transformation of the Holocaust as an event on the fringe of Jewish consciousness to an event at the center of not only American Jewish consciousness but also American consciousness.[9] Such investment, Novick makes clear, came not from a coordinated or unified effort by these organizations—debunking any idea of Jewish "conspiracy"—but from many groups working individually toward the same purpose. Even as Jewish organizations invoked the Holocaust and its memory to rally support for Israel, they also worried over the survival of American Jews. This "survival anxiety" stemmed not from fears of their physical survival from persecution, but rather from the loss of Jewish identity, especially "among the assimilating and intermarrying younger generation." Some Jewish leaders suggested by the early 1970s that this lack of Jewish commitment on the part of younger Jews arose because they lacked "awareness of the Holocaust." At the same time, the growth of "identity politics" allowed "Jews to embrace a victim identity based upon the Holocaust. . . . The only thing that all American Jews shared was the knowledge that but for the immigration of near or distant ancestors, they would have shared the fate of European Jewry. Insofar as the Holocaust became the defining Jewish experience, all Jews had 'honorary' survivorship in common. Insofar as it attained mythic status, expressing truths about an enduring Jewish condition, all were united in an essential victim identity."[10]

By the end of the 1970s, the Holocaust began to attain significance with the American public at large. In April 1978 approximately one hundred million Americans watched the nine-plus-hour production of the television miniseries *The Holocaust*—what Novick calls "the most important moment in the entry of the Holocaust into general American consciousness." In the four nights that the miniseries aired, observers commented, Americans learned more about the Holocaust than they had within the previous thirty years.[11] Later that same year, on the thirtieth anniversary of Israel's birth, Jimmy Carter created the President's Commission on the Holocaust to study the creation of a national Holocaust memorial. In April 1979, the first commemoration was held at the nation's Capitol. Over the next decade, other events, some widely publicized, others not, kept the Holocaust in front of the American public. By the 1990s, the Holocaust had permeated American consciousness, culminating in 1993 with Steven Spielberg's Academy Award–winning *Schindler's List* and the opening of the United States Holocaust Memorial Museum on the National Mall, one of the most visited, if not *the* most visited, attractions in Washington DC. As Novick argues, the Holocaust is central to how American Jews represent themselves to non-Jews, with the US Holocaust Museum "the principle symbol and 'address' of American Jewry, our 'epistle to the gentiles' about what it means to be Jewish."[12]

No one questioned the idea of Jewish silence in the aftermath of the Holocaust or that they remained silent because "deliberate forgetting" remained the accepted narrative, although numerous scholars vigorously challenged Novick's arguments and interpretations.[13] That is, until Hasia Diner's *We Remember with Reverence and Love: American Jews and the Myth of Silence after the Holocaust, 1945–1962*. Diner began her research into American Jewry's postwar silence in 2004, noting that this claim "struck me as wrong in and of itself and because it almost always came with little evidence to back it up."[14] In fact, before she started investigating this myth of silence regarding American Jews and the Holocaust, Diner had argued the same points as previously mentioned scholars in *A New Promised Land: A History of Jews in America* (2003): "Neither *The Diary of Anne Frank* nor the Eichmann trial made American Jews talk about the Holocaust. They did not define their Jewish identities in relation to it. In the late 1960s and 1970s, however, younger Jews began to take a greater interest in the Holocaust. . . . They wanted to know more about what had been an almost forbidden subject."[15]

In the groundbreaking, revisionist *We Remember with Reverence and Love*, Diner argues, with the support of extensive archival research, that American Jews did not remain silent in the years immediately following World War II and "told and retold details of the catastrophe in multiple forms. Over and over, men and women asserted the necessity of revisiting it in their institutions and organs of public opinion, in all its horrors."[16] They did this through sermons, liturgies, songs, poetry, drama, and numerous other ways—what Diner calls a "vast unorganized spontaneous project"—to remember and commemorate the murdered victims of the Holocaust. In copious detail, Diner lays to rest the idea that American Jews remained silent. This myth of silence, she argues, "had been built on slipshod scholarship that put ideology over evidence."[17]

Diner's heavy reliance on the actions and responses of national organizations, in addition to the records of northeastern and midwestern Jewry—admittedly where the bulk of American Jews reside—raises questions of whether her conclusions can be applied to Alabama and the South. Apart from a few of Harry Golden's opinions, one of the only examples of southern Jews speaking out is when the Charleston, South Carolina, Jewish community produced the play *For Those Who Live in the Sun* in 1950 to celebrate two hundred years of Jewish life in Charleston. Written by Sam Byrd, a New Yorker, the play revolved around a family of Polish DPs—Holocaust survivors—who were resettled in Charleston. As Diner notes about the play, "the dramatic device of making Holocaust survivors key characters in a pageant marking two centuries of a southern Jewish community spoke volumes about postwar American Jewry. The play allowed the local Jewish community to show how long it had been present in South Carolina and how crucial a role Jews had played in making America and local history possible. The play also allowed them to demonstrate . . . how deeply they felt their responsibility toward the survivors of the Holocaust . . . and those resettled in Charleston."[18] Birmingham's United Jewish Fund, while it did not produce such a dramatic production, reacted similarly when it used the press to publicize the plight of DPs in postwar Germany. Unfortunately, Diner makes no mention of Charleston Jewry—or little mention of southern Jewry for that matter—beyond *For Those Who Live in the Sun*.

Moreover, Diner's broad claims that the Holocaust caused American Jews and national Jewish organizations to challenge racism and discrimination more forcefully, ignores important regional distinctions. Although many northern Jews linked civil rights and the Holocaust implicitly and explicitly and believed that the murder of European Jewry "contextualized" black suffering, most southern Jews did no such thing. As has been demonstrated, Alabama's Jewish community failed to connect Nazi racism with Jim Crow prior to the war either implicitly or explicitly, and they disavowed national Jewish organizations' actions over civil rights in the 1950s and 1960s, even though Alabamian Irving Engel led the American Jewish Committee. Diner also claims that "American Jewish community leaders had no choice but to see and make the connection between the civil rights movement and the legacy of Hitler and the Nazis," thanks to the racists and antisemitic "enemies" who fanned the flames of racial hatred. Numerous southern rabbis and community leaders spoke out on behalf of civil rights, but it is doubtful that southern Jews would want publicly to connect Nazi racism and the Holocaust with southern white racial beliefs and discriminatory practices in the 1950s and 1960s any more than they did in the 1930s and 1940s. On the other hand, characterizing antisemites such as John Crommelin and J. B. Stoner as Nazi inspired or using the example of Nazism to condemn antisemitism would not be controversial in the least.[19]

With the lack of research pertaining to Jewish Alabama in the postwar years, it is impossible to determine whether Alabama's Jews spoke publicly or often about the Holocaust prior to the mid-1960s and early 1970s. A brief survey of Alabama's Jewish community in the years after World War II does not support Diner's conclusions, but this assessment is hardly conclusive, as the examination of the postwar period thus far has been only cursory. Nevertheless, because the attitudes and actions of Alabama's Jews frequently mirrored national patterns throughout the 1930s and the 1940s, it is reasonable to assume that Alabama's Jewish community did the same in the postwar years, as Diner argues. In fact, given the profound changes within Alabama's Jewish community wrought by Nazism, war, and the Holocaust—changes that "strongly affected [their] basic pattern of thought and feeling" in addition to the trajectory of Jewish life in the state—it is difficult to believe that they remained silent.[20] It is hoped that future scholars will examine just when and how Alabama's Jews, both publicly and privately, began to discuss the horrific events of the Holocaust and memorialize the victims of Nazi crimes.

Holocaust Memory in Alabama

There is little thus far, apart from Diner's comprehensive study of American Jewry, to suggest that the Holocaust became a topic of discussion in Alabama until the late 1970s and early 1980s, except for the brief period surrounding the Eichmann trial in 1961 or mounting Jewish concerns over Israel's conflicts with its Arab neighbors. It is clear, however, that the television broadcast of the miniseries *The Holocaust* in 1978 set in motion events that brought the Holocaust to the attention of the wider public, both in Alabama and throughout the nation.

Only a few months after the broadcast of *The Holocaust*, President Jimmy Carter ordered the creation of a President's Commission on the Holocaust to investigate the creation of a Holocaust memorial museum, as previously mentioned. Regardless of the timing, Carter's decision had little to do with the television broadcast. Edward T. Linenthal argues that Carter's decision to create a Holocaust commission had more to do with ameliorating Jewish concerns over the administration's approach to Israel and the Middle East: "Carter would use the power of government to do something many would perceive as 'good' and, at the same time, reach out to an increasingly alienated ethnic constituency. An act of commemoration could, fortuitously, also serve more pragmatic political ends."[21] Carter announced the creation of the commission on May 1, 1978, to coincide with Israel's thirtieth anniversary, and issued Executive Order 12093 on November 1, 1978, officially creating the President's Commission on the Holocaust.[22] In 1980, Congress established the US Holocaust Memorial Council to create the memorial and to coordinate a national commemoration to the victims of the Holocaust, a commemoration that became known as the Days of Remembrance. Although Carter led the first Days of Remembrance commemoration in 1979, the first council-sponsored commemoration occurred in 1981 at the White House. By 1983, the council planned Days of Remembrance commemorations for all fifty states.

In response, Alabama governor George C. Wallace created a Holocaust Advisory Committee in 1983, appointing University of Alabama professor Charles S. Prigmore as the liaison to the US Holocaust Memorial Council. The advisory committee worked with the Alabama NCCJ to organize a memorial ceremony for victims of the Holocaust, the first of which took place on April 30, 1984, at the governor's mansion in Montgomery.[23] The committee was also charged to "plan, implement, and coordinate programs across the state relating to the Holocaust," in addition to organizing the memorial for the Days of Remembrance.[24] With the enthusiastic backing of Wallace, who took part in rather elaborate commemorations during his tenure as governor, memorial services proliferated throughout the state, with numerous synagogues and other Jewish organizations holding their own commemorations, with survivors, liberators, and children of survivors participating.

Consistent with the objectives of the US Holocaust Council, these events were ecumenical, with Christian ministers, both Protestant and Catholic, taking an active role in remembering the victims of the Holocaust.

Prior to 1983 there had been no public commemorations and little in the way of Holocaust study. Jerome Rosenberg, a professor of psychology at the University of Alabama, began teaching the first Holocaust course in the state in 1977, predating the public interest surrounding the broadcast of *The Holocaust*. By the mid-1980s, he had established a Holocaust studies program at the university, the only such academic program in Alabama to focus specifically on the Holocaust. Rosenberg joined the advisory committee in 1985 and quickly influenced the nature of its Holocaust commemoration. No longer did the committee conduct elaborate ceremonies, but instead planned simpler and more solemn memorials that focused squarely on the victims and survivors of the Holocaust, a pattern that remains to this day.

Moreover, the Alabama Department of Education, apparently influenced by the increased awareness of the Holocaust and prompted no doubt by *The Holocaust* miniseries and the US Holocaust Memorial Council, included *Anne Frank: The Diary of a Young Girl* on its list of required texts for public schools in 1983. The selection, however, was not without controversy. Four members of the Alabama Textbook Commission voted to reject the text because it was "a real downer."[25] Despite the reticence of some of the members of the textbook commission, the diary became part of the Alabama school curriculum.

The Alabama Holocaust Advisory Committee continued to sponsor the Days of Remembrance commemorations throughout the 1980s and 1990s, although the commemoration moved from the governor's mansion to the capitol, where it continues to be held. In 1999 the Alabama legislature created the Alabama Holocaust Commission, a state agency within the executive branch, to replace the advisory committee. This new commission continued to coordinate the Days of Remembrance and Yom HaShoah commemorations, as well as other memorial programs throughout the state, but the legislature also charged the commission to "enhance public awareness of the consequences and significance of the Holocaust" through educational programs by assisting "with the planning, coordinating and enriching of courses of study dealing with the Holocaust."[26] To that end, the commission divided Alabama into four educational regions, with each overseen by an educational coordinator who works with schools and organizations to promote and develop Holocaust education within the region. The commission also sponsors two annual scholarships to the Jewish Foundation for the Righteous Summer Institute for Teachers, offering an opportunity for state educators to develop their knowledge of the Holocaust while deepening the educational resources within the state.

Today, almost all of the Holocaust education within Alabama's secondary schools and for the public at large emanates from the Birmingham Holocaust Education Center (BHEC), created by the commission in 2002.[27] Birmingham serves as one of the four regional divisions and is the home to almost all of the remaining Holocaust survivors in Alabama, many of whom speak to groups large and small throughout the state. The BHEC coordinates traveling Holocaust exhibits and the speaking engagements of the state's Holocaust survivors, selects scholarship recipients, and facilitates teacher workshops throughout the state. It is primarily responsible for the growth of Holocaust education in the secondary school systems in Alabama, although the study of the Holocaust is not mandated by the Alabama Department of Education. While the University of Alabama remains the only postsecondary institution that has a specific program of study devoted to the Holocaust, courses on the subject can be found on almost every college campus in the state, just as it is on college campuses throughout the United States.

Unlike the years that followed the end of World War II, the Holocaust today plays a large, perhaps even a central role in how many Alabamians, and indeed many Americans, remember World War II. It has become unquestionably the grisly epitaph for the Nazi regime, and the standard by which all modern atrocities are measured. In remembering the Holocaust, Alabamians, both Jew and Gentile, look back on the murder of the six million and the unimaginable suffering of those who survived, not with nostalgia, but with respect and reverence.

Notes

Introduction

1. The Czech Memorial Scrolls Trust purchased the scrolls from the Communist Czech government in 1963 in order to preserve the deteriorating scrolls and stored them at Westminster Synagogue in London. Over 1,400 of the Czech scrolls have been entrusted to congregations all over the world. See http://www.czechmemorialscrollstrust.org/index.htm, accessed May 7, 2011. See also http://www.czechtorah.org/home.php, accessed May 7, 2011. The "Survivor of the Fire" pamphlet describes when and why the congregation accepted the Torah scroll. Found in the Ahavas Chesed Papers, University of South Alabama Archives (hereafter cited as USA).

2. "Survivor of the Fire" pamphlet, Ahavas Chesed Papers, USA. In 1986, Birmingham's Reform Temple Emanu-El also received a Torah scroll from the Czech Memorial Scrolls Trust.

3. Nathan Glazer suspects that prior to the Civil War, there was "very likely a higher proportion of Jews among the white population of the South than in the Northeast." Nathan Glazer, *American Judaism* (Chicago: University of Chicago Press, 1957), 23, 44.

4. Stephen J. Whitfield, "The Braided Identity of Southern Jewry," *American Jewish History* 77 (March 1988): 363–87.

5. Lee Shai Weissbach, "East European Immigrants and the Image of Jews in the Small-Town South," *American Jewish History* 85 (September 1997): 231–62. Weissbach notes that second-generation East European Jews in small towns throughout the South became "far less intensively Jewish" than their parents, with the third generation even more removed from immigrant traditions.

6. In 1927 the number of Jews residing in the South totaled 210,646. In 1937 the number had only risen to 214,465. Leonard Dinnerstein and Mary Dale Palsson, eds., *Jews in the South* (Baton Rouge: Louisiana State University Press, 1973), 22. In 1880 the number of Jews living in New York City numbered just over 60,000. By 1937, the Jewish population had grown to 2,035,000. See Jacob Rader Marcus, *To Count a People: American Jewish Population Data, 1585–1984* (Lanham, MD: University Press of America, 1990), 150–52.

7. Stephen J. Whitfield, *In Search of American Jewish Culture* (Hanover, NH: Brandeis University Press and the University Press of New England, 1999), xi–xv;

Eli N. Evans, *The Provincials: A Personal History of Jews in the South* (New York: Atheneum, 1973), vii–viii.

8. Evans, *The Provincials*, vii.

9. Nathan M. Kaganoff and Melvin I. Urofsky, *"Turn to the South": Essays on Southern Jewry* (Charlottesville: University Press of Virginia, 1979), xii. Southern Jewish history is a burgeoning field, beginning with the valuable and groundbreaking work of Evans's *The Provincials*. See also Dinnerstein and Palsson, *Jews in the South*, and Harry Golden, *Our Southern Landman* (New York: G. P. Putnam's Sons, 1974). For the development of southern Jewish historiography, see Mark K. Bauman, "A Century of Southern Jewish Historiography," *American Jewish Archives Journal* (2007): 3–78.

10. Mark K. Bauman, *The Southerner as American: Jewish Style* (Cincinnati: American Jewish Archives, 1996), 1; Bauman, "A Century of Southern Historiography," 24.

11. Marcie Cohen Ferris and Mark I. Greenberg, eds., *Jewish Roots in Southern Soil: A New History* (Waltham, MA: Brandeis University Press, 2006), 18–20. Bauman has acknowledged that regional differences exist, but "that the search for such distinctiveness has been exaggerated and tends to retard the emergence of a more complete, nuanced, and accurate understanding for what it was like for various Jewish subcommunities to live in the South over time." In regard to the Ferris and Greenberg anthology, he writes: "Many of the authors of the articles . . . fall into pitfalls. They find causative relationships with little evidence or logic and ignore comparative information from other suitable locations that make regional distinctiveness questionable. Eastern European Jews, Orthodoxy, Conservatism, and Zionism barely, if at all, appear. In somewhat contradictory fashion, the Jews in many of these essays respond to antisemitism often by doing everything possible to maintain religious practices, although the assumptions remain that the South has been relatively tolerant to Jews and that Jews strove to acculturate." Bauman, "A Century of Southern Historiography," 19, 61–62n75.

12. Eric L. Goldstein, "How Southern Is Southern Jewish History?" Unpublished paper cited with the permission of the author.

13. Ibid. For a fuller treatment of this, see Eric L. Goldstein, *The Price of Whiteness: Jews, Race, and American Identity* (Princeton, NJ: Princeton University Press, 2006).

14. Leonard Rogoff, *Homelands: Southern Jewish Identity in Durham and Chapel Hill, North Carolina* (Tuscaloosa: University of Alabama Press, 2001), 168; Rogoff, "Is the Jew White?: The Racial Place of the Southern Jew," *American Jewish History* 85 (September 1997): 226. Eric Goldstein has noted that this occurred much earlier than the 1930s, since throughout the nineteenth century and into the twentieth, some writers had frequently described Jews as a race but saw them "as unquestionably white in the southern context." Goldstein, *The Price of Whiteness*, chapter 3.

15. Manheim S. Shapiro, "Report on Southern Jewish Opinion," April 11, 1950, 5, Box 302, folder 6, RG347.17.10, American Jewish Committee Papers (hereafter cited as AJC), YIVO Institute for Jewish Research (hereafter cited as YIVO).

16. See Alfred O. Hero Jr., *The Southerner and World Affairs* (Baton Rouge: Louisiana State University Press, 1965), 474–503; Howard K. Rabinowitz, "Nativism, Big-

otry and Anti-Semitism in the South," in *Dixie Diaspora: An Anthology of Southern Jewish History*, ed. Mark K. Bauman (Tuscaloosa: University of Alabama Press, 2006), 280; Bauman, *The Southerner as American Jewish Style*, 11.

17. Bauman, "A Century of Southern Jewish Historiography," 45.

18. South Africa's system of apartheid had not developed to the same stage by this time.

19. Johnpeter H. Grill and Robert Jenkins, "The Nazis and the American South in the 1930s: A Mirror Image?" *Journal of Southern History* 58 (November 1992): 668.

20. For example, see Clive Webb, *Fight against Fear: Southern Jews and Black Civil Rights* (Athens: University of Georgia Press, 2001).

21. Shapiro, "Report on Southern Jewish Opinion," 6.

22. Perhaps the best non-southern example of such attitudes is how Jews on the West Coast responded and reacted to the Japanese and Japanese American internment during the war. See Ellen M. Eisenberg, *The First to Cry Down Injustice? Western Jews and Japanese Removal during WWII* (Lanham, MD: Lexington Books, 2008). Anti-Japanese prejudice on the West Coast, or even anti-Latino prejudice in the Southwest, can be comparable to the southern experience, but neither of those regions of the United States had an all-encompassing social structure to mirror Jim Crow.

23. W. J. Cash, *The Mind of the South* (New York: Alfred J. Knopf, 1941; reprint, London: Thames and Hudson, 1971), 333–34.

24. David Goldfield, "A Sense of Place: Jews, Blacks, and White Gentiles in the American South," *Southern Cultures* 3 (1997): 60.

25. One such example was when members of the Beth Zur B'nai B'rith Lodge in Mobile debated a resolution opposing President Roosevelt's attempt to pack the Supreme Court with justices favorable to his New Deal policies. They declined to speak out publicly after being advised that "every Jew, like citizens of the United States of all faiths and classes, has a right to an opinion on the wisdom of the President's proposal, as on all other matters of State, but those opinions are the opinions of citizens and not adherents to Judaism . . . upon a little further consideration you will readily see how fatal for the best interests of the Jew it would be for him as a group to array himself for or against a matter of governmental concern." J. G. Adler to Alfred M. Cohen, February 19, 1937; S. Rothschild to J. G. Adler, February 22, 1937, Beth Zur Lodge of B'nai B'rith Papers, Springhill Avenue Temple Archives. Once again, there were exceptions to this attempt to remain indistinct. Reform rabbis, for instance, made it a point to make Judaism distinctive relative to Christianity, even as they promoted ecumenism and universal human values.

26. Golden, *Our Southern Landsman*, 100. As Golden wrote in 1951, "The mildest New Deal expression in a 'letter to the editor' signed with a Jewish name sends a shiver through the entire Jewish community—('now we've got someone else to worry about'). But the greatest fear of all is that the next Jewish newcomer to town may be an 'agitator,' a 'pink,' an organizer for the CIO, or even a worker for some Negro cause." Golden's quote can be found in Dinnerstein and Palsson, *Jews in the South*, 20.

27. Robert Singerman, "The Jew as Racial Alien: The Genetic Component of

American Anti-Semitism," in *Anti-Semitism in American History*, ed. David Gerber (Urbana: University of Illinois Press, 1986), 119.

28. See John Higham, *Strangers in the Land: Patterns of American Nativism, 1860–1925* (New Brunswick, NJ: Rutgers University Press, 1955); John Higham, *Send These to Me: Jews and Other Immigrants in Urban America* (New York: Atheneum, 1975); and Leonard Dinnerstein, *Antisemitism in America* (New York and Oxford: Oxford University Press, 1994).

29. Jonathan Sarna, "The 'Mythical Jew' and the 'Jew Next Door' in Nineteenth-Century America," in *Anti-Semitism in American History*, ed. David Gerber (Urbana: University of Illinois Press, 1986), 58. Sarna points out that other minorities also faced this problem, not just Jews.

30. A good example of this can be found in Edward S. Shapiro, "Anti-Semitism Mississippi Style," in *Anti-Semitism in American History*, ed. David Gerber (Urbana: University of Illinois Press, 1986), 129–51.

31. Rita Steinhardt Botwinick, *A History of the Holocaust: From Ideology to Annihilation*, 3rd ed. (Upper Saddle River, NJ: Pearson Prentice Hall, 2004), 59.

32. The Jewish population in Alabama in 1927 was 12,891 (0.5 percent of the population), and in 1937 it had declined to 12,148 (0.42 percent of the population). See Marcus, *To Count a People*, 11. There are few studies of the Jewish community in Alabama. The most helpful are Mark H. Elovitz, *A Century of Jewish Life in Dixie: The Birmingham Experience* (Tuscaloosa: University of Alabama Press, 1974), and Mark Cowett, *Birmingham's Rabbi: Morris Newfield and Alabama, 1895–1940* (Tuscaloosa: University of Alabama Press, 1986). See also Robert G. Corley, *Paying "Civic Rent": The Jews of Emanu-El and the Birmingham Community* (Birmingham: A. H. Cather Publishing, 1982); Yitzchak Kerem, "The Settlement of Rhodian and Other Sephardic Jews in Montgomery and Atlanta in the Twentieth Century," *American Jewish History* 85 (December 1997): 373–91; Jacob Koch, "A Special Heritage: The Demopolis Jewish Community," in *Clearings in the Thicket: An Alabama Humanities Reader: Essays and Stories from the 1983 Alabama History and Heritage Festival*. ed. Jerry Elijah Brown (Macon, GA: Mercer University Press, 1985), 135–45; Robert J. Zietz, *The Gates of Heaven: Congregation Sha'arai Shomayim: The First 150 Years; Mobile, Alabama, 1844–1994* (Mobile, AL: Congregation Sha'arai Shomayim, 1994); Sherry Blanton, *The History of Temple Beth-El, Anniston, Alabama* (Anniston, AL: privately published, 2000); Terry Barr, "A Shtetl Grew in Bessemer: Temple Beth-El and Jewish Life in Small-Town Alabama," *Southern Jewish History* 3 (2000): 1–44; Mary Stanton, *The Hand of Esau: Montgomery's Jewish Community and the Bus Boycott* (Montgomery, AL: River City Publishing, 2006); and Mary Stanton, "At One with the Majority," *Southern Jewish History* 9 (2006): 141–99.

33. Myron Silverman to Milton Grafman, n.d. (probably November 1941); "Historical Statement, n.d."; "Activities B'ham S.S. Council," n.d.; "Religious Census Birmingham Public Schools," May 1940, all found in Milton L. Grafman Papers, held privately by Stephen W. Grafman and the Grafman family.

34. Engel recalled that "the Klan sent an emissary to me—one James Merrill, Deputy Clerk of the Circuit Court, whom I had known all my life, or practically all my life." Irving M. Engel interview by Murray Polner, 1969, tape 2, page 3, box 21,

number 3, William E. Wiener Oral History Library, Dorot Jewish Division, New York Public Library (hereafter cited as NYPL). See also Elovitz, *A Century of Jewish Life in Dixie*, 86; Cowett, *Birmingham's Rabbi*, 137.

35. Elmo Ellis interview by Robert Evans, March 19, 1985, tape 2, side 1, pages 30–31, William E. Wiener Oral History Library, Dorot Jewish Division, NYPL. Ellis grew up as Elmo Israel and changed his name when he got into broadcasting. His first cousin was famous New York Yankees broadcaster Mel Allen, who also changed his name from Israel when he entered the business in the 1930s.

36. Glenn Feldman, *Politics, Society, and the Klan in Alabama, 1915–1949* (Tuscaloosa: University of Alabama Press, 1999), 241.

37. Elovitz, *A Century of Jewish Life in Dixie*, 86–87.

38. Mary Stanton, *The Hand of Esau*, 66–75.

39. Elovitz, *A Century of Jewish Life in Dixie*, 87.

40. Sidney Ziff, Norman Niren, and Sol Kimerling, interview by Dan Puckett, Birmingham, Alabama, August 15, 2006.

41. "Old Muccose and the Lost Tribe of Israel," www.isjl.org/history/archive/al/montgomery.html, accessed June 11, 2009; by 1945, some Orthodox Jews had been accepted as members into the Reform-dominated country club, including Agudath Israel Rabbi Samuel S. Lerer, who "received a tradition-breaking privilege: an invitation to make free use of the facilities of the very swank Standard Club." See "Montgomery, ALA. Visit of Isaiah Terman, May 31–June 1, 1945," July 11, 1945, Box 1, folder "Visits Alabama, Montgomery 40–61," RG347.17.13, AJC, YIVO.

42. The population of Birmingham's Jews in 1937 was 5,300. See Marcus, *To Count a People*, 11. Evans, *The Provincials*, 97. Newfield served Temple Emanu-El from 1895 until 1940, and Blachschleger led Temple Beth-Or from 1934 until 1961.

43. For information on the rabbis' role in the South, see Malcolm H. Stern, "The Role of the Rabbi in the South," in *"Turn to the South": Essays on Southern Jewry*, ed. Nathan M. Kaganoff and Melvin I. Urofsky (Charlottesville: University Press of Virginia, 1979), 21–32; Gladys Rosen, "The Rabbi in Miami—A Case History," in *Turn to the South*, 33–40; Jack D. Spiro, "Rabbi in the South: A Personal View," in *Turn to the South*, 41–43; Mark K. Bauman and Arnold Shankman, "The Rabbi as Ethnic Broker: The Case of David Marx," *Journal of American Ethnic History* 2 (Spring 1983): 51–68; Hollace Ava Weiner, *Jewish Stars in Texas: Rabbis and Their Work* (College Station: Texas A&M University Press, 2006); Hollace Ava Weiner, "The Mixers: The Role of Rabbis Deep in the Heart of Texas," in *Dixie Diaspora: An Anthology of Southern Jewish History*, ed. Mark K. Bauman (Tuscaloosa: University of Alabama Press, 2006), 55–101; Mark K. Bauman, "Role Theory and History: The Illustration of Ethnic Brokerage in the Atlanta Jewish Community in an Era of Transition and Conflict," in *Dixie Diaspora*, 236–61; and George R. Wilkes, "Rabbi Dr. David Marx and the Unity Club: Organized Jewish-Christian Dialogue, Liberalism, and Religious Diversity in Early Twentieth-Century Atlanta," *Southern Jewish History* 9 (2006): 35–68.

44. Scott M. Langston, "Rabbi Morris Newfield: Ambassador to the Gentiles, a Balancing Act," *American Jewish Archives Journal* 59 (2007): 79–88.

45. Marcus, *To Count a People*, 11; Corley, *Paying Civic Rent*, 20–22; Mervyn

Sterne interview, July 12, 1972, 781.4.2.2.7, Mark Elovitz Research Papers, Birmingham Public Library Archives (hereafter cited as BPL); Elovitz, *A Century of Jewish Life in Dixie*, 117–21, 227n4; "Mervyn Hayden Sterne: Biographical Note," Mervyn Sterne Papers, BPL.

46. Ziff, Niren, and Kimerling interview.

47. Milton Grafman to Jeffrey Cohn, April 15, 1982. The letter is courtesy of Stephen W. Grafman.

48. Lee Shai Weissbach, *Jewish Life in Small-Town America: A History* (New Haven, CT: Yale University Press, 2005), 247.

Chapter 1

1. "Report of Anti-Defamation Commissioner," 1937 clipping found in Leon Schwartz Scrapbook no. 13, Mobile Municipal Archives (hereafter cited as MMA).

2. Joseph Lelyveld, *Omaha Blues: A Memory Loop* (New York: Picador, 2005), 104.

3. "Alabama Justice," *The Nation*, April 19, 1933, 434; the *Andalusia Star* editorial was reprinted in the *Prattville Progress*, May 23, 1935.

4. Dan T. Carter, *Scottsboro: A Tragedy of the American South*, rev. ed. (Baton Rouge: Louisiana State University Press), 235. Wright's statement to the jury occurred in the second round of trials in 1933. The first round of trials began only twelve days after the Scottsboro Boys had been arrested. Eight of the nine defendants had been convicted and sentenced to death. A mistrial had been declared in the case of Roy Wright, who, at the time, was only twelve years old. The US Supreme Court overturned the convictions and remanded the cases to the lower court. The state began new trials in 1933, having moved the venue to Decatur. Leibowitz and the ILD joined the case at that time.

5. After witnessing such an apparent miscarriage of justice, Judge James E. Horton Jr. set aside the verdict and ordered a new trial. That decision cost Horton his political future in Alabama, as he was defeated in the 1934 Democratic primary election—*the* election in the South—and he returned to private practice. In a clear rebuke of Horton's decision, Alabamians overwhelmingly elected Thomas Knight, the lead prosecutor in the Patterson trial, as Alabama's lieutenant governor.

6. "Credibility of Witnesses," April 15, 1933, *Birmingham Reporter*, found on Reel 12, frame 0037, International Labor Defense Papers, Schomberg Center for Research in Black Culture, New York (hereafter cited as ILD Papers).

7. Deposition of David Schriftman, Circuit Court, Morgan County, State of Alabama, Reel 2, frame 0916, ILD Papers.

8. Deposition of Victor Elwood, Circuit Court, Morgan County, State of Alabama, Reel 2, frames 0856–0870, ILD Papers.

9. Eleazer and Feidelson quotes found in Carter, *Scottsboro: A Tragedy of the American South*, 241, 259.

10. Feldman, *Politics, Society, and the Klan in Alabama*, 279.

11. See Deposition of Schriftman and Deposition of Elwood, Reel 2, ILD Papers.

12. Robin D. G. Kelley, *Hammer and Hoe: Alabama Communists during the Great Depression* (Chapel Hill: University of North Carolina Press, 1990), 88; Feldman,

Politics, Society, and the Klan in Alabama, 251–54; see John R. Steelman, Arthur Franklin Raper, and Walter R. Chivers, *The Plight of Tuscaloosa: A Case Study of Conditions in Tuscaloosa County, Alabama, 1933* (Atlanta: Southern Commission on the Study of Lynching, 1933). The lynching of Dan Pippen and A. T. Harden occurred on August 13, 1933, and the lynching of Dennis Cross took place on September 24, 1933. Kathleen Lowe generously provided the author with a copy of this report.

13. *Marion Times-Standard*, August 17, 1933; *Birmingham Messenger*, August 19, 1933, 1.

14. Clarence Cason, *90° in the Shade* (Chapel Hill: University of North Carolina Press, 1935; reprint, Tuscaloosa: University of Alabama Press, 1983), 119.

15. Steelman, Raper, and Chivers, *The Plight of Tuscaloosa*, 17.

16. Ibid., 24. Steelman's name does not appear on the report, but according to Kathleen Lowe, Steelman had access to the sources and compiled the report for Raper and Chivers. Kathleen Lowe, "John R. Steelman and Mob Violence in Alabama, 1930–1933," unpublished paper presented at the Alabama Historical Association meeting, Gadsden, Alabama, April 16, 2010, in the possession of the author.

17. Cason, *90° in the Shade*, 113.

18. Stanton, *The Hand of Esau*, 65; see also Stanton, "At One with the Majority," 141–99.

19. "Minutes of the Special Meeting of the Board of Trustees of Kahl Montgomery," March 24, 1933, *Temple Beth-Or Minute Book, 1927–1947*, 211, Temple Beth-Or Archives (hereafter cited as TBO). The board was divided on whether to warn Goldstein against attending.

20. "To the Board of Directors of Kahl Montgomery," March 28, 1933, *Temple Beth-Or Minute Book, 1927–1947*, 208, TBO.

21. Carter, *Scottsboro: A Tragedy of the American South*, 259, 259n40; Feldman, *Politics, Society, and the Klan in Alabama*, 241; Stanton, *The Hand of Esau*, 66–75.

22. *Montgomery Advertiser*, May 26, 1933; Lelyveld, *Omaha Blues*, 109. Lelyveld has written the most complete and insightful account of Goldstein's life and career.

23. Leo Drum interview conducted by author, April 30, 2009.

24. Kelley, *Hammer and Hoe*, 48; Virginia Durr to Olive Stone, January 5, 1975, Box 1, folder 13, Olive M. Stone Papers, Southern Historical Collection, The Wilson Library, University of North Carolina at Chapel Hill (hereafter cited as UNC); Laura Kaufman, "Beatrice Holtzman Schneiderman: Civil Rights Activist and Committed Volunteer, 1904–1996," http://jwa.org/weremember/scheiderman, accessed October 27, 2010.

25. Mark Cowett, "Morris Newfield, Alabama, and Blacks, 1895–1940," in *The Quiet Voices: Southern Rabbis and Black Civil Rights, 1880s to 1990s*, ed. Mark K. Bauman and Berkley Kalin (Tuscaloosa: University of Alabama Press, 1997), 39–49; see also Cowett, *Birmingham's Rabbi*, 148–51.

26. For details concerning the Gelders flogging, see "The Gelders Flogging Case," and "Statement by Joseph S. Gelders," Reel 20, frames 0950–0951, 0956–0960, ILD Papers; Feldman, *Politics, Society, and the Klan in Alabama*, 254–58; Robert P. Ingalls, "Antiradical Violence in Birmingham during the 1930s," *Journal of Southern History* 47 (November 1981): 526–43; and Cowett, *Birmingham's Rabbi*, 139–40. For

information on Joe Gelders, see Hollinger F. Barnard, ed., *Outside the Magic Circle: The Autobiography of Virginia Foster Durr* (Tuscaloosa: University of Alabama Press, 1985), 110–14; and Kelley, *Hammer and Hoe*, 128–31.

27. Feldman, *Politics, Society, and the Klan in Alabama*, 257. According to Bob Kimsey, a labor and industry reporter in Birmingham, the Victor Hansen–owned *Birmingham News/Age-Herald* generally "print stories only favorable to industry." See "Interview with Bob Kimsey, Labor and Industrial Reporter, Birmingham, Alabama, by George C. Stoney," in the Ralph Bunche Papers, Box 83, folder "Alabama: George Stoney—Mable Jones West notes—re Negro in Alabama," University of California at Los Angeles Special Collections (hereafter cited as UCLA).

28. Feldman, *Politics, Society, and the Klan in Alabama*, 257.

29. William Bradford Huie, *Mud on the Stars* (New York: L. B. Fischer Publishing, 1942; reprint, Tuscaloosa: University of Alabama Press, 1996), 70–71.

30. Marianne R. Sanua, *Going Greek: Jewish College Fraternities in the United States, 1895–1945* (Detroit: Wayne State University Press, 2003), 147.

31. Huie, *Mud on the Stars*, 68.

32. Sanua, *Going Greek*, 208.

33. Marcia Graham Synnott, "Anti-Semitism and American Universities: Did Quotas Follow the Jews?" in *American Jewish History*, ed. Jeffrey S. Gurock, vol. 6, *Anti-Semitism in America*, part two (New York and London: Routledge, 1998), 237–38, 245, 262.

34. Arthur Prince, interview by Dan Puckett, Mobile, Alabama, June 15, 2009.

35. "City Commission Deplores Abuse of Jewish Folk," *Mobile Register*, March 29, 1933, 5.

36. The members of the Mobile JDC were Schwarz; Sam J. Ripps, president of Ahavas Chesed; Rabbi Alfred G. Moses; Leo M. Brown; Sol Kahn; Herbert C. Brown; Aaron Lowenstein; and James G. Adler. "To the Jewish Community of Mobile," April 5, 1933, found in Schwartz Scrapbook no. 10, MMA. The funds collected were distributed to the American Jewish Joint Distribution Committee, the American Jewish Committee, the American Jewish Congress, and B'nai B'rith; see also "President's Report, January 25, 1934," folder "Board of Trustees 1934," Springhill Avenue Temple Archives.

37. "Mobile Signs B'nai B'rith Petition," clipping from *Jewish Daily Bulletin*; *Temple Topics*, Government Street Temple Bulletin, September 1933, both found in Schwartz Scrapbook no. 11, MMA.

38. There is no exact date as to when the Montgomery Jewish Federation came into existence. A memo in the federation files states that it "came into being around 1929 or 1930." The federation was incorporated in January 1937. The earliest records date from 1930. See undated memo, binder "Miscellaneous Items," Jewish Federation of Montgomery Papers (hereafter cited as JFM), Jewish Federation of Central Alabama.

39. "Federation—Important," *Temple Bulletin*, January 1933, binder "Temple Beth-Or Bulletin and Index, 1929–1942," TBO.

40. *Temple Bulletin*, April 1933, binder "Temple Beth-Or Bulletin and Index, 1929–1942," TBO.

41. *Temple Bulletin*, September–October 1933, binder "Temple Beth-Or Bulletin and Index, 1929–1942," TBO.

42. "Hull Announces Mistreatment of Jews Ending; German Minister Charges Vilification Renewed," *Birmingham Age-Herald*, March 27, 1933, 1; "Rabbis Score Persecution," *Mobile Register*, March 27, 1933, 10.

43. "Doom of Jews in Germany Is Fear of Rabbi," *Birmingham Age-Herald*, April 29, 1933, 1–2; "Rabbi Addresses Joint Gathering," *Birmingham Age-Herald*, May 6, 1933, 3.

44. "Rabbis Condemn Racial Injustice," *Birmingham Age-Herald*, June 24, 1933, 14.

45. Elovitz, *A Century of Jewish Life in Dixie*, 90, 98.

46. For more information about Roth and the YMHA, see "Birmingham YMHA Dream Come True," *Birmingham Age-Herald*, January 24, 1937, 10.

47. While the federation did not participate in overseas relief efforts, it did provide for "family and transient relief" partly because public relief proved inadequate to provide for the "more expensive foods required by Jewish persons keeping kosher as opposed to the ordinary non-Jewish public relief client." "Reorganization Plan," March 5, 1939, Binder 1936–1940, Birmingham United Jewish Fund Minutes (hereafter cited as UJF), Levite Jewish Community Center.

48. Selma S. Lewis, *A Biblical People in the Bible Belt: The Jewish Community of Memphis, Tennessee, 1840s–1960s* (Macon, GA: Mercer University Press, 1998), 136; Mark K. Bauman, "The Transformation of Jewish Social Services in Atlanta, 1928–1948," *American Jewish Archives Journal* (2001): 86–87.

49. See "Political Stand of Jews Lauded," *Birmingham Age-Herald*, October 19, 1936, 9; "C. N. Feidelson to Talk Sunday," January 27, 1934, 4; "Jews in Germany Called Hopeless," *Birmingham Age-Herald*, March 13, 1934, 9. Feidelson's lecture took place at the Independent Presbyterian Church in Birmingham, across the road from Temple Emanu-El. Henry Edmonds, pastor of the church, often cooperated closely with Emanu-El and was considered one of Newfield's closest friends; "Jewish Unity Is Address Topic," *Birmingham Age-Herald*, October 22, 1936, 9.

50. "Budget Committee," November 24, 1936; "Meeting," November 28, 1938; "Special Meeting with Dr. Kohs," December 15, 1938; "Meeting of State Conference in Montgomery," December 15, 1938, UJF. See also the first edition of the United Jewish Fund's newsletter, *The United Jewish Appeal*, October 5, 1937, folder 781.3.6, BPL.

51. "History of Kahl Montgomery," n.d., TBO; not everyone agreed with this assessment of Blachschleger's interfaith work. Rabbi Samuel S. Lerer stated in 1945 that Blachschleger had been in Montgomery "for more than twelve years during which his interfaith work has been very 'spotty' and his attendance at association meetings sporadic." Lerer also related that when the ministerial association voted to sponsor a Passion Play in Montgomery, that "only after there had been considerable discussion at the meeting of the Ministers' Association and a consensus reached to bring the play to Montgomery did Rabbi Blachschleger trouble to make any objection and then only to state simply that he regretted he could not make the decision unanimous. Rabbi Lerer felt that he could not take the initiative in this matter, due to his brief tenure, and rose to associate himself with Rabbi Blachschleger's statement. The situation was embarrassing to all but no effort was made to explain

why the rabbis disagreed or why bringing the Passion Play to Montgomery might be considered harmful to the community as a whole." See "Visit of Isaiah Terman," Montgomery, Alabama, May 31–June 1, 1945, Box 1, folder "Visits Alabama, Montgomery 40–61," AJC, YIVO.

52. Montgomery's Jewish population was 3,000 in 1927 and 2,400 in 1937. See Marcus, *To Count a People*, 13; Eugene Blachschleger, "Montgomery," in *The Universal Jewish Encyclopedia*, vol. 7, ed. Isaac Landman (New York: The Universal Jewish Encyclopedia, 1939), 632–33. According to Blachschleger, Agudath Israel had a membership of approximately sixty in 1942, and Etz Ahayem had a membership of about forty families; twelve families organized Congregation Kahl Montgomery on May 6, 1849, but they did not draft a charter until 1852. See www.isjl.org/history/archive/al/montgomery.html, accessed June 11, 2009.

53. For more information on Etz Ahayem, see Rubin M. Hanan, *The History of Etz Ahayem Congregation, 1906–1962* (Montgomery, AL: privately published, 1962); for Agudath Israel, see Miriam F. Cohen, *A History of Congregation Agudath Israel, 1902–1987, 5662–5747* (Montgomery, AL: privately published, 1987).

54. Stanton, *The Hand of Esau*, 60.

55. Manheim S. Shapiro, "Report of Field Visit," March 3, 4, 5, 1950, Montgomery, Alabama, Box 1, folder "Visits Montgomery," RG347.17.13, AJC, YIVO.

56. Elchonon Oberstein, "Growing Up in the Heart of Dixie: The Early Years," http://www.wherewhatwhen.com/read_articles.asp?id=244, accessed July 1, 2008.

57. Terman's report was written after meeting with Lucien Loeb, Rabbi Eugene Blachschleger, Simon Wampold, Beatrice Kaufman, Max S. Baum, Adolph Weil, Isidor Weil, Mrs. Florian A. Strassberger, Mrs. Rosenfield, and Rabbi Samuel S. Lerer. "Montgomery, ALA. Visit of Isaiah Terman, May 31–June 1, 1945," July 11, 1945, Box 1, folder "Visits Alabama, Montgomery 40–61," RG347.17.13, AJC, YIVO.

58. Leo Drum, interview by Dan J. Puckett, Montgomery, Alabama, April 30, 2009.

59. "Meeting of the Jewish Federation of Montgomery," October 8, 1940, binder "1935 through 1940," JFM.

60. "History of Kahl Montgomery," n.d., TBO; Brief History of the Jewish Federation of Montgomery, n.d., binder "Miscellaneous Items"; "Constitution and By Laws of the Jewish Federation of Montgomery Alabama," binder "1941 through 1945," JFM. By 1940 the federation included representation from the following groups: Temple Beth-Or, Agudath Israel, Etz Ahayem, Ladies Hebrew Charity Association, Council of Jewish Women, Hebrew Ladies Benevolent Society, B'nai B'rith, Men's Club, United Jewish Charities, and the Zionist Organization of America.

61. "President's Message," January 20, 1936, binder "1935 through 1940"; "President's Report, 1939–40," n.d., binder "1941 through 1945," JFM; Mark K. Bauman, "A Multithematic Approach to Southern Jewish History," in *The Columbia History of Jews and Judaism in America*, ed. Marc Lee Raphael (New York: Columbia University Press, 2008), 277; Judith E. Endelman, *The Jewish Community of Indianapolis, 1849 to the Present* (Bloomington: Indiana University Press, 1984), 159–60.

62. "The Ladies Hebrew Benevolent Association gives direct aid to families, rent, food and medical care when required. The United Hebrew Charities and the Or-

thodox Charities join forces in working toward rehabilitation of the individual, reuniting families, giving immediate and necessary aid to individuals, shelter, food, clothing and medical care. The Council of Jewish Women work along educational lines, maintain a sewing room and cooperate with and in the work of the other organizations." "Federation of Jewish Charities," August 22, 1935, binder "Federation of Jewish Charities, 1925–1935," Springhill Avenue Temple Archives.

63. Mobile's Jewish population was 950 in 1927 and 1,050 in 1937. See Marcus, *To Count a People*, 12; Louis Cassel, "Mobile," *The Universal Jewish Encyclopedia*, vol. 7, 603; "Annual Report Superintendent Sabbath School," January 25, 1934, folder "Board of Trustees," Springhill Avenue Temple Archives. Ahavas Chesed formally identified with the Conservative movement in 1952. Rita S. Whitlock, *A Family Album: The Family of Congregation Ahavas Chesed, 1894–1994, 5655–5755* (Mobile, AL: Ahavas Chesed Synagogue, 1994), 7–9.

64. Milton D. Kulick to Nathaniel Nason, November 6, 1942, Box 38, folder "Mobile," I-180, National Jewish Welfare Board, Army-Navy Division (hereafter cited as NJWB-AN), American Jewish Historical Society Archives (hereafter cited as AJHS); Arthur Prince also observes that the Reform congregation "was literally dying out. The German families had no children, or one child, or maybe two. Well, you don't perpetuate yourself that way." Arthur Prince interview by Dan J. Puckett, Mobile, Alabama, June 15, 2009.

65. Isaiah Terman, "Mobile, Ala.," July 17, 1945, Box 1, folder "Alabama, Mobile 40–62," RG347.17.13, AJC, YIVO.

66. Milton D. Kulick to Nathaniel Nason, November 6, 1942, Box 38, folder "Mobile," I-180, NJWB-AN, AJHS.

67. Report on the Mobile JDC, found in "Federation of Jewish Charities Minutes, 1925–1935," Springhill Avenue Temple Archives.

68. Historian Ellen Umansky notes that Moses, as early as 1903, had to be granted an "extended vacation" from his duties due to physical and mental health problems. Ellen M. Umansky, *From Christian Science to Jewish Science: Spiritual Healing and American Jews* (Oxford and New York: Oxford University Press, 2005), 44. See also Ellen M. Umansky, "Christian Science, Jewish Science, and Alfred Geiger Moses," *Southern Jewish History* 6 (2003): 1–34

69. *New York Times*, January 9, 1934, 13; "Minutes," February 5, 1934, folder "Board of Trustees 1934," Springhill Avenue Temple Archives. Schwarz had been a strong supporter of Black and a member of his reelection committee in Mobile. He even defended Black in print after revelations of Black's Klan membership emerged after Roosevelt appointed him to the Supreme Court. See "Black Admits Once Holding Membership in Klan," *Mobile Register*, October 2, 1937, Schwarz Scrapbook no. 13, and "To the Voters of Mobile County," Schwarz Scrapbook no. 10, MMA; see also Monroe Metzger to Frank W. Boykin, March 20, 1936, and "Minutes," March 19, 1936, B'nai B'rith Papers, Springhill Avenue Temple Archives.

70. Leon Schwarz to Rabbi Sidney E. Goldstein, New York, July 1, 1936, *Jewish Exponent*, clipping found in Schwarz Scrapbook no. 12, MMA. The CCAR later amended the resolution to include only conscientious objectors: "We affirm our conviction that conscientious objection to military service is in accordance with the

highest interpretation of Judaism and therefore we petition the Government of the United States to grant to Jewish religious conscientious objectors the same exemption from military service as has long been granted to members of the Society of Friends and similar religious organizations." See "CONSCIENTIOUS OBJECTORS: Digests of Resolutions Adopted by the Central Conference of American Rabbis Between 1889 and 1974," http://data.ccarnet.org/cgi-bin/resodisp.pl?file=cons&year=1972, accessed July 2, 2010.

71. The speaker was Rabbi Louis Binstock of Temple Sinai in New Orleans. "Nazi Atrocities Depicted in Talk to Mobile Group," March 21, 1934, clipping found in Schwarz Scrapbook no. 11, MMA.

72. "Regular Meeting of Beth Zur Lodge No. 84," February 17, 1938, B'nai B'rith Papers, Springhill Avenue Temple Archives.

73. "Bulletin," December 10, 1935, B'nai B'rith Papers, Springhill Avenue Temple Archives. This was a request by the New Orleans Lodge to the Mobile Lodge. The anti-Nazi boycott began in 1933 and continued through 1941. Americans were urged not to purchase German goods or patronize businesses that sold German goods. Not all Jews supported the boycott, however. Some groups, such as B'nai B'rith and the American Jewish Committee, opposed the boycott, while the American Jewish Congress openly supported it. For more information concerning the boycott, see Moshe Gottlieb, *American Anti-Nazi Resistance, 1933–1941: An Historical Analysis* (New York: Ktav Publishing House, 1982); Moshe Gottlieb, "The Anti-Nazi Boycott Movement in the United States: An Ideological and Sociological Appreciation," *Jewish Social Studies* 35 (July–October 1973): 198–227; and William Orbach, "Shattering the Shackles of Powerlessness: The Debate Surrounding the Anti-Nazi Boycott of 1933–41," *Modern Judaism* 2 (May 1982): 149–69.

74. Botwinick, *A History of the Holocaust*, 126–30; Saul Friedländer, *Nazi Germany and the Jews*, vol. 1, *The Years of Persecution, 1933–1939* (New York: HarperCollins, 1997), 266–79.

75. Mr. Morris Fisher, Mrs. Ida Newman Fisher, Mr. Max Goldberg, and Mrs. Fannie Newman Goldberg interview, July 10, 1972, Elovitz Research Papers, 781.4.1.2.6, BPL.

76. "Views and Interviews," *Birmingham News*, March 5, 1939, 10.

77. S. Davis Wilson to J. M. Jones, November 17, 1938; James M. Jones to Franklin D. Roosevelt, November 21, 1938, James Marion Jones Papers, box 3, folder 3, BPL; Bibb Graves quote cited in Deborah E. Lipstadt, *Beyond Belief: The American Press and the Coming of the Holocaust: 1933–1945* (New York: The Free Press, 1986), 99, 309n58. Lipstadt's notes erroneously cite the governor as "Bill Graves." See also "City Head Assures FDR Backing in Stand for Jews," *Birmingham News*, November 22, 1938, 11; "German Policies Condemned Here," *Mobile Register*, November 17, 1938, found in Schwartz Scrapbook no. 13, MMA.

78. "Ministers Condemn Persecuting Jews," *Birmingham News*, November 14, 1938, 2; see also "German Policy Criticized Here By Churchmen," *Birmingham Age-Herald*, November 14, 1938, 1–2; "Mobile Clergy Assails Nazis' Jewish Policy," *Mobile Register*, November 21, 1938, clipping found in Schwartz Scrapbook no. 14, MMA. The day of prayer was Sunday, November 20, 1938.

79. "Baptists May Rap Jews' Persecution," November 16, 1938, 5; "Alabama Baptists Condemn Nazis, War," *Birmingham News*, November 17, 1938, 22.

Chapter 2

1. David S. Wyman, *Paper Walls: America and the Refugee Crisis, 1938–1941* (Amherst: University of Massachusetts Press, 1968); David S. Wyman, *The Abandonment of the Jews: America and the Holocaust, 1941–1945* (New York: Pantheon Books, 1984).

2. "Special Meeting with Dr. Kohs," December 15, 1938, binder "1936–1940," UJF.

3. *Birmingham Age-Herald*, March 21, 1934, 6; April 13, 1934, 6.

4. "The United States and the Refugee Crisis," www.ushmm.org/museum/exhibit/online/stlouis/teach/supread.htm, accessed June 11, 2010.

5. *Birmingham News*, March 30, 1938, 8; *Birmingham Age-Herald*, July 9, 1938, 4; December 15, 1938, 6.

6. David C. Akins to Editor, *Birmingham News*, November 25, 1938, 12.

7. J. B. Lockhart to Editor, ibid., December 12, 1938, 6.

8. Ibid., November 18, 1938, 14; November 28, 1938, 6.

9. "Special Meeting with Dr. Kohs," December 15, 1938, binder "1936–1940," LJCC; "The National Farm School," June 20, 1897, *New York Times*, SM16; the National Farm School is now known as Delaware Valley College. See http://delval.edu/cms/, accessed November 4, 2012.

10. Lucien Loeb to William Haber, n.d.; Arthur D. Greenleigh to Lucien Loeb, March 19, 1940, MKM 13.50.1038, RG248, National Refugee Service Papers (hereafter cited as NRS), YIVO.

11. *Tuscaloosa News*, "Hillel Group at 'Bama to Support German Refugee," November 25, 1938, *Birmingham Age-Herald*, 15; "United Jewish Appeal to Be Explained at Country Club Dinner," October 18, 1939, 1; "The United Jewish Appeal," October 18, 1939, 4; "Jewish Appeal Receives Inspired Response Here," October 20, 1939, 1; "Jewish Relief Drive Begins," October 29, 1940, 1. The *News* also published a front-page picture of the *St. Louis* being turned away from Cuba. *Tuscaloosa News*, "Jewish Refugees Denied Haven in Cuba," June 5, 1939, 5; see also Monte Kandel, "Field Report," Tuscaloosa, Alabama, December 12, 1940, MKM 13.50.1039, RG248, NRS, YIVO.

12. Milton Klein, interview by Dan J. Puckett, Mobile, Alabama, September 24, 2009.

13. *Opelika Daily News*, July 12, 1935.

14. Henry Stern, interview by Karni Perez, September 16, 1997, Opelika, Alabama, Shoah Foundation Institute for Visual History and Education, University of Southern California (hereafter cited as Shoah Foundation).

15. http://www.bhamholocausteducation.org/bio-stern.htm, accessed August 23, 2011; Stern interview.

16. Charles H. Wampold Jr., interview with Louisa H. Weinrib, October 30, 1991, Montgomery, Alabama, 1–5, box 1, folder 27, Holocaust Survivors and US Liberators Oral History Collection, Alabama Department of Archives and History (hereafter

cited as ADAH). Bertha Manasse's siblings included Samuel Kaufman, the president of Schloss & Kahn Grocery Company; Jacob Kaufman; Clara Kaufman Loeb; and Paula Kaufman Wampold. The Manasses moved to New York in the early 1940s because of the language difficulties in Montgomery.

17. Rabbi Albagli received a nonquota immigration visa as a minister of religion. He was in Naples, Italy. See Lister Hill to Commissioner of Immigration, December 15, 1938; Lister Hill to Thomas D. Bowman, December 19, 1938; Thomas D. Bowman to Lister Hill, January 21, 1939; Lister Hill to Thomas B. Hill, February 20, 1939; Thomas B. Hill to Lister Hill, February 23, 1939; E. Toranto to Thomas B. Hill, March 30, 1939, all in box 161, folder 1, Lister Hill Papers, Hoole Special Collections, University of Alabama (hereafter cited as HSC).

18. Virginia Van der Veer Hamilton, *Lister Hill: Statesman from the South* (Chapel Hill: University of North Carolina Press, 1987), 3, 13; Hill served in the House of Representatives from 1923 until his election to the Senate in 1938, where he represented Alabama until his retirement in 1969.

19. For further information on Luther Patrick's assistance to the Perel family, see Pat Boyd Rumore, *Lawyers in a New South City* (Birmingham, AL: Association Publishing Company, 2000), 86.

20. Joseph L. Abraham to John Sparkman, January 13, 1941, box 13, folder "Joseph L. Abraham," John Sparkman Papers, HSC.

21. John Sparkman to Joseph L. Abraham, May 27, 1941 (first quote); John Sparkman to Joseph L. Abraham, May 17, 1941 (second quote), box 13, folder "Joseph L. Abraham," Sparkman Papers, HSC.

22. Joseph L. Abraham to John Sparkman, December 8, 1941, box 13, folder "Joseph L. Abraham," Sparkman Papers, HSC; the correspondence between Abraham and Sparkman does not reveal exactly when or how the Loew sisters reached America. Joseph L. Abraham to John Sparkman, August 7, 1942, box 13, folder "Joseph L. Abraham," HSC. All of the correspondence pertaining to the Loews and other Abraham family members can be found in box 13, folder "Joseph L. Abraham," Sparkman Papers, HSC.

23. "The United States Department of State," www.ushmm.org/museum/exhibit/online/stlouis/teach/supread.htm#two, accessed June 11, 2010.

24. William Haber, "Resettling New Americans: Out of New York—Into America," 3, MKM 13.10.225, RG248, NRS, YIVO.

25. "Refugees' Relief Drive Is Opened By Mobile Jewry," June 8, 1939, newspaper clipping found in Schwarz Scrapbook no. 14, MMA; "Report Read at Mt. Vernon," May 19, 1941, folder "National Council of Jewish Women, 1897–1969," Springhill Avenue Temple Archives.

26. Beatrice Kaufman was the president of Montgomery's chapter of the National Council for Jewish Women. "Meeting of the Board of Trustees," April 11, 1938, binder "1935 through 1940," JFM; "Special Meeting with Dr. Kohs," December 15, 1938, binder "1936–1940," UJF ; the Montgomery Coordinating Committee consisted of Henry Weil, Lucien S. Loeb, Nathan Segall, Eli Hanan, Beatrice Kaufman, Mrs. Sigmund Weil, and Mrs. Myron Lobman. "Meeting of the Board

of Trustees," April 11, 1938, and May 24, 1938; "The President's Message to the Jewish Federation of Montgomery," January 26, 1939, binder "1935 through 1940," JFM. A thorough study of the American Jewish Joint Distribution Committee is Yehuda Bauer, *American Jewry and the Holocaust: The American Jewish Joint Distribution Committee, 1939–1945* (Detroit: Wayne State University Press, 1981).

27. The national JDC did not participate in direct case work but was "the largest financial contributor to the National Co-ordinating Committee. . . . A number of the officers and members of the Board of Directors of the JDC serve on the National Co-ordinating Committee, thus making for an intimate interrelationship between the two organizations." Erika Mann and Eric Estorick, "Private and Governmental Aid of Refugees," *Annals of the American Academy of Political and Social Science* 203 (May 1939): 147. A particularly good history of rescue operations is Bat-Ami Zucker, *Cecilia Razovsky and the American-Jewish Women's Rescue Operations in the Second World War* (London and Portland, OR: Vallentine Mitchell, 2008).

28. "Problems in the Distribution of the Jewish Refugee Population in the United States," n.d. (1941), MKM 13.48.1001, 3–4; "Resettlement Division: Brief Historical Sketch and Outline of Current Activities," n.d. (1939), 1, MKM 13.4.68, RG248, NSR, YIVO.

29. "Problems in the Distribution of the Jewish Refugee Population in the United States," n.d. (1941), MKM 13.48.1001, 5, NSR, YIVO.

30. "Reorganization Plan," March 5, 1939, binder "1936–1940," UJF.

31. "The President's Message to the Jewish Federation of Montgomery," January 26, 1939, JFM.

32. *Thirteenth Annual Report of the Industrial Removal Office for the Year Nineteen Thirteen*, pamphlet found in Box 1, folder 5, I-91 Records of the Industrial Removal Office (IRO), AJHS. The total number of immigrants resettled in Alabama by the IRO is not known, but a number of these immigrants, like the refugees resettled by the NRS decades later, left the state for opportunities elsewhere.

33. See Jack Glazier, *Dispersing the Ghetto: The Relocation of Jewish Immigrants across America* (Ithaca, NY: Cornell University Press, 1998); Robert A. Rockaway, *Words of the Uprooted: Jewish Immigration in Early Twentieth Century America* (Ithaca, NY: Cornell University Press, 1998); Bernard Marinbach, *Galveston: Ellis Island of the West* (Albany: State University of New York Press, 1984); Gary Dean Best, "Jacob H. Schiff's Galveston Movement: An Experiment in Immigrant Deflection, 1907–1914," *American Jewish Archives* 30 (April 1978): 43–79; Hollace Ava Weiner, "Removal Approval: The Industrial Removal Office Experience in Fort Worth, Texas," *Southern Jewish History* 4 (2001): 1–44; Gur Alroey, "Galveston and Palestine: Immigration and Ideology in the Early Twentieth Century," *American Jewish Archives Journal* (2004): 129–50.

34. "Problems in the Distribution of the Jewish Refugee Population in the United States," n.d. (1941), MKM 13.48.1001, 8; William Haber, "Community Responsibility for Refugees," October 8, 1939, 4, MKM 13.10.225; "Facts about the National Refugee Service: Questions and Answers," n.d., MKM 13.48.1005, 10, NSR, YIVO.

35. In addition to Birmingham, Montgomery, and Mobile, the minutes indi-

cate that representatives from Selma, Florence, and Empire attended the meetings, although undoubtedly many more communities sent representatives. "Meeting of State Conference in Montgomery," December 15, 1938; "Refugee Committee Meeting," January 19, 1939; "State Meeting," October 29, 1939, binder "1936–1940," UJF.

36. "Alabama Field Trip," March 28, 1939, MKM 13.50.1039, RG248, NRS, YIVO.

37. J. W. Pincus to William Haber, August 23, 1939, MKM 13.1.9, RG248, NRS, YIVO. No information concerning the offers, save for the one in Autaugaville, seem to have progressed beyond inquiries, and no replies by the NRS office have been found in the files.

38. E. H. Pearson to Lucien Loeb, June 20, 1939, MKM 13.1.9, RG248, NRS, YIVO. The letter to Loeb included the plan for the details of the proposed settlement of refugee families.

39. Ibid.

40. E. H. Pearson to Lucien Loeb, August 11, 1939, MKM 13.1.9, RG248, NRS, YIVO.

41. Walter Lobman to Lucien Loeb, July 28, 1939, MKM 13.1.9, RG248, NRS, YIVO.

42. William Haber to Lucien Loeb, August 30, 1939; William Haber to Lucien Loeb, October 24, 1939, MKM 13.1.9, RG248, NRS, YIVO.

43. Mr. Gomberg to Mr. Haber, July 1, 1940, MKM 13.50.1038, NRS, YIVO. Other communities, Florence, Selma, Birmingham, and Montgomery also failed to receive refugees requested. Loeb "required almost a year to induce Selma . . . to agree to take a refugee." See Lucien Loeb to William Haber, November 18, 1939; Lucien Loeb to William Haber, November 27, 1939; William Haber to Lucien Loeb, December 7, 1939, MKM 13.1.9, NSR, YIVO.

44. Mr. Gomberg to Mr. Haber, July 1, 1940, MKM 13.50.1038, NRS, YIVO.

45. "Field Report of Kingloff," Birmingham, Alabama, May 19, 1940, MKM 13.50.1039, NRS, YIVO.

46. Aubrey Williams, "The Work of the National Youth Administration," *Living* 1 (November 1939): 65; see also Williams, "Government's Responsibility for Youth," *Annals of American Academy of Political and Social Science* 194 (November 1937): 119–28. For more information on Williams and the creation of the NYA, see John Salmond, *A Southern Rebel: The Life and Times of Aubrey Willis Williams, 1890–1965* (Chapel Hill: University of North Carolina Press, 1983), 78–85.

47. Lucien Loeb reported for the State Coordinating Committee that ten boys had attended the Gadsden school and "5 had been employed in the State, 2 had enlisted in the army, and 1 had returned to New York." Of the two that remained at the school, Loeb stated that one had found employment and the other "would be accepted by Birmingham as its unit if he did not find a job." "May Board Meeting," May 18, 1942, binder "1941 through 1945," JFM; the NYA also had centers in Bessemer and at the University of Alabama in Tuscaloosa.

48. Arnold Krammer, *Undue Process: The Untold Story of America's German Alien Internees* (London: Rowman and Littlefield, 1997), 3.

49. Roosevelt quote in Zucker, *Cecilia Razovsky*, 127–28.

50. "Alien Registration Act of 1940," US Statutes at Large (76th Cong., 3rd

Sess., 670–676), found at http://tucnak.fsv.cuni.cz/~calda/Documents/1940s/Alien Registration Act of 1940.html, accessed October 14, 2010. See Krammer, *Undue Process*, 23.

51. Proclamation 2525 addressed the Japanese and Proclamation 2527 pertained to Italians. See "Presidential Proclamation, No. 2526 Alien Enemies—German," http://www.foitimes.com/internment/Proc2526.html, accessed October 14, 2010; see also Krammer, *Undue Process*, 2.

52. John Christgau, *"Enemies": World War II Alien Internment* (Ames: Iowa State University Press, 1985), 50–51.

53. Christgau, *"Enemies,"* vii. The number of arrests of enemy aliens in Birmingham totaled fifty-four, including three Japanese and twenty-three Italians. See http://foia.fbi.gov/custodet/custode2.pdf, 189, accessed August 17, 2010; Krammer, *Undue Process*, 52. A number of Jewish refugees were ultimately interned as enemy aliens. One hundred German Jews were interned on the West Coast, over nine hundred Italian Jewish refugees were interned in the Fort Ontario Refugee Shelter at Oswego, New York, and eighty-one Jews from Latin America were held in camps in Georgia, Tennessee, Florida, Louisiana, Oklahoma, and Texas. None were held in Alabama. See Harvey Strum, "Jewish Internees in the American South, 1942–1945," *American Jewish Archives* 42 (1990): 27–48.

54. Monte Kandel, "Field Report," Montgomery, Alabama, June 27–29, 1942, MKM 13.50.1039, RG248, NRS, YIVO.

55. "Problems in the Distribution of the Jewish Refugee Population in the United States," n.d. (1941), MKM 13.48.1001, 7, NSR, YIVO.

56. Cecilia Razovsky, Lotte Marcuse, and Blanche Goldman, "Annual Report—1938," MKM8.1.10, RG249, German-Jewish Children's Aid Papers, YIVO. Razovsky was the executive director of the GJCA and Marcuse was director of placements.

57. Mark K. Bauman, "Southern Jewish Women and Their Social Service Organizations," *Journal of American Ethnic History* (Spring 2003): 44.

58. Faith Rogow, *Gone to Another Meeting: The National Council of Jewish Women, 1893–1993* (Tuscaloosa: University of Alabama Press, 1993), 133.

59. Birnbrey landed in Normandy on the second day, June 7, 1944. Henry Birnbrey, interview by Sandra Berman, December 31, 2009, Atlanta, Georgia, Esther and Herbert Taylor Oral History Project, The William Breman Jewish Heritage and Holocaust Museum; "Former Refugee Stationed in England," *Serviceman*, May 1944, folder 1758.1.2, Milton Grafman Papers, BPL; Philip K. Jason and Iris Posner, eds., *Don't Wave Goodbye: The Children's Flight from Nazi Persecution to American Freedom* (Westport, CT: Greenwood Press, 2004), 154–55; Myrna Katz Frommer and Harvey Frommer, *Growing Up Jewish in America: An Oral History* (Lincoln, NE: Bison Books, 1995), 115–16.

60. In 1941 the NRS completely took over the operation of the GJCA. In 1942, to describe better its function, the GJCA changed its name to the European-Jewish Children's Aid. The best study of the GJCA is Jason and Posner, *Don't Wave Goodbye.*

61. "Meeting," November 28, 1938, binder "1936–1940," UJF.

62. "Meeting," November 28, 1938; "Refugee Committee Meeting," January 19, 1939, binder "1936–1940," UJF.

63. "Refugee Committee," March 21, 1939; "Special Meeting Women's Division," August 2, 1939; "Minutes of Meeting," September 12, 1938; "Minutes of Board Meeting," October 19, 1939, binder "1936–1940," UJF; and "Field Report of Monte Kandel," Birmingham, Alabama, February 29–March 1, 1940, MKM 13.50.1039, RG248, NRS, YIVO.

64. Monte Kandel, "Field Report," Birmingham, Alabama, n.d. (1940), MKM 13.50.1038, RG248, NRS, YIVO.

65. "Facts about the National Refugee Service: Questions and Answers," 8, MKM 13.48.1005, RG248, NRS, YIVO.

66. "Roth, Mrs. Benjamin (Dora L.)," "Roth, Benjamin A.," 1871.18.26, Henry Marks Files, BPL; Elovitz, *A Century of Jewish Life in Dixie*, 109–115.

67. Monte Kandel, the field representative of the NRS, had a low opinion of Roth and her abilities to successfully administer the refugee program, at one point writing in his report that she had admitted "that her 'hatred' of refugees has reached a personal level," and she should be "divorced from the refugee program." Kandel's perception of Roth, it seems, stemmed from their tense and rocky relationship rather than from an objective point of view. Evaluations of Roth from representatives of other organizations dealing with the Birmingham community, and from individuals in the Birmingham Jewish community, many of whom did not see eye to eye with Roth, considered her a competent and organized, if spirited, community leader. See "Report of Monte Kandel," Birmingham, Alabama, January 25–27, 1942, MKM 13.50.1039, RG248, NRS, YIVO.

68. Solomon served as caseworker until she resigned in early 1941. Dora Roth continued as caseworker until the fund hired Ruth Gordon in early 1942. In addition, Roth maintained that she never liked to be a social worker and preferred other duties. Monte Kandel, "Field Report," Birmingham, Alabama, February 29–March 1, 1940, MKM 13.50.1039, RG248, NRS; see also "Report of Monte Kandel," Birmingham, Alabama, May 17, 1941, and "Visit to Birmingham," May 5, 1942, MKM 13.50.1039, RG248, NRS, YIVO.

69. Monte Kandel, "Field Report," Birmingham, Alabama, February 29–March 1, 1940, MKM 13.50.1039, RG248, NRS, YIVO. According to Kandel, "Since records were started—25 units—32 individuals were sent here by NRS. 5 units—4 individuals have left. 5 units—10 individuals came namely through affiants either here or in the surrounding territories. The 5 units were those that became known to the local committee. Other refugee families have come to affiants here, who assumed responsibility. The exact number is not known." There were indeed no records kept for refugees who family or friends sponsored, so the total number of refugees who came to Alabama during the 1930s and 1940s is unknown. There are discrepancies in the records of the refugees the NRS sponsored, however. The figures of the NRS office show Birmingham resettled nineteen units (twenty-five individuals) in 1939. See "Units and Individuals Resettled in the Alabama State Region, January 1–December 31, 1939," prepared March 29, 1940, MKM 13.48.1001, RG248, NRS, YIVO.

70. Monte Kandel, "Field Report," Birmingham, Alabama, December 10, 1940, MKM 13.50.1039, RG248, NRS, YIVO; Elovitz, *A Century of Jewish Life in Dixie*, 115. Elovitz, however, does not cite any source for the figure of eighty-seven units.

71. These complaints, NRS field representative Monte Kandel reported in mid-1940, "are well founded." Monte Kandel, "Field Report," Birmingham, Alabama, August 25, 1940, MKM 13.50.1039, RG248, NRS, YIVO.

72. Monte Kandel, "Field Report," Birmingham, Alabama, November 8, 1940, MKM 13.50.1039, RG248, NRS, YIVO.

73. Monte Kandel,"Field Report," Birmingham, Alabama, August 25, 1940, MKM 13.50.1039, RG248, NRS, YIVO.

74. Lee B. Weil, "Community Relations," March 18–19, 1944, Southeastern States Regional Conference—Council of Jewish Federations and Welfare Funds, found in Box 1, folder "Communal Relations–Alabama, Birmingham," RG347.17.13, AJC, YIVO; according to Solomon Fineberg, a field representative of the American Jewish Committee, the defacement of Emanu-El was not reported in the press, "although the editor was reluctant to drop the story, he consented when it was urged that Rabbi Newfield was very ill—in fact, he was dying—and that they wanted to keep knowledge of this from him. . . . To his influence may be attributed considerable of the good feeling existing between Jew and non-Jew. It would have been a tragedy, indeed, had his career terminated, to his knowledge, with this display of bigotry. The editor saw the point. The story was killed." Solomon A. Fineberg, "Birmingham, Alabama," November 6, 1940, Box 1, folder "Visits—Alabama, Birmingham, 44–62," RG347.17.13, AJC, YIVO.

75. Kandel's field report does not mention any names in regard to the "several large Jewish employers," although he reports that "David Feidelson is doing nothing. Mr. [Joseph] Loveman got him to accept the co-chairmanship with the hope that he would hire some refugees in his business or find jobs. He accepted the position under duress, and constantly complains that the Committee members do not cooperate. Mr. Loveman feels that this is his defense mechanism for his own failings." Monte Kandel, "Field Report," Birmingham, Alabama, August 25, 1940, MKM 13.50.1039, RG248, NRS, YIVO; in a later report, Kandel mentions that Sam Phillips of Berger-Phillips Department Store employed two refugees, Isadore Pizitz at Pizitz Department Store employed five refugees, and William Holliner of Parisian Department Store employed four refugees. See Monte Kandel, "Field Report," Birmingham, Alabama, November 8, 1940, MKM 13.50.1039, RG248, NRS, YIVO.

76. "Report of Monte Kandel," Birmingham, Alabama, May 17, 1941; "Report of Monte Kandel," Birmingham, Alabama, September 23, 1941, MKM 13.50.1039, RG248, NRS, YIVO.

77. "Report of Monte Kandel," Birmingham, Alabama, May 17, 1941, MKM 13.50.1039; "Units and Individuals Resettled January–March 1942 by States and Regions and Comparison of Distribution with the Five Year Period 1937–1942," report prepared May 6, 1942, MKM 13.48.1002, RG248, NRS, YIVO.

78. Although Gadsden's Jewish community supported refugee students at the Alabama School of Trades, only by the end of 1940 did the Gadsden community organize themselves to accept the resettlement of a small number of refugees. Monte Kandel, "Field Report," Gadsden, Alabama, September 24, 1941, MKM 13.50.1039, RG248, NRS, YIVO.

79. Gadsden's Jews belonged to the Reform congregation Beth Israel, which had

been established in 1908. Although Gadsden had no full-time rabbi to serve the congregation—the Reform rabbi of Birmingham's Temple Emanu-El often came for special occasions—they had Hugo Hecht, a long-serving lay "rabbi" who stepped in to fill the void of religious leadership for over thirty years. Monte Kandel, "Field Report," Gadsden, Alabama, December 16, 1940, MKM 13.50.1039, RG248, NRS, YIVO; "Gadsden, Alabama," *Encyclopedia of Southern Jewish Communities*, http://www.isjl.org/history/archive/al/gadsden.html, accessed June 11, 2009.

80. "Nat to Mr. Kravitz," October 30, 1939; Monte Kandel, "Field Report," Gadsden, Alabama, December 16, 1940, MKM 13.50.1039, RG248, NRS, YIVO.

81. "Report of Monte Kandel," Gadsden, Alabama, December 29, 1941, MKM 13.50.1039, RG248, NRS, YIVO.

82. "Report of Monte Kandel," Birmingham and neighboring Alabama communities, May 2, 1942, MKM 13.50.1039, RG NRS, YIVO.

83. Kandel reported that Fineberg had "taken over" at Temple Beth-El, and "Orthodox observers are permitted to wear their hats. The rabbi is Conservative." Monte Kandel, "Field Report," Anniston, Alabama, December 17, 1940, MKM 13.50.1039, RG248, NRS, YIVO; for a general history of Anniston's Jews, see Blanton, *The History of Temple Beth-El.*

84. Monte Kandel, "Field Report," Anniston, Alabama, December 17, 1940, MKM 13.50.1039, RG248, NRS, YIVO. The story of a number of those who Lee Freibaum sponsored can be found in Sherry Blanton's study of Holocaust survivors in Anniston. Blanton notes that Friebaum "signed affidavits for twenty-nine relatives still in Germany." Sherry Blanton, *Survivors' Stories: Anniston's Temple Beth-El and the Holocaust* (Anniston, AL: privately published, 2010), 3. It is unclear what happened to Gruneberg's wife and child.

85. "Visit to Anniston, Ala.," May 4, 1942, MKM 13.50.1039, RG248, NRS, YIVO; for the base commanders, see http://www.mcclellan.army.mil/Commanders.asp?TimeFrame=4, accessed October 26, 2010.

86. Monte Kandel, "Field Report," Montgomery, Alabama, August 21, 1940, MKM 13.50.1039, RG248, NRS, YIVO.

87. "The President's Message to the Jewish Federation of Montgomery," January 26, 1939, binder "1935 through 1940"; in regard to fund-raising for 1941, campaign chairman Bernard Lobman wrote, "I am greatly disappointed that I cannot report to you the subscribers of the Federation met their responsibility in the way the committee felt they should. If such had been the case we should have had no trouble in raising $30,000. I deeply regret that the campaign committee failed to make Montgomery Jewry realize that such times as these demand real sacrifices." "Report of the Campaign Committee," n.d., binder "1941 through 1945"; Simon Wampold, the federation president, also commented of the 1941 campaign that "due to the failure of some of our contributors, especially those in the higher brackets, to increase their subscriptions," the federation did not reach its intended goal. "To the Jewish Federation of Montgomery," n.d., binder "Miscellaneous Items," JFM. A report from the NRS stated that "people here have not been educated in contributing to drives i.e. the second largest cotton firm of Weil Bros. only contributes $5000 towards all funds. . . . Mr. Lucien Loeb a very rich man only contributes $900, etc." See N. W.

Bronstein, "Mr. Bronstein's Field Report," Montgomery, Alabama, October 30, 1939, MKM 13.50.1039, RG248, NRS, YIVO; Conversely, a report by the NRS field agent described Loeb as a "top giver." See Monte Kandel, "Report of Monte Kandel," Montgomery, Alabama, June 27–29, 1942, MKM 13.50.1039, RG248, NRS, YIVO.

88. In Hall's editorial, he also reprinted a statement from the United Jewish Appeal for Refugees and Overseas Needs. "The Jewish Federation in Our Town," *Montgomery Advertiser*, September 18, 1939, 4.

89. "Refugees' Cash Is Harvest for Gaming Casinos," April 28, 1940, *Montgomery Advertiser*, 6; "Open Meeting of the Board of Trustees of the Jewish Federation of Montgomery," May 1940, binder 1935–1940, JFM.

90. According to the report, "the consensus of opinion was that this question was raised by a few people in banks because they knew that many affidavits had been signed here and they were under the impression that all these people were coming here." See N. W. Bronstein, "Mr. Bronstein's Field Report," Montgomery, Alabama, October 30, 1939, MKM 13.50.1039, RG248, NRS, YIVO.

91. Manheim S. Shapiro, "Report of Field Visit," March 3, 4, 5, 1950, Montgomery, Alabama, Box 1, folder "Visits Montgomery," RG347.17.13, AJC, YIVO. Shapiro's report also stated that Montgomery Jews "are generally inclined to avoid any real or prominent public role in the community." This observation was demonstrably false as Jews had been and continued to be leaders in civic and economic affairs.

92. "Special Meeting Federation Board," February 25, 1943, binder "1941 through 1945," JFM.

93. "Executive Committee," July 31, 1940; "Meeting of the Board of Trustees," July 1940, binder "1935 through 1940," JFM.

94. "Annual Report of the Coordinating Committee," n.d. (early 1941), binder "1941 through 1945," JFM, JFCA; Monte Kandel, "Field Report," Montgomery, Alabama, September 4, 1942, MKM 13.50.1039, RG248, NRS, YIVO.

95. Fannie G. Steiner, "Field Report," Montgomery, Alabama, December 13, 1944, MKM 13.50.1039, RG248, NRS, YIVO.

96. The Jewish population of Selma in 1937 was 325; by 1948 the population had decreased to 202. Marcus, *To Count a People*, 13.

97. Selma had an Orthodox congregation, B'nai Abraham, but it disbanded in 1944 because of such small membership. The Orthodox Jews in Selma attended Mishkan Israel. See "Selma, Alabama," *Encyclopedia of Southern Jewish Communities*, www.isjl.org/history/archive/al/selma.html, accessed June 11, 2009.

98. Monte Kandel, "Field Report," Selma, Alabama, August 23, 1940, MKM 13.50.1039, RG248, NRS, YIVO. The total number of refugees who resettled in Selma, either sponsored by the NRS or family members, is unknown.

99. Hanna Berger, interview by Louisa H. Weinrib, July 1, 1991, Selma, Alabama, box 1, folder 27, Holocaust Survivors and U.S. Liberators Oral History Collection, ADAH; by the end of 1940, Berger was the only one of seven refugees sent by the NRS. The other six had been sponsored by their families. Monte Kandel, "Field Report," Selma, Alabama, November 2, 1940, MKM 13.50.1039, RG248, NRS, YIVO.

100. Monte Kandel, "Field Report," Selma, Alabama, August 23, 1940; "Field Report," Selma, Alabama, November 2, 1940, MKM 13.50.1039, RG248, NRS, YIVO.

101. Berger interview, 13–14, 18; Hanna Berger, "The Effects of the German Holocaust on One Family—Mine," Box 1, folder 13, Holocaust Survivors and U.S. Liberators Oral History Collection, ADAH. Other family members survived by escaping Nazi Germany, relocating to New York, Chicago, England, Shanghai, China, and Cali, Colombia.

102. Frieda grew up in Niederzissen and Hermann grew up in Burgbrohl. Berger, "The Effects of the German Holocaust on One Family—Mine"; see also Berger interview, 13–14, 18.

103. "Mobilians Discuss Plans to Aid Refugees," January 22, 1939; City's Mayor Aids Refugees," January 22, 1939; "Refugees' Relief Drive Is Opened by Mobile Jewry," June 8, 1939; "Jewish Leaders to Hear Lehman," October 28, 1939, clippings from Schwarz Scrapbook no. 14, MMA; Solomon A. Fineberg, "Mobile, Alabama," November 4, 1940, Box 1, folder "Alabama, Mobile 40–62," RG347.17.13, AJC, YIVO. It is assumed that the clippings from the Schwarz scrapbook came from the *Mobile Register.* By May 1941 the Mobile section of the NCJW had sent cigarettes and candy to homeless refugees interned in "friendly concentration camps in Canada." See "Report Read at Mt. Vernon," May 19, 1941, folder "National Council of Jewish Women, 1897–1969," Springhill Avenue Temple Archives.

104. "Meeting," November 17, 1938; "Regular Meeting," December 15, 1938, B'nai B'rith Papers, Springhill Avenue Temple Archives.

105. One of the reports related that Moses "has been declining toward a state that borders on dementia. He imagines that he is active in the F.B.I. . . . He is, for example, inciting a rumor against a doctor of German descent who, Moses claims, is an agent of the Nazi government. Rabbi Moses is a lovely person with lucid moments, who at the age of sixty-two presents a problem that cannot be disposed of." See J. I. Kingloff, "Field Report," Mobile, Alabama, May 22, 1940, MKM 13.50.1039, RG248, NRS, YIVO; Solomon A. Fineberg, "Mobile, Alabama," November 4, 1940, Box 1, folder "Alabama, Mobile 40–62," RG347.17.13 AJC, YIVO; Zietz, *Gates of Heaven*, 142–43; Umansky, *From Christian Science to Jewish Science*, 44.

106. Zietz, *Gates of Heaven*, 142. It is unclear what Mrs. Moses said to arouse animosity.

107. N. W. Bronstein, "Field Report," Mobile, Alabama, October 29, 1939, MKM 13.50.1039, RG248, NRS, YIVO.

108. The Ladies Aid Society was renamed the Ahavas Chesed Sisterhood in 1954. See "Guide to the Congregation Ahavas Chesed Records, 1923–1989," http://www.southalabama.edu/archives/html/manuscript/chesed.htm, accessed October, 4, 2010.

109. Monte Kandel, "Field Report," Mobile, Alabama, November 2, 1940, MKM 13.50.1039, RG248, NRS, YIVO.

110. Bauman, "Southern Jewish Women," 45.

111. See ibid.; William Toll, "A Quiet Revolution: Jewish Women's Clubs and the Widening Female Sphere, 1870–1920," *American Jewish Archives* 41 (Spring/

Summer 1989): 7–26; and Beth S. Wenger, "Jewish Women and Voluntarism: Beyond the Myth of Enablers," *American Jewish History* 79 (Autumn 1989): 16–36.

112. Monte Kandel, "Field Report," Mobile, Alabama, November 2, 1940, MKM 13.50.1039, RG248, NRS, YIVO.

113. This also included Sol Kahn, who "is still making frantic efforts to bring over additional relatives who are stranded in Holland." See Monte Kandel, "Field Report," Mobile, Alabama, September 25, 1941, MKM 13.50.1039, RG248, NRS, YIVO.

114. Ibid.; Monte Kandel, "Field Report," Mobile, Alabama, April 15–16, 1941, MKM 13.50.1039, RG248, NRS, YIVO.

115. Monte Kandel, "Field Report," Mobile, Alabama, September 25, 1941, MKM 13.50.1039, RG248, NRS, YIVO; "Americanism Talk Is Delivered to Optimist Club Here," n.d., "Clergyman Talks of War's Aftermath at Luncheon," June 11, 1942, "Lions Club Hears War Discussion By Rabbi Berkowitz," n.d., "Welfare Drive for the Oppressed," n.d., "Jewish-Aid Drive Opens Here Today," n.d., clippings found in Sidney M. Berkowitz Papers, Scrapbook, UNC.

116. Pauline A. Berkowitz, interview by Matthew T. Butts, July 22, 1992, Youngstown, Ohio, 4, http://www.maag.ysu.edu/oralhistory/cd1/OH1510.pdf, accessed October 4, 2010. Morgenstern reportedly told Berkowitz that "we have all these great scholars coming over as refugees from Germany, and they're all looking for asylum here because they've been persecuted by Hitler. . . . We're supporting them. We're feeding them. We're housing them, so we feel that as long as we're doing that, we should be giving them jobs."

117. Schlemiel is Yiddish for someone who is clumsy and incompetent and continually bungles things. Monte Kandel, "Field Report," Mobile, Alabama, September 25, 1941, MKM 13.50.1039, RG248, NRS, YIVO.

118. Mary Martha Thomas also explains that "prosperity can also be seen in the wholesale and retail trade figures. By September 1942 the city's $100 million wholesale trade was double its 1940 level. The retail also doubled from $33 million to $65 million." Mary Martha Thomas, "The Mobile Homefront during the Second World War," *Gulf Coast Historical Review* 1 (Fall 1985): 55–58; the John Dos Passos quote can be found in Allen Cronenberg, "Mobile and World War II, 1940–1945," in *Mobile: The New History of Alabama's First City*, ed. Michael V. R. Thomason (Tuscaloosa: University of Alabama Press, 2001), 214–17. The dislocation evident in Mobile during World War II occurred throughout the United States. According to Allan M. Winkler, roughly 20 percent of the American population moved during the war, whether following family to training camps or duty stations or relocating for employment opportunities. Allan M. Winkler, *Home Front U.S.A.: America during World War II*, 2nd ed. (Wheeling, IL: Harlan Davidson, 2000), 47–53.

119. Monte Kandel, "Field Report," Mobile, Alabama, September 25, 1941, MKM 13.50.1039, RG248, NRS, YIVO.

120. C. B. King to Franklin D. Roosevelt, May 25, 1940, Mobile, Alabama, Box 37, folder "Defense," Sparkman Papers, HSC.

121. According to Allen Cronenberg, "at the peak of activity during the war," Gulf Shipbuilding and Alabama Drydock and Shipbuilding Company (ADDSCO)

employed over "40,000 welders, machinists, electricians, and other workers" who produced a ship per week. Allen Cronenberg, *Forth to the Mighty Conflict: Alabama and World War II* (Tuscaloosa: University of Alabama Press, 1995), 53; Monte Kandel, "Field Report," Mobile, Alabama, January 29–30, 1942, MKM 13.50.1039, RG248, NRS, YIVO.

122. Krammer, *Undue Process*, 70.

123. The NCJW had continued to participate in resettlement efforts, although they did not provide the leadership after reorganization. During the war, they turned their attention to war work, which left little time for refugee programs. The Ladies Hebrew Benevolent Society, an affiliate of the federation, also assumed care for the ill and the transients during the war. Fannie Steiner, "Field Report," Mobile, Alabama, February 9–10, 1944, MKM 13.50.1039, RG248, NRS, YIVO.

124. Haberman replaced Rabbi Bertram Korn, who had succeeded Berkowitz. Both Berkowitz and Korn left Mobile to enter the service as chaplains. See Biographical Sketch of Joshua O. Haberman, October 10, 1967, in folder "Haberman, Joshua, Rabbi," Springhill Avenue Temple Archives.

125. See www.ort.org, accessed June 10, 2010.

Chapter 3

1. "The Balfour Declaration," in *The Jew in the Modern World: A Documentary History*, ed. Paul R. Mendes-Flohr and Jehuda Reinharz (New York and Oxford: Oxford University Press, 1980), 458.

2. Melvin I. Urofsky, *American Zionism: From Herzl to the Holocaust* (New York: Anchor Press/Doubleday, 1975; reprint, Lincoln:University of Nebraska Press/Bison Books, 1995), 1–2.

3. "Pittsburgh Platform," http://ccarnet.org/Articles/index.cfm?id=39&pge_id=1606, accessed November 5, 2010.

4. "Christians and Jews, Mobilize!" *Birmingham News*, August 3, 1939.

5. Italics in the original. Theodore Lowi, "Southern Jews: The Two Communities," in *Jews in the South*, ed. Leonard Dinnerstein and Mary Dale Palsson (Baton Rouge: Louisiana State University Press, 1973), 276.

6. Wayne Flynt, *Alabama Baptists: Southern Baptists in the Heart of Dixie* (Tuscaloosa: University of Alabama Press, 1995), ix, 232–33.

7. The study was conducted by Charles Y. Glock and Rodney Stark, *Christian Beliefs and Anti-Semitism* (New York: Harper and Row, 1966), and cited in Leonard Dinnerstein, *Uneasy at Home: Antisemitism and the American Jewish Experience* (New York: Columbia University Press, 1987), 96–97.

8. Flynt, *Alabama Baptists*, ix, 232–33.

9. *Alabama Baptist*, May 4, 1933.

10. Eliza R. L. McGraw, "'How to Win the Jews for Christ': Southern Jewishness and the Southern Baptist Convention," in *Dixie Diaspora: An Anthology of Southern Jewish History*, ed. Mark K. Bauman (Tuscaloosa: University of Alabama Press, 2006), 452–65; Elovitz, *A Century of Jewish Life in Dixie*, 154–55; Flynt, *Alabama Baptists*, 354–55.

11. Elovitz, *A Century of Jewish Life in Dixie*, 135, 138–39.

12. Ibid., 135, 138–39, 230n19.

13. Urofsky, *American Zionism*, 1–2, 88; Elovitz, *A Century of Jewish Life in Dixie*, 133–38; Ehrenreich left his position at Beth-Or in 1921. Byron L. Sherwin, "Portrait of a Romantic Rebel Bernard C. Ehrenreich (1876–1955)," in "*Turn to the South": Essays of Southern Jewry*, ed. by Nathan M. Kaganoff and Melvin I. Urofsky (Charlottesville: University Press of Virginia, 1979), 3, 8.

14. Leo Drum interview.

15. Minutes of the Jewish Federation of Montgomery, May 15, 1944, binder "1941 through 1945," JFM; Leo Drum interview.

16. J. V. W. Shaw, *A Survey of Palestine: Prepared in December 1945, and January 1946, for the Information of the Anglo-American Committee of Inquiry* (Palestine: Government Printer, 1945), 185.

17. "Executive Committee Meeting," September 23, 1938, UJF.

18. Charles Loch Mowat, *Britain between the Wars, 1918–1940* (Chicago: University of Chicago Press, 1955; reprint, Boston: Beacon Press, 1971), 48.

19. "Mandate for Palestine," in *The Jew in the Modern World*, 461–62. The most complete study of Palestine under the mandate is Tom Segev, *One Palestine, Complete: Jews and Arabs under the British Mandate* (New York: Henry Holt, 2000).

20. White Papers were official reports of the British government, usually issued following a governmental investigative commission.

21. See http://avalon.law.yale.edu/20th_century/brwh1939.asp, accessed November 13, 2011.

22. "Special Emergency Meeting," October 9, 1938, UJF.

23. Morris Newfield to Solomon Goldman, October 14, 1938; Ewart H. Wyle to Franklin D. Roosevelt, n.d.; A. H. Reid to Franklin D. Roosevelt, n.d.; "To the Recommendations Committee, International Convention of the Disciples of Christ," n.d., all found in file 817.1.1.1.20, Morris Newfield Papers, BPL.

24. William B. Bankhead to Cordell Hull, October 11, 1938; Cordell Hull to William B. Bankhead, October 15, 1938; William B. Bankhead to Morris Newfield, October 18, 1938, 817.1.1.1.20, Morris Newfield Papers, BPL; "Special Emergency Meeting," October 9, 1938, United Jewish Fund Papers, BJF; "Isaac Abelson," 1871.1.1, Henry Marks Files, BPL. For more information on Ike Abelson, see Karl B. Friedman to editor, *Southern Shofar*, September 1995.

25. Leon Schwarz, "Saga of the Bankheads," *National Jewish Monthly*, March 1939, clipping found in Schwarz Scrapbook no. 14, MMA; Milton H. Fies, "The Man with a Light on His Cap: Being a Brief Chronicle of Coal Mining in Walker County, 1912–1960," 50–51, Hill Ferguson Papers, file 56.4.5.22, BPL.

26. "Democracy in a Changing World," May 9, 1938, box 28, folder 8, William B. Bankhead Papers, ADAH.

27. Walker County Lodge No. 938 to William Bankhead, May 25, 1938, box 28, folder 8; Beth Zur Lodge No. 84 to William Bankhead, June 27, 1938, box 28, folder 8; Leon Schwarz to Sol Bloom, June 9, 1938, box 28, folder 8; Patrick H. Codyre to William Bankhead, May 29, 1938, box 28, folder 8, Bankhead Papers, ADAH. See box 28, folders 6–8, Bankhead Papers, for all of the telegrams concerning the speech.

28. Stephen S. Wise to John Sparkman, October 16, 1938; John Sparkman to Stephen S. Wise, October 20, 1938; Sam J. Israel to John Sparkman, October 17,

1938; John Sparkman to Sam J. Israel, October 20, 1938, box 18, folder "Jews," Sparkman Papers, HSC.

29. Stephen S. Wise to John Sparkman, November 1, 1938, John Sparkman to Stephen S. Wise, November 2, 1938, Box 18, folder "Jews," Sparkman Papers, HSC.

30. Cowett, "Morris Newfield, Alabama, and Blacks, 1895–1940," 42; Cowett, *Birmingham's Rabbi*, 153–54, 169.

31. Cowett, *Birmingham's Rabbi*, 168–69.

32. Temple Emanu-El, *A Century of Reverence, 1882–1982* (Birmingham, AL: Privately printed, 1982), 32.

33. Cyrus Arfa, *Reforming Reform Judaism: Zionism and the Reform Rabbinate, 1885–1948* (Tel Aviv: University Publishing Projects, 1985), 3–4.

34. Elovitz, *A Century of Jewish Life in Dixie*, 64–66, 137–38.

35. "Mr. Lewisohn's Address," *Birmingham Age-Herald*, March 29, 1940, 8. For more information on Lewisohn, see Seymour Lainoff, *Ludwig Lewisohn* (Boston: Twayne Publishers, 1982).

36. Joe H. Radoms to Felix Shevinsky, March 8, 1940, Birmingham, Alabama, found in Elovitz Research Papers, 781.5.19.3.7, BPL.

37. "U.S. Anti-Jewish Fears Allayed," *Birmingham Age-Herald*, March 7, 1940, 7.

38. Elovitz, *A Century of Jewish Life in Dixie*, 140.

39. Radoms to Shevinsky, March 8, 1940, found in Elovitz Research Papers, 781.5.19.3.7, BPL.

40. *Birmingham Age-Herald*, March 8, 1940, 6.

41. "Morris Newfield," *Temple Emanu-El Yearbook: 1945–1946*, 15, "Jewish Synagogues Temple Emanu-El," BPL Subject Files. Mayer Newfield's recollection can be found in *A Century of Reverence, 1882–1982*, 34.

42. Morris Fisher, Ida Newman Fisher, Max Goldberg, and Fannie Newman Goldberg interviews conducted by Mark Elovitz, July 10, 1972, Elovitz Research Papers, folder 781.4.1.2.6, BPL.

43. Irving Beiman to Milton Grafman, n.d. (1943?), folder 1758.1.9, Milton Grafman Papers, BPL.

44. Buddy Marlow to Milton Grafman, n.d., folder 1758.1.77, Grafman Papers, BPL. For more information on Grafman, see Terry Barr, "Rabbi Grafman and Birmingham's Civil Rights Era," in *Quiet Voices: Southern Rabbis and Black Civil Rights, 1880s to 1990s*, ed. Mark K. Bauman and Berkley Kalin (Tuscaloosa: University of Alabama Press, 1997).

45. "Eddy Is Barred By Reich," July 18, 1938, *New York Times*; Eddy quote in unpublished manuscript graciously provided to the author by Stephen W. Grafman, the rabbi's son; Stephen W. Grafman to Dan J. Puckett, July 9, 2011, correspondence in possession of the author. The members of the American Seminar also put together a parody once the tour ended. The words to the parody also provided by Stephen Grafman.

> "Sherwood Eddy" sung to the tune of "There Is a Tavern in the Town"
> Sherwood Eddy is our Pride
> He takes the whole world in his stride

In either hand he holds a hemisphere
With which to biff dictators on the ear.

Chorus
Then three cheers for Sherwood Eddy
For a row he's always ready
The Fascists and the Nazis he abhors
So long so long kind friends so long
Contribute to this little song
Sherwood's on the shoot:
    Sing Tra la la la la
And Devil take the Swastika.

He goes to England and to France
He roams across a vast expanse
He loves the Dane; he loves the Finn
But Germany won't let him in.

The Russians greet him every year;
He's met in Poland with a cheer
To all mankind he feels akin
Yet Germany won't let him in.

He lives with Guide Books and with Maps
He knows—what's fit to know—about the Japs
To eat Sauerkraut he thinks no sin
But Germany won't let him in.
He once pro-German was confessed
The Nordics took him to their breast
Then he criticised the Nazis in Berlin
Now Germany won't let him in.

46. Milton Grafman Travel Diary, 37–38 (unpublished manuscript in possession of the author). The diary was provided to the author by Stephen W. Grafman.

47. Ibid., 39–41.

48. Letter from Milton Grafman to Hiram Weiss, n.d., cited in Stephen W. Grafman, "Out of the Pale: A Grafman Family History," 296–97 (unpublished manuscript in possession of the author).

49. "Temple Emanu-El Schedules an Institute on Judaism," May 9, 1943, *Birmingham News*, 8D. The Emanu-El Men's Club sponsored the institute. Dr. Jacob Rader Marcus headlined the first meeting. Elovitz notes that the institute "brought a prominent Jewish scholar to Birmingham and attracted at least 75 and often more than 150 Christian clergymen to these lectures at Temple Emanu-El." The NCCJ was established in October 1943. Moreover, while it was more common for Reform rabbis to engage in ecumenical endeavors, Temple Beth-El's Abraham Mesch also reached out to Gentiles, conducting "an annual 'inter-faith tea' followed by a presentation for lay Christians." See Elovitz, *A Century of Jewish Life in Dixie*, 153–54.

50. Milton Grafman interview by Mark Elovitz, n.d., 781.4.3.2.8, Mark Elovitz Research Papers, BPL.

51. Membership figures for Temple Emanu-El cited in Elovitz, *A Century of Jewish Life in Dixie*, 151; Morris Fisher, Ida Newman Fisher, Max Goldberg, and Fannie Newman Goldberg interviews conducted by Mark Elovitz, July 10, 1972, Elovitz Research Papers, folder 781.4.1.2.6, BPL.

52. Women were finally granted membership rights in 1954. Although it moved toward being a Conservative congregation, Beth-El kept close ties with the Orthodox K'nesseth Israel. Elovitz notes that compromises between Orthodoxy and practice "became part and parcel of the tradition of Beth El's members whose hearts owed allegiance to traditional Judaism but whose minds strove to accommodate them to the realities of life in Birmingham during the second half of the twentieth century." Elovitz, *A Century of Jewish Life in Dixie*, 94–95, 99, 163–64, 235n4.

53. The Central School of Religion was founded in Indiana in 1896, and students earned their degrees through correspondence courses.

54. Elovitz, *A Century of Jewish Life in Dixie*, 94–95; "Beth-El Forum," *Temple Beth-El Yearbook, 1939*, 18; "Temple Beth-El Now Has Largest Jewish Congregation in State," June 3, 1949, *Birmingham News*, clipping found in 1794.1.12, Temple Beth-El Records, BPL. See also Mark K. Bauman, *Harry H. Epstein and the Rabbinate as Conduit of Change* (Rutherford, NJ: Fairleigh Dickinson University Press, 1994), 53–55.

55. "There'll Be New and Better 'Music in the Air' at Temple Beth-El Soon," September 21, 1935, *Birmingham Post*, clipping found in 1794.1.17, Temple Beth-El Records, BPL.

56. http://www.jewishvirtuallibrary.org/jsource/Judaism/Columbus_platform.html, accessed June 25, 2010; Arfa, *Reforming Reform Judaism*, 1–2.

57. Cowett cites Arfa's dissertation as his source. Cowett, *Birmingham's Rabbi*, 168.

58. It is unclear when Grafman became a Zionist. According to his son, Stephen Grafman, and daughter, Ruth Fromstein, the rabbi most probably embraced Zionism early in his life, well before the Nazis came to power. Stephen Grafman to author, February 22, 2008.

59. Thomas A. Kolsky, *Jews against Zionism: The American Council for Judaism, 1942–1948* (Philadelphia: Temple University Press, 1990), 37.

60. Harry Schneiderman and Morris T. Fine, eds., *American Jewish Yearbook 5703*, vol. 44 (Philadelphia: Jewish Publication Society of America, 1942), 109.

61. "U.S. Reform Rabbis State Principles," August 30, 1942, *New York Times*, 26.

62. Monty Noam Penkower, "The Genesis of the American Council for Judaism," 70–71. See http://www.lekket.com/data/articles/003-001-007_000.pdf, accessed April 3, 2011.

63. Elovitz, *A Century of Jewish Life in Dixie*, 133.

64. Ibid., 133; Mervyn Sterne interview by Elovitz. Mervyn Sterne interview by Billie Sterne, November 20, 1972, tape 1, page 2, box 74, number 6, William E. Wiener Oral History Library, Dorot Jewish Division, NYPL.

65. Manheim S. Shapiro, "Report on Southern Jewish Opinion," April 11, 1950, 4, Box 302, folder 6, RG347.17.10, AJC, YIVO.

66. Henry L. Feingold, *A Time for Searching: Entering the Mainstream, 1920–1945* (Baltimore: Johns Hopkins University Press, 1992), 183–84; Dinnerstein, *Antisemitism in America*, 146–49.

67. "Zionism: An Affirmation of Judaism," November 16, 1942; "Birmingham Rabbis Sign Paper Rebuking Zionism Opponents," *Birmingham News*, November 16, 1942, 2; *Birmingham Age-Herald*, November 17, 1942. The statement was revised later to include 757 signatories: 296 Orthodox rabbis, 247 Conservative rabbis, and 214 Reform rabbis.

68. For the titles of some of Grafman's sermons in the months after his arrival in Birmingham, see the bulletins found in 796.0.1, Temple Emanu-El Records, BPL.

69. "From the Rabbi's Study," March 19, 1943, Temple Emanu-El Bulletin, 796.0.1, Temple Emanu-El Records, BPL.

70. *Birmingham News*, April 4, 1943, 2B; "An Urgent Call to All Jews," newspaper advertisement, n.d., found in 796.7.1, Temple Emanu-El Records, BPL. An article in *Christianity Today* suggested that many evangelicals who joined in the day of prayer "did not advise people to pray for the persecutions to stop, only that Jews might turn to Christ in their despair. The best thing people could do for Jews under the circumstances was send them more New Testaments and missionaries." Timothy P. Weber, "How Evangelicals Became Israel's Best Friend," *Christianity Today*, October 5, 1998, 4. http://www.christianitytoday.com/ct/1998/october5/8tb038.html, accessed April 3, 2011.

71. The Joint Resolution was finally approved on June 10, 1943. Alabama, *General Laws and Joint Resolutions of the Legislature of Alabama* (Birmingham, AL: Birmingham Printing Company, 1943), 136n144; see also "Resolution Is Passed Asking for Creation of Jewish Homeland," *Birmingham News*, May 5, 1943, 1.

72. "Future of Jew Is Talk Subject," May 15, 1943, 12; "Rabbi Discusses Needs of Peace," *Birmingham Age-Herald*, June 5, 1943, 12; "Nazis Can Never Come Back, Says Zionist Leader Lewisohn," *Birmingham News*, May 21, 1943; "With Aid of Christian Nations Anti-Semitism May Go, Says Rabbi," *Birmingham News*, November 1, 1943.

73. Adalien Feidelson Kahn interview conducted by author, January 5, 2002.

74. "Jews Organize Campaign Group," December 21, 1943, 7; "Plan for Aid to Jews Endorsed," *Birmingham Age-Herald*, January 11, 1944, 7; "Palestine Committee Supported in Protest against 'White Paper,'" December 26, 1943; "Black Paper," *Alabama: News Magazine of the Deep South* (January 21, 1944): 15. According to Yad Vashem, the American Zionist Emergency Council was

> created at the beginning of World War II to represent Zionist leadership in the United States, in case the activities of Zionist leaders in London and Jerusalem were to be restricted because of the war. The council's original members included representatives of the Zionist Organization of America and other American Zionist leaders. Until 1941, the council had a weak and disorganized leadership. It did not protest the British White Paper of 1939, which placed further restrictions on Jewish immigration to Palestine. As long as the United States stayed out of the war, the council was afraid to sponsor the establishment of a Jewish fighting organization. AZEC did not rescue Jews

being persecuted by the Nazis; this was mainly done by the American Jewish Congress. AZEC's job was to deal with issues related to the Zionist movement and Palestine, such as immigration. One of its major responsibilities was to convince the American public of the importance of Palestine to the future of the Jewish people. After the war, AZEC turned its attention to supporting the "illegal immigration" of Holocaust survivors to Palestine and lobbying the United States for a Jewish state. In 1949, AZEC became the American Zionist Council.

http://www1.yadvashem.org/odot_pdf/Microsoft%20Word%20-%205737.pdf, accessed September 4, 2011.

75. In his sermon, Grafman sharply criticized anti-Zionists, a number of whom remained at Emanu-El. Grafman stated that if Great Britain did implement the White Paper, it would "be because of aid [and] comfort given her by anti-Zionists. Lines are being drawn [and] each of [us] must ask himself on which side he takes his stand: on the side of perjury [and] injustice [and] heartlessness, or on the side of honesty, of respect for commitments [and] obligations, of justice for all men, including the Jews, on the side where religious-minded people should be found." See "Does the White Paper Portend a Black Future?" October 29, 1943. Sermon found in the private papers of Rabbi Milton Grafman. The papers are privately held by Stephen W. Grafman.

76. *Montgomery Advertiser*, May 19, 1943, 4.

77. *Birmingham News*, December 22, 1943, 8; November 7, 1943, 2D; March 19, 1944, 2D.

78. John Temple Graves, "This Morning," *Birmingham Age-Herald*, December 29, 1943, 1.

79. *Birmingham Age-Herald*, January 12, 1944, 13; January 13, 1944, 4; Zietz, *Gates of Heaven*, 148–49; "Dr. Wise Says Peace Talks Now Will Lead to War III," *Mobile Press*, January 24, 1944, found in folder "Newspaper Clippings," box "Anniversary 100th Brochures"; Bernard Eichold Introduction of Rabbi Korn, n.d., folder "Korn, Bertram Wallace, Rabbi"; Resolution, January 18, 1944, B'nai B'rith Papers, Springhill Avenue Temple Archives.

80. "Minutes of the Annual Meeting," February 14, 1944, binder "1941 through 1945," JFM.

81. Ralph G. Holberg to Frank Boykin, January 25, 1944; A. Lucas to Ralph G. Holberg, January 29, 1944; Ralph G. Holberg to Lister Hill, January 25, 1944; Lister Hill to Ralph G. Holberg, February 1, 1944; Abba Hillel Silber to Rabbi Bertram W. Korn, February 4, 1944, B'nai B'rith Papers, Springhill Avenue Temple Archives; "Chamberlain 1939 Declaration of Appeasement Policy Barring Jewish Immigration to Palestine Brings Censure from Local Council," *Mobile Labor Journal*, January 14, 1944.

82. Stephen S. Wise to Cooper Green, February 4, 1944; Cooper Green to Stephen S. Wise, February 4, 1944; form letter, February 7, 1944; Abe Berkowitz to Cooper Green, February 10, 1944, 9.16, Cooper Green Papers, BPL.

83. John Newsome to Cooper Green, February 14, 1944, 9.16, Cooper Green Pa-

pers, BPL; John Sparkman to Cooper Green, February 8, 1944, box 38, folder "House Legislation: Jews," Sparkman Papers, HSC. Newsome defeated Luther Patrick for Alabama's Ninth District seat in 1942. Patrick recaptured the seat in the 1944 Democratic primary election. Patrick also strongly supported Jewish issues. The Gillette-Rogers Resolution had been initiated in Congress by the Bergson Group. The Bergson Group, headed by Hillel Kook, who operated under the name Peter Bergson, publicized news of the mass killings of Jews in Europe and worked to convince the US government to begin rescue operations. For information on the Gillette-Rogers Resolution, see Haskel Lookstein, *Were We Our Brothers' Keepers? The Public Response of American Jews to the Holocaust, 1938–1944* (New York: Vintage Books, 1988), 173–79. For more information on the Bergson Group, see David S. Wyman and Rafael Medoff, *A Race against Death: Peter Bergson, America, and the Holocaust* (New York: The New Press, 2002), and Judith Tydor Baumel, *The "Bergson Boys" and the Origins of Contemporary Zionist Militancy* (Syracuse, NY: Syracuse University Press, 2005).

84. "Jarman Visions Possible Tangle over Palestine," February 13, 1944, *Birmingham News* clipping; Milton L. Grafman to Pete Jarman, February 4, 1944; Pete Jarman to Cooper Green, February 8, 1944; Pete Jarman to Moses Temerson, February 8, 1944; Pete Jarman to H. C. Pannell, February 8, 1944; Pete Jarman to Milton L. Grafman, February 11, 1944; Abe Berkowitz to Mr. Shapiro, February 14, 1944, all found in Box 1, folder "Cong. Pete Jarman," MS-825 Milton L. Grafman Papers, American Jewish Archives, Cincinnati, Ohio (hereafter cited as AJA). Moses Temerson and H. C. Pannell, both of Tuscaloosa, wired Jarman about supporting the resolution. Pannell was the commander of the American Legion in Tuscaloosa.

85. Ike Abelson to I. L. Kenen, March 1, 1944, c7/877, Central Zionist Archives, Jerusalem, Israel (hereafter cited as CZO).

86. *Birmingham News*, March 19, 1944.

87. Alfred E. Smith to Chauncey M. Sparks, May 20, 1944, box 9, Chauncey Sparks Personal Papers, ADAH.

88. David S. Wyman, *The Abandonment of the Jews: America and the Holocaust, 1941–1945* (New York: Pantheon Books, 1984), 237; Chauncey Sparks to Alfred E. Smith, May 22, 1944, box 9, Sparks Personal Papers, ADAH; see also, "Sparks Endorses Rescue of Jews," *Birmingham Age-Herald*, May 21, 1944.

89. Wyman, *The Abandonment of the Jews*, 237; Chauncey Sparks to Alfred E. Smith, May 22, 1944, box 9, Sparks Personal Papers, ADAH; see also, "Sparks Endorses Rescue of Jews," *Birmingham Age-Herald*, May 21, 1944, 13; Joseph P. Mudd to Chauncey Sparks, May 25, 1944; Chauncey Sparks to Joseph P. Mudd, May 26, 1944, box 9, Sparks Personal Papers, ADAH.

90. A. Berkowitz and I. L. Rosen to Editor, *Birmingham News*, March 18, 1945, 2D.

91. "A Word to Zionists," *Birmingham News*, March 25, 1945, 2D.

92. David Horowitz, "Jewish Colonization and Arab Development in Palestine," October 7, 1945, found at http://www.ismi.emory.edu/PrimarySource/CZAcolanddevOct45.pdf, accessed September 4, 2011.

93. "Visit of Isaiah Terman," June 11, 1945, Birmingham, Alabama, Box 1, folder "Visits Alabama, Birmingham 44–62," RG347.17.13, AJC, YIVO; Kahn interview; William Seidelman Report, May 2, 1945, Birmingham, Alabama, Box 1, folder

"Visits, Alabama, Birmingham 44–62," RG347.17.13, AJC, YIVO. The reason for the conflict between Grafman and Feidelson is not entirely clear. In his field report, Terman stated that Grafman called Feidelson on the telephone and escalated to where "the situation has reached the level of name calling (Grafman to Feidelson)." Grafman supposedly called Feidelson a "son of a bitch," although Terman did not include what was said in his report. In an interview with Feidelson's daughter in 2002, Ms. Kahn recalled that a Birmingham rabbi had called her father a "son of a bitch" in regard to his position on Zionism, although she did not name Grafman specifically. Moreover, few in the community rallied behind Feidelson, who seems to have rubbed many the wrong way. Terman remarked that despite his intelligence and genuine concern for the community, Feidelson "does not conceal the good opinion he holds of himself in distinction to his opinion of some of the other community leaders. And he is not silent on the subject of Zionism."

94. William Seidelman Report, May 2, 1945, Birmingham, Alabama, Box 1, folder "Visits, Alabama, Birmingham 44–62," RG347.17.13, AJC, YIVO.

95. Southern Young Judaea Association Convention Program, August 5–8, 1934, Leon Schwarz Scrapbook no. 11, MMA; S. H. Bucholtz, "Report of Field Representative," July 31, 1944; "Visit of Isaiah Terman," June 4, 1945, Box 1, folder "Alabama, Mobile 40–62," RG347.17.13, AJC, YIVO; Monte Kandel, April 14–16, 1945, MKM 13.50.1039, RG248, NRS, YIVO. May considered his donation to the Zionist organization as "just another charitable contribution."

96. Bernard Eichold introduction of Rabbi Korn, n.d., folder "Korn, Bertram Wallace, Rabbi," Springhill Avenue Temple Archives.

97. "Visit of Isaiah Terman," May 31–June 1, 1945, Montgomery, Alabama, Box 1, folder "Visits Alabama Montgomery 40–61," RG347.17.13, AJC, YIVO. Although the ACJ had great influence among Montgomery's Reform Jews, it did not receive any funds from the federation. Weil had pushed for the federation to include the ACJ in its budget, but after considerable disagreement among board members, Blachschleger stated that it "should be supported by individual subscriptions." See "A Regular Monthly Board Meeting of the Jewish Federation of Montgomery," May 15, 1944, binder "1941 through 1945," JFM.

98. "Board Meeting," February 24, 1941, binder "1941 through 1945," JFM; "Visit of Isaiah Terman," May 31–June 1, 1945, Montgomery, Alabama, Box 1, folder "Visits Alabama Montgomery 40–61," RG347.17.13, AJC, YIVO.

99. Evans, *The Provincials*, 110.

Chapter 4

1. Lee B. Weil, "Community Relations," an address to the Southeastern States Regional Conference of the Council of Jewish Federations and Welfare Funds, March 18–18, 1944. Box 1, folder "Communal Relations, Alabama, Birmingham," RG347.17.13, AJC, YIVO. With a few exceptions, the author has examined the news sections of virtually every daily newspaper and most weeklies in Alabama from 1933 to 1946, and has paid particular attention to the editorial positions of these papers. For a more in-depth analysis of the Alabama press and Nazism, see Dan J. Puck-

ett, "Hitler, Race, and Democracy in the Heart of Dixie: Alabamian Attitudes and Responses to the Issues of Nazi and Southern Racism, 1933–1946" (PhD diss., Mississippi State University, 2005).

2. Drake suggests that this sympathy derived from the acculturation of Jews into North Carolina's small-town culture. "Thus, without any city having a thousand or more Jewish resident," Drake observes, "in North Carolina 'communal constraints and rabbinic authority' did not impede its small-town influence and thus tended to encourage more developed community relationships across religious boundaries." Robert Drake, "*Kristallnacht* and North Carolina: Reporting on Antisemitism in Black and White," *Southern Jewish History* 13 (2010): 113.

3. Deborah E. Lipstadt, *Beyond Belief: The American Press and the Coming of the Holocaust, 1933–1945* (New York: The Free Press, 1986); Laurel Leff, *Buried by the Times: The Holocaust and America's Most Important Newspaper* (Cambridge and New York: Cambridge University Press, 2005).

4. Lipstadt, *Beyond Belief*, 2–3.

5. *Lee County Bulletin*, April 4, 1943, cited in Paul L. Mussleman, "The Editorial Policy of the *Lee County Bulletin*, 1937–1951" (master's thesis, Auburn University, 1952), 7.

6. "Press and Local History," October 7, 1943, 10; "Functions of an Editor," *Birmingham News*, October 5, 1943, 6.

7. Robert H. Kirksey to Editor, *Birmingham Age-Herald*, June 19, 1941.

8. The most penetrating analysis of how the southern press perceived and addressed Nazi Germany is Grill and Jenkins's "The Nazis and the American South in the 1930s," 667–94. Grill and Jenkins examine how southerners condemned Nazi antisemitism but consciously ignored Nazi Negrophobia.

9. *Birmingham Messenger*, March 25, 1933, 1; June 3, 1933, 1; *Birmingham Age-Herald*, April 4, 1933, 4; June 1, 1933, 10; *Cullman Tribune*, April 13, 1933, 6.

10. Leff, *Buried By the Times*, 13–15.

11. See Dan J. Puckett, "In the Shadow of Hitler: Birmingham's Temple Emanu-El and Nazism," *Southern Jewish History* 11 (2008): 1–39.

12. "The Real Issue," *Birmingham Age-Herald*, May 21, 1934, 4.

13. "Nazi Hands Fail to Halt Enemy," *Birmingham Age-Herald*, July 31, 1935, 9; Deborah Lipstadt writes that the "inability to believe that Hitler was directly responsible was a manifestation of the press's difficulty in accepting that his antisemitism was not rhetoric, but a deep-seated ideology." Lipstadt, *Beyond Belief*, 49.

14. *Mobile Register*, March 22, 1933, 4.

15. *Birmingham Age-Herald*, January 31, 1934, 4.

16. Lipstadt, *Beyond Belief*, 48–49.

17. *Southern Jewish Times*, September 1935, 804, drawer 364, folder 2, line 0995, ADAH. The September 1935 paper is the only existing issue found in the archives.

18. Manheim S. Shapiro, "Report on Southern Jewish Opinion," April 11, 1950, 2–6, Box 302, folder 6, RG347.17.10, AJC, YIVO.

19. Botwinick, *A History of the Holocaust*, 124.

20. *Birmingham Age-Herald*, December 6, 1938, 8.

21. Ibid., November 26, 1938, 6.

22. Daniel Webster Hollis III, *An Alabama Newspaper Tradition: Grover C. Hall and the Hall Family* (Tuscaloosa: University of Alabama Press, 1983), 67.

23. "The Egregious Gentile Called to Account," *Montgomery Advertiser*, December 4, 1938, 4.

24. Ibid.

25. "Report on a Beautiful Experience," *Montgomery Advertiser*, December 11, 1938, 4.

26. "From Jew and Gentile," *Montgomery Advertiser*, December 11, 1938, 4.

27. "Report on a Beautiful Experience," 4.

28. "From Jew and Gentile," 4.

29. Hollis, *An Alabama Newspaper Tradition*, 68–69.

30. John Temple Graves, "This Morning," *Birmingham Age-Herald*, January 25, 1939, 1.

31. Hollis, *An Alabama Newspaper Tradition*, 68.

32. "Resolution," n.d., *Minute Book Kahl Montgomery, 1941*, TBO.

33. "Grover Cleveland Hall Memorial Award," Grover C. Hall Jr. Papers, box 1, folder 1, ADAH.

34. Hollis, *An Alabama Newspaper Tradition*, 150.

35. *Catholic Week*, June 23, 1939; June 16, 1939.

36. *Alabama Baptist*, May 4, 1933.

37. *Alabama Baptist*, July 13, 1933, and December 7, 1933; Flynt, *Alabama Baptists*, 397.

38. Charles F. Leek, "A New View of Hitlerism," *Alabama Baptist*, September 6, 1934. The most complete treatment of Gwaltney's views and Alabama Southern Baptist thought in generalis Flynt's *Alabama Baptists*. A brief examination of how Alabama Baptists responded to the growth of Nazi power is found in Jimmy Harper, "Alabama Baptists and the Rise of Hitler and Fascism, 1930–1938," *Journal of Reform Judaism* 32 (Spring 1985): 1–11. For a brief look at the Baptist World Congress in Berlin in 1934, see William Loyd Allen, "How Baptists Assessed Hitler," *Christian Century* (September 1–8, 1982): 890–91.

39. Grover Hall Sr. to H. L. Mencken, May 4, 1936, Microfilm Reel 25, H. L. Mencken Papers, NYPL.

40. *Alabama Baptist*, September 6, 1934.

41. Harper, "Alabama Baptists and the Rise of Hitler and Fascism, 1930–1938," 5; Flynt, *Alabama Baptists*, 397; "The Menace of Hitlerism," *Alabama Baptist*, July 15, 1937, 2.

42. *Alabama Baptist*, December 1, 1938; December 8, 1938.

43. Flynt, *Alabama Baptists*, 397–98.

44. *Birmingham News*, November 11, 1938, 10; *Marion Times-Standard*, November 17, 1938; *Mobile Register*, September 15 and September 16, 1938, found in Leon Schwarz Scrapbook no. 13, MMA.

45. *Clarke County Democrat*, November 24, 1938; one editorial described how "Jews were placed in restricted areas, stripped of their possessions, beaten, abused, and thrown into concentration camps, where they are administered slow death by

the Nazi reign of terror." See *Aliceville Times*, November 17, 1938, 4; November 24, 1938, 1; December 1, 1938, 1, 4.

46. Lipstadt, *Beyond Belief*, 53.

47. *Birmingham Age-Herald*, February 14, 1939, 4; *Aliceville Times*, February 9, 1939.

48. "More Territory, and More Victims of Persecution," *Birmingham News*, March 20, 1939, 6.

49. Steven J. Ross, "*Confessions of a Nazi Spy*: Warner Bros., Anti-Fascism and the Politicization of Hollywood," http://www.Learcenter.Org/pdf/WWRoss.pdf, accessed May 16, 2009.

50. Elmer M. Barke to Editor, *Tuscaloosa News*, May 16, 1939, 4. As Steven Ross points out in his article on *Confessions of a Nazi Spy*, antifascism, particularly by Hollywood Jews, was often considered a front for Communist subversion. Even the House Un-American Activities Committee (HUAC) investigated this claim. See Ross, "*Confessions of a Nazi Spy*."

51. Alfred B. Thomas to Editor, *Tuscaloosa News*, May 21, 1939, 4; while Shelton did not respond directly, the *News* did reprint part of John Temple Graves's article, which addressed the movie on its editorial page. Graves wrote that "the audience in which we saw this motion picture was whipped to a high degree of emotionalism, and the emotions were hate, fear, loathing and a hotly competitive patriotism. When Hitler was shown or some climax of Gestapo villainy was reacted, there would be cries, shouts, exclamations and hisses from all parts of the audience." Shelton called these "timely remarks." "The Wrong Kind of Hissing," *Tuscaloosa News*, June 1, 1939, 4.

52. Paul Locust to Editor, *Tuscaloosa News*, May 21, 1939, 4.

53. Feldman, *Politics, Society, and the Klan in Alabama*, 241.

54. Lipstadt, *Beyond Belief*, 140–41.

55. *Birmingham News*, September 14, 1939, 8; *Birmingham Age-Herald*, February 2, 1940, 6.

56. *Birmingham News*, July 15, 1940, 6.

57. For example, see *Birmingham News*, August 14, 1940, 8; September 22, 1940, 12; December 1, 1940, 16; March 9, 1941, 14; November 23, 1941, 6; J. H. Radoms to Editor, November 3, 1941, 6.

58. Lipstadt, *Beyond Belief*, 140–41; Charles N. Feidelson, "This Evening," *Birmingham News*, February 10, 1942, 6; February 28, 1942, 4.

59. Grill and Jenkins, "The Nazis and the American South," 668; Raymond Parks, one of the charter members of Montgomery's NAACP, kept copies of the *Courier*, the *Defender*, NAACP's *Crisis*, and other northern black newspapers in his barbershop for his customers. See Douglas Brinkley, *Rosa Parks* (New York: Viking, 2000), 38–39.

60. Johnpeter H. Grill, "The American South and Nazi Racism," in *The Impact of Nazism: New Perspectives on the Third Reich and Its Legacy*, ed. Alan E. Steinweis and Daniel E. Rogers (Lincoln: University of Nebraska Press, 2003), 24; Grill and Jenkins, "The Nazis and the American South," 676–77. Grill and Jenkins point to

actions such as the application of the Nuremberg Laws to blacks in Germany and the sterilization of several hundred "Rhineland Bastards," as evidence that "no informed person in the United States, and particularly not American journalists and editors, could be ignorant of Nazi anti-black views and actions by the 1930s"; of the African American newspapers published in Alabama during this period the *Birmingham World* and the *Weekly Review* had the largest circulation.

61. Neil MacMaster, *Racism in Europe, 1870–2000* (New York: Palgrave Macmillan, 2001), 132; see also Tina M. Campt, *Other Germans: Black Germans and the Politics of Race, Gender, and Memory in the Third Reich* (Ann Arbor: University of Michigan Press, 2004); see also Adolf Hitler, *Mein Kampf*, trans. Ralph Manheim (Verlag Frz. Eher Nachf, GMBH, 1925; reprint, Boston: Houghton Mifflin, 1971), 325–27.

62. Unfortunately, most of Alabama's black newspapers in the 1930s are no longer extant. The surviving issues of the two major black newspapers in Alabama, the *Birmingham World* and the *Weekly Review* (Birmingham), begin in 1940 for both papers. K. J. Sullivan began the *Gadsden Call-Post* in either 1934 or 1936, although few copies prior to the 1950s have survived. Thus it is impossible to get a complete picture of the attitudes of the black press during the 1930s. The few black newspapers that have survived are the student newspapers at Tuskegee Institute and Talladega College, both of which make comparisons between the treatment of African Americans in the South and Jews in Nazi Germany. For example, just after *Kristallnacht*, Wilson A. Head of Tuskegee's *Campus Digest* made reference to a campaign to resettle German Jews and opined, "The American Negro is vitally interested in the effects of such a movement into this country. As a minority group he has been subjected to some of the same kind of oppression as the Jews are now undergoing, and he wonders if the United States government is going to rescue the Jews and leave him in his present state. Will the government spend millions of dollars to bring the Jews over here and still do nothing to solve the Negro problem?" "Behind the Headlines," *Campus Digest*, December 17, 1938, 2.

63. Grill and Jenkins, "The Nazis and the American South," 691–92; Robert Durr, "Weekly Digest," *Weekly Review*, June 6, 1941. Durr reproduced black syndicated columnist Gordon B. Hancock's article verbatim without crediting Hancock. This gave the impression that the article was Durr's own work. See Hancock, "Between the Lines," *Birmingham World*, June 3, 1941; see also *Weekly Review*, October 18, 1940.

64. *Birmingham World*, June 10, 1941; Allen Woodrow Jones, "Alabama," in *The Black Press in the South, 1865–1979*, ed. Henry Lewis Suggs (Westport, CT: Greenwood Press, 1983): 44.

65. Robert J. Norrell, "Labor at the Ballot Box: Alabama Politics from the New Deal to the Dixiecrat Movement," *Journal of Southern History* 57 (May 1991): 217; see also Ralph Bunche, "Memorandum on the Political Status of the Negro," *Carnegie Survey of the Negro in America*, 1: 32–33, box 80, Ralph Bunche Papers, UCLA. Durr's passivity and accommodation in matters of race relations and racial justice was not unusual in black journalism in Birmingham. The *Weekly Review* continued in the tradition of Oscar W. Adams and the highly successful *Birmingham Reporter*,

which flourished from 1906 to 1933. Adams, a prominent and wealthy leader in Birmingham's African American community, hewed closely to the accommodationist philosophy of Booker T. Washington. After the *Reporter* shut its doors due to financial hardships caused by the Depression, Adams continued to write a brief social column, "What Negroes Are Doing," for the *Birmingham News*. See Jo Alice Harp, "Oscar W. Adams and *The Birmingham Reporter* 1900–1934," unpublished manuscript (1989), Hill Ferguson Papers, 56.4.16.15, BPL.

66. *Birmingham World*, February 9, 1943; *Weekly Review*, February 13, 1943.

67. Grill, "The American South and Nazi Racism," 24.

68. *Newsweek* described Graves in 1937 as the "first successfully syndicated Southern columnist." Quoted in Margaret E. Armbrester, "John Temple Graves II: A Southern Liberal Views the New Deal," *Alabama Review* 32 (1979): 203.

69. John Temple Graves, "This Morning," *Birmingham Age-Herald*, May 31, 1941.

70. John Temple Graves, "The Southern Negro and the War Crisis," *Virginia Quarterly Review* 18 (1942): 501.

71. *Birmingham World*, June 3, 1941.

72. *Birmingham World*, May 12, 1942.

73. *Weekly Review*, June 13, 1941.

74. See John T. Kneebone, *Southern Liberal Journalists and the Issue of Race, 1920–1944* (Chapel Hill: University of North Carolina Press, 1985).

75. "Hitler Has Ordered All Jews in Nazi Europe Slain by End of Year," November 25, 1942, 3; *Birmingham News*, December 10, 1942, 8.

76. *Birmingham News*, October 5, 1943, 6.

77. *Birmingham News*, August 31, 1943, 8. When the *Birmingham News* used the term *holocaust* to refer to the murder of the Jews in Europe, it used a word that was commonly used to describe massacres or tragedies in general. Not until the 1950s did the term *Holocaust* become synonymous with the mass murder of European Jewry. The Hebrew term *Shoah* was used as early as the 1940s. http://www1.yadvashem.org/yv/en/holocaust/resource_center/the_holocaust.asp, accessed October 8, 2011.

78. S. Merlin to Editor, *Montgomery Advertiser*, November 2, 1943, 4.

79. *Dothan Eagle*, April 24, 1945, 4; Elouise Reagan to Editor, *Dothan Eagle*, April 17, 1945, 4.

80. *Greene County Democrat*, May 10, 1945, 1.

81. *Alabama Baptist*, May 3, 1945, 3.

82. *Birmingham News*, May 14, 1945, 6.

83. Charles Feidelson, "This Evening," *Birmingham News*, April 27, 1945, 10.

84. Peter Novick, *The Holocaust in American Life* (Boston: Houghton Mifflin Company, 1999), 65, 295n9.

85. See Leff, *Buried by the Times*, 307–18.

86. "Uncover Bones of 700,000 Victims of German Murder," *Birmingham World*, January 5, 1945, 1.

87. William A. Fowlkes, "Seeing and Saying," *Birmingham World*, May 1, 1945.

88. W. L. Acuff to Editor, *Birmingham News*, September 14, 1944.

89. Fowlkes, "Seeing and Saying," *Birmingham World*, October 29, 1946.

90. "Nuremberg Verdicts," *Weekly Review*, October 19, 1946.
91. *Clarke County Democrat*, October 17, 1946, 2.
92. Lipstadt, *Beyond Belief*, 262.

Chapter 5

1. Sam Kayser, interview by Dan J. Puckett, Mobile, Alabama, January 12, 2010.

2. http://www.uso.org/history.aspx, accessed December 30, 2010. President Franklin D. Roosevelt had urged the creation of the USO.

3. Milton D. Kulick to Nathaniel Nason, November 6, 1942, Box 38, folder "Mobile"; Maxwell H. Tasgal to David Danzig, October 5, 1942, Box 38, folder "Montgomery," I-180, NJWB-AN, AJHS.

4. Isidore Kaufman, *American Jews in World War II: The Story of 550,000 Fighters for Freedom*, vol. 1 (New York: Dial Press, 1947), 349.

5. Deborah Dash Moore, *GI Jews: How World War II Changed a Generation* (Cambridge, MA: Belknap Press of Harvard University Press, 2004), 141.

6. http://www.mcclellan.army.mil/Info.asp?article_id=2, accessed December 31, 2010. For more information on Fort McClellan, see Mary Beth Reed, Charles E. Cantley, and J. W. Joseph, *Ft. McClellan: A Popular History* (Stone Mountain, GA: New South Associates, 1996).

7. Abba M. Fineberg to Louis Kraft, January 1, 1941; "Circular Letter No. 214," January 2, 1941; Abba M. Fineberg to Benjamin Rabinowitz, January 27, 1941; Abba M. Fineberg to Louis Kraft, February 8, 1941; Julian Rosner to Abba Fineberg, April 21, 1941, Box 15, folder "Anniston," NJWB-AN. For information on the 27th Division, see Charles S. Kaune, *The National Guard in War: An Historical Analysis of the 27th Infantry Division (New York National Guard) in World War II*, http://dmna.state.ny.us/historic/reghist/wwii/infantry/27thInfDiv/27thInfDivKuaneTOC.htm, accessed December 30, 2010. After the United States entered the war, the transient nature of the base made it virtually impossible to ascertain the number of Jewish troops stationed at McClellan.

8. Abba M. Fineberg to Louis Kraft, January 8, 1941; Abba M. Fineberg to Benjamin Rabinowitz, March 24, 1941, Box 15, folder "Anniston"; Morris D. Kronenfeld, "Report of Activities," July 13 to July 26, 1941; Kronenfeld, "Report of Activities," October 9 to October 31, 1941, Box 15, folder "Ft. McClellan Reports," NJWB-AN. Local companies also contributed items to help entertain the men. The Lloyd Baking Company in Anniston donated thirty loaves of bread each week for sandwiches. As Fineberg noted, "we'll have to put in the filling, but it will help us." By late 1941, the JWB and the YMCA were the only two agencies operating in Anniston, as the others had not opened the doors to their centers yet. See Morris D. Kronenfeld to Benjamin Rabinowitz, November 13, 1941, Box 15, folder "Ft. McClellan," NJWB-AN.

9. Morris D. Kronenfeld to David Danzig, May 25 to June 8, 1942, Box 37, folder "Anniston Reports," NJWB-AN. Initially, the rabbis in Birmingham had to cajole their congregations to invite the soldiers from McClellan into their homes. As Rabbi Milton Grafman told his congregation, "These boys are fighting for *us*, and it seems

to me that opening our homes to them during the Festival of FREEDOM [Passover] is the very least we can do to show our appreciation. . . . Morale is very important in the winning of this war. But we do not create morale by talking about it. We create morale among the men in our armed forces by concrete manifestations of our appreciation for the sacrifices they are making." "From the Rabbi's Study," March 20, 1942, Temple Emanu-El Bulletin, 796.0.1, Temple Emanu-El Records, BPL.

10. Nore Piore, "Memorandum on War Industry Areas: Anniston, Alabama," May 6, 1942; Office of Government Reports Memorandum, "United Service Organizations," March 24, 1942, Box 37, folder "Anniston Reports," NJWB-AN.

11. The Workmen's Circle was affiliated with the national Jewish Labor Committee. Abba M. Fineberg to Benjamin Roth, May 27, 1941, Box 15, folder "Anniston," NJWB-AN.

12. Father Charles Edward Coughlin was a Roman Catholic priest whose weekly radio broadcasts and newspaper *Social Justice* were filled with antisemitic vitriol. For information on Coughlin, see Alan Brinkley, *Voices of Protest: Huey Long, Father Coughlin, and the Great Depression* (New York: Knopf, 1982), and Donald Warren, *Radio Priest: Charles Coughlin, the Father of Hate Radio* (New York: The Free Press, 1996).

13. Nathaniel Nason to Benjamin Rabinowitz, May 16, 1942, Box 37, folder "Anniston Reports"; Nathaniel Nason to Benjamin Rabinowitz, May 18, 1942, Box 37, folder "Anniston"; "Summary Narrative," May 29, 1947, Box 140, folder "Anniston Reports," NJWB-AN. Ironically, in May 1945, Father Arthur Terminiello, known as the "Father Coughlin of the South," assumed direction of the NCCS in Anniston and created tremendous friction and dysfunction with the USO operations. See chapter 6 for more information on Terminiello.

14. Abba M. Fineberg to Louis Kraft, January 8, 1941; Abba M. Fineberg to Louis Kraft, January 15, 1941; Abba M. Fineberg to Benjamin Rabinowitz, March 24, 1941, Box 15, folder "Anniston," NJWB-AN.

15. Morris D. Kronenfeld, "Report of Activities," October 9 to October 31, 1941, Box 15, folder "Ft. McClellan Reports"; Nathaniel Nason to Benjamin Rabinowitz, May 16, 1942, Box 37, folder "Anniston Reports"; Morris D. Kronenfeld to David Danzig, May 1–May 11, 1942, Box 37, folder "Anniston Reports"; Morris D. Kronenfeld to David Danzig, June 22 to July 22, 1942, Box 37, folder "Anniston Reports"; Morris D. Kronenfeld, "Report of Activities," May 31 to June 10, 1941, Box 15, folder "Ft. McClellan Reports," NJWB-AN.

16. Morris D. Kronenfeld, "Report of Activities," November 1 to November 15, 1941, Box 15, folder "Ft. McClellan Reports"; Office of Government Reports Memorandum, "United Service Organizations," March 24, 1942, Box 37, folder "Anniston Reports"; Nathaniel Nason to Benjamin Rabinowitz, May 16, 1942, Box 37, folder "Anniston Reports," NJWB-AN.

17. Morris D. Kronenfeld to David Danzig, May 25 to June 8, 1942, Box 37, folder "Anniston Reports," NJWB-AN.

18. "The Coosa River Valley Defense Area, Alabama," n.d., Box 37, folder "Anniston Reports"; Abba M. Fineberg to Samuel Rabinowitz, April 1, 1941; Abba M. Fineberg to Benjamin Rabinowitz, April 8, 1941; Abba M. Fineberg to Benjamin

Rabinowitz, April 23, 1941, Box 15, folder "Anniston"; Donald C. Stuart to Jewish Welfare Board, April 15, 1941, Box 15, folder "Ft. McClellan"; Nore Piore, "Memorandum on War Industry Areas: Anniston, Alabama," May 6, 1942, Box 37, folder "Anniston Reports," NJWB-AN. For the High Holy Days in 1941, Atlanta's four synagogues opened their doors to soldiers, the Standard Club hosted a dance, and the local Army and Navy Committee made arrangements for discounted hotel rates for servicemen who arrived but did not have lodgings. See Eugene Oberdorfer to Mortimer C. Sterne, September 12, 1941, Box 15, folder "Committee," NJWB-AN.

19. Abba M. Fineberg to Benjamin Rabinowitz, March 6, 1941, Box 15, folder "Anniston," NJWB-AN.

20. Blanton, *The History of Temple Beth-El*, 3.

21. Benjamin Rabinowitz to Abba Fineberg, February 28, 1941, Box 15, folder "Anniston," NJWB-AN. *Trefa* means nonkosher. Founded in New York in 1912, the National Council for Young Israel was a coordinating agency for Orthodox synagogues in the United States. According to its constitution, its purpose "shall be to foster and maintain a program of spiritual, cultural, social and communal activity towards the advancement and perpetuation of traditional Torah-true Judaism; and to instill into American Jewish youth an understanding and appreciation of the high ethical and spiritual values of Judaism and demonstrate the compatibility of the ancient faith of Israel with good Americanism. The organization shall promote cooperation among the constituent branches now existing and which may hereafter be formed, establish a close bond of kinship to the end that their individual and common problems may more easily be solved, and act as the federated and central body for the Young Israel Movement so that its influence as a force in Jewry may be felt and recognized in America and the world over." http://www.youngisrael.org/content/history.cfm, accessed January 8, 2011.

22. Moore, *GI Jews*, 54.

23. "Kosher-style" means traditional Jewish food that is nonkosher. Fineberg noted that "no amount of arguing would persuade" Harris to serve food that was "strictly kosher." Moreover, Fineberg claimed in April 1941 that "strangely enough (or is it natural?) among the boys themselves the demand for kosher is almost negligible now." Even Rabbi Joseph Lief, the Jewish chaplain appointed to McClellan in mid-1941, observed that few of the men requested kosher food. Abba Fineberg to Benjamin Rabinowitz, March 6, 1941; Abba M. Fineberg to Benjamin Rabinowitz, April 1, 1941, Box 15, folder "Anniston"; Morris D. Kronenfeld, "Report of Activities," October 8 to October 31, 1941, Box 15, folder "Ft. McClellan Reports," NJWB-AN.

24. Anna Grude to Benjamin Rabinowitz, n.d.; Julian Rosner to Abba Fineberg, April 21, 1941; Abba M. Fineberg to Julian Rosner, May 14, 1941; Abba M. Fineberg to Julian Rosner, May 27, 1941, Box 15, folder "Anniston"; Morris D. Kronenfeld, "Report of Activities," September 27 to October 8, 1941, Box 15, folder "Ft. McClellan Reports," NJWB-AN.

25. Morris D. Kronenfeld, "Report of Activities," October 8 to October 31, 1941, Box 15, folder "Ft. McClellan Reports," NJWB-AN.

26. Ferris argues that "in southern Jewish homes from the mid-nineteenth cen-

tury to the early twentieth century, women were responsible for maintaining traditional foodways, and as a result, controlled one arena of the family's acculturation to the South. Husbands and children might express their wishes about ritual practice and food tastes, but it was women who decided whether or not their kitchens were kosher as they prepared holiday food and incorporated traditional foodways into the family's weekly menus. Women defined this world for themselves and for their families." Marcie Cohen Ferris, "'From the Recipe File of Luba Cohen': A Study of Southern Jewish Foodways and Cultural Identity," *Southern Jewish History* 2 (1999): 136–37, 156.

27. In addition, the JWB held a farewell party upon the closing of the JWB-USO center, at which "JWB certificates of merit were awarded to a group of Jewish volunteers; at the close of the ceremony we learned that many of the non-Jewish guests who were present at the Party indicated that they would be immensely pleased if they too could get JWB awards of merit. The Chairman of the USO Council when the offer was made, stated, 'I would be honored to have such a certificate hanging in my office.' Other friends of the USO who were present at the party expressed themselves in like manner." "Summary Narrative," May 29, 1947, 1, Box 140, folder "Anniston Reports 1947," NJWB-AN.

28. Ibid.

29. For more information on Gadsden and Camp Sibert, see Cronenberg, *Forth to the Mighty Conflict*, 44–48; Joseph T. Robertson and P. Wayne Findley, "Camp Sibert, Alabama's First Chemical Warfare Center, 1942–1945," *Alabama Review* 48 (January 1995): 3–15.

30. Frederick H. Osborn, "Recreation, Welfare and Morale of the American Soldier," *Annals of the American Academy of Political and Social Science* 220 (March 1942): 55; Harold D. Meyer, "A Preview of Community Recreation," *Social Forces* 20 (March 1942): 363. The FSA also secretly administered the War Research Service (WRS), a civilian agency the War Department created in May 1942 to oversee chemical and biological warfare. "Committees on Biological Warfare, 1941–1948," http://www7.nationalacademies.org/archives/cbw.html, accessed January 10, 2011.

31. Louis Kraft to Ray Johns, November 22, 1943; Louis Kraft to Murray Rosenberg, November 17, 1943; handwritten memorandum from Louis Kraft and Nathaniel Nason, n.d., Box 74, folder "Anniston-Montgomery Gen. Correspondence," NJWB-AN.

32. Morris D. Kronenfeld to David Danzig, October 1 to November 1, 1942, Box 37, folder "Anniston Reports"; N. Nason to Morris D. Kronenfeld, November 23, 1942, Box 38, folder "Gadsden"; handwritten memorandum from Louis Kraft and Nathaniel Nason, n.d., Box 74, folder "Anniston-Montgomery Gen. Correspondence," NJWB-AN.

33. Morris D. Kronenfeld to John Sills, March 9, 1943; "Visit to Gadsden," n.d. (1943); Murray Rosenberg to Louis Kraft, n.d. (November 1943), Box 74, folder "Anniston-Montgomery Gen. Correspondence," NJWB-AN.

34. John B. Isom, *As I Remember Me*, http://www.johnbisom.com/AIRMWorldWarII.html, accessed January 10, 2011.

35. Camp Sibert Narrative Report, n.d. (1943), Box 98, folder "Aliceville-Dothan Reports"; Murray Rosenberg to Louis Kraft, n.d. (November 1943), Box 74, folder "Anniston-Montgomery Gen. Correspondence," NJWB-AN.

36. Bernard C. Ehrenreich to H. L. Glucksman, March 22, 1918; "Parents of Toledo Soldiers Thanks Rabbi Ehrenreich," n.d., *Toledo Israelite*; "Will Build Jewish Home Here Soon," February 17, 1918, *Sheridan Reveille*; "Jewish Welfare Home Will Be Formally Dedicated Today," October 6, 1918, *Montgomery Advertiser*; "Jewish Soldiers Made Welcome at Montgomery," n.d., clippings all found in Box 1, Scrapbook 1, Bernard C. Ehrenreich Papers, AJHS.

37. See Jerome A. Ennels and Wesley Phillips Newton, *The Wisdom of Eagles: A History of Maxwell Air Force Base* (Montgomery, AL: River City Press, 2002).

38. J. S. (John S. Sills) to Benjamin Rabinowitz, April 15, 1942, Box 38, folder "Montgomery," NJWB-AN.

39. In addition to his duties in Montgomery, Blachschleger also served as the counselor for the B'nai B'rith Hillel group at Alabama Polytechnic Institute in nearby Auburn. *Temple Beth-Or Bulletin*, October 1944, binder "Temple Beth-Or: Bulletin and Index, 1943–1949; "An Appreciation Written for the Preflight Magazine By a Jewish Soldier Stationed at Maxwell Field," January 1943, *Temple Beth-Or Bulletin*, binder "Temple Beth-Or: Bulletin & Index, 1929–1942," TBO; Jewish Welfare Board Council Meeting, March 18, 1943, Box 74, folder "Anniston-Montgomery Reports"; Eugene Blachschleger to Benjamin Rabinowitz, March 7, 1941, Box 15, folder "Alabama, Montgomery," NJWB-AN.

40. Myron Rothschild to Benjamin Rabinowitz, April 3, 1942; "Survey of the Montgomery Area to determine possible need for additional services for the soldiers of Jewish faith in that area," n.d. (probably April or May 1942), Box 38, folder "Montgomery," NJWB-AN.

41. Mr. Rabinowitz to Mr. Josolowitz, Jewish Welfare Board—Office Memorandum, April 10, 1942; John S. Sills to Benjamin Rabinowitz, April 16, 1942, Box 38, folder "Montgomery," NJWB-AN. Catholics had served as mayors of Montgomery prior to the twentieth century, but according to Wayne Flynt, "anti-Catholicism became increasingly common after 1900, especially among Baptists and Methodists." Wayne Flynt, *Alabama in the Twentieth Century* (Tuscaloosa: University of Alabama Press, 2004), 468–70.

42. Myron Lobman to John S. Sills, May 4, 1942; Myron Lobman to Irving Engel, May 4, 1942; Eugene Blachschleger to John S. Sills, May 4, 1942, Box 38, folder "Montgomery," NJWB-AN.

43. Jack A. Casper to Benjamin Rabinowitz, September 25, 1941; John S. Sills to Jack A. Casper, October 8, 1941; Eugene Blachschleger to Benjamin Rabinowitz, December 10, 1941; Eugene Blachschleger to David Danzig, February 19, 1942, Box 15, folder "Montgomery"; Maxwell H. Tasgal to David Danzig, October 5, 1942; Montgomery Jewish Welfare Board Council Meeting, December 15, 1942, Box 38, folder "Montgomery," NJWB-AN.

44. The Standard Club was so large that for the 1943 Passover seder, Temple Beth-Or hosted approximately three hundred servicemen, in addition to 130 Beth-Or members. In contrast, Agudath Israel's building held 110 soldiers, with room for

only twenty congregants. *Temple Beth-Or Bulletin*, February 1942, binder "Temple Beth-Or Bulletin and Index, 1929–1943"; "President's Message," n.d.; "Minute Book, Kahl Montgomery, 1940–1961"; *Temple Beth-Or Bulletin*, May 1944, binder "Temple Beth-Or: Bulletin and Index, 1943–1949," TBO; Maxwell H. Tasgal to David Danzig, June 8, 1942; Maxwell H. Tasgal to David Danzig, June 15, 1942; Maxwell H. Tasgal to Benjamin Rabinowitz, May 19, 1942, Box 38, folder "Montgomery"; Maxwell H. Tasgal, April 1 to April 30, 1943, Box 74, folder "Anniston-Montgomery Reports," NJWB-AN.

45. Maxwell H. Tasgal to David Danzig, January 9, 1943, Box 38, folder "Montgomery," NJWB-AN.

46. Maxwell H. Tasgal to David Danzig, July 10, 1942, Box 38, folder "Montgomery," NJWB-AN.

47. An NJWB official observed that Lobman "feels he understands the people." Victor H. Taylor, "Visit to Montgomery, Alabama," August 18–19, 1943; Sylvia S. Segall, Narrative Report, November 1–November 30, 1943, Box 74, folder "Anniston-Montgomery Reports," NJWB-AN. Of Schulwolf, she has "so forceful a personality. This enables her to drive our workers rather than work with them. There is no question of her intense desire to serve, her sincere interest and loyalty toward JWB or her role as a leader in the Jewish community." See Harry Hymanson to Nathaniel Nason, September 25, 1945, Box 120, folder "Montgomery Minutes," NJWB-AN.

48. Paul W. Aron to Matthew Penn, December 14, 1943, Box 74, folder "Anniston-Montgomery Reports," NJWB-AN.

49. Nathaniel Nason to Fred Grossman, October 4, 1945; Harry Hymanson to Nathaniel Nason, May 18, 1945; Harry Hymanson to Nathaniel Nason, September 25, 1945, Box 120, folder "Montgomery Minutes," NJWB-AN.

50. The Soldiers Club at the YMCA was white only. Selma had a separate African American club, also operated by the WPA. A. T. Reeves to J. L. Zwingle, July 11, 1942, Box 38, folder "Selma," NJWB-AN.

51. Samson H. Levey to Julian Rosner, March 13, 1942, Box 38, folder "Selma," NJWB-AN.

52. Samson H. Levey to John S. Sills, May 10, 1942; Samson H. Levey to John S. Sills, May 16, 1942; Maxwell H. Tasgal to John S. Sills, November 4, 1942, Box 38, folder "Selma" NJWB-AN; Montgomery Committee Jewish Welfare Board Meeting, July 15, 1942; Maxwell H. Tasgal to Benjamin Rabinowitz, May 22, 1942; Maxwell H. Tasgal to David Danzig, July 17, 1942, Box 38, folder "Montgomery," NJWB-AN.

53. Milton Kulick to Nathaniel Nason, August 11, 1942, Box 38, folder "Mobile," NJWB-AN; a short history of Brookley Army Air Field can be found at http://www.brookleycomplex.com/aboutus_history.html, accessed February 1, 2011.

54. Milton D. Kulick to Nathaniel Nason, September 9, 1942; Milton D. Kulick to Nathaniel Nason, November 6, 1942, Box 38, folder "Mobile," NJWB-AN. Rabbi Sidney Berkowitz volunteered for the service as a chaplain in late 1942. He and his wife, Pauline, had been extremely happy in Mobile, but while in the service, Berkowitz served in the Pacific theater, an experience that shaped his postwar career. After the war, he and his wife returned to Mobile where "he found that, after

having been in Saipan and Okinawa, in that terrible climate, he couldn't stand the southern climate anymore." Instead, they left Mobile and the rabbi took a position with congregation Rodef Shalom in Youngstown, Ohio, where he served until 1983. Pauline A. Berkowitz, interview by Matthew T. Butts, July 22, 1992, Youngstown, Ohio, 7, http://www.maag.ysu.edu/oralhistory/cd1/OH1510.pdf, accessed October 4, 2010.

55. Bernard H. Eichold to Barnett R. Brickner, June 16, 1942; Barnett R. Brickner to Bernard H. Eichold, June 22, 1942, folder "Board of Trustees 1942," Springhill Avenue Temple Archives.

56. Milton D. Kulick to Nathaniel Nason, September 9, 1942; Milton D. Kulick to Nathaniel Nason, November 6, 1942, Box 38, folder "Mobile," NJWB-AN. See also Rita S. Whitlock, *A Family Album: The Family of Congregation Ahavas Chesed, 1894–1994* (Mobile, AL: Corporate Resource Associates, 1994), 63–66.

57. Herbert Kahn to Mrs. Marcuse, August 19, 1942, Box 38, folder "Camp Rucker," NJWB-AN.

58. Napier Field began operating in October 1941. See Jim Noles, "Camp Rucker during the Second World War," *Alabama Heritage* (Summer 2004): 30–36; Saul S. Elgart, Report of Activities, Dothan, Alabama, October 1 to November 1, 1942, Box 38, folder "Dothan," NJWB-AN. Elgart estimated sixty thousand men at Rucker in October 1942.

59. Temple Emanu-El *Book of Memories*, 12, 17–18, The Wiregrass Archives, Troy University, Dothan, Alabama.

60. Nineteen families lived in Dothan, two in Enterprise, one in Ozark, five in Marianna, Florida, about 35 miles from Dothan, while six families lived in Panama City, Florida, approximately 80 miles from Dothan. Louis I. Egelson to John S. Sills, June 29, 1942; Alfred Wolf to John Sills, June 25, 1942, Box 38, folder "Camp Rucker," NJWB-AN.

61. Alfred Wolf to Julian Rosner, February 3, 1942; I. Rimson to Benjamin Rabinowitz, April 1, 1942; John S. Sills to Louis I. Egelson, June 9, 1942; John S. Sills to Alfred Wolf, July 7, 1942, Box 38, folder "Camp Rucker," NJWB-AN.

62. Often the JWB had little ability to assist struggling communities, either due to lack of means or lack of authority. Where the JWB lacked authority, it was often due to USO guidelines. In one instance, an airman from Napier Field had received a furlough for Passover but had no money for a trip home. Temple Emanu-El had no congregational or charity funds for that purpose, so the congregation raised the money to allow him to go home for the holidays. Rabbi Wolf turned to the JWB, but again they had "no funds available for this purpose, but usually as in your recent case, the local JWB Army and Navy Committees has at its own discretion rendered such loans as they saw fit. Unfortunately, we at the national office have no authority to make a loan fund available." Alfred Wolf to John Sills, June 25, 1942; John S. Sills to Alfred Wolf, June 30, 1942, Box 38, folder "Camp Rucker," NJWB-AN.

63. Alfred Wolf to John S. Sills, July 2, 1942, Box 38, folder "Camp Rucker," NJWB-AN.

64. Just prior to the United States entering the war, Wolf was able to secure visas for his family who had been interned at Camp de Gurs, Basses Pyrenees, in Vichy

France. All survived, except for his grandfather who died in the camp. Wolf's wife, Miriam, recalled that he was happy in Dothan where he had "loads to do." Miriam, however, was not happy in the segregated Deep South, a place, she recalled, where "I couldn't raise my children." Wolf left Temple Emanu-El in 1946 for Los Angeles, where he worked with the Union of Hebrew Congregations before accepting the pulpit at the Wilshire Boulevard Temple in 1949. See Mary Rourke, "In Good Faith: Values. Education. Jewish Culture. They're Just a Few of Rabbi Wolf's Passions. No Wonder He Can't Slow Down," October 29, 1995, *Los Angeles Times*, http://articles.latimes.com/print/1995-10-29/news/ls-62447_1_jewish-culture, accessed February 7, 2011; see also "Dothan, Alabama," *Encyclopedia of Southern Jewish Communities*, http://www.msje.org/history/archives/al/dothan.html, accessed February 7, 2011.

65. Interestingly, just as Wolf was a refugee from Germany, so too, in a manner of speaking, was Emanu-El's Torah. The scroll "had been purchased from a refugee who had brought it from Breslau, Germany. There it had, through the foresight and courage of a Jew, escaped the burning of the synagogues of November 10, 1938." Temple Emanu-El *Book of Memories*, 20.

66. Nathaniel Nason to Alfred Wolf, July 8, 1942; Alfred Wolf to Nathaniel Nason, July 12, 1942; J. L. Zwingle to Ray Johns, July 22, 1942, Box 38, folder "Camp Rucker," NJWB-AN.

67. Saul S. Elgart, Report of Activities, Dothan, Alabama, October 1 to November 1, 1942, Box 38, folder "Dothan"; Alfred Wolf to Nathaniel Nason, July 12, 1942; J. L. Zwingle to Ray Johns, July 22, 1942, Box 38, folder "Camp Rucker," NJWB-AN.

68. Father Terminiello will be discussed in greater detail in chapter 6.

69. In November 1942, the USO created a temporary center at the Parish House of the Episcopal Church on the weekends only. Saul S. Elgart, Report of Activities, Dothan, Alabama, October 2 to October 20, 1942, Box 38, folder "Dothan," NJWB-AN.

70. Elgart reported that Hogarty had become "persona non grata to the community leaders in Dothan and he was the handicap that the USO had to overcome." Saul S. Elgart, Report of Activities, Dothan, Alabama, December 1, 1942, to January 1, 1943, Box 38, folder "Dothan," NJWB-AN.

71. Saul. S. Elgart, Initial Report, Dothan, Alabama, September 23 to October 1, 1942; Saul S. Elgart, Report of Activities, Dothan, Alabama, December 1, 1942, to January 1, 1943, Box 38, folder "Dothan"; Dothan, Alabama, Report, n.d. (September 1943), Box 74, folder "Anniston-Montgomery Reports," NJWB-AN.

72. Herbert Kahn to Mrs. Marcuse, August 19, 1942, Box 38, folder "Camp Rucker," NJWB-AN.

73. Saul S. Elgart, Report of Activities, Dothan, Alabama, October 2 to October 20, 1942, Box 38, folder "Dothan," NJWB-AN.

74. Temple Emanu-El *Book of Memories*, 79; Saul S. Elgart, Report of Activities, Dothan, Alabama, October 1 to November 1, 1942, Box 38, folder "Dothan," NJWB-AN.

75. Saul S. Elgart, Report of Activities, Dothan, Alabama, November 1 to December 1, 1942, Box 38, folder "Dothan"; Dothan, Alabama, Report, n.d. (September 1943), Box 74, folder "Anniston-Montgomery Reports," NJWB-AN.

76. See Caraid O'Brien, "Send in the Clown: Molly Picon Endures as the Iconic Face of Yiddish Theater," *Heritage* (Spring 2009): 2–9.

77. Israel H. Mistovsky, Monthly Supplementary NJWB Narrative Report, June 1 to June 30, 1944, Box 98, folder "Aliceville-Dothan Reports," NJWB-AN. Elgart left Dothan in September 1943 and was replaced by Mistovsky in November 1943. Temple Emanu-El *Book of Memories*, 64, 68.

78. *Temple Emanu-El Yearbook*, 21–22, 46–48.

79. *YMHA News*, April 27, 1944, newsletter found in Box 12, folder 2, National Jewish Welfare Board—Bureau of War Records (hereafter cited as NJWB-BWR).

80. The JWB was given desk space at the YMCA-USO center, but operated largely out of the YMHA. Minutes, Regional Staff Conference—Region VII, July 28, 1942, Box 37, folder "Minutes"; Nathaniel Nason to Benjamin Rabinowitz, August 4, 1942, Box 38, folder "Montgomery"; Victor H. Taylor, Visit to Birmingham, Alabama, n.d. (1943), Box 74, folder "Anniston-Montgomery General Correspondence," NJWB-AN; according to the 1940 census, Birmingham had a population of 267,583. See http://www2.census.gov/prod2/decennial/documents/23761117vlch04.pdf, accessed February 1, 2011.

81. *Serviceman*, August 1943, 1, folder 1758, Milton Grafman Papers, BPL.

82. "Devoted Rabbi Gets News to Boys Overseas," *Birmingham Post*, August 1, 1944, folder 1758.1.133, Grafman Papers, BPL.

83. The letters from the various organizations are found in folder 1758.1.132, Grafman Papers, BPL.

84. Report on Birmingham, Alabama, n.d.; Dora Roth to David Turteltaub, June 28, 1946, Box 12, folder 3, NJWB-BWR.

85. Grafman wrote in the *Serviceman* that Birnbrey fled Germany in 1939, but Birnbrey indicated it was 1938. "Former Refugee Stationed in England," *Serviceman*, May 1944, folder 1758.1.2, Grafman Papers, BPL; Jason and Posner, *Don't Wave Goodbye*, 154–55; Frommer and Frommer, *Growing Up Jewish in America: An Oral History*, 115–16.

86. Arthur Prince interview.

87. Bill Kirsch to Edith Weil, copy of letter found in Monte Kandel, "Report of Monte Kandel," June 27–29, 1942, MKM 13.50.1039, RG248, NRS, YIVO.

88. Sidney Ziff, Norman Niren, and Sol Kimerling, interview by Dan J. Puckett, Birmingham, Alabama, August 15, 2006.

89. *Serviceman*, March–April 1945, 7.

90. Malvin Mayer to "Mother & Sis," Germany, June 11, 1945, folder 1758.1.81, Grafman Papers, BPL.

91. Sam Kayser interview.

92. Malvin Mayer to "Mother & Sis."

93. Sam Kayser interview.

94. Sam Kayser interview.

95. Milton Klein, interview by Dan J. Puckett, Mobile, Alabama, September 24, 2009.

96. Arthur Prince, interview by Dan J. Puckett, Mobile, Alabama, June 15, 2009.

97. Herman "Dick" Loeb Jr., interview by Louisa H. Weinrib, November 11, 1990, Montgomery, Alabama, box 1, folder 27, Holocaust Survivors and U.S. Liberators Oral History Collection, ADAH.

98. Roger N. Blum, "Memoirs," n.d. Unpublished manuscript in the possession of the author.

99. Blum wrote that when his parents returned to their house in Brumath, "every item my parents owned was gone from the house when they came back. Some of the household items the neighbors had, they returned everything in good shape. All the furniture, and my parents had some nice furniture, was taken to Germany by a man the Germans installed as postmaster." Blum, "Memoirs."

100. Herman "Dick" Loeb interview, 14.

101. Marks "Bubba" Marcus, interview by Louisa H. Weinrib, November 17, 1991, Montgomery, Alabama, box 1, folder 27, Holocaust Survivors and U.S. Liberators Oral History Collection, ADAH.

102. Article on Harold Marlowe is found in *Serviceman*, June–July 1945, 1, 8.

103. Ibid.

104. See Robert H. Abzug, *Inside the Vicious Heart: Americans and the Liberation of Nazi Concentration Camps* (New York and Oxford: Oxford University Press, 1985).

105. Isaiah Terman, "Birmingham, Alabama," April 1, 1946, Box 1, folder "visits Alabama, Birmingham 44–62," AJC, YIVO.

Chapter 6

1. Dinnerstein, *Antisemitism in America*, 129–32, 187.

2. John Temple Graves, "This Morning," *Birmingham Age-Herald*, January 13, 1939, 1; Graves, "This Morning," *Birmingham Age-Herald*, January 21, 1939, 1.

3. "The Two Daughters," October 15, 1940, John Temple Graves Papers, BPL.

4. *Birmingham Age-Herald*, March 6, 1941, 1; March 10, 1941, 1.

5. Ibid.

6. Augustus Brenners to Gessner T. McCorvey, May 12, 1945, box 2, James A. Simpson Papers, ADAH. The editor of the *Southern Watchman*, Hamner Cobbs, had earlier castigated Feidelson as a "disciple of the *Daily Worker*" and a southern apostate, someone who, "even if he tried, could not be Southern . . . it is beyond his conception of loyalty to defend the South in anything." "Always the Apostate," *Southern Watchman*, May 8, 1943, 5.

7. Feidelson's father, Max, had been born in Russia and immigrated to the United States in 1885. Charles Feidelson had been born in New York City, just prior to the Feidelsons moving to Georgia. For information on the Feidelson family, see 1871.5.24, Henry Marks Files, BPL.

8. Maxine D. Jones and Joe M. Richardson, *Talladega College: The First Century* (Tuscaloosa: University of Alabama Press, 1990), 122; Gabrielle Simon Edgecomb, *From Swastika to Jim Crow: Refugee Scholars at Black Colleges* (Malabar, FL: Krieger Publishing, 1993), 58. In Alabama, the University of Alabama, Alabama College in

Montevallo, and Birmingham Southern College refused to hire any Jewish refugees. See Box 134, folders 9–10, Emergency Committee in Aid of Displaced Foreign Scholars Records, NYPL.

9. F. D. Patterson to Mark Brunswick, June 2, 1939, MKM 13.48.941, RG248, NRS, YIVO.

10. Edward L. Israel, "Jew Hatred among Negroes," *Crisis*, February 1936, 39.

11. See Ziff, Niren, and Kimerling interview; Leo Drum, interview by Dan J. Puckett, April 30, 2009, Montgomery, Alabama; Milton Klein, interview by Dan J. Puckett, September 24, 2009, Mobile, Alabama.

12. J. E. Malone to Editor, *Crisis*, March 1936, 80.

13. John L. LeFlore to Berney L. Strauss, October 12, 1938, Mobile, Alabama. Letter found in Maurianne Adams and John Bracey, eds., *Strangers and Neighbors: Relations between Blacks and Jews in the United States* (Amherst: University of Massachusetts Press, 1999), 378–79.

14. This was a guest editorial from the *Cincinnati Independent*. While the content of the editorial did not originate with the *Birmingham World*, it circulated among Birmingham's black population. The *World* rarely published editorials that strayed too far from its own perspective. "The Die Is Cast," *Birmingham World*, January 10, 1941.

15. F. D. Patterson to Milton Fies, June 2, 1944; Milton Fies to F. D. Patterson, June 6, 1944, Frederick D. Patterson Papers (unprocessed), Booker T. Washington Collection, Tuskegee University; Harry M. Ayers to Dwight Marvin, May 24, 1944, box 143, folder 6, Harry Ayers Papers, HSC.

16. *Birmingham Age-Herald*, January 12, 1944. Wise opposed any alteration to American immigration policy as early as March 1933, despite his belief that the Nazis were attempting to destroy, "if not physically . . . at least economically, and morally to exterminate the Jewish people." He continued his opposition even as the conditions and treatment of European Jews deteriorated. Rafael Medoff, *The Deafening Silence: American Jewish Leaders and the Holocaust* (New York: Shapolsky Publishers, 1987), 24.

17. Transcript of recording made June 27, 1962, 17, found in CTRM 1/01, Arthur W. Terminiello Papers, University of Notre Dame Archives (hereafter cited as UNDA); John Roy Carlson has also written about Terminiello's activities. See John Roy Carlson, *The Plotters* (New York: E. P. Dutton, 1946), 120–30; see also Jeffrey D. Marlett, *Saving the Heartland: Catholic Missionaries in Rural America, 1920–1960* (DeKalb: Northern Illinois University Press, 2002); and Jeffrey D. Marlett, "Rebel Yell: Father Arthur Terminiello and American Catholicism's Conspiratorial Margins," unpublished paper presented at the American Academy of Religion meeting, 2005, in the possession of the author.

18. "Means of Reaching Rural Homes Given by Fr. Terminiello," *St. Teresa's Village News*, October 1941, 1. The newspaper located in CTRM 1/14, Terminiello Papers, UNDA.

19. *Rural Justice* is no longer extant. "'Rural Justice' Circulated Here; Peddles 'Social Justice's' Line," n.d.; "Open Letter to PM," n.d. (Transcript of Terminiello recording indicates article published on May 16, 1943), clippings CTRM 1/03; Ter-

miniello related in his records that shortly after *PM* criticized *Rural Justice* that he was called before Bishop Toolen: "I was told that the committee of the biggest men in Washington had been down to see him. I asked if they were all Jews. He said they were. If they were we can imagine who they were if they were the biggest men in Washington." See transcript of recording made June 27, 1962, 32, 36, 39, CTRM 1/01, Terminiello Papers, UNDA; the estimated 20,000 circulation is cited in Stetson Kennedy, *Southern Exposure* (Garden City, NY: Doubleday), 239–40.

20. "The Cross of War: Is It Due to Stupidity or Cupidity?" October 22, 1944; "Santa Clause or Christ? The Call for a Christian Crusade," December 24, 1944, both sermons found in CTRM 1/04; "Father Terminiello: The Father Coughlin of the South Will Speak Here," flyer advertising Terminiello speech at the Cleveland Public Auditorium on February 1, 1946, in the form of a letter from Gerald L. K. Smith. CTRM 1/07, Terminiello Papers, UNDA.

21. "37 Answer Rev. Terminiello," *Huntsville Times*, March 28, 1945; "Priest Blames Leftist Smear for His Ouster," n.d.; "Rabble Rouser Loses Pulpit," n.d., clippings found in CTRM 1/06, Terminiello Papers, UNDA. While in Anniston, Terminiello served as the head of the NCCS for the Anniston and Ft. McClellan area, where "his influence was not conducive to the most harmonious . . . functioning . . . and affected inter-USO relationships as well as over-all Community attitudes." See "Summary Narrative," May 29, 1947, Box 140, folder "Anniston Reports," NJWB-AN.

22. According to John Roy Carlson, Terminiello opened the Unique Printing Service, which, in addition to publishing *The Crusader*, "served as a clearing house for a large list of nationalist and isolationist literature, which is sold mainly to nationalists north of the Mason and Dixon line." Carlson, *The Plotters*, 122.

23. Copies of the newsletter *The Crusader* prior to February 1946 are not in the Terminiello Papers. Information on Terminiello and his activities in Birmingham came from a series of articles by the political writer Hugh Sparrow of the *Birmingham News*. Hugh Sparrow, "Peacetime Finds Racial Attacks by Ex-Priest Increased in Intensity," *Birmingham News*, November 29, 1945, 1.

24. T. J. Toolen to A. W. Terminiello, November 5, 1945, CTRM 1/05; Charles Feidelson, "This Evening," *Birmingham News*, November 21, 1945, 8.

25. "Effort Made to Force Christian Crusade to Quit," February 1946, 1; "What Is This Unity?" "PM's Hitlerphobia," "For Fear of the Jews," *The Crusader*, February 1946, 2, CTRM 1/14, Terminiello Papers, UNDA.

26. The NCCJ had chapters in Birmingham, Montgomery, Mobile, and Anniston and was directed by Marjorie Rank. Edward Hunvald, the publicity director for Pizitz Department Store, was the most active member from the Jewish community. Pizitz also sponsored a "weekly children's story hour on the radio" for the NCCJ where they awarded the book *One God* to children as a prize. "Visit of Isaiah Terman," June 11, 1945, Birmingham, Alabama, RG347.17.13, Box 1, folder "Visits Alabama, Birmingham 44–62," AJC, YIVO; *Catholic Week* May 4, 1945.

27. "Banned Priest Transfers His Activity Here," *Birmingham Post*, n.d., clipping in CTRM 1/05; "Catholic Priest and Gerald L. K. Smith Join Hands Issue Challenge to the Nation Plan Nationwide Crusade," February 7, 1946, advertise-

ment release for Chicago, CTRM 1/09; "Birmingham Post Prints Retraction," *The Crusader*, February 1946, 1; "Atrocity Stories Part of Zionist Plan," *The Crusader*, February 1946, 7; "Hebrew American Confesses Jews Ruling Europe," *The Crusader*, April 1946, 4, CTRM 1/14, Terminiello Papers, UNDA.

28. Carlson, *The Plotters*, 124–25.

29. Part of Terminiello's speech can be found in "Chicago Riot," CTRM 1/08, Terminiello Papers, UNDA.

30. See http://law.jrank.org/pages/23001/Terminiello-v-Chicago-Significance .html, accessed September 28, 2010.

31. The *Montgomery Advertiser* quote cited in Kennedy, *Southern Exposure*, 227.

32. Terman wrote of the antisemitic incidents: "There is a crackpot in Montgomery who has made slurs against Jews but he has no standing in the community. An instance, of which others in the community had no knowledge, was brought to the attention of the consultant by Rabbi Lerer [of Agudath Israel]. When one Jew was summoned to the OPA board in re violation of ceiling prices, a member of the board remarked that 'we are sending our sons to die for the Jews and this is what they do.'" "Visit of Isaiah Terman," May 31–June 1, 1945; March 29, 1946, Montgomery, Alabama, Box 1, folder "Visits Alabama, Montgomery 40–61," RG347.17.13, AJC, YIVO; "B'nai B'rith convention Report," n.d., B'nai B'rith Papers, Springhill Avenue Temple Archives; Alton Williams to Editor, *Southern Outlook*, February 24, 1946, 6.

33. For an examination of John Crommelin, as well as numerous southern demagogues, see Clive Webb, *Rabble Rousers: The American Far Right in the Civil Rights Era* (Athens: University of Georgia Press, 2010).

34. "Black Paper," *Alabama*, January 21, 1944, 15–16. Although Mordecai and Terminiello operated in Alabama at the same time, most likely there would have been no contact between them despite the antisemitism they had in common. Terminiello viewed British-Israelism in the same light that he viewed Zionism. In fact, when he called for a constitutional amendment banning Zionism, he included British-Israelism as well.

35. Michael Barkun, *Religion and the Racist Right: The Origins of the Christian Identity Movement* (Chapel Hill: University of North Carolina Press, 1994), vii–ix, 52. Barkun states that "Christian Identity is built around three key beliefs. First, Identity believes that white 'Aryans' are descendants of the biblical tribes of Israel and thus are on earth to do God's work. Second, Identity believes that Jews are not only wholly unconnected to the Israelites, but are the very children of the Devil, the literal biological offspring of a sexual dalliance between Satan and Eve in the Garden of Eden. Third, Identity believes the world is on the verge of the final, apocalyptic struggle between good and evil, in which Aryans must do battle with the Jewish conspiracy and its allies so that the world can be redeemed."

36. John Roy Carlson, *Under Cover: My Four Years in the Nazi Underworld—The Amazing Revelation of How Axis Agents and Our Enemies Within Are Now Plotting to Destroy the United States* (New York: E. P. Dutton, 1943), 208–10. The Nazis, too, tried to remove the Jews from Christianity. Susannah Heschel has described how Nazi Germany, in 1939, created an Institute for the Study and Eradication of Jewish Influence on German Church Life "to purge Christianity of all Jewish accre-

tions and restore it to its pristine Aryan origins." While it is unclear if there was any connection between the Nazi Institute and the British-Israelism movement, it is clear that both regarded race as the primary motive for the removal of Jewishness from Jesus. As Heschel explains, "rejecting Jesus's Jewishness and defining him as Aryan was about not only redefining Christianity, but racializing Europe: reassuring Europeans that they were white. Images of Jesus were crucial to racism in establishing the primary criterion of whiteness: Christ himself. It is not the Caucasian male who was the model of the authentic white man, but rather an idealized 'White Man,' namely Christ. For the European male to define himself as a 'white man' he had to fantasize himself as Christ, a Christ who had to be imagined not Jew but as Aryan." Susannah Heschel, *The Aryan Jesus: Christian Theologians and the Bible in Nazi Germany* (Princeton, NJ: Princeton University Press, 2008), 26–28.

37. "Black Paper," *Alabama*, January 21, 1944, 15–16. One element of British-Israelism at the time was anti-Zionism. Barkun explains that "the desire of Jews for an independent homeland in Palestine was seen as a repudiation of the British people's claim to be the true Israel. It was well and good for Britain, as the mandatory power in Palestine, to aid Jewish settlement paternalistically, quite another matter for the Zionist movement to demand British withdrawal." Since Zionists demanded the creation of a Jewish state, Zionism "was taken by British-Israelites to be an affront to God's plan, which required Israel (i.e., Britain) to control the Holy Land." This anti-Zionism, Barkun observes, "remained suppressed through most of the Second World War." Barkun, *Religion and the Racist Right*, xi, 48, 122, 132.

38. "Klan to Launch Drive against Jewish, Catholic Labor Leaders," *Canadian Jewish Chronicle*, February 9, 1945, 3; "Black Paper," *Alabama*, January 21, 1944, 15–16.

39. Lee B. Weil, "Community Relations," March 18–19, 1944, Southeastern States Regional Conference—Council of Jewish Federations and Welfare Funds, found in RG347.17.13, Box 1, folder "Communal Relations-Alabama, Birmingham," AJC, YIVO; Solomon A. Fineberg, "Birmingham, Alabama," November 6, 1940, RG347.17.13, Box 1, folder "Visits—Alabama, Birmingham, 44–62," AJC, YIVO.

40. Weil, "Community Relations," March 18–19, 1944, RG347.17.13, Box 1, folder "Communal Relations-Alabama, Birmingham," AJC, YIVO.

41. Ibid.

42. "Visit of Isaiah Terman," June 11, 1945, 2; "Second visit of Isaiah Terman," April 1 1946, 1; Lawrence L. Koch to Nathan Weisman, August 10, 1948, 6–7, all in Box 1, folder "Visits Alabama, Birmingham 44–62," RG347.17.13, AJC, YIVO. Some of the members of the Birmingham chapter of the Council for American Judaism are noted: Oberdorfer, Milton Fies, Mrs. Julian Adler, Jerome H. Oppenheimer, Samuel Jacobs, Mrs. Bert H. Weisel, and Mrs. Julian Erlick.

43. Memorandum, n.d.; "*Goldman v. Hicks*," *Southern Reporter* 2nd Series, 18–21, both found in Box 1, folder "Goldman v. Hicks," AJC, YIVO.

44. "*Goldman v. Hicks*," *Southern Reporter* 2nd Series, 18–21, both found in Box 1, folder "Goldman v. Hicks," AJC, YIVO.

45. "A Call for Disbarment," February 1, 1941, *Montgomery Advertiser*, 4.

46. Glenn Feldman has produced the only full-length study of Horace Wilkinson's life and career. According to Feldman, the only incident that suggests anti-semitism is found in a 1953 Sunday School lesson: "Carefully distinguishing be-

tween racial pride and racial prejudice, [Wilkinson] argued that the white race was the chosen race, favored by God above all others. Jews, because they could not conceive of God's law given to all people, also could not conceive of a Savior for mankind, and despite popular belief were not really a chosen people." See Glenn Feldman, *From Demagogue to Dixiecrat: Horace Wilkinson and the Politics of Race* (Lanham, MD: University Press of America, 1995), 128–29, 170; Kennedy, *Southern Exposure*, 226–27.

47. Memorandum, n.d.; Leon Schwarz to J. George Fredman, May 13, 1941, Box 1, folder "Goldman v. Hicks," AJC, YIVO.

48. See Dinnerstein, *Antisemitism in America*, 78–104.

49. Leo M. Brown to Edward A. Roberts, June 8, 1942, folder "Board of Trustees 1942," Springhill Avenue Temple Archives.

50. Van Cadenhead to Leo M. Brown, June 2, 1942; E. A. Roberts to Leo M. Brown, June 12, 1942, folder "Board of Trustees 1942," Springhill Avenue Temple Archives.

51. Leo M. Brown to E. B. Peebles, June 18, 1942; E. A. Roberts to Leo M. Brown, June 26, 1942; Leo M. Brown to E. A. Roberts, June 30, 1942; E. B. Peebles to Samuel Eichold, June 30, 1942; Samuel Eichold to E. A. Roberts, July 6, 1942, folder "Board of Trustees 1942," Springhill Avenue Temple Archives.

52. Abba M. Fineberg to Benjamin Rabinowitz, March 6, 1941, Box 15, folder "Anniston"; Morris D. Kronenfeld, "Report of Activities," November 1 to November 15, 1941, Box 15, folder "Ft. McClellan Reports," NJWB-AN.

53. The poem is found in Box 38, folder "Dothan," NJWB-AN. According to Saul Elgart, the JWB representative in Dothan, the poem "was on Army paper and was mimeographed." Elgart turned the poem over to the Intelligence Officer at Camp Rucker who promised to "make a full investigation." No more information was found in the file. See Saul S. Elgart, Monthly Summary Report, November 1–December 1, 1942, Box 38, folder "Dothan," NJWB-AN.

54. Dinnerstein, *Antisemitism in America*, 140.

55. Louis Werfel to Synagogue Council of America, May 11, 1942, Box 38, folder "Montgomery," NJWB-AN.

56. Joseph W. Bendersky, *The "Jewish Threat": Anti-Semitic Politics of the U.S. Army* (New York: Basic Books, 2000), 295–96.

57. Dora Roth to David Turteltaub, November 24, 1943, Box 12, folder 2, NJWB-BWR.

58. Memorandum, "Local Use of the Branch of Service Data Gathered in Birmingham, Alabama," April 27, 1944; S. C. Kohs to Jeanette Rank, April 27, 1944, Box 12, folder 2, NJWB-BWR.

59. "Religious Tolerance to Follow War," *Serviceman*, November 1944, 1.

60. Dinnerstein, *Antisemitism in America*, 150–52.

Chapter 7

1. See "President's Report of the Convention of Union of American Hebrew Congregations," March 1946, 431–33, Temple Beth-Or Minute Book, 1927–1947, TBO.

2. Beatrice Behrman, "Field Trip," Montgomery, Alabama, April 26, 1948, MKM 24.27.612, United Service for New Americans Papers (hereafter cited as USNA); Manheim S. Shapiro, "Report of Field Visit," Montgomery, Alabama, March 3–5, 1950, Box 1, folder "Visits Montgomery," AJC, YIVO.

3. "National Jewish Overseas Relief Supplies Collection," *Bulletin*, January 1946, binder "Temple Beth-Or: Bulletin & Index 1929–1942," TBO.

4. For information about the American Jewish Committee, see Naomi W. Cohen, *Not Free to Desist: A History of the American Jewish Committee, 1906–1966* (Philadelphia: Jewish Publication Society of America, 1972), and Marianne R. Sanua, *Let Us Prove Strong: The American Jewish Committee, 1945–2006* (Waltham, MA: Brandeis University Press, 2007).

5. Lawrence L. Koch to Nathan Weisman, July 9, 1948, Box 1, folder "Visits—Alabama, Birmingham 44–62," AJC, YIVO.

6. For another example of Zionism and community disagreement, see Stuart Rockoff, "Deep in the Heart of Palestine: Zionism in Early Texas," in *Lone Star of David: The Jews of Texas*, ed. Hollace Ava Weiner and Kenneth D. Roseman (Waltham, MA: Brandeis University Press, 2007), 93–107.

7. Lawrence L. Koch to Nathan Weisman, July 9, 1948, Box 1, folder "Visits—Alabama, Birmingham 44–62," AJC, YIVO.

8. Lawrence L. Koch to Nathan Weisman, August 10, 1948, Box 1, folder "Visits—Alabama, Birmingham, 44–62," AJC, YIVO.

9. Ibid.

10. For instance, Karl Friedman, an active Zionist during the period, recalled that "as a little boy we only knew Zionism. We were born into it. We were raised in it." "Full House Honors 'Uncle Bub' for Israel Bonds," *Southern Shofar*, September/October 1997, B-3.

11. W. P. Bloom to Maurice N. Eisendrath, May 22, 1947, C7/877, CZO.

12. Ricky-Dale Calhoun, "Arming David: The Haganah's Illegal Arms Procurement Network in the United States, 1945–1949," *Journal of Palestine Studies* 36 (Summer 2007): 23–24.

13. Leonard Slater, *The Pledge* (New York: Simon and Schuster, 1970), 22–27. In his personal history, David Ben-Gurion omits Berkowitz as one of the seventeen who attended the meeting. See David Ben-Gurion, *Israel: A Personal History* (New York: Funk and Wagnalls, 1971), 55–56.

14. Barbara Goldstein Bonfield, *Hallowed Ground: A History of the K'nesseth Israel/Beth-El Cemetery, Birmingham, Alabama* (Birmingham, AL: privately printed, 2009), 253–54; President Truman invoked the Neutrality Act on December 14, 1947, "imposing a unilateral embargo on weapons to both sides in the Zionist-Arab conflict. From then on, exporting American arms to Palestine was illegal." See Calhoun, "Arming David," 23–24.

15. Elovitz, *A Century of Jewish Life in Dixie*, 142–43.

16. Slater, *The Pledge*, 76.

17. "Birmingham Jews to Celebrate UN Decision on Palestine," *Birmingham News*, December 1, 1947, 16.

18. John J. Beshara to Editor, March 12, 1948, 14; Isadore Sperling to Editor,

March 19, 1948, 4; Alex Rittenbaum to Editor, March 19, 1948, 4, *Birmingham Age-Herald*. Excerpts from the letters from Sperling and Rittenbaum were published together under the title, "The Arab Case against Zionism." See also Daniel Hutchinson, "'We . . . Are the Most Fortunate Prisoners': The Axis POW Experience at Camp Opelika during World War II," *Alabama Review* 64 (October 2011): 285–320.

19. Richard Breitman and Norman J. W. Goda, *Hitler's Shadow: Nazi War Criminals, U.S. Intelligence, and the Cold War* (Washington DC: National Archives, 2010), 17–22. For more information about Husseini, see Philip Mattar, *The Mufti of Jerusalem: Al-Haj Amin al-Husayni and the Palestinian National Movement* (New York: Columbia University Press, 1988).

20. Breitman and Goda, *Hitler's Shadow*, 30; see also Sam Roberts, "Declassified Papers Show US Recruited Ex-Nazis," *New York Times*, December 11, 2010, http://www.nytimes.com/2010/12/12/us/12holocaust.html?_r=2, accessed April 29, 2011.

21. Whitlock, *A Family Album*, 73; Harold Basch, interview by Rhoda Abraham, November 15, 1979, Montgomery, Alabama, Montgomery Section, National Council of Jewish Women Oral History Project, TBO; "Israeli War Heroes Are Welcomed to City," clipping found in 796.7.1, Temple Emanu-El Records, BPL.

22. "ZOA Dinner May 28," *Birmingham News*, May 7, 1967, A-35. See also http://www.jnf.org/about-jnf/, accessed September 13, 2011.

23. "Alabama Monument Unveiled Near Jerusalem," *Southern Shofar*, February 1998, 27; see also, http://thomas.loc.gov/cgi-bin/query/C?r103:./temp/~r103sUE15B, accessed May 6, 2011. By 2012, the American Promenade has not been completed. Only three state monuments have been erected, those to Alabama, Florida, and Michigan, and the monuments are in a state of disrepair. Phyllis Weinstein to Dan Puckett, June 19, 2012, letter in the possession of the author.

24. "Understanding among Jews," *Temple Bulletin*, June 8, 1948, folder "Bulletins, 1917–1949," Springhill Avenue Temple Archives.

25. "President's Message," Temple Emanu-El Annual Reports Year 1948, January 18, 1949, found in 796.5.7, Temple Emanu-El Records, BPL.

26. Lawrence L. Koch to Nathan Weisman, August 10, 1948, Box 1, folder "Visits—Alabama, Birmingham 44–62," AJC, YIVO.

27. Ibid.

28. Ibid.

29. Milton Grafman notes, folder "Temple of Reform Judaism—Corr," Grafman Papers (in possession of Grafman family); Marvin R. Engel to Seymour Samet, December 9, 1955, Box 1, folder "Communal Relations—Alabama, Birmingham," AJC, YIVO.

30. http://www.ushmm.org/wlc/en/article.php?ModuleId=10005459, accessed March 27, 2011. Of those survivors, approximately one-fifth were survivors of the camps. See Novick, *The Holocaust in American Life*, 67–68.

31. Beth B. Cohen, *Case Closed: Holocaust Survivors in Postwar America* (New Brunswick, NJ: Rutgers University Press, 2007), 18–23.

32. Ibid., 13.

33. Beatrice Behrman, "Field Trip," Montgomery, Alabama, April 26, 1948, MKM 24.27.612, USNA, YIVO.

34. Beatrice Behrman, "Field Report," Montgomery, Alabama, June 24, 1948, MKM 24.27.612, USNA, YIVO.

35. Albert Meyers, "Field Report," Montgomery, Alabama, September 17–19, 1949, MKM 24.27.613, USNA, YIVO.

36. Rosenberg quoted in Cohen, *Case Closed*, 22.

37. Ibid.; Bernard Lobman to Walter H. Bieringer, July 11, 1950, MKM 24.27.613, USNA, YIVO.

38. Mrs. Sigmund Weil to Lillian Collins, September 8, 1950, MKM 24.27.613, USNA, YIVO.

39. Lawrence N. Powell, *Troubled Memory: Anne Levy, the Holocaust, and David Duke's Louisiana* (Chapel Hill: University of North Carolina Press, 2000), 370–71.

40. Julius Levins, "Field Report," Montgomery, Alabama, September 17, 1951, MKM 24.27.613, USNA, YIVO.

41. Saul Travin, "Field Report," Montgomery, Alabama, October 6, 1950, MKM 24.27.613, USNA, YIVO.

42. Beatrice Behrman, "Field Report," Selma, Alabama, February 2–3, 1949, MKM 24.27.614, USNA, YIVO.

43. Morton R. Adall, "Field Report," Selma, Alabama, October 27, 1949, MKM 24.27.614, USNA, YIVO.

44. Cohen, *Case Closed*, 5.

45. William B. Helmreich, *Against All Odds: Holocaust Survivors and the Successful Lives They Made in America* (New York: Simon and Schuster, 1992), 266, 276.

46. Seymore L. Cohn to United Service for New Americans, May 26, 1949, MKM 24.27.614, USNA, YIVO.

47. Seymore L. Cohn to United Service for New Americans, June 12, 1950, MKM 24.27.614, USNA, YIVO.

48. "Report of Displaced Persons' Committee," n.d. (1950), folder "1947–1950"; "Minutes of Board Meeting," July 6, 1950, folder "1947–1950," BJF.

49. "Report of Displaced Persons' Committee," n.d. (1950), folder "1947–1950," BJF.

50. Allen Rankin, "The War Is Over, But the Gates to Jewish DP Camps Closed," *Birmingham News*, September 24, 1947, 10.

51. Allen Rankin, "Veteran Charges US Failed Handling DPs in Germany," *Birmingham News*, September 26, 1947, 8.

52. Phone interview with Jack Schniper, April 12, 2011. Information also from the *Darkness Into Life* exhibit. See http://www.bhamholocausteducation.org/bio-schniper.htm, accessed May 1, 2011.

53. Karl Friedman, "Memories," *Deep South Jewish Voice* (September 1999): 28. Friedman was writing about the Nagrodski family, one of the first to be resettled in Birmingham. Szymon Nagrodski became a successful tailor in the city. Friedman noted that "about 30 families" settled in Birmingham. No documentation exists to corroborate this number. Nevertheless, Friedman's recollection is a good estimate as to how many came to Birmingham in the decade following the war, despite few surviving records in this regard.

54. Moore, *GI Jews*, 10.

55. Arthur Prince, interview by Dan J. Puckett, Mobile, Alabama, June 15, 2009.

Postscript

1. Studs Terkel, *The Good War: An Oral History of World War II* (New York: Ballantine Books, 1984); this nostalgia has also overshadowed the difficulties that many veterans faced after returning home. See Thomas Childers, *Soldier from the War Returning: The Greatest Generation's Troubled Homecoming from World War II* (Boston: Houghton Mifflin Harcourt, 2009).

2. Nathan Glazer, *American Judaism* (Chicago: University of Chicago Press, 1957), 114.

3. Leon Jick, "The Holocaust: Its Use and Abuse Within the American Public," *Yad Vashem Studies* 14 (1981): 303–18.

4. Edward S. Shapiro, *A Time for Healing: American Jewry since World War II* (Baltimore: Johns Hopkins University Press, 1992), 212–17.

5. Novick, *The Holocaust in American Life*, 201.

6. Ibid., 101, 114.

7. Ibid., 132–33.

8. Ibid., 148–49.

9. Ibid., 152.

10. Ibid., 190–91.

11. Novick also notes that *The Holocaust* aired in West Germany in January 1979 and "became the turning point in Germany's long-delayed confrontation with the Holocaust. . . . It enabled Germans to connect with the Jewish victims, and with the crime, as never before. It was widely credited with the decisive role in the *Bundestag*'s decision, later that year, to abolish the statute of limitations on war crimes. . . . A double irony. It was an American 'soap opera' that shattered thirty years of German silence on their wartime crimes. It was the German reception of that American 'soap opera' which, as a practical if not theoretical matter, ended the debate in America on the ability of the popular media to present the Holocaust effectively. And—though not for many years on so grand a scale—the American popular media, particularly television, continued to do so: *Playing for Time, Escape for Sobibor, Triumph of the Spirit, War and Remembrance*; there were many, many others." Novick, *The Holocaust in American Life*, 209–14.

12. Ibid., 202.

13. These critics challenge (some harshly) Novick's assumptions and interpretations, but no one questions the idea that silence reigned in regard to the Holocaust until the 1960s. See Hillel Levine, "The Decline of the Incredible," *New Leader* 82 (June 14–28, 1999): 23–25; Lawrence L. Langer, "A Sacred Evil," *New York Times Book Review*, June 27, 1999, 24; Peter Novick to Editor, *New York Times Book Review*, July 18, 1999, 4; Tony Judt, "The Morbid Truth," *New Republic* (July 19–July 26, 1999): 36–40; David G. Roskies, "Group Memory," *Commentary* 108 (September 1999): 62–65; Jeffrey Herf, "Explaining the Holocaust?" *Partisan Review* (Summer 2000): 504–10; Stephen J. Whitfield, "Reflections on Peter Novick's *The Holocaust in American Life*: Two Perspectives," *Judaism* (Fall 2000): 484–92; Severin Hochberg, *Journal of American History* 87 (December 2000): 1099–1101; Marc Lee Raphael, *American Historical Review* 106 (April 2001): 534–35; Berel Lang, "On Peter

Novick's *The Holocaust in American Life*," *Jewish Social Studies* 7 (Spring 2001): 149–58; Eli Lederhendler, "On Peter Novick's *The Holocaust in American Life, Jewish Social Studies* 7 (Spring 2001): 159–68; Peter Novick, "Response to Lederhendler and Lang," *Jewish Social Studies* 7 (Spring 2001): 169–79; Jeremy D. Popkin, "Holocaust Memory: Bad for the Jews?" *Judaism* (Winter 2001): 112–17.

14. Hasia R. Diner, *We Remember with Reverence and Love: American Jews and the Myth of Silence after the Holocaust, 1945–1962* (New York: New York University Press, 2009), ix.

15. Hasia R. Diner, *A New Promised Land: A History of Jews in America* (Oxford and New York: Oxford University Press, 2003), 126–27.

16. Diner, *We Remember with Reverence and Love*, 11.

17. Ibid., 9, 11.

18. Ibid., 197–99.

19. Ibid., 293–311.

20. Novick, *The Holocaust in American Life*, 105, 307n9.

21. Edward T. Linenthal, *Preserving Memory: The Struggle to Create America's Holocaust Museum* (New York: Viking, 1995), 17.

22. Ibid., 23.

23. George C. Wallace to Charles Prigmore, December 2, 1983; Memo "Governor Wallace Names Ex-POW as Liaison to U.S. Holocaust Memorial Council," n.d.; Robert G. Corely to George C. Wallace, January 31, 1984, SG 004759, folder 11, George C. Wallace Administrative Papers, ADAH.

24. Charles S. Prigmore to Jerome Rosenberg, November 20, 1985, Jerome Rosenberg Papers.

25. Nicholas J. Karolides, Margaret Bald, and Dawn B. Sova, *100 Banned Books: Censorship Histories of World Literature* (New York: Checkmark Books, 1999), 341.

26. The Alabama Holocaust Commission was charged with the following responsibilities and duties:

> (1) Provide assistance and advice to the public and private schools, colleges, and universities with respect to implementation of Holocaust education and awareness programs.
>
> (2) Meet with appropriate education officials and other interested public and private organizations, including service organizations, to assist with the planning, coordinating, and enriching of courses of study dealing with the Holocaust.
>
> (3) Survey and catalog the extent and breadth of Holocaust and genocide education presently incorporated into the curricula and taught in the educational systems of the state; to inventory those Holocaust memorials, exhibits, and resources which could be incorporated in courses of study; to assist other educational agencies in the development and implementation of Holocaust and genocide education programs. In furtherance of this responsibility, the commission may contact and cooperate with existing resource organizations.
>
> (4) Compile a roster of individual volunteers who are willing to share

their knowledge and experience in classrooms, seminars, and workshops on the subject of the Holocaust. These volunteers may be survivors of the Holocaust, liberators of concentration camps, scholars, clergy, artists, community relations professionals, or other persons who, by virtue of their experience or interest, have acquired personal or academic knowledge of the Holocaust.

(5) Coordinate events commemorating the Holocaust and to seek volunteers who are willing and able to participate in events that will enhance public awareness of the consequences and significance of the Holocaust.

(6) Prepare reports for the Governor and the Legislature regarding findings and recommendations to facilitate the inclusion of Holocaust studies and commemorative programs throughout the state.

(7) Act as a liaison in matters concerning the United States Holocaust Memorial Museum.

See http://www.legislature.state.al.us/SearchableInstruments/1999rs/bills/hb140.htm, accessed July 8, 2012.

27. http://bhamholocausteducation.org/index.htm, accessed July 8, 2012.

Bibliography

Manuscript Sources

Atlanta, Georgia

THE WILLIAM BREMAN JEWISH HERITAGE AND HOLOCAUST MUSEUM
Esther and Herbert Taylor Oral History Project

Birmingham, Alabama

BIRMINGHAM PUBLIC LIBRARY ARCHIVES
Birmingfind Collection
Cowett, Mark, Research Papers
Edmonds, Henry M., Papers
Elovitz, Mark, Research Papers
Ferguson, Hill, Papers
Grafman, Milton L., Papers
Graves, John Temple, II, Papers
Green, Cooper, Papers
Hamilton, Virginia, Research Papers
Jones, James Marion, Papers
Marks, Henry, Files
Mendel, Leo, Papers
Newfield, Morris, Papers
Patrick, Luther, Papers
Sterne, Mervyn, Papers
Temple Beth-El, Birmingham, Records
Temple Emanu-El, Birmingham, Records, 1887–2000

LEVITE JEWISH COMMUNITY CENTER
Birmingham United Jewish Fund Minutes

SAMFORD UNIVERSITY SPECIAL COLLECTIONS
Bell, Charles R., Jr., Papers
Gwaltney, L. L., Papers
Stivender, James C., Papers

UNIVERSITY OF ALABAMA AT BIRMINGHAM ARCHIVES
Sterne, Dorah, Memoir
Sterne, Mervyn H., Memoir

Chapel Hill, North Carolina

SOUTHERN HISTORY COLLECTION, THE WILSON LIBRARY
Berkowitz, Sidney M., Papers
Stone, Olive M., Papers

Cincinnati, Ohio

AMERICAN JEWISH ARCHIVES
Fineberg, Solomon A., Papers
Grafman, Milton L., Papers
Korn, Bertram W., Papers
Newfield, Morris, Papers

College Park, Maryland

NATIONAL ARCHIVES AND RECORDS ADMINISTRATION
Federal Bureau of Investigation
Office of the Secretary of War
Office of War Information
Provost Marshal General
Records of the Office of Government Reports
Works Progress Administration

Dothan, Alabama

TROY UNIVERSITY, THE WIREGRASS ARCHIVES
Temple Emanu-El *Book of Memories*

Jerusalem, Israel

CENTRAL ZIONIST ARCHIVES
Papers of the American Jewish Conference

Los Angeles, California

UNIVERSITY OF CALIFORNIA SPECIAL COLLECTIONS,
UNIVERSITY RESEARCH LIBRARY
Bunche, Ralph, Papers

UNIVERSITY OF SOUTHERN CALIFORNIA
Shoah Foundation Institute for Visual History and Education

Mobile, Alabama

MOBILE MUNICIPAL ARCHIVES
Schwartz, Leon, Scrapbooks

SPRINGHILL AVENUE TEMPLE ARCHIVES
Congregation Sha'arai Shomayim Board of Trustee Minutes

Congregation Sha'arai Shomayim Bulletins
Federation of Jewish Charities Minutes
Rabbi Files
Beth Zur Lodge of B'nai B'rith Papers

UNIVERSITY OF SOUTH ALABAMA ARCHIVES
Ahavas Chesed Congregation Papers
LeFlore, John L., Papers

Montgomery, Alabama

ALABAMA DEPARTMENT OF ARCHIVES AND HISTORY
Alabama State Council of Defense Papers
Bankhead, William Brockman, Papers
Boykin, Frank, Papers
Dixon, Frank M., Personal and Administrative Papers
Feldman, Eugene, Papers
Durr, Virginia Foster, Papers
Graves, David Bibb, Papers
Hails, Francis M., Files
Hall, Grover C., Jr., Papers
Hall, Grover C., Sr., Papers
Holocaust Survivors and United States Liberators Oral History Collection
Jarman, Pete, Papers
Lila Bess Olin Morgan Family Papers
Public Information Subject Files
Simpson, James A., Papers
Sparks, Chauncey, Personal and Administrative Papers
State Democratic Executive Committee Papers
Wallace, George C., Administrative Papers

JEWISH FEDERATION OF CENTRAL ALABAMA
Jewish Federation of Montgomery Minute Books

TEMPLE BETH-OR ARCHIVES
Montgomery Section, National Council for Jewish Women Oral History Project
Temple Beth-Or Minute Books
Temple Beth-Or Bulletins

Nashville, Tennessee

VANDERBILT UNIVERSITY ARCHIVES
Owsley, Frank L., Papers

New York City, New York

AMERICAN JEWISH HISTORICAL SOCIETY ARCHIVES
Ehrenreich, Bernard C., Papers
National Council for Jewish Women, Birmingham, Alabama Section
National Jewish Welfare Board, Army-Navy Division Papers
National Jewish Welfare Board, War Bureau Records

AMERICAN JEWISH JOINT DISTRIBUTION COMMITTEE ARCHIVES
JDC Administration Collection

NEW YORK PUBLIC LIBRARY ARCHIVES AND MANUSCRIPTS
Emergency Committee in Aid of Displaced Foreign Scholars Records
Joint Boycott Council of the American Jewish Congress and Jewish Labor Committee Records
Mencken, H. L., Papers

NEW YORK PUBLIC LIBRARY DOROT JEWISH DIVISION
American Jewish Committee Oral History Collection

NEW YORK UNIVERSITY, TAMIMENT LIBRARY/ROBERT F. WAGNER LABOR ARCHIVES
Jackson, James and Esther, Papers
Jewish Labor Committee Papers

SCHOMBERG CENTER FOR RESEARCH IN BLACK CULTURE
Bunche, Ralph, Papers
Carnegie-Myrdal Research Memoranda
International Labor Defense Records

YIVO INSTITUTE FOR JEWISH RESEARCH
American Jewish Committee Papers
German Jewish Children's Aid Papers
National Coordinating Committee for Aid to Refugees Coming from Germany Papers
National Refugee Service Papers
United Service for New Americans Papers

South Bend, Indiana

UNIVERSITY OF NOTRE DAME ARCHIVES
Terminiello, Arthur W., Papers

Tuscaloosa, Alabama

JEROME ROSENBERG
Rosenberg, Jerome, Papers

W. S. HOOLE SPECIAL COLLECTIONS, UNIVERSITY OF ALABAMA
Ayers, Harry M., Papers
Hill, Lister, Papers
Hillel Foundation Papers
Nolen, Roy N., Papers
Sparkman, John J., Congressional Papers

Tuskegee, Alabama

BOOKER T. WASHINGTON COLLECTION, TUSKEGEE UNIVERSITY
Patterson, Frederick D., Papers

Washington, DC

LIBRARY OF CONGRESS, MANUSCRIPT DIVISION
Black, Hugo, Papers

STEPHEN W. GRAFMAN AND THE GRAFMAN FAMILY
Grafman, Milton L., Papers

Public Documents

Alabama Department of Archives and History. *Alabama Official and Statistical Register, 1943*. Wetumpka, AL: Wetumpka Printing Company, 1943.

Alabama Legislature. Senate. Senate Joint Resolution. No. 144. *General Laws and Joint Resolutions of the Legislature of Alabama* (June 10, 1943). Birmingham, AL: Birmingham Printing Company, 1943.

Interviews

Capouya, Morris. Interview by author, July 17, 2008, Montgomery, Alabama.

Drum, Leo. Interview by author, April 30, 2009, Montgomery, Alabama.

Kahn, Adalien Feidelson. Interview by author, January 5, 2002, Berkeley, California.

Kayser, Sam. Interview by author, December 10, 2009, Mobile, Alabama.

Klein, Milton. Interview by author, September 24, 2009, Mobile, Alabama.

Miller, Joseph. Interview by author, December 11, 2009, Mobile, Alabama.

Prince, Arthur. Interview by author, June 15, 2009, Mobile, Alabama.

Ziff, Sidney, Norman Niren, and Sol Kimerling. Interview by author, August 15, 2006, Birmingham, Alabama.

Alabama Newspapers and Magazines

Alabama Baptist
Alabama Christian Advocate
Alabama News Digest
Alabama: News Magazine of the Deep South
Birmingham Age-Herald
Birmingham News
Birmingham World
Catholic Week
Centreville Press
Clarke County Democrat
Cullman Tribune
Deep South Jewish Voice
Dothan Eagle
Greene County Democrat
Greensboro Watchman
Labor Advocate

Marion Times-Standard
Mobile Labor Journal
Mobile Press-Forum Weekly
Mobile Register
Montgomery Advertiser
Southern Jewish Times (Birmingham)
Southern Outlook (Clanton)
Southern Shofar
Southern Watchman (Greensboro)
Tuscaloosa News
Tuskegee News
Weekly Review (Birmingham)

Other Newspapers and Periodicals

Life
Pittsburgh Courier
Southern Israelite

Books

Abzug, Robert H. *Inside the Vicious Heart: Americans and the Liberation of Nazi Concentration Camps*. New York and Oxford: Oxford University Press, 1985.

Adams, Maurianne, and John Bracey, eds. *Strangers and Neighbors: Relations between Blacks and Jews in the United States*. Amherst: University of Massachusetts Press, 1999.

Alpers, Benjamin L. *Dictators, Democracy, and American Public Culture: Envisioning the Totalitarian Enemy, 1920s–1950s*. Chapel Hill: University of North Carolina Press, 2003.

Arad, Gulie Ne'eman. *America, Its Jews, and the Rise of Nazism*. Bloomington: Indiana University Press, 2000.

Atkins, Leah Rawls. *The Valley and the Hills: An Illustrated History of Birmingham and Jefferson County*. Tarzana, CA: Preferred Marketing, 1981.

Atlas, Seymour. *The Rabbi with the Southern Twang: True Stories from a Life of Leadership Within the Orthodox Jewish Congregations of the South*. Victoria, BC: Trafford Publishing, 2007.

Baldwin, Neil. *Henry Ford and the Jews: The Mass Production of Hate*. New York: Public Affairs, 2001.

Bankier, David, ed. *Probing the Depths of German Antisemitism: German Society and the Persecution of the Jews, 1933–1941*. New York: Berghahn Books, 2000.

Barkun, Michael. *Religion and the Racist Right: The Origins of the Christian Identity Movement*. Chapel Hill: University of North Carolina Press, 1994.

Barnard, Hollinger F., ed. *Outside the Magic Circle: The Autobiography of Virginia Foster Durr*. Tuscaloosa: University of Alabama Press, 1985.

Bartley, Numan V. *The New South, 1945–1980*. Baton Rouge: Louisiana State University Press, 1995.

Bauer, Yehuda. *My Brother's Keeper: A History of the American Jewish Joint Distribution Committee, 1929–1939*. Philadelphia: Jewish Publication Society of America, 1974.

Bauman, Mark K. *Harry H. Epstein and the Rabbinate as Conduit for Change*. Rutherford, NJ: Fairleigh Dickinson University Press, 1994.

———. *The Southerner as American: Jewish Style*. Cincinnati: American Jewish Archives, 1996.

Bauman, Mark K., and Berkley Kalin, eds. *The Quiet Voices: Southern Rabbis and Black Civil Rights, 1880s to 1990s*. Tuscaloosa: University of Alabama Press, 1997.

Bauman, Mark K., ed. *Dixie Diaspora: An Anthology of Southern Jewish History*. Tuscaloosa: University of Alabama Press, 2006.

Ben-Gurion, David. *Israel: A Personal History*. New York: Funk and Wagnalls, 1971.

Bendersky, Joseph W. *The "Jewish Threat": Anti-Semitic Politics of the U.S. Army*. New York: Basic Books, 2000.

Berman, Aaron. *Nazism, the Jews, and American Zionism, 1933–1948*. Detroit: Wayne State University Press, 1990.

Besmann, Wendy Lowe. *A Separate Circle: Jewish Life in Knoxville, Tennessee*. Knoxville: University of Tennessee Press, 2001.

Biographical Sketches of Citizens of Birmingham and Jefferson County. Indianapolis, IN: Citizens Historical Association, 1936–44.

Black, Edwin. *War against the Weak: Eugenics and America's Campaign to Create a Master Race*. New York: Four Walls Eight Windows, 2003.

Blanton, Sherry. *The History of Temple Beth-El, Anniston, Alabama*. Anniston, AL: Privately published, 2000.

———. *Survivors' Stories: Anniston's Temple Beth-El and the Holocaust*. Anniston, AL: Privately published, 2010.

Blumenthal, L. Roy. *Fighting for America: A Record of the Participation of Jewish Men and Women in the Armed Forces during 1944*. New York: National Jewish Welfare Board, 1944.

Bonfield, Barbara Goldstein. *Hallowed Ground: A History of the K'nesseth Israel/Beth-El Cemetery, Birmingham, Alabama*. Birmingham, AL: Privately printed, 2009.

Botwinick, Rita Steinhardt. *A History of the Holocaust: From Ideology to Annihilation*. Upper Saddle River, NJ: Pearson Prentice Hall, 2004.

Breitman, Richard, and Norman J. W. Goda. *Hitler's Shadow: Nazi War Criminals, U.S. Intelligence, and the Cold War*. Washington, DC: National Archives, 2010.

Breitman, Richard, and Alan M. Kraut. *American Refugee Policy and European Jewry, 1933–1945*. Bloomington: Indiana University Press, 1987.

Brown, James M., T. Horton Walker, and Horace R. Evans. *History Department of Alabama Veterans of Foreign Wars of the United States: Golden Jubilee Edition, 1899–1949*. Montgomery, AL: Paragon Press, 1949.

Brown, Jerry Elijah, ed. *Clearings in the Thicket: An Alabama Humanities Reader: Essays and Stories from the 1983 Alabama History and Heritage Festival*. Macon, GA: Mercer University Press, 1985.

Browning, Christopher R. *The Path to Genocide: Essays on Launching the Final Solution*. London: Cambridge University Press, 1992.

———. *The Origins of the Final Solution: The Evolution of Nazi Jewish Policy, September 1939–March 1942*. Lincoln: University of Nebraska Press, and Jerusalem: Yad Vashem, 2004.

Bullock, Alan. *Hitler: A Study in Tyranny*. Completely rev. ed. New York: Harper and Row, 1962.

Bush, George S. *An American Harvest: The Story of Weil Brothers-Cotton*. Englewood Cliffs, NJ: Prentice-Hall, 1982.

Carageorge, Ted, ed. *Gulf Coast Politics in the Twentieth Century*. Pensacola, FL: Historic Pensacola Preservation Board, 1973.

Carlson, John Roy. *The Plotters*. New York: E. P. Dutton, 1946.

———. *Under Cover: My Four Years in the Nazi Underworld—The Amazing Revelation of How Axis Agents and Our Enemies Within Are Now Plotting to Destroy the United States*. New York: E. P. Dutton, 1943.

Carter, Dan T. *Scottsboro: A Tragedy of the American South*. Rev. ed. Baton Rouge: Louisiana State University Press, 1979.

Cash, W. J. *The Mind of the South*. New York: Alfred A. Knopf, 1941.

Cason, Clarence. *90° in the Shade*. Chapel Hill: University of North Carolina Press, 1935; reprint, Tuscaloosa: University of Alabama Press, 2001.

Cesarani, David, and Eric J. Sundquist, eds. *After the Holocaust: Challenging the Myth of Silence*. London: Routledge, 2012.

Childers, Thomas. *Soldier from the War Returning: The Greatest Generation's Troubled Homecoming from World War II*. Boston: Houghton Mifflin Harcourt, 2009.

Christgau, John. *"Enemies": World War II Alien Internment*. Ames: Iowa State University Press, 1985.

Cobb, James C. *Redefining Southern Culture: Mind and Identity in the Modern South*. Athens: University of Georgia Press, 1999.

Cobb, James C., and Michael V. Namorato, eds. *The New Deal and the South*. Jackson: University Press of Mississippi, 1984.

Cohen, Beth B. *Case Closed: Holocaust Survivors in Postwar America*. New Brunswick, NJ: Rutgers University Press, 2007.

Cohen, Edward. *The Peddler's Grandson: Growing Up Jewish in Mississippi*. New York: Dell Publishing, 1999.

Cohen, Miriam F., ed. *Congregation Etz Ahayem, 1912–1987*. Montgomery, AL: Privately published, 1987.

———. *A History of Congregation Agudath Israel, 1902–1987, 5662–5747*. Montgomery, AL: Privately published, 1987.

Cohen, Miriam F., and Gaby Capp, eds. *Congregation Etz Ahayem, 1912–1997*. Montgomery, AL: Privately published, 1987.

Cohen, Miriam F., and Jo Anne Rousso, eds. *Congregation Etz Ahayem: Tree of Life, 1912–1982*. Montgomery, AL: Privately published, 1982.

Cohen, Naomi W. *Not Free to Desist: A History of the American Jewish Committee, 1906–1966*. Philadelphia: Jewish Publication Society of America, 1972.

Corley, Robert G. *Paying Civic Rent: The Jews of Emanu-El and the Birmingham Community*. Birmingham, AL: A. H. Cather Publishing, 1982.

Cowett, Mark. *Birmingham's Rabbi: Morris Newfield and Alabama, 1895–1940*. Tuscaloosa: University of Alabama Press, 1986.

Cronenberg, Allen. *Forth to the Mighty Conflict: Alabama and World War II*. Tuscaloosa: University of Alabama Press, 1995.

Dabney, Virginius. *Below the Potomac: A Book about the New South*. New York: D. Appleton-Century, 1942.

———. *Liberalism in the South*. Chapel Hill: University of North Carolina Press, 1932.

Daniels, Jonathan. *A Southerner Discovers the South*. New York: Macmillan, 1938.

Dawidowicz, Lucy S. *The War against the Jews, 1933–1945*. New York: Holt, Rinehart and Winston, 1975; Bantam trade edition, 1986.

Deakin, F. W. *The Brutal Friendship: Mussolini, Hitler and the Fall of Italian Fascism*. New York: Harper and Row, 1962.

Diner, Hasia R. *In the Almost Promised Land: American Jews and Blacks, 1915–1935*. Westport, CT: Greenwood Press, 1977; reprint, Baltimore: Johns Hopkins University Press, 1995.

———. *We Remember with Reverence and Love: American Jews and the Myth of Silence after the Holocaust, 1945–1962*. New York: New York University Press, 2009.

Dinnerstein, Leonard. *America and the Survivors of the Holocaust*. New York: Columbia University Press, 1982.

———. *Antisemitism in America*. New York and Oxford: Oxford University Press, 1994.

———. *Uneasy at Home: Antisemitism and the American Jewish Experience*. New York: Columbia University Press, 1987.

Dinnerstein, Leonard, and Mary Dale Palsson, eds. *Jews in the South*. Baton Rouge: Louisiana State University Press, 1973.

Dobbs, Michael. *Saboteurs: The Nazi Raid on America*. New York: Alfred A. Knopf, 2004.

Dwork, Debórah, and Robert Jan van Pelt. *Flight from the Reich: Refugee Jews, 1933–1946*. New York: W. W. Norton, 2009.

Edgcomb, Gabrielle Simon. *From Swastika to Jim Crow: Refugee Scholars at Black Colleges*. Malabar, FL: Krieger Publishing, 1993.

Edmonds, Henry M. *A Parson's Notebook*. Birmingham, AL: Elizabeth Agee's Bookshelf, 1961.

Egerton, John. *Speak Now against the Day: The Generation before the Civil Rights Movement in the South*. New York: Alfred A. Knopf, 1994.

Eisenberg, Ellen M. *The First to Cry Down Injustice? Western Jews and Japanese Removal During WWII*. Lanham, MD: Lexington Books, 2008.

Ellison, Rhoda Coleman. *History of Huntingdon College, 1854–1954*. Montgomery, AL: NewSouth Books, 2004.

Elovitz, Mark H. *A Century of Jewish Life in Dixie: The Birmingham Experience*. Tuscaloosa: University of Alabama Press, 1974.

Endelman, Judith E. *The Jewish Community of Indianapolis, 1849 to the Present*. Bloomington: Indiana University Press, 1984.

Ennels, Jerome A., and Wesley Phillips Newton. *The Wisdom of Eagles: A History of Maxwell Air Force Base*. Montgomery, AL: River City Press, 2002.

Evans, Eli N. *The Provincials: A Personal History of Jews in the South*. New York: Atheneum, 1973.

Feingold, Henry L. *A Time for Searching: Entering the Mainstream, 1920–1945*. Baltimore: Johns Hopkins University Press, 1992.

Feldman, Glenn. *From Demagogue to Dixiecrat: Horace Wilkinson and the Politics of Race*. Lanham, MD: University Press of America, 1995.

———. *Politics, Society, and the Klan in Alabama, 1915–1949*. Tuscaloosa: University of Alabama Press, 1999.

Ferris, Marcie Cohen, and Mark I. Greenberg, eds. *Jewish Roots in Southern Soil: A New History*. Waltham, MA: Brandeis University Press, 2006.

Fest, Joachim C. *Hitler*. Translated by Richard and Clara Winston. New York: Harcourt Brace Jovanovich, 1974.

Fiebig-von Hase, Ragnhild, and Ursula Lehmkuhl, eds. *Enemy Images in American History*. Providence, RI: Berghahn Books, 1997.

Fischer, Klaus P. *The History of an Obsession: German Judeophobia and the Holocaust*. New York: Continuum Publishing Group, 1998.

Flynt, Wayne. *Alabama Baptists: Southern Baptists in the Heart of Dixie*. Tuscaloosa: University of Alabama Press, 1998.

———. *Alabama in the Twentieth Century*. Tuscaloosa: University of Alabama Press, 2004.

Friedländer, Saul. *Nazi Germany and the Jews*. Vol. 1, *The Years of Persecution, 1933–1939*. New York: HarperCollins Publishers, 1997.

Friedman, Saul S. *No Haven for the Oppressed: United States Policy toward Jewish Refugees, 1938–1945*. Detroit: Wayne State University Press, 1973.

Gerber, David A., ed. *Anti-Semitism in American History*. Urbana: University of Illinois Press, 1986.

Gerstle, Gary. *American Crucible: Race and Nation in the Twentieth Century*. Princeton, NJ: Princeton University Press, 2001.

Glass, Charles. *Americans in Paris: Life and Death under Nazi Occupation, 1940–44*. London: Harper Press, 2009.

Glass, James M. *"Life Unworthy of Life": Racial Phobia and Mass Murder in Hitler's Germany*. New York: Basic Books, 1997.

Glazer, Nathan. *American Judaism*. Chicago: University of Chicago Press, 1957.

Glazier, Jack. *Dispersing the Ghetto: The Relocation of Jewish Immigrants across America*. Ithaca, NY: Cornell University Press, 1998.

Golden, Harry. *Our Southern Landsmen*. New York: G. P. Putnam's Sons, 1974.

Goldfield, David R. *Black, White, and Southern: Race Relations and Southern Culture, 1940 to the Present*. Baton Rouge: Louisiana State University Press, 1990.

Goldstein, Eric L. *The Price of Whiteness: Jews, Race, and American Identity*. Princeton, NJ: Princeton University Press, 2006.

Gottlieb, Moshe. *American Anti-Nazi Resistance, 1933–1941: An Historical Analysis*. New York: Ktav Publishing House, 1982.

Graves, John Temple. *The Fighting South*. New York: G.P. Putnam's Sons, 1943; reprint, Tuscaloosa: University of Alabama Press, 1985.

Greenberg, Cheryl Lynn. *Troubling the Waters: Black-Jewish Relations in the American Century*. Princeton, NJ: Princeton University Press, 2006.

Greene, Joshua M. *Justice at Dachau: The Trials of an American Prosecutor*. New York: Broadway Books, 2003.

Gurock, Jeffrey S., ed. *American Jewish History*. Vol. 6, *Anti-Semitism in America*. New York and London: Routledge, 1998.

Hacker, Louis M., and Mark D. Hirsch. *Proskauer: His Life and Times*. Tuscaloosa: University of Alabama Press, 1978.

Hale, Grace Elizabeth. *Making Whiteness: The Culture of Segregation in the South, 1890–1940*. New York: Vintage Books, 1998.

Hamerow, Theodore. *Why We Watched: Europe, America, and the Holocaust*. New York: W. W. Norton, 2008.

Hamilton, Virginia Van der Veer. *Hugo Black: The Alabama Years*. Baton Rouge: Louisiana State University Press, 1972.

———. *Lister Hill: Statesman from the South*. Chapel Hill: University of North Carolina Press, 1987.

Hanan, Rubin M. *The History of Etz Ahayem Congregation, 1906–1962*. Montgomery, AL: Privately published, 1962.

Handlin, Oscar. *A Continuing Task: The American Jewish Joint Distribution Committee, 1914–1964*. New York: Random House, 1964.

Harris, Leon. *Merchant Princes: An Intimate History of Jewish Families Who Built Great Department Stores*. New York: Harper and Row, 1979.

Helmreich, William B. *Against All Odds: Holocaust Survivors and the Successful Lives They Made in America*. New York: Simon and Schuster, 1992.

Hero, Alfred O., Jr. *The Southerner and World Affairs*. Baton Rouge: Louisiana State University Press, 1965.

Herschel, Susannah. *The Aryan Jesus: Christian Theologians and the Bible in Nazi Germany*. Princeton, NJ: Princeton University Press, 2008.

Higginbotham, Jay. *Mobile: City by the Bay*. Mobile, AL: Azalea City Printers, 1968.

Higham, John. *Send These to Me: Jews and Other Immigrants in Urban America*. New York: Atheneum, 1975.

———. *Strangers in the Land: Patterns of American Nativism, 1860–1925*. New Brunswick, NJ: Rutgers University Press, 1955.

Hitler, Adolf. *Mein Kampf*. Translated by Ralph Manheim. Verlag Frz. Eher Nachf, GMBH, 1925; reprint, Boston: Houghton Mifflin, 1971.

Hollis, Daniel Webster, III. *An Alabama Newspaper Tradition: Grover C. Hall and the Hall Family*. Tuscaloosa: University of Alabama Press, 1983.

Huie, William Bradford. *Mud on the Stars*. New York: L. B. Fischer Publishing, 1942; reprint, Tuscaloosa: University of Alabama Press, 1996.

Jones, Larry Eugene, ed. *Crossing Boundaries: The Exclusion and Inclusion of Minorities in Germany and America*. New York: Berghahn Books, 2001.

Jones, Margaret Jean. *Combing Cullman County*. Cullman, AL: Modernistic Printers, 1972.

Jones, Maxine D., and Joe M. Richards. *Talladega College: The First Century*. Tuscaloosa: University of Alabama Press, 1990.

Kaganoff, Nathan M., and Melvin I. Urofsky, eds. "*Turn to the South*": *Essays on Southern Jewry*. Charlottesville: University Press of Virginia, 1979.

Kaufman, Isidore. *American Jews in World War II: The Story of 550,000 Fighters for Freedom*. 2 vols. New York: Dial Press, 1947.

Kaufman, Menahem. *An Ambiguous Partnership: Non-Zionists and Zionists in America, 1939–1948*. Jerusalem: Magnes Press; Detroit: Wayne State University Press, 1991.

Kelley, Robin D. G. *Hammer and Hoe: Alabama Communists during the Great Depression*. Chapel Hill: University of North Carolina Press, 1990.

Kennedy, Stetson. *Southern Exposure*. Garden City, NY: Doubleday, 1946.

Kershaw, Ian. *Hitler, 1889–1936: Hubris*. New York: W. W. Norton, 1998.

———. *Hitler, 1936–1945: Nemesis*. New York: W. W. Norton, 2000.

Key, V. O., Jr. *Southern Politics in State and Nation*. New ed. New York: Alfred A. Knopf, 1949; reprint, Knoxville: University of Tennessee Press, 1984.

Kneebone, John T. *Southern Liberal Journalists and the Issue of Race, 1920–1944*. Chapel Hill: University of North Carolina Press, 1985.

Kolsky, Thomas A. *Jews against Zionism: The American Council for Judaism, 1942–1948*. Philadelphia: Temple University Press, 1990.

Koonz, Claudia. *The Nazi Conscience*. Cambridge, MA: Belknap Press of Harvard University Press, 2003.

Krammer, Arnold. *Undue Process: The Untold Story of America's German Alien Internment*. London: Rowman and Littlefield, 1997.

Kühl, Stefan. *The Nazi Connection: Eugenics, American Racism, and German National Socialism*. New York and Oxford: Oxford University Press, 1994.

Lainoff, Seymour. *Ludwig Lewisohn*. Boston: Twayne Publishers, 1982.

Larson, Edward J. *Sex, Race, and Science: Eugenics in the Deep South*. Baltimore: Johns Hopkins University Press, 1995.

Leff, Laurel. *Buried by the Times: The Holocaust and America's Most Important Newspaper*. Cambridge and New York: Cambridge University Press, 2005.

Lelyveld, Joseph. *Omaha Blues: A Memory Loop*. New York: Picador, 2006.

LeMaster, Carolyn Gray. *A Corner of the Tapestry: A History of the Jewish Experience in Arkansas, 1820–1990s*. Fayetteville: University of Arkansas Press, 1994.

Lewis, Selma S. *A Biblical People in the Bible Belt: The Jewish Community of Memphis, Tennessee, 1840s–1960s*. Macon, GA: Mercer University Press, 1998.

Liebman, Arthur. *Jews and the Left*. New York: John Wiley and Sons, 1979.

Lifton, Robert Jay. *The Nazi Doctors: Medical Killing and the Psychology of Genocide*. New York: Basic Books, 1986.

Linenthal, Edward T. *Preserving Memory: The Struggle to Create America's Holocaust Museum*. New York: Viking, 1995.

Lipstadt, Deborah E. *Beyond Belief: The American Press and the Coming of the Holocaust, 1933–1945*. New York: The Free Press, 1986.

Lookstein, Haskell. *Were We Our Brothers' Keepers? The Public Response of American Jews to the Holocaust, 1938–1944*. New York: Random House, 1985.

Lusane, Clarence. *Hitler's Black Victims: The Historical Experiences of Afro-Germans, European Blacks, Africans, and African Americans in the Nazi Era*. New York and London: Routledge, 2003.

MacMaster, Neil. *Racism in Europe, 1870–2000*. New York: Palgrave, 2001.

Marcus, Jacob Rader. *To Count a People: American Jewish Population Data, 1585–1984*. Lanham, MD: University Press of America, 1990.

Marinbach, Bernard. *Galveston: Ellis Island of the West*. Albany: State University of New York Press, 1984.

Marlett, Jeffrey D. *Saving the Heartland: Catholic Missionaries in Rural America, 1920–1960*. DeKalb: Northern Illinois University Press, 2002.

McMillen, Neil R., ed. *Remaking Dixie: The Impact of World War II on the American South*. Jackson: University Press of Mississippi, 1997.

Medoff, Rafael. *The Deafening Silence: American Jewish Leaders and the Holocaust*. New York: Shapolsky Publishers, 1987.

Mendes-Flohr, Paul R., and Jehuda Reinharz, eds. *The Jew in the Modern World: A Documentary History*. New York and Oxford: Oxford University Press, 1980.

Michie, Allan A., and Frank Ryhlick. *Dixie Demagogues*. New York: Vanguard Press, 1939.

Miller, Joseph B. *A Doctor! Who—Me???: One Physician's Incredible Journey through Life, Medicine, and Miracles*. Coral Springs, FL: Llumina Press, 2003.

Moore, Deborah Dash. *GI Jews: How World War II Changed a Generation*. Cambridge, MA: Belknap Press of Harvard University Press, 2004.

Moss, Florence Hawkins Wood. *Building Birmingham and Jefferson County*. Birmingham, AL: Birmingham Printing Company, 1947.

Mowat, Charles Loch. *Britain between the Wars, 1918–1940*. Chicago: University of Chicago Press, 1955; reprint, Boston: Beacon Press, 1971.

Myrdal, Gunnar. *An American Dilemma: The Negro Problem and Modern Democracy*. New York: Harper and Brothers, 1944.

Nadell, Pamela S., and Jonathan D. Sarna, eds. *Women and American Judaism: Historical Perspectives*. Hanover, NH: University Press of New England, 2001.

Newton, Wesley Phillips. *Montgomery in the Good War: Portrait of a Southern City, 1939–1946*. Tuscaloosa: University of Alabama Press, 2000.

Niewyk, Donald, and Francis Nicosia. *The Columbia Guide to the Holocaust*. New York: Columbia University Press, 2000.

Noakes, Jeremy, and G. Pridham, eds. *Nazism, 1919–1945: A Documentary Reader*. Vol. 2, *State, Economy, and Society, 1933–1939*. Exeter: University of Exeter Press, 1984; reprint, Exeter: University of Exeter Press, 1997.

Noll, Steven. *Feeble-Minded in Our Midst: Institutions for the Mentally Retarded in the South, 1900–1940*. Chapel Hill: University of North Carolina Press, 1995.

Norman, Corrie E., and Don S. Armentrout, eds. *Religion in the Contemporary South: Changes, Continuities, and Contexts*. Knoxville: University of Tennessee Press, 2005.

Norwood, Stephen H. *The Third Reich in the Ivory Tower: Complicity and Conflict on American Campuses*. Cambridge: Cambridge University Press, 2009.

Novick, Peter. *The Holocaust in American Life*. Boston: Houghton Mifflin, 1999.

Packer, George. *Blood of the Liberals*. New York: Farrar, Straus and Giroux, 2000.

Percy, William Alexander. *Lanterns on the Levee: Recollections of a Planter's Son*. New York: Alfred A. Knopf, 1941.

Peters, Joan. *From Time Immemorial: The Origins of the Arab-Jewish Conflict over Palestine*. New York: Harper and Row, 1984.

Polenberg, Richard. *One Nation Divisible: Class, Race, and Ethnicity in the United States since 1938*. New York: Penguin Books, 1980.

Powell, Lawrence N. *Troubled Memory: Anne Levy, the Holocaust, and David Duke's Louisiana*. Chapel Hill: University of North Carolina Press, 2000.

Proctor, Robert N. *Racial Hygiene: Medicine under the Nazis*. Cambridge, MA: Harvard University Press, 1988.

Proctor, Samuel, and Louis Schmier, eds. *Jews of the South: Selected Essays from the Southern Jewish Historical Society*. Macon, GA: Mercer University Press, 1984.

Proskauer, Joseph M. *A Segment of My Times*. New York: Farrar, Straus, 1950.

Rabinowitz, Dorothy. *New Lives: Survivors of the Holocaust Living in America*. New York: Alfred A. Knopf, 1976.

Raphael, Marc Lee. *Jews and Judaism in a Midwestern Community: Columbus, Ohio: 1840–1975*. Columbus: Ohio Historical Society, 1979.

Raphael, Marc Lee, ed. *The Columbia History of Jews and Judaism in America*. New York: Columbia University Press, 2008.

Reed, Mary Beth, Charles E. Cantley, and J. W. Joseph. *Ft. McClellan: A Popular History*. Stone Mountain, GA: New South Associates, 1996.

Riley, Sam G. *The American Newspaper Columnist*. Westport, CT: Praeger, 1998.

Rockaway, Robert A. *Words of the Uprooted: Jewish Immigration in Early Twentieth Century America*. Ithaca, NY: Cornell University Press, 1998.

Roediger, David R. *The Wages of Whiteness: Race and the Making of the American Working Class*. Rev. ed. London and New York: Verso, 2007.

Rogers, William Warren, Robert David Ward, Leah Rawls Atkins, and Wayne Flynt. *Alabama: The History of a Deep South State*. Tuscaloosa: University of Alabama Press, 1994.

Rogow, Faith. *Gone to Another Meeting: The National Council of Jewish Women, 1893–1993*. Tuscaloosa: University of Alabama Press, 1993.

Ross, Robert W. *So It Was True: The American Protestant Press and the Nazi Persecution of the Jews*. Minneapolis: University of Minnesota Press, 1980.

Rumore, Pat Boyd. *Lawyers in a New South City*. Birmingham, AL: Association Publishing Company, 2000.

Sacco, Jack. *Where the Birds Never Sing: The True Story of the 92nd Signal Battalion and the Liberation of Dachau*. New York: Regan Books, 2003.

Salmond, John A. *The Conscience of a Lawyer: Clifford J. Durr and American Civil Liberties, 1899–1975*. Tuscaloosa: University of Alabama Press, 1990.

———. *A Southern Rebel: The Life and Times of Aubrey Willis Williams, 1890–1965*. Chapel Hill: University of North Carolina Press, 1983.

Sanua, Marianne R. *Going Greek: Jewish College Fraternities in the United States, 1895–1945*. Detroit: Wayne State University Press, 2003.

———. *"Here's to Our Fraternity": One Hundred Years of Zeta Beta Tau, 1898–1998*. Hanover, NH: Zeta Beta Tau Foundation; distributed by Brandeis University Press and University Press of New England, 1998.

———. *Let Us Prove Strong: The American Jewish Committee, 1945–2006*. Waltham, MA: Brandeis University Press, 2007.

Schad, Kathleen White. *They Call Me Kay: A Courtship in Letters*. Edited by Nancy G. Anderson. Montgomery, AL: Black Belt Press, 1994.

Segev, Tom. *One Palestine, Complete: Jews and Arabs under the British Mandate*. New York: Henry Holt, 2000.

Shaw, J. V. W. *A Survey of Palestine: Prepared in December 1945, and January 1946, for the Information of the Anglo-American Committee of Inquiry*. Palestine: Government Printer, 1945.

Shirer, William L. *Berlin Diary: The Journal of a Foreign Correspondent, 1934–1941*. New York: Alfred A. Knopf, 1941.

Slater, Leonard. *The Pledge*. New York: Simon and Schuster, 1970.

Sosna, Morton. *Southern Liberals and the Race Issue: In Search of the Silent South*. New York: Columbia University Press, 1977.

Stanton, Mary. *The Hand of Esau: Montgomery's Jewish Community and the Bus Boycott*. Montgomery, AL: River City Publishing, 2006.

Steelman, John R., Arthur Franklin Raper, Walter R. Chivers. *The Plight of Tuscaloosa: A Case Study of Conditions in Tuscaloosa County, Alabama, 1933*. Atlanta: Southern Commission on the Study of Lynching, 1933.

Steinweis, Alan E., and Daniel E. Rogers, eds. *The Impact of Nazism: New Perspectives on the Third Reich and Its Legacy*. Lincoln: University of Nebraska Press, 2003.

Stevens, Richard. *American Zionism and US Foreign Policy, 1942–1947*. New York: Pageant Press, 1962; reprint, Beirut, Lebanon: Institute for Palestine Studies, 1970.

Sundquist, Eric J. *Strangers in the Land: Blacks, Jews, Post-Holocaust America*. Cambridge, MA: Belknap Press of Harvard University Press, 2005.

Svonkin, Stuart. *Jews against Prejudice: American Jews and the Fight for Civil Liberties*. New York: Columbia University Press, 1997.

Takaki, Ronald. *Double Victory: A Multicultural History of America in World War II*. Boston: Little, Brown, 2000.

Temple Beth-Or. *150 Years of Kahl Montgomery, 1852–2002*. Montgomery, AL: Privately printed, 2002.

Temple Emanu-El. *A Century of Reverence, 1882–1982*. Birmingham, AL: Privately printed, 1982.

Terkel, Studs. *The Good War: An Oral History of World War II*. New York: Ballantine Books: 1984.

———. *Hard Times: An Oral History of the Great Depression*. New York: Pantheon Books, 1970.

Thomason, Michael V. R., ed. *Mobile: The New History of Alabama's First City*. Tuscaloosa: University of Alabama Press, 2001.

Thornton, J. Mills, III. *Dividing Lines: Municipal Politics and the Struggle for Civil Rights in Montgomery, Birmingham, and Selma*. Tuscaloosa: University of Alabama Press, 2002.

Tindall, George Brown. *The Emergence of the New South, 1913–1945*. Baton Rouge: Louisiana State University Press, 1967.

Toll, William. *The Making of an Ethnic Middle Class: Portland Jewry over Four Generations*. Albany: State University of New York Press, 1982.

Trommler, Frank, and Elliot Shore, eds. *The German-American Encounter: Conflict and Cooperation between Two Cultures, 1800–2000*. New York: Berghahn Books, 2001.

Umansky, Ellen M. *From Christian Science to Jewish Science*. Oxford and New York: Oxford University Press, 2005.

Urofsky, Melvin I. *American Zionism: From Herzl to the Holocaust*. New York: Anchor Press/Doubleday, 1975; reprint, Lincoln: University of Nebraska Press/Bison Books, 1995.

Van Paassen, Pierre, and James Waterman Wise, eds. *Nazism: An Assault on Civilization*. New York: H. Smith and R. Haas, 1934.

Wallace, Max. *The American Axis: Henry Ford, Charles Lindbergh, and the Rise of the Third Reich*. New York: St. Martin's Press, 2003.

Ward, Geoffrey C., and Ken Burns. *The War: An Intimate History, 1941–1945*. New York: Alfred A. Knopf, 2007.

Webb, Clive. *Fight against Fear: Southern Jews and Black Civil Rights*. Athens: University of Georgia Press, 2001.

———. *Rabble Rousers: The American Far Right in the Civil Rights Era*. Athens: University of Georgia Press, 2010.

Weiner, Hollace Ava. *Jewish Stars in Texas: Rabbis and Their Work*. College Station: Texas A&M University Press, 1999.

Weiner, Hollace Ava, and Kenneth D. Roseman, eds. *Lone Stars of David: The Jews of Texas*. Waltham, MA: Brandeis University Press, 2007.

Weissbach, Lee Shai. *Jewish Life in Small-Town America: A History*. New Haven, CT: Yale University Press, 2005.

Wells, Leon Weliczker. *Who Speaks for the Vanquished? American Jewish Leaders and the Holocaust*. Edited by Michael Ryan. New York: Peter Lang, 1987.

Whitfield, Stephen J. *In Search of American Jewish Culture*. Hanover, NH: Brandeis University Press, 1999.

———. *Voices of Jacob, Hands of Esau: Jews in American Life and Thought*. Hamden, CT: Archon Books, 1984.

Whitlock, Rita S. *A Family Album: The Family of Congregation Ahavas Chesed, 1894–1994*. Mobile, AL: Corporate Resource Associates, 1994.

Winkler, Allan M. *Homefront U.S.A.: America during World War II*. 2nd ed. Wheeling, IL: Harlan Davidson, 2000.

Wistrich, Robert S. *Antisemitism: The Longest Hatred*. New York: Schocken Books, 1991.

———. *Who's Who in Nazi Germany*. London: Weidenfeld and Nicolson, 1982; London and New York: Routledge, 1995.

Wyman, David S. *The Abandonment of the Jews: America and the Holocaust, 1941–1945*. New York: Pantheon Books, 1984.

———. *Paper Walls: America and the Refugee Crisis, 1938–1941*. Boston: University of Massachusetts Press, 1968.

Wyman, David S., and Rafael Medoff. *A Race against Death: Peter Bergson, America, and the Holocaust*. New York: The New Press, 2002.

Zellner, Bob. *The Wrong Side of Murder Creek: A White Southerner in the Freedom Movement*. Montgomery, AL: NewSouth Books, 2008.

Zietz, Robert J. *The Gates of Heaven: Congregation Sha'arai Shomayim: The First 150 Years, Mobile, Alabama, 1844–1994*. Mobile, AL: Congregation Sha'arai Shomayim, 1994.

Articles

Adler, Selig. "The United States and the Holocaust." *American Jewish History* (September 1974): 14–23.

Allen, William Loyd. "How Baptists Assessed Hitler." *Christian Century* (September 1–8, 1982): 890–91.

Barr, Terry. "A Shtetl Grew in Bessemer: Temple Beth-El and Jewish Life in Small-Town Alabama." *Southern Jewish History* 3 (2000): 1–44.

Bauman, Mark K. "A Century of Southern Jewish Historiography." *American Jewish Archives Journal* (2007): 3–78.

———. "The Transformation of Jewish Social Services in Atlanta, 1928–1948." *American Jewish Archives Journal* (2001): 83–111.

Bauman, Mark K., and Arnold Shankman. "The Rabbi as Ethnic Broker: The Case of David Marx." *Journal of American Ethnic History* 2 (Spring 1983): 51–68.

Bayme, Steven. "American Jewish Leadership Confronts the Holocaust: Revisiting Naomi Cohen's Thesis and the American Jewish Committee." *American Jewish Archives Journal* (2009): 163–86.

Berman, Aaron. "American Zionism and the Rescue of European Jewry: An Ideological Perspective." *American Jewish History* (March 1981): 310–30.

Breitman, Richard. "The Allied War Effort and the Jews, 1942–1943." *Journal of Contemporary History* 20 (January 1985): 135–56.

Calhoun, Ricky-Dale. "Arming David: The Haganah's Illegal Arms Procurement Network in the United States, 1945–1949." *Journal of Palestine Studies* 36 (Summer 2007): 22–32.

Cowett, Mark. "Rabbi Morris Newfield and the Social Gospel: Theology and Societal Reform in the South." *American Jewish Archives Journal* (1982): 52–74.

Dalin, David G. "Cyrus Adler, Non-Zionism, and the Zionist Movement: A Study in Contradictions." *American Jewish Studies Review* 10 (Spring 1985): 55–87.

Daniel, Pete. "Going among Strangers: Southern Reactions to World War II." *Journal of American History* 77 (December 1990): 886–911.

Duff, Earl D. "A Study of a Successful Interest Group: The American Zionist Movement." *Western Political Quarterly* 25 (March 1972): 109–24.

Falk, Gerhard. "The Reactions of the German-American Press to Nazi Persecutions, 1933–41." *Journal of Reform Judaism* 32 (Spring 1985): 12–23.

Feist, H. J. "The Status of Refugees." *Modern Law Review* 5 (July 1941): 51–53.

Feldman, Glenn. "Soft Opposition: Elite Acquiescence and Klan-Sponsored Terrorism in Alabama, 1946–1950." *Historical Journal* 40 (September 1997): 753–77.

Ferris, Marcie Cohen. "'From the Recipe File of Luba Cohen': A Study of Southern Jewish Foodways and Cultural Identity." *Southern Jewish History* 2 (1999): 136–37.

Ferris, William R. "John Dollard: Caste and Class Revisited." *Southern Cultures* 10 (Summer 2004): 7–18.

Gal, Allon. "The Zionist Influence on American Jewish Life." *American Jewish Archives* 41 (1989): 173–84.

Genizi, Haim. "American Interfaith Cooperation on Behalf of Refugees from Nazism, 1933–1945." *American Jewish History* (March 1981): 347–61.

Golden, Harry L., and Albert Vorspan. "Unease in Dixie." *Midstream: A Quarterly Jewish Review* 2 (Autumn 1956): 38–51.

Goldfield, David. "A Sense of Place: Jews, Blacks, and White Gentiles in the American South." *Southern Cultures* 3 (1997): 58–79.

Gottlieb, Moshe. "The Anti-Nazi Boycott Movement in the United States: An Ideological and Sociological Appreciation." *Jewish Social Studies* 35 (July–October 1973): 198–227.

Grill, Johnpeter Horst, and Robert L. Jenkins. "The Nazis and the American South in the 1930s: A Mirror Image?" *Journal of Southern History* 58 (November 1992): 667–94.

Halperin, Samuel. "Ideology or Philanthropy? The Politics of Zionist Fund-Raising." *Western Political Quarterly* 13 (December 1960): 950–73.

Harper, Jimmy. "Alabama Baptists and the Rise of Hitler and Fascism, 1930–1938." *Journal of Reform Judaism* 32 (Spring 1985): 1–11.

Hellendall, F. "Status of Refugees." *Modern Law Review* 7 (November 1944): 235–38.

Hollis, Daniel Webster, III. "Grover Cleveland Hall: The Anatomization of a Southern Journalist's Philosophy." *Alabama Historical Quarterly* 42 (Spring and Summer 1980): 87–101.

———. "The Hall Family and Twentieth-Century Journalism in Alabama." *Alabama Review* 32 (April 1979): 119–40.

Hutchinson, Daniel. "'We . . . Are the Most Fortunate Prisoners': The Axis POW Experience at Camp Opelika during World War II." *Alabama Review* 64 (October 2011): 285–320.

Ichheiser, Gustav. "The Jews and Antisemitism." *Sociometry* 9 (February 1946): 92–108.

Ingalls, Robert P. "Antiradical Violence in Birmingham during the 1930s." *Journal of Southern History* 47 (November 1981): 521–44.

Karp, Abraham J. "A Century of Conservative Judaism in the United States." *American Jewish Yearbook* (1986): 3–61.

Kelley, Robin D. G. "'Comrades, Praise Gawd for Lenin and Them!': Ideology and Culture among Black Communists in Alabama, 1930–1935." *Science and Society* 52 (Spring 1988): 59–82.

———. "Resistance, Survival, and the Black Poor in Birmingham, Alabama, 1929–1970." Madison, WI: Institute for Research on Poverty Discussion Paper no. 950–91, 1991.

Kerem, Yitzchak. "The Settlement of Rhodian and Other Sephardic Jews in Montgomery and Atlanta in the Twentieth Century." *American Jewish History* 85 (December 1997): 373–91.

King, Richard H. "Reflections on Southern Intellectuals." *Southern Cultures* 1 (Spring 1995): 335–46.

Klarman, Michael J. "Scottsboro." University of Virginia Law School Public Law and Legal Theory Working Paper Series, Paper 17, 2005.

Knee, Stuart E. "Jewish Non-Zionism in America and Palestine Commitment, 1917–1941." *Jewish Social Studies* 39 (Summer 1977): 209–26.

Laqueur, Walter. "Zionism and Its Liberal Critics, 1896–1948." *Journal of Contemporary History* 6 (1971): 161–82.

Leff, Laurel. "'Liberated by the Yanks': The Holocaust as an American Story in Postwar News Articles." *Journal of Ecumenical Studies* 40 (Fall 2003): 407–30.

Mann, Erika, and Eric Estorick. "Private and Governmental Aid of Refugees." *Annals of the American Academy of Political and Social Science* 203 (May 1939): 142–54.

Mart, Michelle. "The 'Christianization' of Israel and Jews in 1950s America." *Religion and American Culture: A Journal of Interpretation* 14 (Winter 2004): 109–46.

Meyer, Harold D. "A Preview of Community Recreation." *Social Forces* 20 (March 1942): 357–63.

Norwood, Stephen H. "Legitimating Nazism: Harvard University and the Hitler Regime, 1933–1937." *American Jewish History* 92 (June 2004): 189–223.

Orbach, William. "Shattering the Shackles of Powerlessness: The Debate Surrounding the Anti-Nazi Boycott of 1933–41." *Modern Judaism* 2 (May 1982): 149–69.

Osborn, Frederick H. "Recreation, Welfare, and Morale of the American Soldier." *Annals of the American Academy of Political and Social Science* 220 (March 1942): 50–56.

Peck, Sarah E. "The Campaign for an American Response to the Nazi Holocaust, 1943–1945." *Journal of Contemporary History* 15 (April 1980): 367–400.

Penkower, Marty Noam. "The Genesis of the American Council for Judaism: A Quest for Identity in World War II." *American Jewish History* 86 (June 1998): 167–94.

Puckett, Dan J. "In the Shadow of Hitler: Birmingham's Temple Emanu-El and Nazism." *Southern Jewish History* 11 (2008): 1–39.

Robertson, Joseph T. "Fort McClellan's POW Camp, 1943–1946." *Alabama Review* 49 (October 1996): 276–91.

Robertson, Joseph T., and P. Wayne Findley. "Camp Sibert, Alabama's First Chemical Warfare Center, 1942–1945." *Alabama Review* 48 (January 1995): 3–15.

Rogoff, Leonard. "Is the Jew White?: The Racial Place of the Southern Jew." *American Jewish History* 85 (September 1997): 195–230.

Rudman, Floyd, Rüdiger M. Trimpop, Ilona-Patricia Kryl, and Pawel Boski. "Gustav Ichheiser in the History of Social Psychology: An Early Phenomenology of Social Attribution." *British Journal of Social Psychology* (1987): 165–80.

Shapiro, Edward S. "The Approach of War: Congressional Isolationism and Anti-Semitism, 1939–1941." *American Jewish History* (September 1984): 45–65.

Sheppard, Judith. "Mobile's Own Ozymandias: Ralph B. Chandler and His Newspapers." *Alabama Heritage* 51 (Winter 1999): 26–37.

Stanton, Mary. "At One with the Majority." *Southern Jewish History* 9 (2006): 141–99.

Strum, Harvey. "Jewish Internees in the American South, 1942–1945." *American Jewish Archives* 42 (1990): 27–48.

Szajkowski, Zosa. "Relief for German Jewry: Problems of American Involvement." *American Jewish History* (December 1972): 111–45.

Thomas, Mary Martha. "The Mobile Homefront during the Second World War." *Gulf Coast Historical Review* 1 (Fall 1985): 55–75.

Toll, William. "A Quiet Revolution: Jewish Women's Clubs and the Widening Female Sphere, 1870–1920." *American Jewish Archives* 41 (1989): 7–26.

Webb, Clive. "Jewish Merchants and Black Customers in the Age of Jim Crow." *Southern Jewish History* 2 (1999): 55–80.

Weissbach, Lee Shai. "East European Immigrants and the Image of Jews in the Small-Town South." *American Jewish History* 85 (September 1997): 231–62.

Williams, Aubrey. "The Government's Responsibility for Youth." *Annals of American Academy of Political and Social Science* 194 (November 1937): 119–28.

———. "The Work of the National Youth Administration." *Living* 1 (November 1939): 65–66.

Dissertations and Theses

Campbell, Kathryn H. "Sojourn of a Southern Liberal: The Life and Ministry of Charles R. Bell, Jr." Master's thesis, Auburn University, 1986.

Cannady, Lauren Elizabeth. "'*For Those Who Live in the Sun*': Holocaust Commemoration in the Southeastern United States." Master's thesis, Clemson University, 2011.

Crider, Robert F. "The Social Philosophy of L. L. Gwaltney, 1919–1950." Master's thesis, Samford University, 1969.

Greear, Wesley P. "American Immigration Policies and Public Opinion on European Jews from 1933 to 1945." Master's thesis, East Tennessee State University, 2002.

Mussleman, Paul LaFayette. "The Editorial Policy of the *Lee County Bulletin*, 1937–1951." Master's thesis, Alabama Polytechnic Institute, 1952.

Lippert, Amy Katherine DeFalco. "The Rationalization of Righteousness: Nazi Ideology, the Holocaust and the African-American Community in World War II." Honor's thesis, University of California, Berkeley, 2001.

Sprayberry, Gary S. "'Town among the Trees': Paternalism, Class, and Civil Rights in Anniston, Alabama, 1872 to Present." PhD diss., University of Alabama, 2003.

Wagnon, Judy. "Grover C. Hall, Jr.: Profile of a Writing Editor." Master's thesis, University of Alabama, 1975.

Whitten, Clinton William. "Alabama Editorial Opinion on American Entry into World War II, 1939–1942." Master's thesis, Auburn University, 1961.

Index

Abelson, Annie, 84
Abelson, Frank, 60, 76, 78, 83–84, 212, 221
Abelson, Isaac, 76, 80, 83–84, 97–98, 184, 209, 210, 212, 221
Abraham, Joseph, 44, 46
Adams, Oscar W., 20, 270–271n65
Adath Israel (Lexington, Kentucky), 86
Adler, James G., 35, 68
African Americans, 7–8, 9, 17, 19–22, 76, 81, 110, 114, 118, 120–124, 133, 141, 147, 150, 185–190, 200, 217, 222, 230; black press, 121–124, 128–129, 189, 270n62; view of Jews, 188–189
Agudath Israel (Montgomery), 12, 31, 32, 90, 102, 114, 143–147; Sisterhood, 32
Ahavas Chesed (Mobile), 1, 13, 26, 27, 34–35, 67, 68–69, 90, 101–102, 150, 163, 212, 223, Ladies Aid Society, 69
Alabama Baptist, 76, 115–117, 127
Alabama Bar Association, 14
Alabama College, 22
Alabama Department of Education, 232, 233
Alabama Fuel and Iron Company, 123
Alabama Holocaust Advisory Committee, 231, 232
Alabama Holocaust Commission, 18, 232, 291–292n26
Alabama National Guard, 120
Alabama Novelty Company, 83, 221
Alabama Polytechnic Institute (Auburn University), 43
Alabama River, 32
Alabama School of Trades, 53, 61–62, 250n47
Alabama Southern Baptist State Convention, 38–39, 76
Alabama Supreme Court, 199
Alabama Textbook Commission, 232
Albagli, Moses, 45, 248n17
Alexander, John, 38
Alexander City, 63
Aliceville Times, 118
Alien Registration Act (1940), 54
Alpha Epsilon Phi, 25
Altneuschule, 1
Altschukl, Harold, 89
America First Party, 192
American Council for Judaism (ACJ), 77, 92–93, 101, 102, 198, 206–208, 213–214
American Federation of Labor (AFL), 97
American Jewish Committee (AJC), 7, 35, 166, 223, 230
American Jewish Congress, 35
American Jewish Joint Distribution Committee (JDC), 28, 30, 34, 35, 48, 72, 73, 207, 215
American Legion, 36, 155; Lamar Y. McLeod Post (Mobile), 38
American National Conference against Racial Persecution in Germany, 26
American Promenade, 212, 288n23
American Seminar, 86–87
American Zionist Emergency Council, 95, 96, 97, 263–264n74
Andalusa Star, 20
Anglo-Saxon Federation of America, 195–197
Anne Frank: The Diary of a Young Girl, 228, 232
Anniston, Alabama, 62–63, 132–140, 141, 142, 148, 149, 155, 158, 192; Anniston Army and Navy Committee, 134, 138; Federal Recreation Center, 135–137, 140; Grude Kosher Kitchen, 139; holidays, 137, 138; observance

of *kashrut*, 138–140; as wartime boomtown, 138
Anniston Star, 190
Anschluss, 39, 72
Anti-Defamation League (ADL), 193, 195, 197
Antisemitism, 9, 11, 17–18, 19–21, 26, 40, 55, 59–60, 75, 99, 113, 115, 119–120, 154–155, 185–205, 284n32
Arab-Israeli War (1948–1949), 211
Arabs, 79, 95, 99, 210–211, 231; prisoners of war in Opelika, 211; support of Nazi war effort, 99–100, 211
Arfa, Cyrus, 83, 90
Arkansas, 77
Aron, Paul W., 148
Art-Craft Publishing, 200
Associated Press (AP), 105, 107, 109, 125
Atkins, David, 42
Atlanta, Georgia, 30, 31, 57, 133, 134, 137, 139; Federation of Jewish Charities, 30; Junior Hadassah, 136
Atlanta Constitution, 107
Atlantic City, New Jersey, 91
Attala, 61, 62
Auschwitz-Birkenau extermination camp, 98, 165
Austria, 39, 40, 41, 57, 72, 118, 165
Autauga County, 51
Autaugaville, Alabama, 51–52
Ayers, Harry M., 190

Bailes, George Lewis, 24–25
Balfour, Arthur James, 74
Balfour, J. Gilbert, 21
Balfour Declaration, 40, 74, 79
Bankhead, John H., Jr., 80–81, 83
Bankhead, John H., Sr., 81
Bankhead, William B., 80–82, 83
Baptists, 38; Fifth Baptist World Congress, 115–116; Southern Baptist Convention, 76, 115; Southern Baptists, 76, 115–117
Barke, Elmer, 119–120
Barkun, Michael, 196
Basel, Switzerland, 74, 76
Baum, Max, 52
Bauman, Mark K., 5, 33, 69
Baumhower, Charles A., 67
Bavaria, Germany, 32, 45
Bear, Joseph, 101, 102
Behrman, Beatrice, 207, 216, 218–219
Bendersky, Joseph, 204
Ben-Gurion, David, 209–210
Bergen-Belsen Concentration Camp, 127, 165
Berger, Hanna, 66
Berger, Hermann and Frieda, 66–67, 72, 175, 218
Berger-Phillips Department Store, 60
Berkowitz, Abe, 77, 94, 97–98, 99–100, 181, 212; Israeli Freedom Medal, 212; participation in the Sonnenborn Institute, 209–210
Berkowitz, Pauline, 70
Berkowitz, Sidney, 35, 68, 69–70, 71, 72, 103, 150–151, 180, 277–278n54
Berlin, Germany, 37, 86–87, 115–116
Berlin Institute for Jewish Studies, 153
Beshara, John J., 211
Biloxi, Mississippi, 71, 151
Birmingham, Alabama, 10, 11, 12, 16, 23, 24–25, 27, 29–31, 33, 35, 38, 50, 52, 55, 63, 74, 76–77, 78, 79–91, 94–101, 105, 118, 122–124, 132, 133, 134, 136–137, 149, 158–160, 164, 192–193, 195–198, 204, 206–214, 233; Birmingham Refugee Committee, 49, 57, 59, 61–62, 69, 197; Birmingham Refugee Committee, Women's Division, 57; cultural and religious differences of Birmingham's Jews, 13–15; Federation of Jewish Charities, 29, 243n47; Jewish Community Council, 197–198; Jewish population, 13, 239n42; Ladies Auxiliary of the Jewish War Veterans, 142, 158; number of Birmingham's Jews to serve in armed forces, 160, 204; refugee employment committee, 59; resettlement of DPs in Birmingham, 220–222, 289n53; resettlement of pre-war refugees, 56–61, 252n69, 253n75; United Jewish Fund, 29–30, 48, 49, 53, 57, 58–60, 78, 79, 85, 92, 196, 198, 204, 208, 213, 220, 221, 229; Young Judaean Club, 76, 84; Youth Aliyah, 84
Birmingham Air Base, 159
Birmingham Age-Herald, 20, 24, 41–42, 85, 106, 107–110, 111–112, 114, 117–118, 120, 127, 169–170, 182, 187, 210–211
Birmingham Baptist Association, 80
Birmingham Bar Association, 14

Birmingham Board of Education, 14
Birmingham Catholic Club, 28
Birmingham Chamber of Commerce, 14
Birmingham City Commission, 95, 97
Birmingham Community Chest, 14
Birmingham Country Club, 13
Birmingham Emergency Committee for Palestine, 95
Birmingham Holocaust Education Center (BHEC), 233
Birmingham Messenger, 21–22
Birmingham Methodist Layman's Club, 28
Birmingham News, 24, 41–43, 94, 96, 98, 99–100, 106, 108, 117–118, 120–121, 125–126, 127, 129, 187, 193, 220–221
Birmingham Pastors Union, 80
Birmingham Reporter, 20
Birmingham Rotary Club, 75
Birmingham Sunday School Council, 10
Birmingham World, 122, 124, 128–129, 171–172, 189
Birmingham Zion Association, 76, 84
Birmingham Zionist Organization, 77, 83, 99, 209, 211
Birnbry, Edmund, 56
Birnbry, Henry, 56–57, 161
Birnbry, Jenny, 57
Blachschleger, Eugene, 12, 13, 31, 65, 77, 102, 104, 132, 143–145, 148, 153, 177, 243–244n51
Black, Hugo L., 36, 245n69
Blanton, Sherry, 138
Bloom, Otto, 58
Bloom, William P., 22, 209
Blum, Roger N., 164, 281n99
Blumberg, Rebecca, 220
B'nai B'rith, 30, 35, 37, 43, 50, 66, 81–82, 144, 192; Beth Zur Lodge, 27, 68, 81, 96–97, 237n25; Walker County Lodge, 81
Boblasky, Harry, 161–162
Bolling, Alabama, 190
Bonfield, Barbara, 210
Boston, Massachusetts, 190
Botwinick, Rita Steinhardt, 10
Boykin, Frank, 97
Brandeis, Louis, 84
Brandon, William Woodward, 36
Breitman, Richard, 211
Brenners, Augustus, 187
Brickner, Bernard, 151
Brill, Henry, 63
British-Israelism, 196, 285n37
Brodsky, Joseph, 19
Brookley Army Air Field (Mobile, Alabama), 71, 150–151; Bates Field, 150; Air Material Command, 150
Brown, Herbert C., 35
Brown, Leo M., 35, 101, 102, 201, 206
Brumath, France, 164
Buchenwald Concentration Camp, 127, 163, 220
Bunche, Ralph, 188
Burnham, Louis, 188
Byrd, Sam, 229

Cadenhead, Van, 201
Calhoun County, Alabama, 135, 141
Cambridge University, 70
Cameron, William J., 196
Camp de Gurs, Basses Pyrenees, 46
Camp Kawaga, Wisconsin, 77
Camp Rucker, Alabama, 132, 146, 152–157, 202–203, 204; German POWs, 156; Ozark Triangular Division Camp, 152; Servicemen's Religious Council, 157
Camp Shelby, Mississippi, 133
Camp Sheridan, Alabama, 143
Camp Sibert, Alabama, 140–142, 158
Canada, 48
Caravan of Hope, 211–212
Carlson, John Roy (Avedis Boghos Derounian), 196
Carnegie Corporation, 188
Carter, Jimmy, 228, 231; Executive Order 12093, 228, 231
Cash, W. J., 8, 9
Cason, Clarence, 22
Catholic Church, 46, 151, 191–195; anti-Catholicism, 75, 76, 135, 145, 154–155, 191; motor missions, 191
Catholic Week, 115
Central Conference of American Rabbis (CCAR), 27, 28, 36, 74–75, 82, 90, 91; Columbus Platform, 90, 91; Committee on Social Justice, 28; Pittsburgh Platform, 75, 82, 91; Committee of Chaplains, 151
Central Missions of Alabama, 190

Central School of Religion, 89
Charleston, South Carolina, 229
Cherson Work Camp, Ukraine, 221
Chicago, Illinois, 41, 194, 197
Chicago Defender, 121
Christian Identity, 196, 284–285n52
Christian Veterans of America, 194
Church of the Visitation (Huntsville), 191
Cincinnati, Ohio, 70, 139, 218
Cincinnati Independent, 189
Civil War, 32
Clanton, Alabama, 195
Clark, Leigh M., 199
Clarke County Democrat, 117, 130
Classe Ribbon Works, 63
Cleveland, Ohio, 194
Cohen, Beth, 215, 219
Cohen, Nace, 207
Cohen, Ralph, 31
Cohn, Seymore, 220
Cold War, 226–227
Coleman, James, 127
Coleman, W. S., 135
Columbiana, Alabama, 12
Commission on Interracial Cooperation (CIC), 20
Committee on Displaced German Scholars, 188
Communism, 19, 21, 22, 23–24, 25, 115, 117, 186, 187–188, 194, 227
Confessions of a Nazi Spy (1939), 119–120
Congressional Record, 114
Congress of Industrial Organizations (CIO), 123
Cooper, Jerome "Buddy", 166, 220, 223
Coughlin, Charles Edward, 135, 191–192, 200, 202
Cowett, Mark, 24, 82–83
Craig Army Air Field (Selma, Alabama), 66, 146, 148–149
Crisis, 123, 188
Crommelin, John G., 195, 205, 230
Crossley, John, 44
Czech Memorial Scrolls Trust, 1, 235n1
Czechoslovakia, 1, 39, 41, 118

Dachau Concentration Camp, 127, 163
Daugette, Clarence W., 136
Davis, Neil O., 106
Days of Remembrance, 231, 232
D-Day, 57
Dearborn Independent, 196
DeBardeleben, Charles, 122–123
DeBardeleben Coal Company, 14, 190
Decatur, Alabama, 20–21
Denver, Colorado, 80
Der Judenstaat (1896), 74
Der Stürmer, 193
Dickenson, Alfred J., 39
Diner, Hasia, 228–230
Dinnerstein, Leonard, 5, 185, 203, 204–205
Displaced Persons (DPs), 18, 206, 212, 214–222, 229; psychological problems of adjustment, 218–219
Dixiecrat Party, 200
Dixon, Frank M., 36, 199–200
Dos Passos, John, 71
Dothan, Alabama, 10, 132, 146, 148, 152–157; Dothan Army and Navy Committee, 153, 155–156
Dothan Eagle, 126–127
Dothan Recreational Center, 154, 157; Victory Belles, 157
Doylestown, Pennsylvania, 43
Drake, Robert, 105
Drum, Leo, 33, 77
Durr, Clifford and Virginia, 186–187
Durr, Robert, 122–124, 129

Eberbach, Germany, 153
Eddy, George Sherwood, 86, 260–261n45
Egelson, Louis I., 152
Ehrenreich, Bernard C., 77, 143, 147
Eichhold, Bernard, 69, 101, 150–151
Eichmann Trial, 227, 228, 231
Eichmann, Adolf, 225, 226
Eisendrath, Maurice, 209
Eldridge, Elizabeth, 25
Eleazer, Robert Burns, 20
Elgart, Saul S., 155–157
Ellis, Elmo (Elmo Israel), 11, 239n35
Elovitz, Mark, 12, 29, 59, 85, 89, 92, 210
Enemy Aliens, 54–55, 72; Enemy Alien Internment Program, 55
Engel, Irving M., 11, 145, 208, 230, 238–239n34

Engel, Marvin, 214
Engel, William P., 58, 79, 80, 208, 213
Engelberg, Louis, 142
England. *See* Great Britain
Enterprise, Alabama, 152, 154
Eppstein, Arthur, 35
Erlick, Bertha, 213
Etz Ahayem, 31, 45, 102, 143–144, 147
Evans, Eli, 5, 13, 103
Evansville Packing Company, 49

Fair Employment Practices Committee (FEPC), 110, 128, 172, 185
Fairmont Club (Birmingham), 13
Federal Bureau of Investigation (FBI), 54–55, 119, 210
Federal Security Agency (FSA), 140–141, 154
Federation of American Zionists, 76, 77
Feidelson, Charles N., Sr., 20, 85, 94, 95, 98, 100–101, 108, 121, 127–128, 173, 187, 192, 265–266n93, 281nn6–7
Feldman, Glenn, 11, 21, 120
Ferris, Marcie Cohen, 5, 139
Fies, Jacob, 81
Fies, Milton, 14, 81, 92, 190, 214
Fifteenth Amendment, 186
Fifth Column, fear of, 54
Final Solution. *See* Holocaust
Fineberg, Abba M., 63, 133–134, 136–139, 202
First Amendment, 194
First Baptist Church of Mobile, 39
First Christian Church (Birmingham), 80
First Presbyterian Church (Birmingham), 195–196
Fisher, Ida Newman, 38
Florence, Alabama, 51
Flynt, Wayne, 76
Ford, Henry, 113, 196
For Those Who Live in the Sun (1950), 229
Fort McClellan, Alabama, 62, 63, 93, 132–134, 136–139, 142, 158, 202–203; Basic Immaterial Replacement Training Center, 133; Infantry Replacement Training Center, 133; New York National Guard, 27th Infantry Division, 134, 137
Foster, Henry B., 21–22
Fourteenth Amendment, 186
Fowlkes, William A., 128–129
France, 123
Freibaum, Lee, 63, 141
Friedman, Karl, 221
Friend, Edward M., Jr., 166, 223

Gadsden, Alabama, 10, 38, 53, 61–62, 133, 137, 140–142, 253–254n79; Gadsden Refugee Committee, 61; JWB Women's Committee, 142; observance of *kashrut*, 142; Soldier Service Center, 140–141; Travelers Aid Troop Transit Lounge, 141; as wartime boomtown, 140–141
Gadsden Ordinance Plant, 140
Galveston, Texas, 50
Galveston Movement, 49–50
Gelders, Joseph, 24–25
German-Jewish Children's Aid (GJCA), 56–57, 161, 251n60
Gestapo, 37, 127
Gillette-Rogers Resolution (1944), 97–98, 264–265n83
Glazer, Nathan, 226
Goda, Norman, 211
Goebbels, Joseph, 37, 162, 192
Goldberg, Fannie Newman, 85, 88
Goldberg, Joseph, 95
Golden, Harry, 5, 9, 229, 237n26
Goldfield, David, 8
Goldman, Godfrey, 198–199, 200
Goldman, Solomon, 80, 83, 84
Goldman v. Hicks, 198–199, 202
Goldstein, Benjamin, 22–24, 28, 31, 110, 186, 187
Goldstein, Eric L., 6
Göring, Herman, 55
Government Street Temple. *See* Sha'arai Shomayim
Grafman, Milton L., 85–91, 103–104, 166, 174, 193, 208, 212, 213; conflict with Charles Feidelson, 100–101, 265–266n93; European trip, 86–88; World War II, 142, 158–161, 272–273n9; Zionism, 83, 88, 90–91, 92, 93–97, 264n75. *Serviceman*, 159–161
Grand Hotel, 200–202
Graves, David Bibb, 36, 38, 200
Graves, John Temple II, 96, 114, 123–124, 185–186

Great Britain, 16, 40, 41, 63, 65, 70, 74, 99, 103; British Colonial Office, 79; British Labour Party, 78; White Paper (1938), 79–82, 95, 96–98, 190
Great Depression, 41, 71, 190
Green, Cooper, 97, 212
Greenberg, Mark I., 5
Greene County Democrat, 127
Grude, Anna, 139
Gruneberg, Joseph, 63
Grynszpan, Herschel, 37
Gunter, William A., 23, 143
Gunter Field (Montgomery, Alabama), 65, 143–144, 146, 148, 158, 177; Municipal Basic Flying Field, 143
Gup, Samuel M., 212, 213
Gwaltney, L. L., 38, 76, 115–117, 127
Gypsies, 163

Haber, William, 47, 52
Haberman, Joshua O., 72
Hadassah, 30, 68, 72, 77, 83, 84, 101, 102–103, 144, 207, 144, 158; Junior Hadassah, 30, 136, 146, 158
Haganah, 209–210
Hagedorn, Amelia, 44
Hagedorn, Joseph, 44–45
Hagedorn, Julius S., 44–45
Hagedorn, Merlin, 141–142
Hagen, Germany, 63
Hall, Grover Cleveland, Sr., 24, 51, 64, 106, 185, 199; "The Egregious Gentile," 112–115, 117, 120; Grover Cleveland Hall Memorial Award, 114, 120
Hammel's Department Store, 70, 189
Hanson, Victor, 108
Harwell, Hoyt Horace, 38
Hebrew Immigrant Aid Society, 35
Hebrew Theological College, 89
Hebrew Union College, 70, 72, 86, 90, 101, 153, 218
Hebron Yeshiva, 89
Helmreich, William B., 219
Henry Harris's Delicatessen, 139
Hernfeld, Harry, 63
Herzl, Theodore, 74
Hess, Emile Carl, 204–205, 223
Heydrich, Reinhard, 55
Hicks, Lorraine, 198–199
Hicks, Madge Hardy, 198–199
Hicks, William H., 198–199
Highland Avenue Baptist Church (Montgomery), 116
Hilberg, Raul, 226
Hill, Lister, 45–46, 97, 114, 143, 164, 248n18
Hillcrest Club (Birmingham), 12, 13
Hillel Foundation, 43, 46, 86, 159
Himmler, Heinrich, 55, 123
Hindenburg, Paul von, 107
Hirsch, Jeanette, 164
Hirsch, Jimmy, 164
Hitler, Adolf, 1, 2, 7, 8, 15, 17, 18, 19, 28, 36, 37, 38, 44, 54, 55, 67, 71, 74, 84, 85, 93, 94, 96–97, 99, 107–109, 113, 115–117, 127, 128, 131, 152, 165, 185–186, 194–195, 210–211, 230
Hogarty, Alexander, 155
Hollis, Daniel, 114
Hollywood, California, 76, 119, 192
Holocaust, 1, 2, 3, 130, 162–164, 215; Final Solution, 1–2, 15, 17, 18, 55–56, 73, 85, 90, 92–99, 109, 123, 125–129, 130, 160–161, 163, 164, 209, 214, 222, 225; Holocaust denial, 185, 193–194; liberation of the camps, 126–128
Holocaust, The (1978), 225, 227, 231, 232, 290n11
Hoover, J. Edgar, 210
Horton, James E., Jr., 240n5
Huie, William Bradford, 25–26
Hull, Cordell, 79, 80–81
Hungary, Hungarian Jews, 98–99
Huntingdon College, 23, 31
Huntsville, Alabama, 46, 191
Husseini, Haj Amin al-, Grand Mufti of Jerusalem, 211

Immigration, 40–42, 78, 98–99, 125; immigration quotas, 40–41, 103; visa application process, 46–47
Indianapolis, Indiana, 34
Industrial Removal Office (IRO), 49–50
Institute on Judaism for Christian Clergy, 88
International Convention of the Disciples of Christ, 80
International Day of Prayer for the Jews in Palestine, 94

International Labor Defense (ILD), 19–22, 23, 43, 120
Isom, John B., 142
Israel, 3, 16, 18, 61, 75, 76, 83, 206–207, 212, 215, 224, 227–228, 230; establishment of state of Israel, 209–213, 223, 226
Israelsohn, Rosalie Hagedorn, 44–45

Jackson, Emory O., 122, 124
Jackson, Robert H., 194
Jacksonville, Alabama, 137
Jacksonville State Teachers College, 136
Japanese, 55, 131, 191
Jarman, Pete, 97
Jarvis, Reynolds Fletcher, 62
Jasper, Alabama, 42, 52, 80, 81
Jefferson County, Alabama, 24
Jefferson County Commission, 95
Jenkins, John, 63
Jerusalem, Israel, 226
Jewish Agency for Palestine, 209
Jewish Federated Charities (Tuscaloosa), 43
Jewish Foundation for the Righteous, 232
Jewish Immigrants' Information Bureau, 50
Jewish Institute of Religion, 23
Jewish National Fund, 212
Jewish Progress Club (Montgomery), 215
Jewish Progressive Club (Mobile), 35, 47, 101, 150–151
Jewish Welfare Board (JWB), 3, 17, 63, 132, 153; Anniston, 133–140; Birmingham, 158–159; Bureau of War Records (BWR), 160, 204; Dothan, 153–157; Gadsden, 140–142; Jewish Welfare Home, 143; Mobile, 151–152; Montgomery, 143–148; National JWB Committee on Army and Navy Religious Activities, 153; Selma, 149–150
Jewish Welfare Fund (Memphis), 30
Jews: Alabama Jewish population, 10, 235n6, 238n32; Central European Jews, 2–4, 9, 12–15, 19, 25–26, 29, 65, 74, 140, 143, 166, 213, 215; cultural differences between Jewish sub-communities, 3–4, 12–13, 25–26, 31–33, 35, 60–61, 65, 68, 72–73, 103, 108, 147–148, 151–152, 166, 209, 215–216; Eastern European Jews, 3, 4, 9, 11–15, 19, 25–26, 29–33, 65, 74, 76–77, 78, 83–85, 88, 90, 92, 102–103, 143, 166, 206, 213, 215; Reform Jews desire to acculturate, 16, 75, 84, 108; regional distinctiveness, 5–8, 236n11; Sephardim, 4, 12, 15, 25–26, 31–33, 45, 65, 78, 85, 103, 143, 213
Jim Crow, 6–8, 16, 17, 107, 110, 111, 118, 121, 123–124, 129, 130, 187, 215, 217, 222, 230
Jones, Jimmie, 38

Kahl Montgomery. *See* Temple Beth-Or
Kahn Manufacturing Company, 69
Kahn, Ben, 61
Kahn, Herbert, 156
Kahn, Julius, 67
Kahn, Sol, 35, 44, 69, 101, 206
Kandel, Monte, 69, 70
Kanter, Joe, 220–221
Kaplan, Robert, 12
Kappa Nu, 26
Kashrut, 133, 274n23, 274–275n26
Kaufman, Beatrice, 23, 48
Kaufman, Louis, 23
Kayser, Sam, 131, 132, 162–163
Keesler Field, 71
Kelley, Robin D. G., 24
Kilby Prison, 23
Kimerling, Max, 210, 212
Kimerling, Tillie, 210, 212, 220
Kirsch, Bill, 161
Klein, Alex, 38
Klein, Margaret, 135
Klein, Milton, 163, 223
K'nesseth Israel, 13, 14, 29, 30, 31, 38, 83, 85, 89, 95, 204, 208; Ladies Auxiliary, 158
Koch, Lawrence, 208
Kohn, Jacob, 32
Kohs, Samuel C., 48
Kolsky, Thomas A., 91
Korn, Bertram Wallace, 72, 96, 101–103, 151, 180
Kraft, Louis, 141
Krammer, Arnold, 54
Kristallnacht. *See* Nazi/Nazi Germany
Kronenfeld, Morris D., 134, 136, 139, 142
Ku Klux Klan, 11–12, 19–21, 23, 24, 75, 106, 109, 113, 117, 120, 129, 176, 190, 199–200, 205
Kulick, Milton D., 151

Lake Kawaguesaga, Wisconsin, 77
League of Nations, 78
Lee County Bulletin, 106
Leek, Charles F., 116–117
Leff, Laurel, 106, 107, 108, 128
LeFlore, John L., 189
Lehman Brothers, Henry, Emanuel, Mayer, 32
Leibowitz, Samuel, 19–20
Lelyveld, Joseph, 19
Lerer, Samuel S., 32, 102–103
Levey, Samson H., 93, 149
Levin, David, 220
Levinson, Peter, 218–219
Lewisohn, Ludwig, 84, 94
Lewy, Ludwig and Dora, 67
Lexington, Kentucky, 86
Lief, Joseph H., 138
Linenthal, Edward T., 231
Linnick, Jake, 35
Lipstadt, Deborah, 106, 107, 118, 120–121, 130
Lithuania, 90
Livingston, J. Edwin, 199
Lobman, Bernard, 216–217
Lobman, Myron, 145, 147
Lobman, Walter, 33, 49, 52, 64
Lockhart, J. B., 42
Locust, Paul, 119–120
Loeb, Herman, Jr., 163–164, 223
Loeb, Herman, Sr., 44, 45
Loeb, Lucien, 50, 51–53
Loeb, Robert, 223
Loew, Elsa and Sofie, 46
Los Angeles, California, 119
Louisiana, 77
Louisville, Kentucky, 58
Loveman, Joseph, 80, 92, 190
Lowenstein, Aaron, 35
Lowi, Theodore, 75
Ludwigslust Work Camp, 163–164
Lynching, 20, 21–22, 120, 129

Malone, J. E., 188–189
Manasse, Moritz and Bertha, 45
Marcus, Marks "Bubba", 164–165
Mardi Gras, 13
Marianna, Florida, 152, 155
Marianna Army Air Field, Florida, 152
Marion Times-Standard, 21
Marlowe, Harold, 165–166
Marseilles, France, 46
Marshuetz, Joseph, 218
Marx, Karl, 115
Mauthausen Concentration Camp, 162–163
Maxwell Army Air Field (Montgomery, Alabama), 65, 143–144, 146, 148, 158, 177
May, Ben, 36, 70
May, Paul, 69, 70, 101
Mayer, Ernest, 27
Mayer, Malvin, 162
Mazer, Isadore, 210
Meadows, Ruth, 44
Megginson, Ernest, 212
Mein Kampf, 37, 122
Memphis, Tennessee, 30
Mencken, H. L., 113
Mesch, Abraham, 89–90, 93, 95, 142, 158, 212
Meyers, Albert, 216
Millennialism, 75
Miller, Benjamin M., 26
Milwaukee, Wisconsin, 28
Minda, Alfred, 86
Minneapolis, Minnesota, 86
Mistovsky, Israel H., 157
Mitchell, Reba, 69
Mobile, Alabama, 4, 10, 11, 13, 15, 16, 19, 25, 26–27, 34–37, 38, 44, 47, 53, 105, 189, 191, 200–201, 206, 213; Hadassah, 101; Jewish population, 245n63; Ladies Hebrew Benevolent Association, 34; Mobile Federation of Jewish Charities, 27, 35, 36; Mobile JDC, 27, 35, 37, 67, 68, 242n36; Mobile Jewish Federation, 67, 201; Mobile JWB Army and Navy Committee, 151; Mobile Refugee Committee, 51; Mobile Resettlement Agency, 68–71; Mobile ZOA, 101; Orthodox Federation of Jewish Charities, 34; Philanthropic Committee of the Council for Jewish Women, 34; resettlement of pre-war refugees, 67–72; United Hebrew Charities, 34; USO Club for Soldiers, 151; USO Women's Club, 151; World War II, 131, 150–152, 161, 162–163; Young Judaean Club, 101; Zionism in Mobile, 74, 76, 90, 96–97, 101–104

Mobile Central Trades Council, 97
Mobile City Commission, 26
Mobile Country Club, 34–35
Mobile County, 71
Mobile County Federation of Women's Clubs, 38
Mobile Register, 109, 110, 117
Monsky, Harry, 192
Monsky, Leroy, 166
Montevallo, Alabama, 22
Montgomery, Alabama, 10–12, 15, 22–24, 25, 27, 31–34, 35, 45, 48–51, 53, 61, 105, 112–114, 116, 195, 206–207, 231; entertaining soldiers at Oak Park, 145, 178; Hadassah, 102–103, 144, 207; Hebrew Ladies Benevolent Society, 33, 144; Hospital Visitation Committee, 146; intermarriage, 33; Jewish Federation of Montgomery, 27, 34, 45, 48, 49, 52, 63–65, 79, 97, 102, 144, 165, 207, 218, 242n38, 254n87; Jewish population, 31, 244n52; JWB Council, 144–145, 147, 149; Montgomery Coordinating Committee, 63, 64; Montgomery Refugee Committee, 65, 69; Montgomery ZOA, 102; Public Relations Committee, 195; resettlement of DPs in Montgomery, 215–218, 222; resettlement of pre-war refugees, 63–65; United Hebrew Charities, 33; World War II, 143–148, 149, 153, 161; YMCA-USO Soldiers Center, 145; Zionism in Montgomery, 74, 76, 77–78, 90, 96, 101–104
Montgomery Advertiser, 24, 64, 96, 106, 112–115, 117, 120, 126, 195, 199
Montgomery Country Club, 12
Montgomery County, 31
Montgomery Ministerial Association, 27, 31
Montor, Henry, 209–210
Moore, Deborah Dash, 133, 139, 166, 223
Mordecai, Abraham, 31
Mordecai, Trevor P., 195–198
Morgan County, Alabama, 20–21
Morgenstern, Julian, 70, 153, 257n116
Moritz, Charles, 23
Moses, Alfred Geiger, 35, 38, 68, 70, 104, 256n105
Moses, Mordecai, 32
Mudd, Joseph, 99
Mud on the Stars, 25
Munich Conference (1938), 39, 164
Murphy High School (Mobile), 213

Napier Army Air Field (Dothan, Alabama), 152, 156
Naples, Italy, 165
Nashville, Tennessee, 48
Nason, Nathaniel, 135, 137, 141
National Association for the Advancement of Colored People (NAACP), 123, 188–189
National Catholic Community Service (NCCS), 132, 135, 145–146, 151, 154–155, 157
National Committee for the Defense of Political Prisoners (NCDPP), 24
National Conference on Christians and Jews (NCCJ), 88, 193, 204, 231, 283n26
National Coordinating Committee for Aid to Refugees Coming from Germany (NCC), 16, 34, 48, 57, 72; origins, 48–49; Resettlement Division, 48, 50
National Council for Young Israel, 138–139, 274n21
National Council of Jewish Women (NCJW), 48, 69; Birmingham section, 56, 158, 161; Mobile section, 47, 67, 68, 69, 72; Montgomery section, 32, 144, 148, 207, 218; Selma section, 149; Service for the Foreign Born, 214
National Farm School, 43
National Labor Committee for Palestine, 30
National Opinion Research Center, 41
National Refugee Service (NRS), 16, 34, 43, 47, 48–51, 52–53, 56, 57–60, 62–66, 69, 70, 188, 214, 218; friction between local and national groups, 52–53, 59; resettlement process, 47; Social and Cultural Adjustment Division, 50
National Travelers Aid Association, 132, 141
National Youth Administration (NYA), 53, 61–62
Nazi/Nazi Germany, 1, 2, 15, 16, 48, 49, 54, 74, 78, 131; African Americans' views of Nazism, 122–124, 128–129, 189, 270n62; anti-Nazi boycott, 37, 168, 246n73; Aryan supremacy, 7, 107, 111; Baptists support of Nazis, 115–117, 268n38; effect on Zionism, 77, 82–85, 92, 94, 103, 211, 263–264n74; *Ein-*

satzgruppen, 55, 111; German Consul General, 119; *Kristallnacht*, 15, 37–39, 41–43, 45, 56, 63, 68, 72, 83, 105, 112–113, 117–118; Jewish soldiers' view of Nazism, 160–166; Nazi view of blacks, 121–123, 267n8, 269–270n62; Nuremberg Laws, 111; Operation Barbarossa, 55, 121; persecution of European Jews, 3, 15, 17, 19, 86–88; policy of forced emigration, 40–41, 55; press's perception of Nazism, 105–110; reactions to Jewish persecution, 26–39, 40–41, 42, 44, 45, 56–57, 69, 72, 75, 82, 222, 230; spread of antisemitism in the United States, 18, 59–60, 112–114, 119–120, 185, 188; SD (*Sicherheitsdienst*), 37; SS (*Schutzstaffel*), 37, 127, 211; Stalag Luft IV, 165. *See also* Holocaust
Newberger, John, 61
New Deal, 191, 194
Newfield, Mayer, 83
Newfield, Morris, 27–28, 29, 31, 77, 79–80, 85, 86, 103–104, 253n74; racial issues, 24, 28, 187; spokesman for Birmingham's Jews, 13–14, 30; Zionism, 82–83, 88
Newfield, Seymon, 92
New Orleans, Louisiana, 200, 217
Newsome, John, 97
New York, 4–5, 23–25, 32, 40, 43, 44, 48–50, 52, 53, 56, 62–64, 66, 67, 79–80, 96, 98, 108, 134, 138, 139, 145, 156, 191, 197, 209–210, 215, 217, 219, 222
New York Times, 36, 105, 107, 108, 128
Niagara Falls, New York, 133
Nice, France, 65
Niren, Norman, 12, 161
Nobel Prize, 99
Normandy, France, 57
North Alabama Network, 191
North Carolina, 105, 187
Novick, Peter, 127, 226–228
Nuremberg Trials, 17, 110–111, 129–130
Nyons, France, 164

Oberdorfer, Leo, 14, 80, 92, 198
Oberstein, Elchonon, 32
Olmert, Ehud, 212
Omicron Delta Kappa (ODK), 43, 46
Opelika, Alabama, 44–45, 211
Opelika Kiwanis Club, 44
Opelika POW Camp, 211
Organization for Rehabilitation and Training (ORT), 72, 89
Ottoman Empire, 74, 78
Ozark, Alabama, 152, 154

Paassen, Pierre Van, 99–100
Palestine, 3, 16, 27, 29, 34, 39–42, 73–75, 78–85, 125, 166, 207, 209–211, 214, 220; British Mandate for Palestine, 78–80, 82, 126, 210; Jewish immigration totals, 78
Panama City, Florida, 152, 155
Paris, France, 36, 37
Parisians Department Store, 60
Patterson, Frederick D., 188, 190
Patterson, Haywood, 20
Patton, George S., 164
Pearl Harbor, Hawaii, 46, 85, 131, 138, 143, 191
Pearson, Abe, 68
Pearson, E. H., 51–52
Peebles, E. B., 201
Penkower, Monty Noam, 92
Phillips High School (Birmingham), 221
Pi Tau Pi, 57
Picon, Molly, 157
Pittsburgh, Pennsylvania, 86
Pittsburgh Courier, 121, 167
Pizitz, Isadore, 15, 53, 58, 59
Pizitz, Louis, 14, 190
Pizitz Department Store, 60
PM Magazine, 191
Point Clear, Alabama, 200
Poland, 32, 89, 90, 120, 165, 218
Posey, J. F., 51
Powell, Lawrence, 217
President's Commission on the Holocaust, 228, 231
Prigmore, Charles S., 231
Prince, Arthur, 26, 161, 163, 223
Pritchard National Bank, 201
Production Code Administration (PCA), 119
Progressive Club (Mobile), 13
Prohibition, 33
Proskauer, Hans, 72

Protocols of the Elders of Zion, 192, 196
Pulitzer Prize, 106, 199

Racial Issues, 147; poll tax, 99, 187; similarities between Nazi and southern racism, 109, 110–112, 114, 129, 171, 186, 222, 230; southern white supremacy, 6–8, 17, 99, 107, 111, 124, 129, 187, 200; white reaction to black civil rights, 186
Radoms, Joe, 85
Rank, Jeanette, 204
Rasmussen, Donald and Laura, 188
Rath, Ernst vom, 37
Reconstruction, 32
Red Cross, 48, 72, 131
Refugees, 15, 169, 190, 206; Alabama State Coordinating Committee, 50, 52–53, 59, 61, 62, 69, 134; German Jewish refugee scholars at black colleges, 187–188
Rheydt, Germany, 162
Rhodes, 31, 32
Rimson, Ike, 153
Ripps, Sam J., 35, 101
Rittenbaum, Alex, 211, 212, 221
Rittenbaum, Sol, 212, 221
Roberts, Edward A., 201
Robinson, Edward G. (Emanuel Goldenberg), 119
Rogoff, Leonard, 6
Romania, 163
Roosevelt, Eleanor, 194
Roosevelt, Franklin D., 2, 27, 36–38, 53, 54, 71, 80, 82, 98, 103, 191; Executive Order 9106, 55; Presidential Proclamation 2526, 54
Rosenberg, Ethel and Julius, 227
Rosenberg, Jerome, 232
Rosenberg, Murray, 141–142
Rosenbush, Bert and Mary Louise, 183
Roth, Benjamin A., 29, 58–59, 136, 158, 180
Roth, Dora Landau, 29, 58–59, 61, 160, 180, 204, 208, 212, 220, 252n67
Rothschild, Lionel Walter, 74
Rothschild, Myron, 144
Rowno, Poland, 221
Rund, Jeanette, 137
Rund, Margaret Alabama Bond, 137
Rund, Samuel Issac, 137
Rural Justice, 191, 194–195
Russia, 55, 60, 72, 83, 127, 165, 227

Sacred Heart Church (Anniston), 192
Salvation Army, 132
San Remo Conference (1920), 79
Sarna, Jonathan, 9, 11, 200
Schniper, Chaim and Chana, 221
Schniper's Dry Goods, 221
Schulwolf, Lena, 147
Schwarz, Leon, 19, 26, 35–36, 38, 68, 81, 179, 200, 245n69
Scottsboro Trials, 8, 10, 17, 19–21, 23–26, 28, 110, 185, 187, 240n4
Sears Roebuck, 44
Seattle, Washington, 82
Sedlin, Elias, 213
Selb, Germany, 221
Selective Training and Service Act (1940), 72, 133
Selma, Alabama, 10, 65–67, 72, 146, 148–150; Army and Navy Committee, 149; JWB Committee, 149; Refugee Committee, 66; resettlement of DPs, 218–220, 222; Selma-Dallas County Defense Recreation Committee, 148; YMCA Soldiers Center, 149
Sha'arai Shomayim (Mobile), 13, 19, 26, 27, 34–37, 38, 67–68, 69–70, 72, 96, 101–102, 150–151, 163, 212, 213
Shanghai, China, 67
Shapiro, Aaron, 212
Shapiro, Edward S., 226
Shapiro, Isadore, 11
Sheffield, Alabama, 10, 82
Shelton, Bruce, 43, 51, 119–120
Sherman, Eliot, 212
Sherwin, Byron L., 77
Shugerman, Harry P., 80
Silverman, Myron, 75
Simon, Hannah, 218
Simpson, James A., 94
Six-Day War (1967), 225, 226, 227
Slater, Leonard, 209
Smith, Alfred E., 98
Smith, Gerald L. K., 192, 194

Smyer, Sid, 94
Social Justice, 191, 202
Solomon, Marjorie, 59
Sonnenborn, Rudolf G., 209–210
Sonnenborn Institute, 209–210
Southern Commission of the Study of Lynching, 22
Southern Conference for Human Welfare (SCHW), 118
Southern Jewish Times, 110
Southern liberals, 123–124, 186–187; policy of Gradualism, 186
Southern Negro Youth Congress, 188
Southern Outlook, 195, 200, 205
Southern Watchman, 187
Soviet Union. *See* Russia
Spanish-American War, 36
Sparkman, John, 46, 82, 97
Sparks, Chauncey, 99
Sperling, Isadore, 211
Spielberg, Steven, 228
Standard Club (Montgomery), 12, 13, 145–146, 149, 215, 276–277n44
Stanton, Mary, 32
Steelman, John R., 22
Steiner, Bernard, 213
Steiner, Leo, 80
Stern, Arnold, 44–45
Stern, Hedwig, 44–45
Stern, Henry (Heinz), 44–45
Stern, Lora (Hannalora), 44–45
Stern, Morris, 101
Sterne, Carrie, 62, 135
Sterne, Leon A., 62, 135, 141
Sterne, Mervyn H., 14, 52–53, 59, 63, 80, 92
Sterne, Mortimer C., 62, 134, 135, 139, 141
St. Mary's Episcopal Church (Birmingham), 186
Stone, Olive, 23
Stoner, J. B., 230
Strauss, Bernie, 70, 189
Straussburger, Leo, 23
Streicher, Julius, 193
St. Teresa's Village, 190
Sulzberger, Arthur Hayes, 108
Swedlaw, Alfred, 166
Switzerland, 211
Sznur, Clara, 218–219
Sznur, Joseph, 218–219

Talladega College, 187–188
Talladega, Alabama, 42, 137, 187–188
Tallahassee, Florida, 155
Tallapoosa Sharecropper's Union, 23
Talmud Torah (Louisville, Kentucky), 58
Tarrant, Alabama, 220
Tasgal, Maxwell H., 145–149
Tau Gamma Nu, 146
Taylor, R. V., 26
Taylor Field (Montgomery, Alabama), 143
Teitelbaum, Samuel, 93, 138
Telz-Stone, Israel, 212
Temple Beth-El (Anniston), 63, 133–134, 138
Temple Beth-El (Bessemer), 158
Temple Beth-El (Birmingham), 13, 14, 29–31, 83–85, 88–90, 93, 95, 161, 208, 214; Beth-El Forum, 89; Junior Congregation, 89; Sisterhood, 89, 158; transition to Conservative movement, 89, 262n52
Temple Beth Israel (Gadsden), 62, 141–142
Temple Beth-Or (Montgomery), 12, 22–23, 27, 28, 31–33, 45, 65, 77, 102, 114, 143–147, 163, 165, 178, 207; Kahl Montgomery Religious School, 23
Temple B'nai Israel (Florence), 93
Temple Emanu-El (Birmingham), 11, 13–15, 24, 27, 29–31, 60, 75, 83, 85–86, 88, 89–90, 93, 95, 100–101, 103, 108, 161–162, 164, 165, 190, 193, 197, 213–214; Sisterhood, 158, 160
Temple Emanu-El (Dothan), 152–153, 156–157
Temple Emanu-El (Tuscaloosa), 43
Temple for Reform Judaism (Birmingham), 214
Temple Mishkan Israel (Selma), 66, 93, 149, 218
Tennessee Coal and Iron Company (TCI), 24
Terman, Isaiah, 166
Terminiello, Arthur W., 155, 190–195, 197, 198, 200, 205
Terminiello v. Chicago, 194
Terre Haute, Indiana, 70
The Crusader, 192–195
Tikwath Zion, 76, 84
Tollison, Louise, 44
Toolen, Thomas J., 38, 191–193, 195
Transylvania College, 86

Travin, Saul, 218
Troy, Alabama, 191
Truman, Harry S., 215
Turrou, Leon G., 119
Tuscaloosa, Alabama, 10, 21–22, 25, 51, 59, 98, 114, 119–120, 158, 209; Jewish Federated Charities of Tuscaloosa, 43
Tuscaloosa News, 22, 43, 119–120
Tuskegee Institute, 188, 190
Tutwiler Hotel, 94, 212
Tydings, Millard, 36
Tyndall Army Air Field (Panama City, Florida), 152

Ullman, Samuel, 14
Under Cover (1943), 196
Union of American Hebrew Congregations, 152, 209
Union of Christian Crusaders, 192–194, 195, 197
United Jewish Appeal (UJA), 30, 48, 72, 209, 212, 215, 220–221
United Nations (UN), 210, 220–221
United Negro College Fund (UNCF), 190
United Palestine Appeal (UPA), 72, 73, 78, 102, 207
United Press (UP), 105
United Service for New Americans (USNA), 214–221
United Service Organizations (USO), 3, 17, 63, 72, 131–132; Anniston, 133–137, 140; Birmingham, 158–159; Dothan, 154–157; Federal Recreation Center in Anniston, 135–137, 140; Gadsden, 141; "V" (Victory) Girls, 136–137; Mobile, 151; Montgomery, 144–148; Selma, 148–149
United States Army: Third Army, 164; 30th Infantry Division, 57; 82nd Airborne, 163; 88th Infantry Division, 162; 92nd Infantry Division, 133
United States Government Printing Office, 114
United States Holocaust Memorial Council, 231–232
United States Holocaust Memorial Museum, 228
United States House of Representatives, Foreign Affairs Committee, 97
United States State Department, 40, 46, 80, 82, 86, 92
United States Supreme Court, 200
University of Alabama, 22, 24, 25–26, 43, 120, 231–232, 233; B'nai B'rith Hillel Foundation, 114, 120; Holocaust Studies program, 232; Law School, 36
University of Cincinnati, 86
University of Georgia, 187
University of Kentucky, 86
University of Louisville Law School, 58
Urofsky, Melvin, 5, 74

Vichy, France, 46
Virginia, 187

Wales, 196
Wallace, George C., 231
Wampold, Charles, 44, 45
Wampold, Simon, 195
Wannsee Conference, 55, 125
War Assets Administration, 209
Warner Brothers' Studio, 119
War Refugee Board (WRB), 98
Warsaw Ghetto, 72
Washington, DC, 81, 82, 86, 97–98, 228
Waterman Steamship Corporation, 201
Wayland, Yaakov, 212
WBHP (Huntsville), 191
Weekly Review (Birmingham), 122–124, 129
Weil, Adolph, Sr., 102
Weil, Edith, 161, 217
Weil, Eugene, 61–62
Weil, Harold S., 200–201
Weil, Henry A., 48, 52, 63, 64, 145, 207
Weil, Lee B., 49, 196–197
Weil brothers (Josiah, Heinrich, and Jacob), 32
Weiner, William, 191
Weingarten, Sam, 101
Weissbach, Lee Shai, 15
Werfel, Louis, 204
West Blocton, Alabama, 11
West End Baptist Church (Mobile), 38
West Germany, 226
Westheim, Germany, 44
Westphalia, Germany, 44
Whitfield, Stephen, 4
Wiesel, Elie, 226
Wilkinson, Horace, 198–200, 285–286n46

Williams, Aubrey, 53
Wilson, Woodrow, 78
Winchell, Walter, 192, 202
Wise, Stephen S., 22, 23, 82, 96–97, 125, 180, 190, 196, 282n16
Wolf, Alfred, 132, 152–157, 278–279n64
Woodlawn Baptist Church (Birmingham), 200
Workmen's Circle, 135, 158
Works Progress Administration (WPA), 53, 140, 148, 154, 157
World War I, 36, 78, 136, 143, 144, 158
World War II, 14, 15, 17, 18, 32, 54, 77, 131–166, 225; Jews serving in war, 133
Worms, Germany, 44
Wright, Wade, 20
Wrightstown, New Jersey, 152
Wyle, Ewart H., 80
Wyman, David, 40

Yom HaShoah, 18, 232
Yom Kippur War (1973), 225, 227
Young Men's Christian Association (YMCA), 86, 132, 136–137, 145–149, 159
Young Men's Hebrew Association (YMHA), 29, 30, 58, 84, 93, 94, 136, 158–159, 190, 210
Young Women's Christian Association (YWCA), 132
Young Women's Hebrew Association (YWHA), 158

Zeta Beta Tau (ZBT), 25
Zietz, Robert, 68
Ziff, Sidney, 14
Zionism, 3, 16, 39, 60, 73, 74–103, 166, 193, 197–198, 206–214, 215–216, 224; anti-Zionism, 3, 17, 77, 78, 90, 91–93, 101, 102–103, 198, 206–208, 213–214; First Zionist Congress, 74, 76; non-Zionism, 3, 73, 78, 79, 82–83, 92, 95, 96, 98, 100, 101–103, 198
Zionist Organization of America (ZOA), 77, 79–80, 83, 84, 96, 212